Mexican New York

The publisher gratefully acknowledges the generous contribution to this book provided by the General Endowment Fund of the University of California Press Foundation.

Mexican New York,

Transnational Lives of New Immigrants

ROBERT COURTNEY SMITH

University of California Press

BERKELEY   LOS ANGELES   LONDON

University of California Press, one of the most distinguished university presses in the United States, enriches lives around the world by advancing scholarship in the humanities, social sciences, and natural sciences. Its activities are supported by the UC Press Foundation and by philanthropic contributions from individuals and institutions. For more information, visit www.ucpress.edu.

Unless otherwise noted, all photographs are by the author.

Portions of chapter 8 were originally published as Robert C. Smith, "Social Location, Generation and Life Course as Social Processes Shaping Second Generation Transnational Life," in *The Changing Face of Home*, ed. Peggy Levitt and Mary C. Waters, 145–68 (New York: Russell Sage Foundation, 2002).

University of California Press
Berkeley and Los Angeles, California

University of California Press, Ltd.
London, England

Library of Congress Cataloging-in-Publication Data
Smith, Robert C., 1964–.
    Mexican New York : transnational lives of new immigrants / Robert Courtney Smith.
        p.   cm.
    Includes bibliographical references and index.
    ISBN 0-520-24412-5 (cloth : alk. paper).—ISBN 0-520-24413-3 (pbk. : alk. paper)
    1. Mexican Americans—New York (State)—New York—Social conditions.   2. Immigrants—New York (State)—New York—Social conditions.   3. Transnationalism.   4. United States—Relations—Mexico.   5. Mexico—Relations—United States.   6. New York (N.Y.)—Emigration and immigration.   7. Puebla (Mexico : State)—Emigration and immigration.   8. New York (N.Y.)—Ethnic relations.   I. Title.
F128.9.M5S64   2006
304.8'7471072'090511—dc22   2005001616

Manufactured in the United States of America

15 14 13 12 11 10 09 .08 07 06
10 9 8 7 6 5 4 3 2 1

This book is printed on New Leaf EcoBook 60, containing 60% postconsumer waste, processed chlorine free; 30% de-inked recycled fiber, elemental chlorine free; and 10% FSC-certified virgin fiber, totally chlorine free. EcoBook 60 is acid-free and meets the minimum requirements of ANSI/ASTM D5634-01 *(Permanence of Paper).* ♾

Contents

Illustrations

MAPS

TABLE

Acknowledgments

Many people and institutions have aided the writing of this book over seventeen years. Most critical was support for two years of leave, from 1999 to 2001, funded by fellowships from the Spencer Foundation/National Academy of Education; the Social Science Research Council, the Program on International Migration, with funds from the Andrew W. Mellon Foundation; and the Oral History Research Office at Columbia University, with funds from the Rockefeller Foundation. A generous grant and supplement from the Sociology Program of the National Science Foundation (grant number SES-9731280) funded critical travel, teaching relief, and research assistance; thanks to William Bainbridge, Patricia White, and Joane Nagel. The Social Science Research Council, through its Urban Underclass Program, and the National Science Foundation, through its Grants to Improve Doctoral Dissertations, supported the dissertation that began this research. A $2,500 seed grant and 40 percent sabbatical leave were provided by Barnard College.

My intellectual debts are also numerous. Saskia Sassen, Alejandro Portes, and Marcelo and Carola Suarez-Orozco have written countless letters on my behalf and opened up ways of looking in their work that readers will see reflected in this book. Chuck Tilly, Sudhir Venkatesh, Beth Bernstein, Nicole Marwell, and Nick de Genova read large portions of the manuscript and offered valuable comments. Herb Gans and Kathy Neckerman offered insights that helped me secure funding to finish the book. Manuel Garcia y Griego, Meg Crahan, John Mollenkopf, Phil Kasinitz, and Roger Waldinger offered excellent advice, almost none of which, alas, I followed. My year as a Rockefeller Fellow in Oral History at Columbia opened up my interviewing, thinking, and writing; thanks to Mary Marshall Clark, Ron Grele, and the Fellows. I also thank Wayne Cornelius, Roger Rouse, David Kyle, Ari

Zolberg, Josh DeWind, Carlos Gonzalez Gutierrez, Luin Goldring, Sergio Zendejas, Gail Mummert, Mercedes Gonzalez de la Rocha, Juan Flores, Rodolfo de la Garza, "Padre" Federico Besserer and his family, Gaspar Rivera Salgado, Juan Manuel Sandoval, Michael Kearney, Larry Donnelley, James Soles, James McGee, and especially Mark Miller and the Honors Program at the University of Delaware. At Columbia, I thank Douglas Chalmers, Ira Katznelson, Mark Kesselman, and Peter Bearman; at Barnard, Kelly Moore, Lynn Chancer, Flora Davidson, and Robert Remez. Finally, I thank my student researchers, Sandra Lara (now Dr. Sandraluz Lara-Cinisomo), Sara Guerrero-Rippberger, Agustín Vecino, Griscelda Perez, Carolina Perez, Lisa Peterson, Katie Graves-Abe, and Erika Flores. As my citations indicate, their work on the second-generation school and work project contributed significantly to this book.

My greatest debts are to the Ticuanenses, United States– or Mexico-born, without whose *confianza* this book would not exist. While confidentiality precludes my mentioning their names, I thank them for their patience in explaining things to a *gringo muy preguntón*. I hope that the portrait of Ticuani given here resonates with their experience. I also thank Salvador Beltran del Rio, Gerry Dominguez, Jaime Lucero, Joel Magallan Reyes, Angelo Cabrera, Arturo Sarukhan Casamitijana, and others. I thank Don Pedro Lara, a mushroom picker from Moroleon, Guanajato, for opening his world to me when I was a college student. As a small gesture of thanks, half of all my royalties from this book will be donated to projects to benefit the Mexican communities in New York and the Mixteca.

Finally, I must thank my family for their continued support as I worked on the book: my parents, Mr. and Mrs. Walter Smith; my sister, Vicky Farhi, and her family; my brother, David Smith; my aunt, Sister Anne Courtney, and the late Sister Mary Eugene Gotimer for their spiritual, human, and scholarly examples; and my late grandmother, Mary Messenger—Mom Mom—whose toughness has helped all of us.

This book is for my wife, Maura, and our two sons, Owen and Liam. Here words simply don't serve. Maura's love has centered my life for two decades. Owen and Liam have enriched our lives in ways I could not even have imagined. I watch in wonder as four-year-old Liam sings his way into boyhood and Owen sprints into his own at age seven. While writing a book is fun, nothing compares to Liam's forty-pound and Owen's fifty-five-pound running hugs that knock me over at the start and end of each day, or to Maura's delighted smile and my own at all of us together.

1. Transnational Life in Ethnographic Perspective

THREE VIGNETTES

> There's a time you can't believe you're here [in Ticuani]. You're like, "Oh, it's probably a dream down here." . . . Since I have dreams that I'm over there and I wake up. . . . But I'm like, "Oh, I'm really here." And I have fun. And in the nights you can't wait to leave your house at eight o'clock and go to the *centro,* and you see all the lights from the house.
>
> LINDA, age fifteen

Linda's wonder at actually being in the town I call Ticuani—a small *municipio* (county) of less than two thousand people in southern Puebla, in the Mixteca region of Mexico—is not just an enthusiastic teenager's response to a favorite vacation spot: it attests to Ticuani's central place in her social world. Although she says that she cannot visit her cousins in Manhattan because it is "mad far" from her apartment in Brooklyn and her parents will not let her go, they permit her to travel more than two thousand miles with her brother or cousins (but without her parents) to stay for several weeks in Ticuani during winter and summer vacation each year. While in Ticuani, Linda can stay out all night to dance, drink beer (with discretion), and walk around freely outside, whereas in New York she is a "lockdown" girl who must come straight home from school and await her parents' return. In Ticuani she participates in the overnight Antorcha (torch run) for Padre Jesús and other religious rituals, which simultaneously give her freedom from her parents and a closer connection, as she practices traditions in which they have also participated. Such patterns transnationalize adolescent rituals for her and her second-generation immigrant friends and give Ticuani an enhanced place in their lives.

· · ·

Tomás Maestro got up at 5 A.M. on the morning of January 26, 2001, and went quickly to the zocalo, or town center, of Ticuani, wincing as he put pressure on the swollen leg that had kept him home from the Grand Dance the previous night. Normally, he would have spent the entire night at the dance, to which he had been looking forward all year. He had brought his wife and four children down to Ticuani from New York to enjoy such rituals with him. This year he went to the zocalo to keep an eye on his oldest son, Toño, as the dance ended. It was fortunate that he did. He arrived soon after Toño had screamed, "¡Pendeja!" (Asshole!) at his younger sister, Magda, when she refused to get out of a car with several youths he did not like, including some *pandilleros*, or gang members, from New York. One *pandillero*, thinking the insult was directed at him, got out of the car to confront Toño. Older relatives separated them, warning Toño how dangerous the *pandilleros* could be. Toño listened to Tomás, but the next morning Tomás got up early again, this time to hear his son angrily ordering his girlfriend, Julia, to go home despite her desire to stay in the zocalo and eat tacos with her friends.

These conflicts show how transnational life emerges and how gender figures into that process. Tomás, Toño, Julia, and Magda are all attempting to negotiate the different meanings of gender in New York and Ticuani. The relative autonomy of Mexican women in New York can be challenged by men in Mexico as they claim expanded masculine authority, often with support from local Ticuanenses. These assertions of authority, such as Toño's "defending" Magda, are also assertions of masculine honor—of "heart"—because Toño stands up to *pandilleros* who inspire fear in both New York and Ticuani.

· · ·

"The water pipes have come in!" Don Emiliano tells me and the members of the Ticuani Solidarity Committee with excitement. Months of work are paying off for Ticuani. Committee members explain to me again how the old one-inch pipes cannot handle the pressure needed to pump water to distant parts of the growing *municipio*, and how the committee and the municipal government are working together to install three-inch pipes. The committee members are going to inspect the new pipes, which they tell me are plastic and will not corrode like the old ones. "We will be able to shower at any time of day or night," says one committee member, "and plant trees right in our backyard and water them without any trouble, too. It will make life better in Ticuani."

This ordinary civic scene takes place not in Ticuani but on a Brooklyn street corner in 1993. We say goodbye to committee members headed to John F. Kennedy Airport in Queens. They will travel to Mexico City and then five hours overland to Ticuani for the weekend to consult with authorities and contractors on the work they are funding, returning the following Monday to their jobs in New York City. Moreover, the committee is the Ticuani Solidarity Committee *of New York* (hereafter the Committee), which has substantially funded most major Ticuani public works projects over three decades by soliciting donations from Ticuanenses in New York. For this, the largest Ticuani project ever, the Committee raised more than two-thirds of the $150,000 cost of the project, exceeding the Mexican federal, state, and local government contributions combined. The Committee has also become involved in Ticuani politics, helping to fashion a set of rules and practices for participating in transnational public life. Fundraising in New York by Ticuanenses has become increasingly important in Ticuani electoral politics. That fundraising in Brooklyn basements matters so much to the public life of a remote village some twenty-five hundred miles away points to how much life has been transnationalized in some places in the United States and Mexico.

· · ·

This is a book about how the lives of many contemporary immigrants and their children are being lived transnationally. In each of these three vignettes, the actors have adopted practices in use both in the United States and in Mexico and which are understood by means of social and moral maps encompassing both Ticuani and New York.[1] *Globalization* and, to a lesser extent, *transnationalization* have become buzzwords describing how the "local becomes global,"[2] how distant people are becoming linked through economic markets, communications, and cultural dissemination and homogenization. But what do these processes mean in people's everyday lives? Why are increasing numbers of migrants so interested in maintaining relations with their home towns and countries?[3] More compellingly, why are so many of their children also participating in these practices, and how does this participation change their experiences of assimilation in the United States? My book sets out to provide interesting answers to these questions, drawing on an extended case study of migrants and their children from Ticuani, in Puebla, Mexico, who migrate to New York.

The tremendous growth in Mexican migration to New York over the last fifteen years reflects a larger trend. While most Mexican migrants still settle in the Southwest of the United States, during the 1990s migration to the East Coast increased: today, for example, more than half a million people of Mexican origin live in New York State. Transnational life emerges from attempts by migrants and their children to live meaningful lives, to gain respect and recognition, within the context of the larger processes of migration from Mexico, on the one hand, and assimilation in the United States, on the other.

I trace the emergence and evolution of transnational life through fifteen years of ethnography in the Ticuanense community, focusing on the formation of political community by first-generation migrant men; on how gender structures transnational life; and on second-generation assimilation and participation in transnational life. Migration itself has changed with the closer economic integration of Mexico and the United States, along with other forms of globalization, which foster, limit, or otherwise affect transnational life. Similarly, settlement and assimilation pressures in New York urge Ticuanenses and their children toward transnational action but also constrain it. Studying both migration and assimilation helps explain why and how Ticuanense migrants and their children remain attached to Ticuani. This attachment and the transnational life it supports are crucially affected by secondary processes affecting the lives of migrants and their children, such as adolescence and racialization. Finally, changes in communications and travel technology (including the postmodern concept of "time-space compression"),[4] large-scale integration, and government intervention facilitate creation of transnational structures on the local level that are experienced differently than were earlier long-distance migrations and diasporas.[5]

My analytical strategy is dialectic, emphasizing how local and larger forces, structures, and actors influence each other over time in a generative historical process. I explain how migrants and their children in New York and Puebla are affected by political or economic events both local and global; I show how their responses to these new situations help institutionalize transnational life. The contours of local-level transnational life emerge through the repetition of certain political, gender, and cultural practices, which gradually become normative and structural—"social facts," external to and coercive of individuals, in the words of Émile Durkheim—but also continue to evolve through the actions of migrants and their children and outside forces.[6] My goal is more to tell how things came to be as they are today than to predict what they will be like in the future, though I also reflect on the direction I think transnational life will take.[7]

The evolution of Ticuani transnational life reflects my own sustained engagement with Ticuanenses and their children. I first did research in Ticuani and its neighboring town, which I call El Ganado, during the summer of 1988, and I followed up this visit with five- or six-week trips from 1991 through 1993, while doing ongoing ethnography in New York. From 1990 through 1994 I worked especially closely with Ticuanense men on the Committee, but also with women and the second generation. From 1994 to 1997 I stayed in touch with Ticuanenses and began a second major project, on the school and work fates of their children in the United States. This second period of intensive fieldwork, from 1997 to 2002, gave me the chance to revisit Ticuani and Ticuanenses in New York and to apply gender and generation as important analytical lenses, focusing more explicitly on the experiences of the second generation and of women. In reworking transnational issues, I deepened old friendships. And after I had worked alone for ten years, grant funds enabled me to hire several excellent researchers, whose influence is also felt in this book.[8]

My reentering Ticuani life from 1997 to 2002 has made this a better book. Attending the Feast of Padre Jesús (Ticuani's patron saint) in January 1999 for the first time since 1993, I was surprised not just by how warmly I was received but also by how deeply I was moved. Although I had participated in Ticuani life in Brooklyn in the interim, returning to Ticuani made me deeply happy—and also made possible new insights. I was able to see, for example, how age affected participation in transnational life: Some younger children who had not liked returning to Ticuani seven or even ten years earlier now embraced its rituals as adolescents, and some who had been adolescents in the early 1990s now participated less. At the same time I had been making my own journey from graduate student to professor, and from engagement to marriage to my wife, Maura, and the birth of my two children, Liam and Owen. Meeting my wife and children led Ticuanenses to see me as more real and gave us more in common. Finally, my reentry into Ticuani life led even my Ticuanense friends to ask when the book would be done, giving me more *ganas* (desire) to finish.[9]

TRANSNATIONAL LIFE IN SCHOLARLY AND HISTORICAL CONTEXTS

The image of the "clean break" with the old country, embodied in the title of Oscar Handlin's 1951 book *The Uprooted*, guided most research on immigration from the 1920s through the 1980s.[10] A transnational perspective emerged in response to the failure of this and other dominant theories of immigrant assimilation to explain the growing trend of close ties between migrants and their home countries, illustrated in the vignettes above. Whereas early work on transnational life saw it as wholly new, and newly discovered, recent work has detailed and compared its historical, contemporary, and theoretical contours. One study, for example, draws on random samples of migrant populations to gauge the frequency of transnational practices among them.[11]

In its most common version, derived from the work of Nina Glick-Schiller and her colleagues, transnational theory has several elements.[12] First, it disputes the inevitability of severing ties to the old country, once assumed to be part of the inexorable transition from "immigrant" to "ethnic" to "native" in two or three generations. Rather, it argues, migrants and their children may remain linked to their home countries for long periods, in part to resist racial and other forms of inequality in the host country. Second, it argues that capitalism has created a set of global markets and processes that have increased migration and superseded the nation-state, creating a kind of global civil society that threatens the state's monopoly on politics. This change opens possibilities for subversive action, aided by new technology such as the Internet. Finally, some argue or imply that transnationalization creates a kind of "third way," or what the historian David Gutiérrez has called a "Third Space," for immigrants, enabling them to somehow escape the grasp of the nation-state and the host and home societies.[13] While all of these positions are correct to some extent, they fail to sufficiently consider factors limiting or extending the longevity of transnational life or to illuminate some of its dimensions, such as the role of adolescence and the life course in creating and shaping transnational life. They also sometimes err through what the anthropologist Sherry Ortner describes as an "ethnographic refusal"[14] to investigate, for example, local conflicts and meanings, because the research is framed mainly in terms of resistance to domination by larger processes such as globalization.

I analyze transnational life or transnationalization by emphasizing lived experience and process, purposely avoiding the more common terms *transnationalism* and *transmigrants*. I also differentiate between transnational processes, which involve particular migrant populations and nation-states, and global ones, which involve economic, institutional, cultural, and other changes that reconfigure power on a planetary scale.[15] As I use the term, *transnational life* includes those practices and relationships linking migrants and their children with the home country, where such practices have significant meaning and are regularly observed, as in the studies by the sociologist Alejandro Portes and his colleagues.[16] But, for me, transnational life is also embodied in identities and social structures that help form the life world of immigrants and their children and is constructed in relations among people, institutions, and places. Transnational life usually involves travel between the home and host destination, but it can also include the experience of stay-at-homes in close relationships with travelers.[17] Finally, I understand transnational life not as an all-encompassing identity, but as one of several that migrants can hold and exercise. Involvement in transnational life is generally stronger than that in purely associational forms of social life, such as political parties, but less strong than that envisioned in the primordial notion of "natural community"[18] as formulated by the German sociologist Ferdinand Tonnies or the American anthropologist Robert Redfield in the early to mid-1900s. I do not intend to fall on my theoretical sword in arguing for a transnational perspective. I point up ways in which transnational life seems strong and institutionalized and those in which it seems limited, and I reflect on factors that affect how long it endures and how it is experienced.

Most transnationalists avoid the concept of *assimilation*, which they conceive of in its mid-twentieth-century form, positing conformity to an imagined set of white, Anglo-Saxon Protestant norms. Yet while we should criticize this harsh Americanization project—for example, for its uncritically viewing differences in life chances as the result of inherent group traits (such as race)—we still face the fundamental question of how immigrants become part of the larger American society. Many scholars prefer the term *incorporation* to describe this process because it is free of the Americanization overtones of *assimilation*. Although I use both terms, I more often use *assimilation* because it more accurately describes what immigrants perceive to be a coercive process with often negative consequences for them and their children. I do not endorse this coercive dimension of immigrant experience, but I think we cannot get a good picture of the current reality without acknowledging it, especially among groups with lower levels of education and income.

Some scholars see assimilation overwhelming transnational life as the second and subsequent generations become largely monolingual English-speakers.[19] Yet this is not always the case, and even if it were, the transnational relationship would persist among new waves of immigrants. The relationship between assimilation and transnational life is complex, changing across the life course, by generation, and by class. Indeed, assimilation pressures are refracted through transnational processes: just as assimilation can be "segmented" into upward and downward mobility (into either more schooling and better jobs, or leaving school without graduating and poorer jobs),[20] transnational life can extend such tendencies. Hence gang members on negative assimilation paths and students on positive ones in New York live out these experiences when they return to Ticuani. By so doing, they transnationalize both gangs and a culture of educational mobility, and this experience then affects assimilation and incorporation when they return to New York. Moreover, assimilation and transnationalization are not mutually exclusive processes: being more transnational does not necessarily mean being less assimilated. Indeed, leaders in migrant communities in the United States who engage in collective action there also tend to participate more in transnational life.[21] Some evidence suggests that this was also the case in the past, as in the Swedish temperance or franchise-reform movements, which were pushed by the same adherents in both countries in the late 1880s and early 1900s.[22] Hence, I think the biggest danger to positive assimilation is not transnationalization but negative assimilation pressures in the United States. Transnational life in fact has great potential to facilitate positive assimilation in the United States.

Transnationalization affects life differently in Mexico and New York. Life in Mexican sending villages like Ticuani (the communities from which migrants come to the United States) becomes oriented toward *el norte*, while life in New York is dominated by the daily struggles of surviving. Yet, among the more than 40 percent of Ticuanenses in New York and their children who become significantly involved in transnational life, it changes how they understand their own Mexican identity and their attitude toward various economic, racial, and ethnic assimilation pressures in New York. (I estimate that between 100 and 150 youths and 300 to 400 adults return to Ticuani each year, figures that represent at least 10 percent of all Ticuanenses in the United States and Mexico. Thus some 30 to 40 percent of all Ticuanenses return to Ticuani over the course of three years.) That transnational action does not directly involve all migrants does not detract from its pervasive influence. Indeed, a generation ago, the urban sociologist Gerald Suttles showed that, as with unions or political parties, the actions of leaders and a few active followers have disproportionate effects on collective life and on the less active members of a community.[23]

Transnational life and reciprocal effects on assimilation and migration are not new, but they require a new theoretical lens to see them as such. Indeed, essays in "historical retrieval" are now documenting patterns of transnational action in immigration history that were not previously seen as such.[24] Immigrants during the late 1800s and early 1900s engaged in many of the transnational practices described in this book, including involvement in local politics and religious movements in communities of both origin and destination. Migrant-sending countries also took many of the same measures in the past as they have done today, such as attempting to cultivate a closer relationship with their diaspora by establishing special programs for them, using their emigrants to lobby for national interests, and pursuing nationalist goals from abroad. Yet transnational life today is different from that of the past. These differences result in part from communications and travel technologies that enable migrants to participate in communities in both countries. A different regime of assimilation in the United States today also encourages ethnic identification and links with the home country rather than stressing Americanization. Moreover, today's migrants are likely to come with an identity linked to their country of origin, whereas migrants a hundred years ago might have identified themselves more strongly with their home village. And the current international system exerts contradictory pressures on migration. It controls most potential migration through passport and other state controls—what the political scientist Ari Zolberg calls "remote control"[25]—which did not exist during most of the last wave of migration, from the 1880s to the 1920s. But it also promotes economic and cultural globalization, which fosters migration. More than two hundred million people around the world are now migrants, the largest number in human history.

The conditions supporting transnational life will persist for the foreseeable future.[26] With regard to transnationalization between Mexico and the United States, these conditions include globalization (ably analyzed by Saskia Sassen) and continuing labor market and migration pressures in Mexico. One-third of all Mexicans will travel to the United States during their lifetime, and half have a relative who has done so.[27] Changes in U.S. immigration and other laws and closer integration with the United States have also led to quicker long-term settlement in the United States.[28] U.S.-born children of Mexican migrants are the largest foreign-born group in Mexico outside Mexico City.[29] More than twenty million people of Mexican origin live in the United States; Mexico's population is now more than one hundred million. Without a major disruption of these conditions—on the scale of the Great Depression and World War II, which combined with restrictionism to end the last wave of migration—transnational life should continue to grow strongly in the future.

KEY SITES FOR ANALYZING TRANSNATIONAL LIFE

I analyze local-level transnational life at three of its key sites: in politics in the first generation, in gender relations in the first and second generations, and in the assimilation experiences of teenage students and gang members. Analyzing these themes in this order traces the migration process and its partner, the assimilation process, through various steps from the causes of migration through the effect of continued attachment to Ticuani to the reasons for and links between positive and negative assimilation in New York and returning to Ticuani among the second generation. By focusing over an extended period on both the community of origin in Ticuani and the community of destination in New York, I document how politics, gender relations, and second-generation assimilation evolve within the context of transnational life. In contrast to many other researchers,[30] I not only celebrate migration and transnationalization's positive aspects—such as the democratic catalyzation of politics—but also depict their darker sides, such as extended, painful family separations and transnational gang formation, and I relate these elements to assimilation. Ticuani provides transnational theory with what the late Robert Merton calls a "strategic research site," where the object of study presents itself with unusual clarity, thus permitting detailed examination.[31]

Common to all three sites is the struggle for respect and recognition in difficult circumstances, what Doreen Massey calls "a sense of place."[32] The committee leaders want their efforts on behalf of Ticuani recognized, second-generation girls and boys want their Mexicanness and masculinity or femininity recognized, and gang members want respect from others. People's attempts to create a place for themselves are simultaneously oriented toward particular geographical spaces, such as Ticuani's zocalo or schools in New York; to social space, the myriad social locations formed in relation to gender, ethnic, and racial images and hierarchies in Mexico and the United States and social relations among Ticuanenses; and to "emergent" (temporary) spaces (such as Mexican DJ parties in clubs in New York), whereby masculinity, Mexicanness, and that social space are jointly constituted.[33] Space is both a geographical place and an existential freedom to feel that one belongs fully amid difference. This analysis resonates with what the Latino studies scholars William Flores, Rena Benmayor, and Renato Resaldo call "Latino cultural citizenship," the right to feel at home in claiming space or rights despite one's ethnic or racial difference from others in the community.[34] While this notion of cultural citizenship usually theorizes a Latino right to belong and make claims within the dominant, white society, my analysis of claims to rights and existential belonging by Ticuanenses in New York is more often set within other kinds of unequal power relations. Returning migrants and their children negotiate with the local Ticuanense power elite; children of Ticuani immigrants in New York negotiate with Puerto Rican, Black, and white youth; and (first-generation) teenage migrants negotiate with U.S.-born children of Ticuani immigrants and other groups. I return to the meanings and function of geographic, social, and emergent, or constituted, space periodically.

I turn first to the formation of a transnational political community, by which I mean the formally and informally institutionalized patterns and practices of public life in Ticuani and in New York. The Mexican government—at the municipal, state, and federal levels—is crucial in creating transnational public life. The municipality is most involved in and affected by transnational public life because it cannot raise the money it needs for public works without the contributions of Ticuanenses in New York. But the governments of Mexico and of several Mexican states, including Puebla, have also created programs to strengthen their links with Mexicans abroad in order to do public works, to keep remittances flowing, and to control the transnational political participation of Mexicans in the United States, especially in Mexican electoral politics. The Mexican president Vicente Fox has credited migrants' influence with helping him win the 2000 election, and migrants have become an integral part of what Benedict Anderson would call Mexico's "imagined political community" during Fox's presidency.[35] This participation of the state in creating and maintaining transnational life is at odds with the views of scholars such as the anthropologist Arjun Appadurai, who sees the state as being "on its last legs," transcended by migrant action.[36] But the state matters in at least two ways. First, the territoriality of the state and its monopoly over the legitimate use of violence in that territory enable the Mexican state, for example, to use force to stifle dissent. But migrants can leave Mexico to protest from the safety of the United States.[37] Second, the state, especially at the municipal level, is key to creating a sense of community, belonging, and social closure (knowing where the community starts and stops), and to linking these concepts to certain places and practices, among both the first and the second generations.[38] Being a Ticuanense is not a cosmopolitan, placeless identity but rather begins as its opposite, a local, deeply rooted traditional identity that is lived in two countries at once, and evolves into something transnational but still local. Because migrants and their U.S.-born children can return regularly to Ticuani, its traditions and ability to confer authenticity make it important to many second-generation youths for whom being Mexican in New York has negative connotations of victimization and difficulty in school. In this way, assimilation and transnationalization become intimately bound.

All this is not to imply that harmony, equality, and fraternity reign within the community or that all forms of transnational life fall under its rubric. Ticuani public life is riven by political, factional, and class conflicts. But by negotiating such conflicts simultaneously in New York and Puebla, Ticuanenses create and reproduce a transnational political community, a Ticuanense "we" that is understood in the zocalo in Ticuani as well as on the baseball and soccer fields of Brooklyn. Even if politicians use the rhetoric of community to advance their own aims, many Ticuanenses believe in a transnationally constituted Ticuani community and act on that belief, thus creating and sustaining communal goals, views, and practices. Moreover, the Mexican state and other groups treat Ticuanenses in New York and in Ticuani as members of the same community, thus reinforcing the Ticuanense sense of community through what Suttles would term their "foreign relations" with migrants.[39] Finally, a Ticuanense identity can coexist with others, such as Mexican American, Hispanic, or New Yorker; the Ticuani identity may not always be ascendant but can still be important. Focusing on the community level elucidates the developing logic of relationships among actors over time, illuminating the factors that affect the transnational sense and practice of community. This focus is precluded if one takes the individual as the key unit of analysis in transnational studies, as others have done.[40]

My relational, long-term focus has enabled me both to see how transnational life depends on actors in both countries and to register the effects of changes inside and outside Ticuani. For example, it has become common for the Ticuani municipal president to visit New York seeking support for projects in Ticuani. Contributions by Ticuanenses living in New York are governed by conditions set by the Committee. Yet the Committee too must play by rules set by local leaders in Ticuani. Hence anyone who wishes to run for municipal president must return to Ticuani for at least one year. Such transnational practices acquire a normalcy—for Ticuanenses and researchers studying them—that becomes noticeable when it is upset by external forces. Thus when the then-dominant political party in Mexico, the Partido Revolucionario Instiucional (PRI), changed its rules for selecting local candidates for election, it occasioned a split in the PRI in Ticuani and among Ticuanenses in New York. This division ended the Committee's monopoly on representing those in New York and led to the defeat of the Ticuani political boss's candidate through financial and moral support from an insurgent political group in New York. Such two-way influence is testimony to the extent to which the town's political community is now transnational.

In addition to examining transnational local politics, my second task in this book is to show how transnationalization and assimilation are affected by gender and the life course.[41] The prevailing view of gender in migration studies emphasizes such phenomena as the "crisis of masculinity"[42] and "liberating femininity," by which, for example, first-generation men, usually assumed to be undocumented, are seen to want to return home or to imagine themselves returning, whereas women want to settle or imagine themselves settling, because men lose status and power in the United States and women gain them. Although there is truth to these perceptions, many Ticuanense men and women in New York create institutional and social settings affording men real power, and not just its symbolic form, which, as the sociologist Pierrette Hondagneu-Sotelo insightfully argues, compensates for diminished power.[43] Ticuanense men exercise power in New York as community leaders and from New York as absent Ticuanense leaders. Their wives enjoy enhanced status, derived in part from their husbands' power and in part from the opportunities for service and status display afforded by their own transnational activities.

The life course too affects transnational life in gendered ways. While many retired first-generation men become more involved in politics from New York, many retired women bring their third-generation grandchildren back to Mexico for vacations while their adult children remain in the United States working. In the second generation, men's and women's involvement in transnational life varies according to their divergent experiences of assimilation, adolescence, and school in New York. Some second-generation men attempt to reclaim the lost male privilege they imagine their fathers to have had in Mexico. These men are in many ways allowed to live that privileged life in Ticuani, whereas their second-generation girlfriends attempt to reclaim some aspects of their lost traditions while resisting pressure to surrender the autonomy they enjoy in New York.[44]

Toño's case is instructive. In Ticuani, Toño attempts to renegotiate the "gender bargains" he has with his sisters and girlfriend. When Toño fails to assert masculine authority over his sister Magda, he angrily asserts it over his girlfriend, who accedes to his will. Although his girlfriend and sister move quite autonomously in New York, in Mexico—and especially in Ticuani where he feels everyone is watching—Toño feels he has not only the right but also the responsibility to watch out for the women in his life; if anything happens to them, it will be his fault. At the same time, Toño is showing everyone that he will tolerate no disrespect from his girlfriend, his sister, or even intimidating gang members. His family and girlfriend report that in Ticuani he gets into more fights with other men and attempts to control the behavior of women more than in New York. These renegotiations of the gender bargains in his family and with his girlfriend are part of transnational life for them.

My third approach to the study of transnational life is through the experiences of the second generation. This term is a conscious simplification: the transnational social world of Ticuanense youth encompasses three other groups. The "1.5 generation" is composed of youth born in Mexico but raised from the age of about ten in the United States; the "−1.5 generation" was born in the United States but raised for several years in Mexico before returning to the United States; and there has been a large influx of first-generation teenage migrants who came to New York in the 1990s under the family reunification policies accompanying the Immigration Reform and Control Act of 1986. I usually include the first three groups within the category of "second generation" and treat teen migrants as a separate group to reflect their substantially different experiences of migration and assimilation. I make the cut at age ten because the younger children do not enter middle school or high school or go through puberty on arrival in the United States; they thus avoid a number of the challenges of urban adolescence imposed on teen migrants.[45]

For many second-generation Ticuanenses, adolescence itself is practiced transnationally, even while it is engaged with migration and assimilation pressures. They use Ticuani's communal rituals, such as feasts and dances, to negotiate their place in New York. Being transnational helps many in the second generation to differentiate themselves, as ethnic Mexicans, from Blacks and Puerto Ricans, other ethnic minorities with whom they feel they are often equated. And in contradistinction to the inherent danger perceived in adolescent rituals in New York, Ticuani offers the second generation a safe site for rituals and enables parents both to offer their children more freedom and to establish closer connections with them, a hard trick during adolescence.[46] Economically or educationally successful second-generation returnees enter Ticuani at the top of its social hierarchy, in contrast to their often-diminished place in New York. Yet, unlike their parents, they are not always received as beloved *hijos ausentes* (absent sons and daughters). They are sometimes seen as *presumidos*, arrogant outsiders who flaunt their material wealth and New York styles and lack authentic Mexican values, customs, and language.

Life course also affects second generation transnational life. Second-generation participation in transnational life alters with age. Typically, younger children take less interest in their connection with Ticuani; this takes on an urgent meaning and intensity as they reach adolescence and persists through the late teens and the early twenties. Later, permanent jobs, children, and other adult obligations leave less time for travel to Ticuani but also bring another set of rituals practiced in Ticuani: baptizing children, building or inheriting houses, and returning for family vacations.

The dual processes of migration and assimilation have disrupted the safe haven that returning second-generation youth once enjoyed in Ticuani. Family reunification under the 1986 amnesty caused a surge of emigration by children and adolescents who would otherwise have stayed in Mexico until their late teens or early twenties. Their difficult incorporation in New York and other factors caused a great increase in Mexican gangs in New York during the 1990s and the exportation from New York to Ticuani of associated social problems such as drug use and violence. As some teen migrants encountered legal or gang troubles in New York, they fled to Ticuani and took up gang life there, virtually unchallenged by other youth or by an adult male population severely depleted by migration. This long-term ethnographic analysis of the transnationalization of adolescence and then of gangs illustrates the iterative process by which transnational life emerges, often including contestation over the meaning and possession of place.[47]

Despite its title, this book does not attempt to analyze the entire Mexican community in New York.[48] It analyzes one case of local-level transnational life over an extended period. I cannot generalize my findings to a broader population, as can many statistical studies. However, I use the continuities and anomalies in the Ticuanense case to gain deeper insight into both individual experience and the larger processes—national or global, or of gender or race or adolescence—shaping transnational life. Through ongoing engagement with my informants, with knowledge of the contexts within which their lives are set, and with theory, I develop what the sociologist Michael Burawoy calls an "extended case analysis."[49]

Ticuani represents one of the strongest instances of local-level transnational life documented thus far, but it is not unique. Other cases in Oaxaca, Zacatecas, and elsewhere in Latin America show high levels of transnational life, which are likely to persist.[50] Other communities in the Mixteca region seem to be following Ticuani northward. Migration has virtually emptied parts of the Mixteca, which lost more than 100,000 people to migration between 1985 and 2000, resulting in population losses ranging from 5 percent to more than 60 percent in some *municipios* over the last twenty years despite high birth rates (3 percent or more). Some 70 percent of these migrants go to New York, and the Mixteca region accounts for some two-thirds of Mexicans in New York.[51] Such demographics have sustained transnational life and significantly affected local politics. All of the thirty-five *municipios* in the Mixteca region have hometown associations similar to the one studied in this book, and the current governor of Puebla has opened an office in New York to maintain links with *poblanos* there. Moreover, government officials told me that electoral outcomes were changed profoundly by migrants in one-third of the Mixteca *municipios* in 1998, and that by 2002 migrants had affected electoral politics in more than 50 of the state's 217 *municipios*. And the governor formed a special unit of the State Judicial Police during the late 1990s to deal with public security issues, including gangs, especially during periods of high return, such as the religious feasts.

THE PLAN OF THE BOOK

Chapter 2 describes both how Ticuani has been transformed by migration and how Mexicans, including Ticuanenses, fit into New York's economic, ethnic, and racial hierarchies. The remaining eight chapters work in pairs. Chapters 3 and 4 trace how cooperation and the negotiation of conflict in New York and Ticuani have institutionalized a transnational political community and how changes in Mexican national politics have affected local Ticuanense politics in Mexico and New York. Chapter 5 shows how gender affects settlement, return, and transnational life among men and women in the first generation; chapter 6 examines the same issues among the second generation. Chapters 7 and 8 focus on the life course and transnational life. The former analyzes the transnationalization of adolescence for second-generation U.S.-born Ticuanenses, showing how their participation in Ticuani rituals both distinguishes them, in their eyes, from native-born U.S. minorities and links them with their parents and their Mexican culture in positive ways. Chapter 8 charts how changes in the life course account for both the failed attempts of an earlier cohort of second-generation Ticuanenses to institutionalize transnational life and for the current cohort's strong embrace of Ticuanense identity and rituals. Chapters 9 and 10 analyze the causes of the emergence and transnationalization of Mexican gangs in New York and rural Puebla during the 1990s and how gangs have changed the experience of Ticuani both for gang members and for the transnationalized adolescence of returning "regulars." The conclusion considers conditions that will affect the durability and scope of transnational life and makes policy recommendations to address some issues raised in the book.

This demonstration of the effects of transnational life in the United States and Mexico should begin to allay Roger Waldinger's frustrated but ultimately useful plea in 1997 for "transnationalists" to demonstrate how transnationalization has affected some social reality beyond identity. I hope this book helps to establish transnational life as a social reality in the minds of skeptics and to legitimize the transnational perspective as a useful lens for studying the twin processes of migration and assimilation.

Most Ticuanenses and their children asked me to use their real names in the book, saying they were "proud of the things they were doing" and wanted their stories told. However, to foster frankness and safeguard confidentiality, all names of persons in this book are pseudonyms, except for those of public persons, such as the governor of Puebla. Each pseudonym refers to the same person throughout the book. For example, the Tomás Maestro and Linda who appear in the opening paragraphs of this chapter are the same Tomás Maestro and Linda who appear throughout the book; thus I trace the same person through different spheres of Ticuani transnational life. Where public figures, such as politicians' staff members, requested anonymity, I have not named them.

I have translated Spanish-language quotations into English but have left the two languages mixed where the speaker did so, translating Spanish words in brackets immediately following the quotation. This mixing of two languages, especially among the second generation, reflects the speaker's engagement with two cultures. Sometimes one language expresses an idea better than the other, or does so in a way that seems more relevant to the speaker and his or her audience. I felt it was important to preserve this sense of ease in both languages.

2. Dual Contexts for Transnational Life

More than two hundred young men and women dressed in white sweat-shirts adorned with the image of Ticuani's patron saint, Padre Jesús, ran across the Manhattan Bridge on a frigid January morning to the Cathedral of Saint Bernard on Fourteenth Street, following their New York City Police escorts. This 1997 run from the heart of Brooklyn to downtown Manhattan—a distance of six or seven miles—was the first enactment in New York of a pilgrimage run, or Antorcha, for Ticuanense youth, corresponding to the annual thirty-six-hour relay from the Cathedral of the Virgin in Mexico City to Ticuani. Older Ticuanenses spoke proudly of the devotion their young people showed toward "Padrecito" and their town's customs, and they reminisced about their own Antorchas in Mexico. I ran with these young pilgrims in my dual role as an ethnographer and a founding member of the Mexican Athletic Club of New York; my job was to make sure no stragglers were lost en route. As we ran, they described how hard their lives were and how hard it was to run, but also the importance of this devotion in their lives.

During and after the event, Leobardo, the organizer, repeated several times how the police captain supervising the run had complimented him on the organization of the run and the evident devotion of the youths to Mexican customs: "I don't want to take away from any other groups, but the captain said he had not seen any other groups in New York that had such devotion and culture," he said. Others said that Blacks and Puerto Ricans lacked such a culture. Moreover, the adults argued that Padre Jesús protects Ticuani youths even in New York. In the 2004 Antorcha in New York, the organizers emphasized at the beginning of the run that what they most wanted to demonstrate to New Yorkers was their *educación*—proper upbringing. As we ran through Brooklyn's various neighborhoods, the cheers went up—"¡Que vive [Long live] Padrecito!" "¡Que vive los Mexicanos!" and, for the first time I can remember, "¡Que vive los Latinos!" So even as these U.S.-born youths embarked on the traditional Ticuani ritual of the Antorcha, transplanted into a new environment, they were also running and searching for their place within New York's racial, economic, and educational hierarchies.

This event illustrates how engagement with New York's racial, economic, and educational hierarchies creates a context for transnational life. It first provides a motivation for immigrants and their children to participate in transnational life. This motivation enables them to preserve positive meanings of being Mexican—to positively redefine, or at least escape briefly, the often-negative meanings of being Mexican in New York. Yet transnational life also serves as a locus in which the positive and negative trajectories of assimilation develop. Mexicans experiencing downward mobility and racialization in New York carry this experience with them as they return to Mexico; so too the upwardly mobile bring their perspective to Ticuani. Because I argue that transnational life emerges from the migration and assimilation processes, in this chapter I offer a detailed look at how each of these works among Ticuanenses, linking these processes to larger changes in Mexico-U.S. migration, to economic, ethnic, and racial hierarchies in New York, and to transformations in Ticuani and the Mixteca resulting from migration.

MEXICAN MIGRATION TO AND SETTLEMENT IN NEW YORK

During the 1990s, various nicknames were coined to describe Mexicans' place in, or between, New York and Mexico: "Puebla York," "NewYorktítlan," and "Manhatítlan."[1] One Ticuanense made and sold T-shirts showing the silhouette of the New York skyline at night over the name "Ticuani City." Each of these names juxtaposes the two places in which many Mexican immigrants make their lives. The nicknames suggest both the presence of Mexicans as a visible part of New York's ethnic landscape and their close links with their country of origin.

In 2000 the Mexican-origin population in New York City, including both immigrants and native-born Mexican Americans, was 275,000 to 300,000, about half of whom were between the ages of twelve and twenty-four. This figure represents a remarkable increase from 40,000 Mexicans in 1980 and 100,000 in 1990.[2] Moreover, "Little Mexicos" have sprung up in various neighborhoods in New York: Jackson Heights in Queens; El Barrio, or Spanish Harlem, in Manhattan; Sunset Park and Williamsburg in Brooklyn; in the south Bronx; and even on Staten Island. Reports by the New York City Board of Education show that the number of new Mexican immigrant students jumped from 996 in 1990 to 5,850 in 1993.[3] It dropped to 5,140 in 1996 and leveled off at 4,389 in 1999 and 4,285 in 2000. Mexicans have also become a presence in Hudson Valley towns like Newburgh and in New Jersey cities like Paterson in the north and Bridgeton in the south. In 2000, there were about 420,000 Mexicans in New York State and 700,000 to 750,000 in New York, New Jersey, and Connecticut combined. Moreover, new Mexican-origin populations have sprung up all over the East Coast, from Georgia and the Carolinas to Pennsylvania and Rhode Island. Census experts predict that Mexicans will soon become the largest Latino minority on the East Coast;[4] in some of these places, they already are.

The Mexican population in New York has grown faster than any other major ethnic group in the city[5]—witness the 232 percent increase in births to Mexican mothers between 1988 and 1996, as reported by the New York City Department of Health—and further growth is probable. For at least the next twenty years, new entrants to Mexico's labor market will far outstrip the number of available jobs. Migration to the United States is likely to increase from nontraditional sending regions, thereby initiating new migration chains. And there is a growing tendency for migrants to stay longer or to settle permanently in the United States.[6] Because of the size of Mexico's population—100,000,000 people in 2000, compared with, for example, the Dominican Republic's 8,000,000—it also seems likely that Mexicans will continue to account for a larger percentage of New York's Latino population. The Puerto Rican population (down to about 750,000 in 2000) is now falling, and the Dominican population (about 650,000 in 2000) is growing more slowly.

We can divide migration from Mexico to New York over the past sixty years into four phases, each implicating different forces that push and pull migrants. The first two phases involve migration mainly from the Mixteca region, a cultural and ecological zone that includes the contiguous parts of Puebla, Oaxaca, and Guerrero. Map 1 shows the Mixteca's location in Mexico. In surveys done in 1992 and in 2001–2, the Mixteca accounted for two-thirds of Mexican migrants to New York, just under half of whom came from Puebla.[7] The first phase of migration, from the mid-1940s to the mid-1960s, involved individuals from a few towns in southern Puebla who already had relatives in New York. Indeed, we can date the onset of migra-

MAP 1.   General location of the Mixteca, southern Mexico. (Based on Cederstrom 1993: 146.)

tion from this region to July 6, 1943, when Don Pedro and his cousin and brother (all from Ticuani) crossed the border. In an interview several years before he died, Don Pedro told me he remembered the date because it was "two days after your Independence Day." They had been living in Mexico City and had been trying to bribe their way into a labor contract to go to the United States when they were introduced to a New Yorker named Montesinos, who was vacationing in Mexico City. He drove them back to New York, put them up in a hotel, and helped them get jobs, which Don Pedro said were easy to get "because of the war."

The second phase, from the mid-1960s to mid 1980s, still involved a small and tight network, but it encompassed increasing numbers of people, including the first appreciable number of women. The attractions in New York included much higher wages than in Puebla and modern conveniences that most people could not even imagine, given that Ticuani had no electricity until the mid-1960s.[8] Many "pioneer" migrants from Puebla were seeking to escape political violence: Don Pedro had fled to Mexico City to escape violence in Ticuani when he met Montesinos.

The third stage of migration was the explosion of the late 1980s to mid-1990s, which arose from several factors. First, by the late 1980s, Mexico's "lost decade" ("lost" in the sense that the economy did not grow) seemed sure to continue into the 1990s. Puebla was among the states hardest hit, experiencing a net contraction of its economy from 1981 to 1985.[9] The Mixteca was one of the worst-off regions in Mexico.[10] Mexicans' loss of faith in Mexico's economy coincided with U.S. employers' identification of Mexicans as plentiful and diligent workers. By linking up with non-Mexican immigrant employer networks, Mexican immigrants became a preferred labor source.[11] Because New York's Mexican population had reached a critical mass by the late 1980s, the social and economic costs of migration decreased: new migrants could draw on the support of friends and relatives already there.[12] Arguably most important was the amnesty provision of the 1986 Immigration Reform and Control Act, or IRCA, which enabled certain undocumented immigrants to apply for temporary residence and eventually become eligible for permanent resident status. Many were surprised that Mexicans were the ethnic group accounting for the second highest number of amnesty applications in New York City—about nine thousand, behind roughly twelve thousand from Dominicans.[13]

The amnesty program profoundly changed Mexicans' relationship to their hometowns. After years of being unable to leave the United States, migrants could return home at will and bring family members from Mexico to join them. The Mexican sociologist Sergio Cortés Sánchez has documented how tens of thousands of wives and children left the Mixteca and moved to New York after 1986.[14]

The last phase of migration, which began in the late 1990s, differs from previous phases in several respects. First, by the late 1990s, many towns in the Mixteca region were mature migrant communities: that is, most people who wanted to leave had already done so, and those remaining behind were unlikely to migrate soon.[15] The number of settled Mexican migrants, both legal and undocumented, who planned to remain permanently in New York increased. Hence migration from the Mixteca has now reached a kind of consolidated stability, and fewer new migrants are leaving the Mixteca. Second, quicker long-term settlement is becoming more common as a result of changes in the political economy of migration; these have been analyzed by the sociologists Douglas Massey and Nolan Malone and the Mexican anthropologist Jorge Durand.[16] Leigh Binford at the University of Puebla has documented "accelerated migration,"[17] by which the time from first migration to whole-town migration is reduced from two or more decades to less than one, especially in urban areas in Puebla with little previous history of migration. He attributes this boom in migration to the collapse of local industries, such as construction, in the wake of Mexico's 1994–95 peso crisis. Many of these migrants left in what I have elsewhere called a "backdraft" migration, whereby rural migrants to Mexican cities travel to the United States through contacts in their own or their parents' rural hometowns. Hence, migrants crossing illegally are now less likely to engage in circular migration, a pattern in which the family stays in Mexico and the migrant returns. This change is partly an ironic but predictable response to tightened U.S. border controls and partly due to the logic of family reunification fostered by the amnesty program. These changes have also increased the migration of unaccompanied adolescents, including some of the teen migrants I discuss later. Third, the origins and destinations of migrants have changed. The East Coast has become an important site of Mexican immigration. Areas such as the states of Tlaxcala, Tabasco, Morelos, and Mexico City and its neighboring conurbation in the state of Mexico, Ciudad Nezahualcoyotl (or "Neza," as migrants call it), are sending an increasing number of migrants. Some 11 percent of the immigrants in New York City are from Mexico City, and its population of twenty million promises more to come.[18] Migrants from Neza now say that they live in "Neza York."[19]

Bifurcated Prospects and "In-Between" Status

Ticuani transnational life reflects Mexicans' bifurcated fates in New York and their constant engagement with the city's economic, educational, and racial hierarchies. This dynamic of incorporation is embodied in the immigrant analogy, which poses the question: Why are descendants of Black slaves in the United States in so much worse shape, on average, than the descendants of white immigrants, if both faced discrimination in the United States? The formulation of the question mistakenly equates the historical experiences of Blacks and immigrants and leads to the facile answer that Blacks have failed through their own lack of effort and moral shortcomings, whereas immigrants have prospered because of their strong work ethnic and moral virtue. My grandparents suffered when they came here, goes the refrain, but we prospered. Why can't Blacks and their descendants do the same?

The intellectual roots of the immigrant analogy can be traced to W. E. B. DuBois, who observed in the 1930s that poor Southern whites got a "public, psychological wage" from being white that enabled them to feel superior to Blacks despite living in similarly miserable material conditions. When Irish immigrants started coming to the United States in significant numbers in the 1830s, they had much in common with Blacks. Both groups did dirty work for wealthier whites, both had been victimized by systematic prejudice, and they often lived side by side in the poorest parts of town. David Roediger and others use DuBois's insight to analyze how the "Irish became white." The Irish learned that to be full members of American society, it did not suffice to be "not black"; one also had to be "anti-black." This attitude was fostered by the Catholic Church and the Democratic party.[20]

The phenomenon recurs among recent nonwhite immigrants, such as the second-generation Caribbeans studied by the sociologist Mary Waters.[21] Mexicans in New York are just one of many new immigrant groups who must negotiate New York's and America's social and racial hierarchies, but Mexicans deserve special attention for several reasons. First, they are a growing population on the East Coast. Second, Mexicans do not fit into any obvious place in social and racial hierarchies. That is, in the United States most conceptions of race are based in America's "original sin" of slavery, with blackness historically signaling that a group is unfit and whiteness that it is fit for full membership in society. The darker your skin, the lower your place in the hierarchy. But this categorization is complicated in New York City—and increasingly in other places too—by the messy realities of race and class. Blacks in New York share the most stigmatized position at the bottom of the hierarchy with a Latino group, Puerto Ricans, and there are also stronger degrees of white ethnicity and racialization, due in part to the presence of white immigrants such as Greeks, Russians, and Italians, that introduce further complications into membership. Many Puerto Ricans appear "black" and experience consonant levels of racial segregation and discrimination, but they also speak Spanish and are identified as Latinos. Racial categorization is further complicated by class. A visible middle class is emerging among Blacks, Puerto Ricans, and other Latinos, especially Latino immigrants with higher educational levels and incomes, and those, such as Colombians, who tend to have lighter skin. Hence, many Mexican parents and their New York–born children wonder whether their futures will look more like the hard lives they associate with Puerto Ricans and Blacks or the upwardly mobile lives they associate with white ethnic immigrants and more prosperous Latino immigrants. Will Mexicans in New York become a marginalized, racialized minority or an upwardly mobile, incorporated ethnic group?

Segmented assimilation theory, as developed by Alejandro Portes, Ruben Rumbaut, Min Zhou and their colleagues, posits three possible paths for second-generation immigrants.[22] They can assimilate to the white middle class by surrendering their ethnicity, taking the path of upward mobility posited by classic assimilation theory. They can assimilate to an oppositional, inner-city culture that constitutes what Paul Willis called "doomed resistance" and which Herb Gans feared would contribute to "second-generation decline" for children of immigrants. Youths in this culture drop out of the schools and the labor market they see as oppressive.[23] This resistance seals their fate and creates a "rainbow underclass" composed of oppositional youth from many races. Or, finally, second-generation immigrants and their communities can use their ethnicity to circumvent discrimination and define themselves as different from both the white mainstream and their less successful inner-city counterparts.

This theory powerfully describes the fears and perceptions of first-generation parents and the reality for many second-generation Mexicans in New York. But it also leaves out important possibilities, for example the minority culture of mobility posited by Kathryn Neckerman and her colleagues, by which minorities develop nonoppositional ways to negotiate racism while being upwardly mobile.[24] In its first incarnation, segmented assimilation theory also failed to give enough attention to gender. But if we consider minority cultures of mobility, and carefully splice racialization and gender processes into the explanation, this theory can help us understand the contemporary immigrant and second-generation experience.

The prospects for Mexican immigrants in New York are divergent. On the one hand, the Mexican-origin population showed alarming signs of social distress in the 1990 census compared to 1980. For example, Mexicans in New York went from having one of the highest per capita incomes among Latinos in New York in 1980, nearly equivalent to that of Cubans, to among the lowest in 1990; incomes rose only slightly in 2000. The decline was particularly pronounced for those without a high school education: it dropped from $17,495 in 1980 to $13,537 in 1990, a net drop in unadjusted dollars of 22.6 percent, constituting a more than 50 percent drop in per capita income, adjusted for inflation, for this group.[25] The per capita income in 2000 of Mexican workers increased nominally, to $15,631 for men and $11,731 for women, but this gain represented no real increase in buying power over their 1990 earnings. Indeed, it placed them at least $2,000 behind their nominal earnings of twenty years earlier! Not surprisingly, a cohort analysis shows that fully 81 percent of men and 70 percent of Mexican American women were not upwardly mobile in their occupations during the 1980s.[26]

A further sign of social distress is that in 1990 and again in the 2000 census Mexicans had the highest rate of sixteen- to nineteen-year-olds who were not in high school and had not graduated: 47 percent, compared with the next-highest groups, Dominicans and Puerto Ricans, with 22 percent each in 1990.[27] Perhaps most disturbing, in 2000 school enrollment rates for Mexican boys and girls dropped from 95 percent and 96 percent at ten to fourteen years to 25 percent and 31 percent among those aged eighteen to nineteen.[28] This confirms my ethnographic findings that Mexicans drop out of school in large numbers by the end of the sophomore year.

It is not a tale of straight decline, however. In part, these distressing trends are artifacts of the high levels of Mexican immigration, especially teen immigration, during the 1980s and 1990s. The influx of young Mexican immigrants with low levels of education masks the progress of a significant minority of Mexicans and Mexican Americans, especially Mexican American women, in New York. Between 1980 and 1990, cohort analysis shows, Mexican Americans' levels of education were improving steadily, though not dramatically. Nineteen percent of men and 31 percent of women were upwardly mobile in terms of occupational prestige and associated pay and conditions. An important path for mobility in the 1990s, especially for women, has been skilled secretarial and retail work. Indeed, some 34 percent of Mexican-heritage women (compared with 15 percent of Mexican-heritage men) worked in technical and administrative support positions, such as legal or medical secretary. This "pink-collar economy" of skilled support staff[29] requires a high-school diploma and vocational training or an associate's degree. Our informants and their immigrant parents see these jobs as real progress—"clean" jobs, "in an office," with health insurance and paid vacations. Second-generation women were also nearly twice as likely as men to work in the professional and technical sector of the economy—17 percent versus 9 percent in the 1990 and 2000 censuses.

The contingency in Mexican prospects is linked to the way they enter New York's labor market. Research on immigrants and labor markets indicates that the more "niched" an ethnic group is—the more highly concentrated in specific industries and jobs—the better for the group, because its members have greater access to job opportunities and training. Having a niche in a growing industry enables the group to advance itself. Even a niche in a shrinking industry allows at least some members of the group to use ethnic ties to move up or maintain their positions, especially if another ethnic group is leaving that industry.[30] Mexicans in New York—like those in California—were among the least niched of all immigrants in 1990,[31] and most niches in New York included only about 2 percent of the Mexican working population.

A wide dispersion across industries and jobs has negative long-term consequences for the group's advancement and development of human and social capital. Immigrant parents of Mexican Americans have few resources to help their children move up within their own industries, often being unable or reluctant to get them jobs in their own firms. In fact, many second-generation Mexicans we interviewed ended up getting their first jobs in the same industry as their parents, but often not in the same firm. When parents do help their children get jobs, they are the kinds of entry-level jobs that undocumented immigrants occupy.

Yet Mexicans were more niched in 1990 than they were in 1980, and some niche concentrations seem to have grown during the 1990s. In 1990, the census showed that 10 percent of Mexican men worked in restaurants,[32] but this percentage has certainly grown, as can be shown by a quick glance into the kitchen of almost any New York restaurant. Ticuanenses have been established in the restaurant industry for a long time—some 25 percent of them worked in restaurants in 1993. Many Ticuanenses work in private dining clubs or hotels in midtown Manhattan and have advanced through the clubs' "internal labor market," gaining seniority and excellent salaries with benefits. As a result, they have gained a foothold in New York's middle class, enabling their children to graduate from high school and get some form of postsecondary education.

A larger niche for Ticuanenses has been work in Greek and other ethnic restaurants. In these cases, Ticuanense and other Mexican immigrants have been able to move from being busboys to cooks or waiters, with commensurate increases in pay, through what I call "fictive coethnicity"—an identification of employer and employees as fellow immigrants (and sometimes also as Christians), making them different from those born in the United States. The demand for Mexican instead of Greek (or Korean, or other group) labor stems from Greeks' (or Koreans') very high rates of self-employment in New York and the lack of cheap immigrant labor from these countries. Greek immigrants want to own restaurants, not work for others. During the 1990s, Greek employer networks sought Mexican employees, and Mexican immigrants became aware of this need, with the result that nearly every Greek restaurant now employs Mexicans. My research shows that Greek restaurants have offered Mexican immigrants an internal labor market—the chance to start with few skills and learn and advance on the job and in many cases to enjoy the "enclave effect," by which one earns more than one's educational level would predict.[33] Such results do not show up in the census per capita income data because the earnings of the upwardly mobile segments of the Mexican community are outweighed by miserable wages of new workers.

The implication that the life chances of the second generation are partly determined by the economic niches entered by the first generation is borne out by comparing the restaurant and garment industries. My informants tell me that not only did workers make less money in garment factories, but the internal labor market there was also more constrained, offering fewer chances for advancement. Moreover, the garment industry is a shrinking industry and one in which other immigrant groups are already ahead of Mexicans in the queue to become the next owners. Roger Waldinger has shown that immigrant groups such as Koreans were able to advance to ownership despite a shrinking of the garment industry because of the massive exodus of Jewish and Italian owners during the 1970s and 1980s.[34] But because Mexicans in the garment industry work for employers from different ethnic groups, they are easier to exploit. And because new groups such as Koreans are not leaving the industry, there are fewer opportunities to become business owners. The lower earnings among Mexicans in the garment than restaurant industry are also partly due to the fact that, among Mexicans, the former industry employs mainly women, while the latter employs mainly men. Hence, Mexicans whose networks direct them into the garment industry face a bleaker future than those who work in restaurants.

This quick evaluation of Mexicans' economic prospects contradicts the predictions of much of the academic literature on immigrants. Many scholars approach immigrant economic life with the model of a primary labor market, in which some workers, usually in major companies, earn good salaries, benefits, and job security, while other workers, especially immigrants, women, and minorities, are channeled into the secondary labor market, with its poor wages, insecurity, and lack of benefits. Yet this two-part model reflects the labor market of the 1960s and 1970s more than today's. Although most immigrants do start in the secondary labor market, a significant minority of immigrants and their children have been able to move beyond it. And there are intermediate markets, such as the pink-collar economy, that offer real opportunity to some children of immigrants. None of this denies that most children of Mexican immigrants will face a hard future; but it suggests that there are alternative routes to upward mobility.

The educational future of Mexicans and Mexican Americans appears bright for some and grim for many. The influx of younger migrants has made dropping out of school more common, in part because it has dramatically increased the size of the population at risk. Before the 1990s, young people generally stayed in Mexico until they were eighteen or twenty and then came to New York to work, not study. By this age they saw themselves as adults and were less likely to become involved in adolescent tribulations such as gangs. Today, Mexican youth encounter the schools, the *sonidos* (dance parties), and other youth arenas as adolescents and undergo a secondary socialization that can negatively affect their futures. Moreover, the dramatic influx of Mexicans into New York City's schools has led to abuse from other groups.[35] Teenage boys, especially, are likely to join gangs or negotiate a looser association known as "hangin'" with gangs, for their own protection.[36] High dropout rates for Mexicans and Mexican Americans are at least partly attributable to these dynamics.

The presence of a growing percentage of urban migrants, especially from Mexico City, may have exacerbated these problems. While migrants from Mexico City tend to be more educated (with eight or nine years of education instead of five or six for rural immigrants) and more accustomed to an urban environment, they also seem more likely to come to New York without their parents and join less tightly organized communities in New York, with fewer resources and less adult supervision. Moreover, some teen migrants have prior experience in Mexico with drugs and gangs; some may even bring their gangs with them. The increase in gang activity among Mexican youths might also damage the public perception of Mexicans in New York as diligent workers and conscientious students, closing opportunities for them.

Mexicans' ambiguous locations in New York's racial and ethnic hierarchies make it possible to analyze the process of racialization as it is happening, when outcomes are still contingent, and see how it is linked to transnational life. These processes can be observed in urban social spaces, such as schools, parks, and neighborhoods, that Mexicans occupy along with other ethnic groups. Many are "emergent" spaces, constituted ephemerally, as when groups of Mexicans informally occupy a park on a Sunday for their basketball league or rent a club for a dance.[37] Their occupation of that space makes it Mexican or Ticuanense for that time, asserting what William Flores, Rena Benmayor, and Renato Resaldo might call Mexican (or Ticuanense) "cultural citizenship." This claim to space sometimes occasions ethnic antagonism from other groups, but more often there is ethnic accommodation, or coexistence. But even here, Mexicans sometimes attribute particular cultural meanings to their gathering. Cultural citizenship theory posits such claims of belonging as being made with respect to a dominant white society; here, they are usually made with respect to Blacks or other Latinos. They create a racialized meaning even in the absence of racial or ethnic confrontation. They also help create a context for transnational life because these same events are used to reinforce attachment to Ticuani and Padre Jesús.

New York City's great diversity means that most immigrant groups or other groups, including Puerto Ricans, do not constitute a majority of the population, even in "their own" neighborhoods or in immigrant majority areas. So, although many Chinese, Dominicans, West Indians, or Puerto Ricans do make up a majority in their neighborhoods, most other groups—including Ecuadorans, Pakistanis, Indians, and Koreans—experience themselves as being both foreign and a minority among minorities. And many, if not most, Puerto Ricans, for example, live in neighborhoods where they are not a majority.

Mexican locations in social and ethnic hierarchies have been reinforced by Mexicans' geographic dispersal in New York City, which was surprisingly high until the mid 1990s. Hence most Mexicans in New York experienced being Mexican as being a minority, usually among other minorities. The "Mexican" neighborhoods that began to emerge during the 1990s are not as fully "Mexican" in population as East Los Angeles or the Pilsin District in Chicago. Mexicans in Mexican neighborhoods in New York are usually not a majority of the population, although they may be the largest minority and have a strong public presence.

These points are illustrated by maps 2 and 3. Map 2a shows the numbers of Puerto Ricans per census tract in the year 2000. Map 2b shows the change from 1990 to 2000 in numbers of Mexicans per census tract. As can be seen, many of the census tracts and neighborhoods experiencing the largest influx of Mexicans during the 1990s had much larger numbers of Puerto Ricans. Map 3 shows the percentage change in Mexican population per census tract between 1990 and 2000. The map shows about twenty census tracts throughout the city that were more than 20 percent Mexican and a much larger number with lower percentages. If we focus on Sunset Park, an important, emerging Little Mexico in Brooklyn (which is just south and west of the two large white areas, a cemetery and a park, in the lower left-hand corner of map 3), the census tells us that within the neighborhood's main zip code (11232), Mexicans constituted only 13 percent of the total population and 20 percent of the Latino population, while Puerto Ricans made up 22 percent of the total population and 38 percent of the Latino population. This settlement pattern has very frequently placed Mexicans in neighborhoods with large numbers of Puerto Ricans. Often, the Mexican immigrant experience has been that of newcomers in a neighborhood understood to be Puerto Rican.

Given this high degree of overlap in areas of settlement, Mexicans often seek energetically to differentiate their children's futures from the social

Puerto Ricans

☐ 0 to 50
▨ 50 to 200
▰ 200 to 1,000
■ 1,000 to 4,439

MAP 2a. Number of Puerto Ricans living in each census tract, New York City, 2000.

distress of the Puerto Rican community they see around them. In this context, the immigrant analogy is not a theoretical lens but rather a ready explanation of the fate of Puerto Ricans in New York, and a reassurance to Mexican immigrants there that they and their children will not turn out as they believe Puerto Ricans have—too assimilated, too Americanized, ignorant of their culture, and dependent on welfare and crime. They fear the Puerto Rican present will become their Mexican future. I often hear the classic statement "Not all Puerto Ricans are like that—I have Puerto Rican

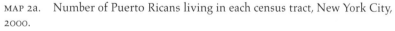

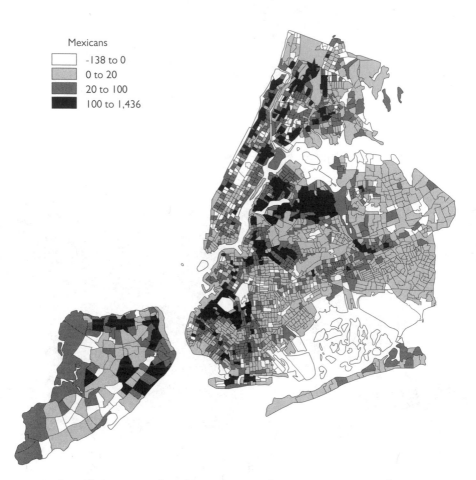

Mexicans

☐ -138 to 0
▨ 0 to 20
▦ 20 to 100
■ 100 to 1,436

MAP 2b.   Change in number of Mexicans in each census tract, New York City, 1990–2000. (Thanks to John Mollenkopf of CUNY's Urban Research Center for producing and generously sharing these maps.)

MAP 3 (FACING PAGE).   Mexicans as percentage of population, by census tract, New York City, 1990 and 2000. (Thanks to John Logan of Brown University for producing and generously sharing this map.)

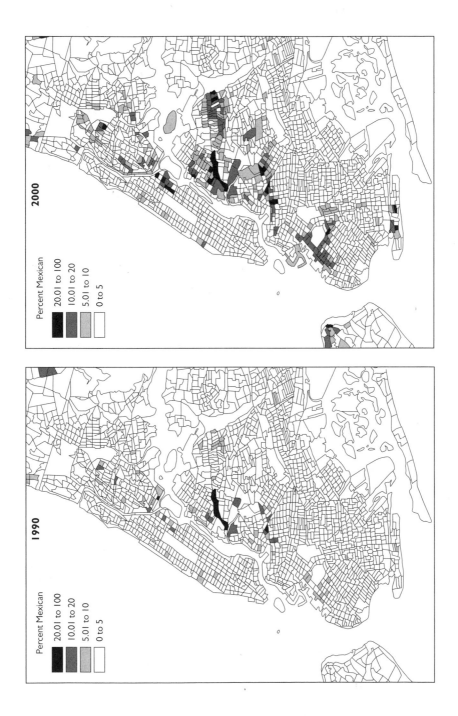

friends who are good people—but many of them are like this." This formula is not a simple repetition of the contemporary American custom of always making an individual exception to any disparaging ethnic or racial generalization. Rather, it reflects two dimensions of Mexican–Puerto Rican relations. While Mexicans fear that the Puerto Rican present could be their future, they also have had very positive experiences with Puerto Ricans and other Latinos in New York. They often feel indebted to Puerto Ricans who helped them when they came to New York, back when few Mexicans lived there. Many Mexicans have married Puerto Ricans or benefited from the extended family networks and social customs of Puerto Ricans. For example, Doña Selena recalled of a Puerto Rican neighbor: "Doña Silvia took care of our girls for years, we worked and she took care of them, she lived below us."[38] First-generation Mexicans tend to value the help of their Puerto Rican friends but to lament and fear the social distress Puerto Ricans as a group are thought to experience. In imagining a different future for their own children, Mexicans use the readily available American tool, the immigrant analogy, to posit a racialized difference between themselves and Puerto Ricans.

I observed this pattern of regular engagement and intermittent conflict with Puerto Ricans in several Brooklyn neighborhoods with many Ticuanenses. In one neighborhood where a sizable Mexican group emerged during the 1990s, they lived among Bangladeshis—whom they called "Hindus"—and other Latinos, especially Dominicans and Puerto Ricans. I saw or heard of no serious conflict with the Bangladeshis, and little with the Dominicans, but the young Mexicans did talk about their victimization by Puerto Ricans. Another neighborhood included Italians, Hasidic Jews, and some Latinos, among them Puerto Ricans. Here again, I was never told of serious conflict with Italians or Hasidic Jews, but stories of Puerto Rican aggression were plentiful. A third neighborhood consisted mainly of Puerto Ricans, Dominicans, and African Americans, and here the dominant stories of conflict involved African American and Puerto Rican youth gangs, or crews, from the nearby housing projects. It seemed that the Bangladeshis and Hasidic Jews inhabited a kind of parallel universe in the same physical space as the Mexicans but had little to do with them, while the Puerto Rican and Mexican universes overlapped. For example, walking through these neighborhoods with Mexican immigrant or second-generation friends, I saw that they rarely greeted any of their neighbors or were acknowledged by them. Even second-generation store or restaurant owners did not seem to know those living on their immediate block; the public they served was a Mexican one that came from other parts of town to transact business.

Given how much Puerto Rican–Mexican conflict is discussed here, I should state that I do not think there is anything essential about being Mexican or Puerto Rican that makes these groups more susceptible to conflict, nor about being Italian, "Hindu," Hasidic, or white that makes them less so. I think the higher apparent rates of conflict with Puerto Ricans arise from the sudden appearance of a large Mexican population settling in Puerto Rican areas of the city and attending the same schools, combined with perceived workforce competition and a common language other than English. If these conditions applied equally to other groups, I would expect similar conflicts. Howard Pinderhughes documents how some of the Italian teens he talked to in the late 1980s and early 1990s purposely targeted Mexicans (as well as Blacks and Puerto Ricans) in an attempt to show their toughness to their peers and to make sure their neighborhoods stayed Italian.[39] The two neighborhoods he worked in, Gravesend and Bensonhurst, were at the time getting small but more visible concentrations of Mexicans in areas where none had been before. My focus on Puerto Rican–Mexican conflict results from its frequent appearance in stories from my young informants and from my sense that this conflict in particular served a strategic function in Mexican narratives of migration and settlement in New York.

The second generation's engagement with the immigrant analogy is more complex for a variety of reasons, including the fact that this group has grown up more immersed in New York's racial hierarchies and in its public schools, parks, and other social spaces. They are likely to have Puerto Rican friends and to identify with Blacks and Puerto Ricans. Most Mexicans, Puerto Ricans, and Blacks attend schools that are mostly Black or Latino. This tendency to identify with Blacks and Puerto Ricans as oppressed minorities—which fits with the concept of a rainbow underclass[40]—competes with the tendency to adopt the immigrant-analogy position of their parents, in which Mexican is better.

The first and second generations also engage racialization and the immigrant analogy in different ways in the labor market. The first generation's experience in the labor market usually engages racialization through what one can call "doubly bounded solidarity"—bounded on one side by not being white and on the other by not being Black.[41] While many Korean, Greek, Italian, or native-born American employers explicitly or implicitly compare Mexican immigrants favorably with native-born Blacks and Puerto Ricans, they also see the Mexicans as immigrants like themselves (or their parents or grandparents). This comparison can lead an employer to identify strongly with the employee, emphasizing their common ground and their shared difference from native minorities.[42] Even in the most exploitative work relationships, Mexican immigrants' willingness to work for lower wages is understood by both sides to be a mark of their stronger work ethic compared with U.S.-born minorities. Even when Mexican workers say they are exploited, unlike native-born employees they also point proudly to their desire to work hard.

The second generation's experiences in the labor market are more diverse. Their conditions of incorporation yield both significant upward mobility and frustrated prospects. About a fifth of the second-generation boys and a third of the girls are upwardly mobile in terms of occupation and education; the rest are showing little progress, and a small number are slipping backward. These numbers are roughly consistent with the results of large-scale studies using the census in California.[43] In highly racialized contexts such as New York, such a pattern of limited mobility often leads to pressures on young people to reject American institutions like school.

The growing minority of upwardly mobile second-generation workers has a less highly charged engagement with racialization than do their parents or other second-generation youth. For example, many second-generation college students hold decently paid part-time jobs in work-study or in retail companies like the Gap, Borders Books, and Bed, Bath and Beyond. These jobs offer what Victoria Malkin incisively describes as a "Benetton" context—one in which their ethnicity is cool and chic, not racialized and stigmatized. This is an especially important pathway for young men who can take advantage of it, because their alternatives lie in factories, restaurants, or other sectors of the service economy with limited prospects. Young women, who are more likely to work as professionals than their male counterparts, are also likely to experience their Mexicanness as having a positive or neutral effect on their status at work.[44]

Yet most second-generation men and women are stuck in jobs offering similar pay and conditions to those of their parents. Some parents of second-generation children who do badly in school drag their children to work in garment factories beside them, to dissuade them from working young and dropping out of school. Although the children dislike the factory work, many end up following their parents into this type of job. Some even contrast their immigrant parents' good jobs with their own limited chances. One young man, who dropped out of college and now works for a very low wage in the kitchen of a large institution, spoke with envy of his father's job as a cook at a fancy restaurant. He said that his father could not help him get a job there, partly because they wanted to hire only immigrants, not U.S.-born workers. Thus, among the upwardly mobile segment of the second generation, Mexicanness is more likely to carry a positive connotation of ethnicity in the labor market, whereas among those who are stuck or downwardly mobile, it often carries a stigmatized racial connotation.

The engagement with racialization can vary at different times of day and in different contexts. Consider a Mexican immigrant working in a factory that offers little chance to advance, whose Korean boss pays bad wages and yells at his Mexican workers, hiring them only because he can pay them one-third what he would have to pay Korean workers.[45] Now imagine this immigrant's home in a Puerto Rican neighborhood, where large numbers of new Mexican arrivals are seen as unfair competition and some are targeted by youth gangs. For maximum contrast, consider a second Mexican working in a much larger Greek restaurant in which he can expect to advance and where his employer sees the two of them as sharing the virtues of hardworking immigrants. Next, put him in a white Italian neighborhood with few Mexicans, who are seen as fellow immigrants and Catholics, struggling as their own grandparents did. The first immigrant is likely to be called "Mexico" as he walks on the street and to be or at least feel threatened, while the second is likely to go about his daily routine and be left alone. Being "Mexican" for the first one has a completely different meaning than for the second.

Similarly, second-generation youths born or raised in the United States experience their Mexicanness differently depending on where they live, hang out, and go to school. Imagine the son of the first immigrant above, living in a largely Puerto Rican neighborhood where youth gangs pick on Mexicans and attending a school where various youth gangs, especially other Mexican gangs, challenge him. Imagine the son of the second immigrant in the Italian or Greek neighborhood, and put him in a school that is academically stronger, where Mexicans have not become a target. The life chances of the second youth are better than the first, all other things being equal, and the meaning of Mexicanness for the two of them will be very different. (Of course, if the Mexicans begin to settle in large numbers in Italian or Greek areas and come to be seen as invaders or underbidding competitors, such positive scenarios will be harder to imagine.)

Mexicans encounter an in-between status, where they do not fit easily into any one category, in a somewhat different way within larger American institutions. For example, the American Catholic Church has been both slow and eager to embrace Mexicans. While some forward-thinking parish priests and administrators pushed to have a Jesuit brother, Joel Magallan, brought up to New York to organize Asociación Tepeyac—the first pan–New York Mexican religious organization—in 1997, my informants report that the larger Catholic Church has been slower to respond. When trying to persuade archdiocesan officials of the importance of Tepeyac's mission in ministering to Mexican Catholics in New York, I have always been politely received. But there is a perception in the church, described to me by priests and laypersons alike, that Mexican parishioners' needs can be taken care of by "Mr. Rodriguez, who speaks Spanish." Mr. Rodriguez is usually a Puerto Rican layman with years of service in the parish. The perception behind this statement is that language is the only issue. The administrators fail to understand that, as predominantly U.S. citizens, Puerto Ricans face different issues from the mainly undocumented Mexican members of the Church. This is one example of how Mexicans' in-between status complicates their position in New York.

For Mexicans in New York, engagement with racialization, the immigrant analogy, and segmented assimilation together provide a compelling impetus to participate in transnational life. A person's attitude toward and involvement in transnational life depend to some degree on how he or she is doing in the United States. An upwardly mobile person is likely to see the engagement with transnational life and return trips to Mexico as positive. Someone on a downward trajectory or struggling in New York is more likely to see transnational life as negative or mixed. Returning to Mexico, for instance, may represent a kind of exportation back to Mexico of the problems with assimilation in the United States. Hence assimilation, far from being incompatible with transnational life, greatly affects it. And immigrants' experiences in New York also shape and influence the transnational life of their hometowns in Mexico.

THE MIXTECA: TRANSFORMED BY AND ANCHORING TRANSNATIONAL LIFE

"We build houses that nobody lives in," the workmen tell me.[46] Like many poor Ticuanenses, these workmen toil in one of the few thriving industries in the Mixteca: building houses for migrants in New York who use the houses for a few weeks' vacation every year or two. Indeed, the construction of empty houses has been extensive, and the nearest available building sites to the center of town are now more than two miles down the main road. Land prices in the center of Ticuani are said to be higher than in the city of Puebla. And these houses are not the old adobe houses that were common when I first went to Ticuani in the late 1980s. They are huge, built of cinderblock, with two floors, large foyers and windows, a patio, and amenities unimaginable to Ticuanense locals. Some even have American-style pitched roofs instead of the flat ones typical of the Mixteca. (Similar changes in housing construction were noted in Swedish and Italian sending communities during the last wave of migration.)[47] Being in Ticuani during the Feast of Padre Jesús, when the migrants return, and afterward, when they have left, feels like being in two different towns: the first is a bustling town where young people dance late into the night, families eat and laugh together, and money flows, and the second is a nursery and nursing home where the young and old await the return of their relatives in New York.

Driving from the city of Puebla to Ticuani, one sees how the Mixteca region is both marginalized and transnationalized. Descending from the mountains that separate the Mixteca from the rest of Puebla, one finds that the roads are in worse repair, vegetation is sparser, and the mountains are covered with sere shrubs; yet, numerous travel agencies list prices for flights to New York, signs advertise videos and cell phones, and parabolic television antennas—which the locals call "metal flowers"—sprout from the roofs of the houses. Internet cafes have popped up, linking migrants and stay-at-homes by e-mail. As the Mixteca drives people north, technology moves in to keep them in touch with their relatives who stay behind.

The changes caused by migration have transformed Ticuani and the Mixteca and affected the dynamics of politics and generation in several ways. First, migration juxtaposes new and old forms of social organization, exacerbates inequalities, and creates new possibilities, including transnational ones, for political and social action. Second, the nature of transnational dynamics changes as the process of migration itself matures. Hence, these transnational ties are durable—meaning that they persist long enough to produce further identifiable social patterns that last at least a decade. But they are not necessarily permanent, and evidence suggests that some are attenuating. Relations between those in the sending communities and their relatives abroad go through three stages. In the "migration" phase, migration involves most of the town's population. In the "settlement" phase, large numbers of migrants settle in the new country, and influence flows in both directions. In the "consolidation" phase, as local outmigration decreases and settlement in the United States increases, new kinds of relationships emerge.[48] Ticuani is now entering the consolidation phase. It still evidences a great deal of transnational activity, despite a decrease in outmigration, because of the established links between those settled in New York and those in Ticuani. This three-phase approach draws on the work of Robert Ostergren and of Douglas Massey and his colleagues on how the migration process itself matures[49] but goes beyond that analysis

FIGURE 1.   Two views of Ticuani. *Top:* view of the chapel on the hill, circa 1920; note the preponderance of adobe houses (photo by Adan Lazaro Fortoso). *Bottom:* the same view, 2004; note the two- and three-story houses (photo by author).

to examine the effects on transnational life—the relations between those in Mexico and in the United States. I begin with a brief history of the Mixteca and move through Ticuani's demographic, social, and economic changes with the goal of conveying a palpable sense of the tensions and changes underpinning transnational life.

Introduction to the Mixteca

During my first visit to the Mixteca, in 1988, I stared in awe from the bus window at the cactuses standing taller than telephone poles. The Mixteca is hot, mountainous, dry, and poor. The population has lower levels of education than the rest of Puebla, and a higher percentage live at or near subsistence level. Agriculture, the main livelihood, is singularly unsuited to the Mixteca's dry climate and has spurred outmigration, first to Puebla, Veracruz, and Mexico City, and since then to the United States. According to Don Andrés, a former municipal president and teacher in Ticuani, "Farming did not give you enough to live on, never mind to live decently, and from that surges the necessity to . . . go to the United States." Indigenous industries in the Mixteca, such as the weaving of palm mats, have declined since the 1960s. Raising livestock, especially goats suited to the terrain, can be profitable but requires significant wealth to purchase the animals.[50] The marginalization of the Mixteca both contributes to outmigration and is exacerbated by it.

Socially and politically, the Mixteca is syncretic and local, and these conditions have affected the emergence of transnational life. By syncretic, I mean that some old forms of organization persist even while new ones are superimposed on them. The Mixteca shows a fascinating mix of pre-Columbian and pre-Mexican indigenous practices and modern ones, arising from attempts by first the Spanish and then the Mexican government to "modernize the Indians." Thus two primary forms of local governance coexist: the cacique system and what Eric Wolf has called the "closed corporate peasant community system," also known as the *council of elders* system. *Caciquismo* as a form of political organization emerged in steps in the Mixteca, first as the Spanish imposed it on more collective, indigenous forms of social organization and then as the Mexican state and the PRI, the long-dominant political party, used the caciques as building blocks. Caciques are local political bosses who derive their power from brokering relations between the community and the outside world and by controlling both the use of force and access to outside resources.[51] In the closed corporate peasant community, authority and honor derive from participating in the rotating system of religious-political office holding (called the cargo system), in which all honorable men must take their turn at leadership, overseeing such events as the feast of the patron saint. The closed corporate peasant community survived the destruction of higher-level, pre-Columbian forms of political and social organization to coexist to various degrees in Mexico, especially in areas in Puebla, Oaxaca, and Chiapas, with a significant indigenous population. The cacique system and the closed corporate community often reinforce each other, but they come into conflict in Ticuani transnational politics.

The Mixteca's localism is manifest in rivalries between neighboring villages. Competition between Ticuani and El Ganado has at times been particularly fierce. Local lore, an academic history of Spanish settlements in the 1500s, and outside observers tell the same story. Ticuani was a point of passage for indigenous peoples, including Chinantecos, Olmecs, and Mixtecos. The Spanish strategically built a new settlement adjacent to it, in El Ganado, in order to impose Spanish religion and governance. This new, artificially created community caused friction and resentment. The enduring rivalry between El Ganado and Ticuani comes out in Ticuanenses' referring to Ganadenses as "immigrants," "more white-skinned," "Spanish," and "rich," while they describe themselves as "more indigenous, more authentic," with more "pure blood." Ganadenses say that Ticuanenses speak Spanish with odd indigenous intonations. Differences in the economy and customs of the towns were also described in 1958 by Denise O'Brien, who noted, among other observations, how few bicycles Ticuani had. Recalling those years, Leobardo told me he and his friends used to run after the man with the first bicycle in the town, so awed were they by it. O'Brien noted that everyone in Ticuani made their living by farming, whereas El Ganado had many merchants. Ganadenses were lighter-skinned, had European names like Blanca Rosa (white rose), and had disposable incomes sufficient to buy things like bicycles, which Ticuanenses did not have. Such historical differences shed some light on why Ticuani transnational life is more collectively oriented, whereas those at the center of El Ganado transnational life tend to be successful businessmen in New York (who still attempt to use communal practices to raise funds).

This rivalry is reflected in how Ticuanenses explain the meaning of the Dance of the Tecuanis, which is practiced throughout the Mixteca region, though local interpretations and variations are myriad. *Tecuani*, also spelled *Tecuane*, means "tiger" in Nahuatl, an indigenous language that until recent years was widely used as a first language in the Mixteca region. According to state anthropological museums, the consistent theme in the dance is that the peasants, represented by dancing youths dressed in masks and traditional hats, seek and after several tries kill the tiger or jaguar that has been killing their farm animals.[52] In Ticuani, there is another interpretation, which is that the peasants are, according to Leobardo, "making fun of the Spaniards . . . by dressing in old, torn clothes and really big coats." Hence, by dressing like Spanish dandies, but in worn-out clothes, the Ticuanenses are making fun of those with power. Moreover, the jaguar (who is now also joined by a wolf, *la loba*) is no longer a threat to the Ticuanenses but rather protects the town against outward menaces, be they thieves, other animals, or Spaniards. This inversion of the story speaks to the rivalry between Ticuani and El Ganado and the use of images of authentic, indigenous people versus immigrant Spaniards.

The Mixteca's syncretism and localism underpin transnational life. They provide compelling communal practices that migrate with its migrants. These include religious and cultural events for Ticuani migrants and their children; especially important for the second generation are the Antorcha and the Dance of the Tecuanis. They also include political practices, such as collecting funds in New York for Ticuani communal projects. At the same time, the local power of the cacique often conflicts with the "external" power exerted by migrants in the United States, who feel they have earned authority, according to the logic of the closed corporate peasant community, by their sacrifice and communal labor. Juxtaposing these two forms of governance and honor creates a dynamic tension that alters the possibilities for thought and action in Ticuani politics, helping to create a transnational political community.[53]

Migration and Durable Transnational Life

How profoundly Ticuani had changed by the mid-1990s can be gauged by how its main coyote—a smuggler of undocumented immigrants to the United States—responded to my asking him how business was. Was he bringing many people north? He laughed: What people? Everyone in Ticuani had already left. He was expanding his markets in Oaxaca and Guerrero. As we stood in the zocalo after the Feast was over, his point was clear. Around us were old men and women and young children, some with their mothers, but almost no one of working age. The extensive social, economic and demographic changes, and the decrease in the number of new migrants, make Ticuani a mature migrant community, subject to conflicts and inequalities that are played out transnationally.

Migration from the Mixteca over the last twenty years has reached levels comparable to those in classic sending states such as Zacatecas, which have had high levels of migration for more than sixty years, with similar changes in social structure and transnational life. Ticuani's population dropped from about 4,000 in 1958 and 4,600 in 1970 to about 3,800 in 1980, 2,500 in 1990, and 1,800 or fewer in 2000.[54] Ticuani lost 38 percent of its population during the 1980s, and 28 percent of that already depleted population left during the 1990s. Don Andrés, speaking of all Ticuanenses, whether in Ticuani or New York (including New York–born children) told me in 2000 that "we who live here permanently are like 45 percent or 40 percent—and 60 percent live outside the town." A survey I conducted in February 1992 showed that 41 percent of all Ticuanenses (U.S.- or Mexico-born) resided in New York City and 48 percent in Ticuani itself.[55] That Ticuani only lost about 700 migrants during the 1990s, compared with about 1,300 during the 1980s, suggests that its potential migrant population was virtually exhausted.

Telephone records from Ticuani also indicate its orientation toward New York. Before the mid-1990s, when direct dialing service was installed, all calls had to be routed through an operator using a switchboard. International calls involved waiting hours for an operator in Mexico City. For me, this meant that my wife and I could talk for twenty minutes a week after waiting three hours for the call to go through. The silver lining for me was that these calls were logged by hand in the local telephone operators' notebook, so that I was able to count how many calls went to which area codes and draw inferences about migrant destinations. During a typical month in 1992, there were roughly ten times as many calls placed to the United States as to all long-distance destinations in Mexico—288 versus 28. Of these, 209 were to New York City and 36 to other parts of the New York metropolitan area (New York, New Jersey, and Connecticut).

The 1986 Amnesty

The amnesty provision of the 1986 Immigration Reform and Control Act (IRCA) facilitated the conduct of transnational life by making it cheaper, faster, and easier to travel between Ticuani and New York. Undocumented immigrants could legalize their status if they met certain conditions, and many Ticuanenses did.[56] Table 1, opposite, shows the legal status of migrants on their first and their most recent trip to the United States. Whereas 66 percent of these migrants report being undocumented on their first trip back to Mexico, only 16.3 percent were undocumented on their most recent trip. A further 23.5 percent used a tourist visa on their first trip to the United States; assuming that most of these overstayed their visas, roughly 89.6 percent of the sample were either undocumented or likely to become so on their first trip. Of the migrants with legal status, 41.8 percent

TABLE 1. *Migrants' U.S. Immigration Status on First Trip and Most Recent Trip to Ticuani*

	First Trip		Most Recent Trip	
	Number	*%*	*Number*	*%*
Undocumented	76	66.1	16	16.3
Documented	8	6.9	36	36.7
Tourist visa	27	23.5	2	2.0
U.S. citizen	3	2.6	3	3.1
Covered by 1986 amnesty	1	0.9	41	41.8
Total	115	100.0	98	100.0

SOURCE: Author's survey, February 1992.

had legalized their status through amnesty. Another 36.7 percent did so through other means, yielding a return migrant population that was 78.5 percent documented and 18.5 percent undocumented.

The legal status afforded by IRCA allowed migrants to travel between Mexico and the United States without paying a coyote or running the risks of an illegal crossing. They could plan visits without risking losing their jobs in New York if they were caught reentering the United States or if they stayed in Ticuani longer than planned because of the uncertainty of when they would next be able to return. "Having papers" has also changed the psychological orientation of both migrants and stay-at-homes. The mother of one Committee member told me, with a smile, that having papers now gave her son no excuse for not visiting her. Her son said that with his papers, he would return more often, and that it made sense to "invest in a video camera" with which he could tape the Feast and watch the tapes in New York with his Ticuanense friends.

Yet amnesty has spurred outmigration that in the long run weakens local transnational life. The single biggest jump in outmigration from Ticuani came during the amnesty program,[57] much of it because children of migrants were able to join their parents in the United States. Ticuani's middle school opened in 1981 with 139 students, all of them born in Ticuani. By January 2000, 63 percent of the schools' students came from outside Ticuani—6 percent born in the United States, 57 percent born in other towns in the Mixteca. The exodus from Ticuani means that its middle-school enrollment numbers must be maintained by bringing children in from elsewhere. School records indicate that during the peak years of student outmigration, between 1993 and 1998, 24 percent of the students left in the middle of the year—almost all, according to teachers, to join their parents in New York. More students left to rejoin their parents during the summer, after the school year had ended. And 84 of 96 students surveyed in 2000 had family members in the United States, making them also likely to migrate. The director of Ticuani's secondary and high schools told me that one of his classes lost 25 of 60 students one summer during the amnesty program. Their departure triggered an investigation by state educational officials in the capital of Puebla, who suspected that school leaders had been stealing funds allotted for students who did not exist. Yet the same story of family reunification was repeated all throughout the Mixteca during the late 1980s to mid 1990s.

This surge in youth migration, including teen migration, to New York is apparent in the increasing numbers of young Mexicans coming legally to New York in the 1990s compared with the 1980s, as measured by Joe Salvo of the New York City Department of City Planning, using Office of Immigration Statistics data.[58] These statistics enumerate only those Mexicans coming as legal immigrants to New York (not as tourists), and hence do not accurately reflect the magnitude of the increase in this population, which by some measures is more than 90 percent undocumented. But these numbers are useful because my ethnographic work indicates that many youths who saw their friends and relatives going legally to New York followed them without benefit of legal status. The exodus of spouses and children from the Mixteca after amnesty was both legal and undocumented, with the latter, larger flow driven in part by the former. Hence, we can take the changes in these relatively small numbers of legal entrants as proxies for what was happening in the larger population. During the 1980s, an average of 394 Mexicans came legally to New York each year (a total of 3,938), and 75 were age twenty-five or under. During the 1990s, an average of 772 per year (a total of 7,718) were legally admitted each year, and 387 were age twenty-five or under. Hence the percentage of legally admitted immigrants under age twenty-five increased from 19 percent in the 1980s to 50 percent in the 1990s.

Amnesty also plays a causal role in an argument developed in this book that the increase in Mexican youth immigration, especially teen migrants, increased anti-Mexican sentiment and supported Mexican gang formation, especially during the mid-1990s. The numbers of Mexican youths under age twenty-five coming into New York each year increased from an average of 183 for 1990–91 to 567 for 1992–94, precisely the time when my informants told me that teen migrants were coming in large numbers to New York and affecting intra-Mexican relations and their relations with other ethnic groups. The numbers fell to just under 400 per year between 1995 and 1999. Much of this bump can be traced to those youths admitted through the amnesty programs, whose numbers went from zero in 1990 and 1991 to an average of 256 for 1992–94, and back to zero or one for 1995–99. These statistics tend to confirm the impressions of my informants that many undocumented youths followed their legally admitted friends and relatives north.

Transnational Life and Changes in Ticuani

As a mature migrant community, Ticuani has moved from the migration phase through settlement to the consolidation phase, which supports transnational life in several ways. First, productive labor in New York, where people earn money, is separated from "reproductive" labor, in Ticuani,[59] where babies are born and raised until they are reunited with parents or migrate on their own. Don Andrés described this division of labor this way: Ticuani consists of those who are "less than fifteen years of age and older than fifty years of age," while Ticuanenses between the "ages of fifteen and fifty years go to the U.S. . . . The majority of the youths in their productive years, those who are strong and healthy and ambitious to make their life a better life, they go to the United States. The few that are here, we who are between twenty and fifty years old, well, we are ones who in one way or another have a profession that enables us to survive here, in this pueblo, no?" In 1993, children aged one to fourteen accounted for only 4.5 percent of the population in New York but for 33.6 percent of the Ticuani population. Similarly, the elderly accounted for only 2.7 percent of Ticuanenses in New York but for 15.6 percent of those in Ticuani. On the other hand, among Ticuanenses in New York, 45.0 percent of the total population are in the 25–40 age group, and 27.0 percent in the 41–60 age group. Among those in Ticuani, only 19.5 percent of the population are in the 25–40 age group, and another 16.4 percent are in the 41–60 age group.

Migration has also altered the previous class structure beyond recognition. Whereas every family in Ticuani in the 1950s was linked to agriculture, Ticuani in the mid-1990s showed roughly equal percentages of campesinos—13.4 percent—and professionals—11.8 percent, the result of the outmigration of the former and the strong demand for the latter. Of the rest, 67.7 percent of the population was in either the "homemaker" or "stu-

dent or pre–school age" occupational category (as compared with 21.7 percent in New York). Remittances from the United States pay for the teachers and doctors for the young and elderly who remain behind. Among the
local professionals, Ticuani even has its own "transnational architect" who
flies to New York to sketch out new house designs at kitchen tables, charging upwards of US$60,000 for design and construction of a Ticuani house.
He himself is the result of another migration-induced pattern, wherein
younger brothers remaining in Mexico are supported in their professional
studies by their migrant elder brothers.

Teachers have been affected especially strongly. Teaching has traditionally provided stable, professional employment in rural areas, and teachers
have played central roles in organizing social, cultural, and political life,
often countering the political power of the local caciques.[60] Few teachers
migrated from the Mixteca before the 1980s, but many have left since, as
their buying power has been eroded so much that they cannot afford modest luxuries, such as meat or a car. Teachers have experienced this erosion
while watching their former students, whose education seldom extends beyond the sixth grade, return from the United States flush with money to
supervise the building and lavish furnishing of their new houses. Many
teachers have followed their students north, first as "target earners" in-
tending to return once they have earned a certain sum of money (for example, enough for a house), but later becoming long-term migrants. State
teachers' union officials told me that in the Mixteca in the early 1990s,
20 percent of the teachers in the whole region and 100 percent of those in
small ranchos had migrated to the United States, as opposed to about 5 percent in the state of Puebla as a whole. This meant that 50 to 80 percent of
rancho schools were closed at some time during the 1980s and 1990s.
Moreover, a black market in teaching posts emerged as migrant teachers
sold their jobs for limited terms for about seven hundred dollars in the
early 1990s, sometimes to unqualified people who could not get a position
otherwise. By the late 1990s, the state of Puebla stopped renewing "migrant leaves" for teachers, forcing many living in the United States to decide whether to stay permanently or return to Puebla.

These changes have affected Ticuani transnational life in two ways.
First, they have cemented a natural partnership between the teachers in
Ticuani and the Committee in New York, because a number of the teachers
have had direct contact with the Committee. Both groups must negotiate
with the cacique and his elite. The teachers do this as middle-class Ticuani
leaders, and the Committee does it as an alternative, transnational power
structure. For example, the teacher who defeated the cacique's candidate in

the 1998 municipal election had previously taken leave to earn money in New York, working with the Committee and developing close relations with other Ticuanense leaders in New York whose support was crucial to his campaign. Second, several teachers who had taken leave decided to stay in New York. Tomás Maestro told me, "The union [in Mexico] told me, 'No more. You come back or you stay there, but we will not give you any more leave.'" With his employer in New York offering to sponsor his application for U.S. residency, he decided to stay. From New York, Tomás has become a central player in Ticuani's public life, hosting Ticuani's priest and municipal president when they visited New York for Ticuani meetings and advising the Committee on a strategy for negotiations with the *municipio*. The migration-induced changes that pushed the teachers north, and the teachers' presence in New York, have in turn spurred further transnational activity and conflict.

The Transnationalization of Ticuani's Economy

That once economically secure teachers have begun migrating in large numbers is one sign that a remittance economy has emerged in Ticuani and the Mixteca.[61] Remittances are the largest source of income in the region, exceeding even the state funds allocated for the area, according to local politicians. Indeed, almost every peso spent in the Mixteca can be linked to someone washing dishes in New York. Corn vendors make change from thick wads of bills composed of both multicolored pesos and greenbacks. Using postal money orders as a base, I estimated that US$3 million to US$5 million came into Ticuani each year in the early 1990s, an average of more than $500 per local resident. Local dollar changers estimate the figure at more than $1,300 per person. Their estimate seems plausible considering that remittances accounted for more than US$11 billion in foreign exchange for Mexico in 2002, second only to oil, and for more than 10 percent of gross domestic product in Mexico during the 1990s.[62] Don Andrés believes that "the pueblo could not live without the economic help [from remittances]. Why? Because . . . half of the family is there and half is here. Or sometimes it's entire families that are there, no? And those that stay here are grandparents or children, they depend on the people in their productive years, who are working." This dependence can be seen in how much household income is reported by Ticuanenses as coming from remittances. In my 1993 survey, some 32.5 percent of Ticuanenses in my sample reported that their households in Ticuani received 99 percent or more of their income from remittances from the United States, and another 18.7 percent reported that 90 percent of their income came this way, yielding a total of 51.2 percent of the households in Ticuani receiving 90 percent or more of their income from U.S. remittances. Households that did not report receiving any of their income from this source accounted for only 36.1 percent of the total, and many of this group lived in absolute poverty.

A remittance economy exacerbates inequalities by "dollarizing" the local economy, inflating prices as migrant families pay for goods with dollars, and widening class differences in Mexico, which become defined by whether one has relatives in the United States and how much they earn and remit.[63] This produces both a "remittance bourgeoisie," who live more comfortably because of the flow of dollars, and a "transnational underclass," who receive no remittances. This underclass includes the very poor, who cannot afford to migrate and must earn locally in pesos but pay for goods in the dollarized local economy, and the elderly, who have no income at all. Don Cuahuatemoc, Ticuani's president in 1999, described this class structure as Ticuani's "two economies," in which families with a migrant remitting money can live reasonably comfortably but "the ones that don't have family here . . . go to the level of just surviving . . . because there in the Mixteca, you have seen it, life is more expensive" because of migration.[64] He estimated that about 20 percent of Ticuanenses live in abject poverty and have no one sending money, and more than half of Ticuanenses have unmet economic needs. Demand for food aid in the town was so great, he said, that they had to rotate which of the 335 eligible families (over half of Ticuani's population of 600 families) received help boxes from the municipal government through an antipoverty program. As more migrants settle and raise their families in New York, they have less money to remit, and more people in Ticuani need government assistance.[65]

Ticuani's "two economies" contribute to the emergence of and tensions within transnational life. First, dependence on remittances has made it impossible for the municipal authorities to raise the needed funds for municipal projects, so they rely on migrant cooperation. Second, the two economies also exacerbate class tensions, marginalizing those left behind and rendering young men vulnerable to the pressures of returning gang members. If these marginalized teens in turn emigrate, they are more likely to experience negative assimilation in the United States, while their wealthier, better-connected peers are more likely to experience positive assimilation. The dual economy has also created a labor shortage in the town that has occasioned an influx of indigenous migrants from the state of Oaxaca, who build houses for returning Ticuanenses in New York. Finally, those able to locate themselves strategically in this remittance economy

FIGURE 2. Old one-story stone house next to two-story house with patio, Ticuani, 2004.

FIGURE 3. New housing construction in front of Ticuani's church, 2000.

have profited from those unable to do so. For example, with no banks or other financial institutions to compete with, the cacique and his friends had a virtual monopoly on currency exchange in the late 1990s, setting rates advantageous to themselves. Moreover, because the cacique owned the franchise for the state dry-goods store, he also had a monopoly on most of the building materials in the town during the twenty-five-year building boom driven by migrant dollars and dreams of home ownership. However, this exploitation of the transnational economy did not go unnoticed; it was later used effectively by the teachers in challenging the cacique's stranglehold on municipal elections.

CONCLUSION

Transnational life is anchored simultaneously in the assimilation of Ticuanense migrants and their children in New York and in the transformation of Ticuani and the Mixteca by migration. In New York, assimilation does not preclude involvement in transnational life. Rather, it provides a context that makes transnational attachments valuable for immigrants and their children. Ticuanenses and their children experience New York as minorities among other minorities, especially among Puerto Ricans, and this experience is one motivation for their transnational attachment.

Migration has changed demographic, population, and social structures in Ticuani in ways that have helped generate and structure a durable transnational life, affecting politics and second-generation experiences. Although Ticuani is a mature migrant community in the consolidation phase of migration, its transnational life is ongoing because of its economic dependence on and other links with Ticuanenses in New York. For example, migration has profoundly changed social class structure in Ticuani in ways that have contributed to an increase in both migration and involvement in transnational politics for its teachers, and to the emergence of gangs. The maintenance of Ticuani as effectively a nursery and nursing home for the young and aged and as a vacation spot for those in their working years also promotes a durable transnational life.

3. "Los Ausentes Siempre Presentes"

Making a Local-Level Transnational Political Community

The phrase *los ausentes siempre presentes* (the absent ones always present) beautifully evokes different dimensions of transnational life. As part of the New York Committee seal, stamped onto documents such as receipts for contributions to the water project, it expresses the Committee's imagined presence in Ticuani and the joint authority it exercises with the *municipio*. Yet when a municipal president says, "Los ausentes siempre presentes— sounds like a threat, no?" it represents an unwelcome external vigilance and imposition. In these different contexts the expression illustrates the dance of assertion, recognition, and resistance between the Committee and the *municipio*. The Committee wants to assert its place in Ticuani public life and shares power with the *municipio*, but the municipal authorities can always redefine their relationship by withholding recognition, thus trying to constrain the power of the Committee.

Tracing the cooperation and power struggles of the Committee and the municipal authorities over the last thirty years shows how a local-level transnational political community is formed. Not only has the Committee become the institution through which Ticuanenses living in New York participate in Ticuani public life, it has also become their advocate with the elected authorities in Ticuani, who are often perceived to work in the interests of Ticuani's locate elites and to treat migrants as second-class citizens. Yet as the Committee has funded more and more of Ticuani's public works—providing two-thirds of the funding for the town's largest project ever, the potable water system—it has demanded a greater say in Ticuani politics. These two structures of power—the Committee in New York and the cacique and municipal authorities in Ticuani—have pounded out a political settlement governing the ways those in New York can participate in Ticuani politics. Understanding the dynamics of membership in Ticuani should help illuminate political life in the scores of other, similarly transnationalized *municipios*. Moreover, the claims and contestation arising in the Ticuani case also animate the larger debates in Mexico about whether and how migrants in the United States should be included in the political community. By the summer of 2003, migrants living in the United States were running as migrants for office in the Mexican Congress, through major political parties, with the stated intent of living in the United States and advocating for "our people" there. The migrant issue also looms large in Mexican presidential politics. In this context, Ticuani politics may represent an interesting and growing aspect of Mexico's political future and the contested place of migrants in it.

In this chapter I trace how the Ticuani transnational community has been created and how it works. The Committee's work with Ticuanenses in New York and its negotiations with the *municipio* create not only a moral map but also institutions that embody this transnational vision. Committee members not only seek recognition and political influence but now demand them of the community on the basis of their economic power.

Focusing specifically on struggles over political community puts me at odds with some scholars using a transnational perspective who see the state as marginal to creating transnational life and others, such as the anthropologist Nina Glick-Schiller, who see community as too "bounded" a concept to be of use, emphasizing instead that the nation-state is now "deterritorialized."[1] But these scholars throw the baby out with the bathwater. They rightly object to the "natural community" concept, which presumes that earlier forms of community were more pure and harmonious and directly expressed a given, often indigenous, people's essential qualities. Such essentialist notions of community are routinely invoked in self-interested ways to justify claims and draw the boundaries of moral communities. But even if Ticuanenses (or any politicians) strategically or even cynically use community in pursuing their interests, when they negotiate and institutionalize settlements to guide their actions in addressing public issues, they form a functioning political community. Community is indeed a bounded concept, but it is precisely the contestation of these boundaries that creates a sense of place and animates action. Ticuani is what I have elsewhere called a "transnational locality,"[2] in which the sense of place is anchored in geographical space (especially in Ticuani and the zocalo, but also in New York, as in the basement of Casa Zavala, the Committee's meeting place in Brooklyn, with its shrine to Padre Jesús) and in the social space created by the relations among Ticuanenses and by their institutions (such as the Committee); and it is experienced in the constituted space of their gatherings (for example, at the Antorcha celebration in New York). My goal here is to describe the struggles and accords that make a transnational community.

Ticuani and other migrant politics can also be understood through the approach of the political scientist Albert Hirschman in his classic book *Exit, Voice, and Loyalty*. While most theories of immigration or politics would predict that Mexican migrants would leave Mexico's political system and either become politically dormant in the United States or move into politics as U.S. ethnics, Ticuanenses and other Mexican migrants have done neither. Although they live in the United States, they have remained loyal to their home localities by contributing money to them. At the same time they exercise *voice*, for example by demanding democratization in Mexico as a condition of their continued economic support. I study the various uses of exit, voice, and loyalty in my examination of relations between the Committee and the *municipio*. This process involves, among other things, the adaptation of older indigenous practices to a context of modern technology. By mapping out how Ticuani political community is formed in New York and Ticuani, and showing how immigrants' participation in Ticuani public life became normal, I refine and extend theories about transnational life.

THE NEW YORK COMMITTEE AND TICUANI'S MUNICIPAL AUTHORITY

The Committee began much as it persists today, during a long Sunday afternoon gathering with talking, joking, and drinking. Don Manuel, the Committee's president, recalled that it started "in 1968 in a house in Brooklyn, talking about the news of the pueblo . . . and we thought that we were lucky to be in New York and not in Mexico. . . . We decided to visit house by house during our days off . . . to call attention to the conditions in the pueblo, and to do something about it." The Committee's list of more than two hundred Ticuanense households in New York puts them in contact with at least as many Ticuanenses as still live in the *municipio*. The Committee's first public work was to repave the zocalo, or town square, in 1970 and 1971. Don Manuel described the Committee's strategy this way: "It was necessary to gain the confidence of the people, and because of this we chose a small project, so we could prove with deeds that what we had said, we would do." They succeeded, he said, "thanks to our people." His narrative of this project, which locates credit with the people and not the Committee who did most of the work, resonates with the emphasis on communal responsibility. The Committee's list of projects is impressive:

1970–71:	Paving the zocalo
1972:	Installing fluorescent lights in the zocalo
1977–79:	Constructing a primary school
1980–82:	Repairing and refurbishing the church after earthquake damage
1984–87:	Constructing a secondary school
1985:	Contributing to the digging of a community well
1988:	Making additional contributions to the digging and setting up of another deep community well, with drainage
1991–92:	Beginning the potable water project, after several years of discussion
1992:	Incorporating the Committee as a not-for-profit organization in New York State
1993:	Installing the potable water system
1998–2000:	Fixing a small chapel and a large church exterior, repairing the path leading to the church, and repairing a nearly two-hundred-year-old church mural; no collaboration with the *municipio* was involved

As the Committee's projects grew in size, its relationship with the *municipio* changed. According to its members, the Committee first approached the municipal authorities deferentially, as emigrant sons asking only for the chance to help their pueblo. Yet by the time of the potable water project in the early 1990s, the Committee had come to relate to the *municipio* as a self-constituted player in Ticuani politics, asserting that it and not the *municipio* controlled access to Ticuani dollars in New York and defended the interests of Ticuanenses there. During the early 1990s, the Committee ceased dispersing money directly to the *municipio* because funds were disappearing. For the water project, for example, the New York Committee established a corresponding work committee in Ticuani, headed by teachers, to handle money and supervise the work of contractors hired by the *municipio*. (For clarity's sake, I refer to this as the "Ticuani potable water committee"; "the Committee" always refers to the one in New York.) The result is that the *municipio* and most Ticuanenses look to the Committee for funding, effectively giving it a veto on projects by politicians it does not support (as happened in 2000).

This northward quest for municipal dollars stems, first, from the contradiction between massive outmigration and the mechanics of public funding.

In Mexico local public projects are often completed with equal contributions from the federal, state, and local governments, the last being gathered by house-to-house collections. (Donations are nominally voluntary but socially coerced, because Ticuanenses know others are donating.) But with more than half of its population—including its most economically productive members—in New York, how can Ticuani, or other *municipios* with large numbers of migrants, raise funds for anything? Moreover, the relative distribution of tax receipts to the local (.5 percent), state (1.5 percent), and federal (98 percent) governments in Mexico, and legal restrictions on developing municipal tax bases,[3] make the *municipio*'s position even more precarious and dependent on migrant dollars. The *municipio* must cajole the Committee into funding its projects. On a 1999 visit to New York, the Ticuani municipal president (or mayor) Don Cuahuatemoc beseeched Ticuanenses to help fund the new high school, which, in the absence of a building, was holding classes in the municipal offices. He said: "If you don't give what you should give, it will go under. . . . People will take their kids out of the school. This is anti-Ticuanense! You can help if you talk to your family by telephone—tell them: don't send the kids to another school!" Committee members understand the power they hold, which one described this way: "Economically, this *is* the Presidencia! Here, we have the power."

The Committee, which has never failed to finish a project, has been run by the same men for thirty years, whereas the *municipio*'s leadership changes every three years, and each outgoing administration is accused of scandalous accounting. In a public meeting with a visiting Ticuani president, one Committee member gave credit to the Ticuanenses and the Committee, but not the *municipio*, for completed projects: "Thanks to God and also to the people who live in New York, who have given their confidence to the Committee. . . . The specific works for which the Committee here in New York has solicited money from the *paisanos* are proved to be complete. The greatest one, the potable water project, is a blessing and a great work the pueblo did, for the same reason, that the people have confidence in the Committee." While this statement obviously seeks leverage for dealing with the municipal president, that Ticuanenses keep giving money to the Committee suggests that it does enjoy their confidence. The Committee has also cultivated relationships with allies in Ticuani, especially local teachers, who benefit from the new schools and other projects and with whom many Committee members have *compadrazgo*, or godchild-godparent relations, which are important in political life in rural Mexico.[4]

The Committee has also become the institution through which the eroding tradition of *faenas* is fulfilled. *Faenas* (literally, tasks) are communal projects to which one is expected to donate labor.[5] In Ticuani, the poor were fed on the days they did *faenas,* while the rich paid someone else to work for them. Migrant Ticuanenses came to act like the rich, giving money to the Committee instead of participating directly in *faena* labor. Although the Committee's first project was done with *faena* labor, by the late 1990s only the very poor, who could not pay for surrogates, were obliged to do actual work—and some were briefly jailed for not doing so. Don Miguel, a Committee member, explained: "Before, you could give someone food, and they would work. Now . . . they don't want to work voluntarily to do their *faenas.* Why? 'Because I have my son here in New York and he gave his contribution. . . . I have money. . . . You can't oblige me to work, because I gave money.' And he makes sense, our friend. The times are changing." Ticuanenses now contribute more reluctantly to such projects and ask how they will benefit. Moreover, out of more than one hundred second-generation youth we interviewed, none even knew what *faenas* were, and few felt obligated to contribute to Ticuani projects. Yet the Committee was still able, in a few months in 1999 and 2000, to raise tens of thousands of dollars for a new project by soliciting house to house.

Despite the Committee's increasing power, neither it nor the *municipio* forgets that the Committee's power has been premised on the *municipio*'s active participation and assent. Just as the *municipio* depends on the Committee to extract funds from Ticuanenses in New York, so too the Committee depends for its legitimacy on the *municipio.* Because the vast majority of its projects have been for the benefit of Ticuani, the Committee relies on a collaborative relationship with Ticuanenses to justify its existence. This interdependence is the reason the Committee must be sensitive to the threats of the *municipio* and the cacique and his friends to withdraw recognition from the Committee. If the *municipio* does not participate, and if those in power in Ticuani say a project is illegitimate, many in New York will not want to contribute.

THE LEGACY OF "LA VIOLENCIA"

Changing power relations have caused local Ticuani leaders to describe the Committee as sometimes overstepping the limits of *apoyando* (supporting) Ticuani public life and instead *imponiendo* (imposing) its demands. This description invokes the Mixteca's violent and divisive political history, ranging from protests against the unjust conditions in the haciendas to supporting the Church against liberal reforms[6] to the use of violence as a political tool. Indeed, the first Ticuani migrant to New York told me that "we left because of the divisions in politics [in Ticuani]. I could not even leave [the house]. I went, my mother and everyone went, to the Federal District to live to escape the violence."

As described to me by officials of the state of Puebla, *caciquismo* was an essential cause of this violence. (*Caciquismo* is the political and social system organized around local political bosses, or caciques; a *cacicazgo* is the political and social machine controlled by one cacique.) According to one official, "The PRI, the government was sustained by local *cacicazgos*. In the small communities these *cacicazgos*—one feels them more strongly, no? So lots of people left their communities for fear of being killed by the caciques, or because they had killed someone. . . . In the Mixteca it is very common for people to kill each other over questions without a lot of importance, no?" Caciques derive power from their role as conduit to the world outside the village, from their positions as political patrons and employers, and especially from the social cement of *compadrazgo,* giving them control over the ostensibly democratic mechanisms of government, such as elections.[7] In rural Mexico, *cacicazgos* became the building blocks of the PRI and government in mid-twentieth-century Puebla. The result was a political system based directly on personal relations, wherein caciques used illegal means, including murder, to keep power. The Mexican state could not easily exercise control over places like the Mixteca because the state itself was largely under the control of the caciques. The resulting *caciquismo* was "large in number but small in resources," according to a Puebla state assembly representative. For example, a special unit of the state police had to be formed to dislodge the losers of local elections, as I observed in El Ganado in 1993.[8]

In Ticuani, the cacique system and its violence impoverished the town. In 1949, the municipal president, a friend of the regional cacique, tried to eliminate Ticuani's main competition in the lucrative chicken trade by ambushing the distributor, who purchased his chickens from neighboring El Ganado. But the plan went awry, they killed the Ticuani distributor instead, and, as locals describe it, "the businessmen lost all their trust" and moved their sales to El Ganado. This attack occurred at the start of the period known as "la violencia" and "la división," which lasted until the late 1970s. The local Ticuani cacique, Don Gregorio, systematically used terror and assassination to maintain power, even killing his own nephew, Don Jorge. This instability reflected the erosion of the political machine of the Avila Camacho family, which helped the PRI establish control over Puebla from the 1930s to the 1950s. But during the 1960s and 1970s, this power structure was challenged by labor unions, student movements, and the left-leaning President Luis Echeverria (who served from 1970 to 1976), who tried to integrate such groups into the PRI. Where the Avila Camacho machine would once have been able to adjudicate the rivalry between Don Gregorio and Don Roberto, its eroded authority led to the burgeoning of such local disputes and increasingly to their bloody resolution during the 1960s and 1970s. A former Ticuani school teacher living in New York, unaffiliated with the Committee, described how Don Gregorio had "a hired assassin who lived in the hills and killed for a wage! . . . People didn't want, physically, to enter the presidential palace [town hall] for fear they would become targets." In 1970, federal troops were sent to quiet the town, and "the assassins stood in the streets with guns and shot at the soldiers up there in the hills." During this period, Ticuani had more than two dozen municipal presidents. Most fled before their terms were up, fearing Don Gregorio's assassins. But suddenly, in 1977, seven of Don Gregorio's gang died in quick succession—"No one knows who did it," says one local leader, a former teacher—so that, in 1978, "democracy started again."

Migrants, including future Committee members, experienced this violence directly and collectively. The current Ticuani cacique, Don Chucho, a returned migrant, lost his father. Don Manuel served as a municipal secretary under several presidents, including Don Jorge, during the 1960s, and is said to have left in fear of violence because he knew "lots of secrets." A friend says he still "lives in that time . . . so he's distrustful." Migrants were also involved in the democratic restoration. In 1978 Ticuani leaders asked Don Zoriano to return, after two decades of living in Brooklyn and Mexico City, to become president. Don Zoriano had always participated in projects, but, having lived so long abroad, was not deeply involved in Ticuani politics. This long absence was what made him a good candidate.

"La violencia" is a backdrop to the Committee's relations with the *municipio* and the cacique. Its members refer to this period strategically as they negotiate, underlining the need to avoid violence and to prize achievements possible in its absence. That all sides have managed their interests without violence for more than thirty years attests to their political skill, though New York Ticuanenses' demands have sometimes strained relations.

PARTICIPATION OR MEDDLING?

Local Ticuani leaders and the cacique see the Committee's first step from "supporting" to "imposing" in Don Juan's ill-fated 1989 candidacy for municipal president. Returning after thirty years in New York, Don Juan was supported by the local campesino organization but shut out by the cacique in the short selection *(pre-candidato)* period the PRI started in 1988 after an important national PRI leader, Cuahuatemoc Cardenas, left the PRI. Although the migrant Don Juan was easily defeated, migration was instrumental in the victory of Don Trinidad, who had lived in New York but returned to Ticuani years earlier, over Don Geronimo, a teacher who had never migrated. Don Trinidad argued that his campesino roots and migration experience made him more representative of the pueblo than Geronimo, a nonmigrant "professional." The Committee later sent Trinidad a videotape warning him to avoid his predecessors' abuses, such as refusing to meet with them or demanding larger *mordidas*, or bribes, from migrant families than from others, or they would withdraw support.

The Committee understood itself as being responsible to "our people in New York" *(nuestra gente en Nueva York)*, exercising authority it had gained through years of sacrifice under the religious cargo system supporting public works for Ticuanenses. Committee members were angry that municipal authorities refused to acknowledge their sacrifice, even as they prepared in December 1991 to deliver a five-thousand-dollar payment for the water project. "We are Ticuanenses! We have sacrificed a great deal!" they lamented. They applauded another who said: "Always, always, they want the money, . . . but when you need some service, . . . they don't take you into account. [Our] sacrifice should be respected!" That the cacique and local leaders could deny them recognition violated their view of Ticuani's normative order. The cacique's local power structure triumphed over the Committee's transnational one, but the contestation itself helped legitimize the Committee's participation in Ticuani public life. Indeed, Don Cuahuatemoc, a teacher who had worked with the Committee in New York and on the corresponding committees in Ticuani, expressed strong support and measured criticism for the Committee's increasing demands to participate. "They have the right to participate . . . as Ticuanenses, because they are participating as members of the community. . . . The problem is that they do not know enough anymore about the problems of the pueblo."

This criticism is echoed by other Ticuanenses in New York, not linked to the Committee. One such person told me, during a visit to Ticuani, that the Committee "want[s] to do everything the way you do it there [in the U.S.] . . . to do everything [in Ticuani] with money from there . . . so they can have more influence. They think that because they send money that we are going to do it in the way they want. . . . But they have to come down to see how to organize the pueblo . . . [and] understand the problems here." Again, migrants' desire to participate is seen as legitimate, but they require a few months of "renaturalization" to know the problems in Ticuani. One critic who knows both the Committee and the cacique well argued that Don

Juan had "lived for many years outside the pueblo, is old, and does not know what the needs of the people really are here in Ticuani." Moreover, the Committee's video went too far, and its withholding of funds was irresponsible because "the money is needed now in Ticuani and they are not giving it over. They want to keep the money until the last minute, and they want to do the whole project with money from the U.S."

Some critics raise the issue of democracy, painting Don Manuel as a cacique. They observe that he has been the only Committee president and say the Committee does not consult Ticuanenses in New York. One municipal president asked me, "How do they select the president, do you know? Do they elect him? It's always Don Manuel." Another criticized the Committee's conduct in the public meeting in New York at which he had unsuccessfully sought funding: "I viewed the Committee badly Saturday. They took decisions among themselves when they should do it democratically. . . . They should have all those assembled decide if they are going to give their hundred dollars or two hundred or a thousand. . . . The Committee is not giving democracy to our countrymen . . . in New York. . . . The Committee [said it] was going to agree so that they could tell society, the countrymen, how much they will have to give. Well then, I call this an imposition." The same issue was raised pointedly by a Ticuanense not affiliated with the Committee in the meeting about how a proposed project was being decided on: "Many of us do not agree that we should redo the floor [in the church]. Well, if you are going to ask for cooperations [contributions], if we are all going to cooperate, it would also be a good idea [to] go with the majority of votes. Because how are we going to cooperate in something that we do not agree with?"

Committee members responded that meeting times are well known, all are welcome, and convening a full meeting of all Ticuanenses to make decisions is impractical. Tomás Maestro defended the Committee leadership, saying that it "is nothing more than direct democracy . . . the president is an ideal person, responsible, honorable, and capable of directing the Committee. [But] if there is some concept that we don't approve of, then we don't approve it." He further compared Don Manuel to President Clinton and the Committee members to Congress. "He leads, but we also have power." My observations over a decade largely accord with his defense. Committee members agree that Don Manuel is a good leader, that no one else wants his huge job, and that he leads by consensus and allows contestation. Yet the Committee is a hybrid—part *cacicazgo*, part religious cargo system, part town meeting—and thus cannot function to everyone's satisfaction.

Nevertheless, even the Committee's harshest critics see its participation in Ticuani politics as legitimate. For example, even Don Trinidad tempered his ire at the Committee's "meddling" by acknowledging their right to "help" Ticuani, though he observed that they should hand over the money more quickly and without conditions.[9] This recognition is partly due to the *municipio*'s need for New York dollars and partly to the Committee's skill in presenting itself as representing Ticuanenses in New York while depicting the municipal authorities as representing Ticuani's elite, especially the cacique and his circle.

INSTITUTIONALIZING A NEW YORK TICUANI COMMUNITY

The Committee has created a sense of community among Ticuanenses in New York by three mechanisms: its collection of funds and the related exercise of authority, its emergence as a center of Ticuani public life in New York, and its self-definition in contradistinction to the municipal authorities. (In contrast, this group displays a marked lack of engagement with American politics despite its members' deep links to American labor markets, schools, and churches.) The feeling of a nearly "institutionally complete"[10] engagement with Ticuani politics has been encouraged by Mexico's outreach toward migrants and by the barriers migrants face in engaging with American political institutions. Ticuani transnational life is thus not cosmopolitan but local and parochial, an extraterritorial conducting of Mexican politics in New York that creates linked political practices at both sites.

The Committee has created a normative order supporting its work through thirty years of, in the Committee's oft-repeated phrase, "knocking on doors, house to house" seeking monetary "cooperations."[11] By Committee rules, this collecting is done by a group. Visits can last a few minutes or a few hours. The visitors begin by asking after the health of the family and then explain the current project. Often they are offered a beer. Such encounters give Ticuanense men a chance to enjoy the company of other men in the conduct of public life. The leisurely, considered pace of the encounter recalls social encounters in Ticuani and conveys mutual respect. These practices have created a huge reserve of *confianza* (deep trust), a social expectation that Ticuanenses will donate, and the knowledge that others are giving. They help counteract the atomizing effects of Ticuanense dispersal in New York. If Ticuanenses no longer meet each other on Ticuani roads or fields or in the zocalo, nevertheless most households are visited by and give money to the Committee. Each beer drunk, each dollar donated, and each bit of gossip *(chisme)* traded creates community and places the Committee at the center of the process. Moreover, the Committee's long history of public works and diligence in visiting every house create a socially coercive context. Ticuanenses give out of a love of their pueblo and also to avoid becoming the object of gossip.

The Committee exercises public authority for the *municipio* and for itself when it collects funds in New York. For the water project, it threatened to cut off water in Ticuani to the relatives of New York residents who did not contribute. Its influence extends further: for example, it adjudicated a dispute between two Ticuanenses in Brooklyn, voting to split the market between them for T-shirt sales in Ticuani during the Feast. The disputants accepted the Committee's decision. The Committee also hosts public Ticuanense events, including a monthly prayer group, visits by Ticuani presidents and priests, and open meetings. When a rumor circulated that the governor of Puebla had already paid for the water project, raising the question of where the New York Ticuanenses' money had gone, Don Manuel held a meeting to deny the rumor and to ask Committee members to spread the word.

Technology facilitates these community-building efforts. The use of videotapes has become standard practice in transnational public meetings and enables both Committee members and municipal leaders to document their efforts on behalf of constituents. When the Committee sent a delegation to consult with the *municipio* on the water project's progress and to dispense its largest payment (twenty thousand dollars), its official videographer taped the daylong meeting. Back in New York, Don Manuel held a screening of the video, which showed Committee members and elected Ticuani officials touring the project, meeting contractors, and seeing pipes being laid. Don Manuel was shown on tape vigorously demanding that the sacrifice of Ticuanenses in New York be recognized, saying the reason he placed conditions on the release of funds was his obligation to "our people in New York," and thereby disputing Trinidad's charge of "meddling." The audience in Brooklyn applauded. Over the years, I have seen Don Manuel and Don Cuauhatemoc directly address New York Ticuanenses on similar videos. Such tapes offer both a view of the work that oral description alone cannot and a simultaneity that builds community: all those who watch the tape see the open trenches being dug in the streets and dilapidated buildings that need to be fixed. Technology facilitates transnational political life in part by "compressing" time and space, aiding the creation of a continuous Ticuani political community in New York and Ticuani.

Hosting Ticuani municipal presidents in New York also casts the Committee as the defender of migrant interests. When the newly elected president of Ticuani, Don Cuauhatemoc, appealed for aid in the wake of a small earthquake and a state budget cut in 1999, Don Manuel criticized those in Ticuani for abandoning its customs: "Our predecessors left to us all that we see there [in Ticuani] . . . without asking anything from New York. And there was a unity that they all had, people gave their work, you asked them, and you did not have to push them. So now, there are people—but I have seen it!—who instead of working, do not lend a hand. . . . We [in New York] give, but where are the cooperations of the people [in Ticuani]? . . . We sacrifice a lot, we walk house to house, . . . and the people [in Ticuani]—what?" Don Manuel argued that those in New York had upheld their obligations to the pueblo more than those in Ticuani had done. Speaking in front of fifty politically active Ticuanenses in New York, he honored their sacrifice and placed the burden of showing legitimacy onto the *municipio*. While Don Manuel asserts the Committee's power, his comments also reflect a lack of understanding of how extensive migration itself has helped weaken the logic of communal work. As more Ticuanenses move their families to New York, some do not want to donate money for Ticuani.

These Ticuanense political practices also invest certain geographical spaces in Ticuani, such as the zocalo, and in New York, such as the basement in Casa Zavala, with special community-affirming meaning. Although not religious, they become sacred, powerful spaces for this community.[12] They also create social space through institutions embodying the social relations between Ticuanenses in New York and Ticuani. Finally, such practices create constituted space, for example when the Committee presides at a sports tournament or religious celebration in New York. Although the geographical space is only "Mexican" for the time Mexicans occupy it, that the community brings itself together in that space for that time has great symbolic importance for Ticuanenses.

This engagement with Ticuani coexists with disengagement from American politics. Whereas Mexico has attempted to cultivate relations with emigrants, the United States seems to discourage immigrant political participation. In the early 1900s, American institutions (spurred by political machines seeking immigrant votes) made it easy to become a citizen and vote; now naturalization is a tortuously long, expensive process. Even those holding U.S. citizenship encounter barriers to participation.[13] Ticuanenses have higher rates of legal residence and citizenship than most Mexicans in New York because their earlier arrival made them eligible for the amnesty of the late 1980s. Yet they still face the "Puerto Rican problem": many institutions see "Latino" or "Hispanic" issues as being adequately addressed by a Puerto Rican presence in politics, not realizing that immigrant Latinos and Puerto Ricans face different issues.[14] Although New York–based Mexican organizations are emerging, they cannot yet mobilize groups like the Committee into citywide Mexican organizations. The Committee's utter disengagement with New York politics was clear when they politely took but then discarded literature for a candidate for a Brooklyn office, saying: "This is not for us. We do not vote." Their place, they implied, is in Ticuani. Their main step toward incorporation into American institutions has been to register as a not-for-profit organization in New York State, a move they saw as giving them rights in the United States and an institutional, legal identity independent of the *municipio*'s recognition.

Ticuanenses have more sustained, substantive contact with the Mexican state, both through routine consular interactions and through its policy of *acercamiento* (closer relations) with the United States. This policy attempts to create a diaspora and lobby in the United States by empowering Mexicans in the United States and orienting them positively toward Mexico.[15] For example, Mexico has organized delegations of municipal presidents to visit New York, and the state of Puebla has established an office in New York. Yet the Committee and other Ticuanenses participate in consular activities warily. They proceeded with the water project without applying for the special help for migrants available from the Mexican federal government. And another Ticuani leader in New York told me he tried to avoid consular activities because "I don't want the Consulate to control me."

CONFLICT AND NEGOTIATED MEMBERSHIP IN A TRANSNATIONAL COMMUNITY

The tensions between the Committee's increased demands for inclusion and the *municipio*'s attempts to set limits on its power erupted publicly at the inauguration of Ticuani's potable water project in 1993. While a crowd of Ticuanenses, state officials, and journalists sat in the sun in shocked silence outside the presidential palace, Committee members and municipal leaders inside screamed at each other about whether to compare the Committee's and the *municipio*'s lists of donors before or after the ceremony. The Committee wanted it done before, to ensure that no names were mistakenly omitted or included, while Don Trinidad said it was inappropriate to raise the issue with people outside listening to this "division." I believe the setting and issue had been carefully chosen by Don Manuel to provoke a public conflict wherein the Committee could defend "its people" in New York and display its economic power. While flying to Mexico from New York the day before, I had asked if there would be enough time to review

FIGURE 4. Ticuanenses gather for the ceremony inaugurating the potable water project, 1994. Note the five video cameras used for reporting the event to donors in New York.

both lists before the ceremony, given that we would arrive less than an hour before it started. Don Manuel's curt answer that there would be, and his management of the ensuing conflict, suggest that this was his first strike in a week-long effort to renegotiate the place of New York Ticuanenses in Ticuani public life. Don Chucho, the cacique, knew the comparison of the lists was no trivial detail, as one Committee member had suggested, and quipped that saying so was like saying *el mole*—a traditional dish in Puebla taking days to prepare—is a detail in a dinner party. Using Hirschman's language, local leaders would have said that Ticuani migrants had acquired too much voice and were insufficiently loyal in their return after their exit.

The proximate issue was whether twenty-two nonpayers, including Don Chucho and his friends, would be forced to pay the same US$300 water fee as all other able Ticuanenses in New York and Ticuani. The real issue was who had the right to require payment. Although this group had not paid as of 2005 and seem unlikely ever to do so, the ensuing negotiations did reset the parameters of the Committee's role, further institutionalizing the participation of New York migrants in Ticuani public life. The

Committee's hand was strengthened by the fact that it had raised most of the cost of the project and that its work resonated strongly with the Mexican state's new orientation toward migrants.[16] Examining the negotiation over this issue affords insight into how preexisting structures of power, such as the *cacicazgo,* relate to new, transnational structures created through migration, such as the Committee.

The debate between the new and old structures of power unfolded in steps. Don Trinidad, the municipal president, responded angrily to Don Manuel's demand to compare the lists before the ceremony. He claimed that these remarks and others made clear the Committee had "some bad information . . . and we have to rectify this." First, he declared that the project had been done in three phases—drilling the well, installing the water pump, and installing the water pipe system—and that the Committee had contributed money only to the last phase, whereas the others had been funded by the state of Puebla and the Federal Solidarity Program and well managed by his administration. Moreover, the value of the Committee's contribution was equaled by the joint contributions in the other phases, including the labor and *faenas* of Ticuanenses in Ticuani. Don Trinidad demanded that the New York Committee stop saying it had done the project itself and recognize Mexican government and Ticuani contributions.

The Committee demanded that everyone be made to pay in order to keep "a promise with our people" in New York, so that those who had paid would not feel "like fools." According to Don Manuel, rumors that certain people (the cacique and his friends) would not have to pay were already circulating—a Ticuanense asking this question had come to the Committee meeting in New York—and he argued that maintaining the Committee's *confianza* required cutting off the water for nonpayers. He again recited the numbers to Don Trinidad: the Committee had raised $100,000 of the $150,000 total, and the state and federal governments had given about $48,000, while the money raised in Ticuani itself was a paltry $1,600. To this Don Trinidad screamed: "They made me the municipal president to control the pueblo! . . . [You will] divide the pueblo!" He continued to say that they were definitely *not* going to turn off anyone's water just *because the New York Committee told them to,* which would "divide the pueblo, not unite it!" He advised them to act more responsibly, thus invoking *la violencia.* The Committee members saw Trinidad's desire to control the pueblo as evidence that he served the interests of the nonpaying cacique, to whom he owed his election. Trinidad accepted that it would be fair to make everyone pay but disputed the Committee's right to make demands. Don Andrés, the president-elect, broke the stalemate by proposing a dinner meeting later that week. Then the New York and Ticuani leaders went out together into the afternoon heat to inaugurate Ticuani's largest public works project ever.

Don Trinidad's physical organization of the ceremony reflected his tripartite view of the project. Speeches were given at the municipal palace, at the water pump installation and water tank outside the town, and at the spigot in Ticuani's town square. At each stop, the municipal president hammered home his message that the "unity of the pueblo" had made this great work possible. He used each space to orchestrate an experience of the project, reflecting his attribution of credit for it only to Ticuani locals. He was the only speaker who did not specifically thank the Committee and those in New York, an omission he privately told me was deliberate, since he had thanked them without naming them when he thanked "el pueblo." Don Andrés hedged his bets: he was beholden to the cacique for his election but knew he would need the Committee's help in future large projects. He explicitly thanked the Committee but in the same breath named state government and "all the citizens of our population."

Neither Don Trinidad's exclusion nor Don Andrés's attempts to broaden the project's parentage could stem the tide of praise from others for the Committee and Ticuanenses in New York, nor their assertions of ownership of the project. The highest-ranking government official present, representing both the federal Solidarity Program and the state teachers' union, extended "deep recognition" to the municipal authorities, but his thanks went "principally to the Committee of Solidarity that worked so arduously in the City of New York. . . . This embodies the concept of the National Solidarity Program." He proposed that they "receive the community-action prize from the hands of the President of the Republic." At several points he turned directly to migrants who were videotaping the event and said, "Go to New York and take your videos of this event, and show the people in New York what has been done with the money." By directly addressing those in New York, he reinforced the link between the potable water project and the Committee and Ticuanenses in New York. Don Cuahuatemoc, the teacher who played a central role in electoral changes in 1999 (see chapter 4), speaking for the potable water committee, thanked all parties but gave special recognition to the Committee for sacrificing their family time on weekends to collect money "in cold weather," and he chastised those who did not contribute this time to be "more conscientious" in the future. The report of the event in Puebla's main newspaper highlighted the Committee's contribution, resonating with the idea of a diasporic Mexico that was promoted by the government.

The speaker representing the Committee was Don Miguel, a founding member. He laid out clearly the sacrifices the Committee had made for Ticuani and challenged its critics and Don Trinidad's definition of the project. Greeting assembled dignitaries "in the name of the New York Committee," he apologized for not knowing their names and then delineated the relative contributions of various entities to the project:

> It is well known by all of us that this work has been made a reality, in the first place, mentioned in order of economic contribution by the Ticuanenses residing in the City of New York. In second place, by the federal and state governments, and in third place, by the few citizens who live here and who enjoy a good economic position. My congratulations to these who have made it in our pueblo without leaving. Nevertheless, we Ticuanenses who are living in the city of New York are permanently informed, in all senses, about what goes on in our pueblo. For that reason, on March 15, 1991, came the idea to endow our pueblo with a new potable water system. . . . To live in New York is not an easy thing. [It is a] a voluntary dispossession, but still one. Nevertheless, engaged in this difficult chore we were deceived by people who do not open the door, who peek through the mail slot, and exclaim, "Those damn water guys [*viejos del agua*] are here!" We are deceived too [by] negative criticisms because at the end of a day of collecting we finish a little inappropriate [drunk]. . . . But we forgive them, because they are informed badly.[17] . . . To these critics I do not send congratulations, but, yes, I invite them to participate with us. This project was completed with the true sacrifice of the Committee. It is dignified to recognize this labor. Our people told us: Son, cousin, husband, et cetera, even if you can't also send me my monthly payment, give them your cooperation there so that we have water. . . . But there are people who in spite of already seeing the project done, refuse to give us their cooperation. (Spanish, translated by the author)

That Don Miguel asserts the position of the Committee directly in this speech, without deference to the municipal authorities, reflects how powerful the Committee has become. The Committee also asserts that it is "permanently informed" about Ticuani and can thus legitimately judge whether to offer or withhold support. (This position is partly contradicted by Don Miguel's admission that he does not know the names of the invited notables.) And Don Miguel presents the Committee's sacrifice as part of the larger story of migration itself. He links the histories of the migrant Committee members with the those of the majority of Ticuanenses (in contrast to the economically privileged few who had the luxury of staying in Ticuani). He attacks the Committee's critics and contrasts them with other, self-sacrificing Ticuanenses who tell their relatives to send their monthly check to the Committee for its water project. Even those who accuse the Committee members of getting drunk with the money have their accusations turned around; the beer they drink comes not from "cooperations," but from neighbors' goodwill (e.g., they offered them a beer). Such hospitality offers a strong contrast to those who close the door and pretend not to be home. By such rhetoric, the Committee attempts to shape Ticuani's normative order to hew more closely to the religious cargo system by which it operates. By publicly defining those who gossip about them as morally deficient and lacking loyalty to the pueblo, the Committee attempts to appropriate the authority to define good and bad Ticuanenses. The Committee members no longer publicly stand as deferential, humble servants but rather represent an economically powerful migrant community demanding a voice in Ticuani politics. In this they are at least partly successful.

The perception that the project was carried out by the Committee resulted not simply from rhetoric but also from its exercise of municipal authority. Most Ticuanenses in New York gave their $300 contribution to the Committee, which enabled them to tell their relatives in Ticuani that their water could be turned on. In another exercise of authority, the municipality also went to the Committee to ask the New York relatives to quiet down a man in Ticuani who had menaced his neighbors. And the Committee paid the full-time worker who maintained the pump. As a result, Ticuanenses in Ticuani and New York now routinely approach Committee members to complain about Ticuani's municipal services. Tomás Maestro told me in 1999 that Ticuanenses returning from Mexico complained to him about the "deficiencies in the care" of the water system, which the Committee reported to the authorities in Mexico. He also followed up himself: "I tell you that I listen to the complaints of the people. . . . [And] I go to Mexico twice a year." The quotidian nature of these interactions reflects the belief that the Committee has the municipal authority to get results.[18]

Other demonstrations of municipal authority by the Committee have brought criticism, as with its handling of the Grand Dance at the Feast of Padre Jesús in 1993. Although attendance at the dance is a status marker showing that one has sufficient disposable income, the custom had been to hold it in a place where even those not attending could look on and listen to the music. In 1993 the Committee hired a professional concert organizer from New York, who put up corrugated metal fencing instead of the customary chicken wire, obstructing the view of the band in the outdoor town market, and instituted a badge system and security personnel to control backstage access. As a result many Ticuanense leaders, including the cacique, could not enter, while Committee members (and I) did so freely.

Some Ticuanenses felt the Committee had violated the spirit that the Feast is for everyone, citing this as evidence that the Committee was trying to impose its will on Ticuani and was out of touch with the community.

NEGOTIATED LIMITS TO MEMBERSHIP

Observing the negotiations between the Committee and the incoming and outgoing Ticuani presidents during the Feast week—one of the few occasions when the Committee and municipal leaders meet face to face—offered me a direct look at coexisting local and transnational structures of power in Ticuani politics. Each side offered its own vision of Ticuani's future and migrants' place in it. The cacique was absent, which I took as a sign of power: he could trust the two presidents to defend his interests, and he could not be directly confronted about paying for the water project. The Committee's rhetoric reflected their economic power and institutional weakness. While Don Manuel could threaten to stop cooperating with the *municipio* if the nonpayers were not confronted, he had to appeal to the presidents: "You have the law, . . . [and] we are not here." When Don Trinidad denied that the Committee even had a right to ask such a political question, the Committee set a date one month in the future by which they would withdraw their cooperation if everyone had not paid. They demanded a letter of agreement from the *municipio*.

President-elect Don Andrés stepped in, agreeing that everyone, including the cacique, had to pay, and that nonpayers should have their water cut off. But he asked the Committee for two extra weeks so that "we will not have to cut [the water of] even one, because we are going to convince them" to pay. He appealed for their help by referring to his inexperience: "Imagine what will happen to me if the first thing I do is cut the water" of people like Don Chucho. "I want to work with you, but you have to be aware of the constraints we face here in Ticuani." While apparently conceding the Committee's point, Don Andrés cleverly put the Committee on the defensive by asking them to "imagine" what his position was like: he implied that their long absence from Ticuani might have made them lose touch. Indeed, Don Andrés later told me, "The *paisanos* there [in New York] live in another way and live in another situation." And the cacique, Don Chucho, told me of New York, "It is impossible to see the issues from there." Most important, the two-week extension meant that most Committee members would be back in New York by the deadline.

A contingent settlement on the nature and limits of the Committee's participation in Ticuani public life emerged. First, the legitimacy of the

Committee's participation was acknowledged. Unlike past presidents, both Don Trinidad and Don Andrés agreed to meet with the Committee to negotiate on issues and allowed the Committee to speak for itself at the inauguration. Second, both sides agreed that funds owed by families with relatives in New York should be collected only in New York, simplifying accounting and reinforcing the Committee's exercise of municipal authority. Third, over two years, the Committee and Ticuani leaders converged on a position that migrants must live for a minimum of one year in Ticuani to be eligible for municipal office. This "renaturalization" period highlights the belief that returning migrants need time to relearn the needs of the pueblo.

Finally, the two sides agreed that everyone must pay the $300 contribution for the water system. This issue pitted local and transnational power structures directly against one another. When I told the cacique and his brother that the Committee believed that Don Andrés had broken his promise to collect from nonpayers, they responded in a 1999 interview:

> He [Don Andrés] never asked us [to pay]. That was an issue from there [New York]. . . . Nobody can demand that you pay your cooperations—it's voluntary. Andrés could not have cut the water. . . .
> And they think that it was an issue for Andrés, but only in that he told them he would try to convince us to pay. . . . No committee can order a president, when things are in order. . . . Yes, they [the Committee] can make recommendations: If you find it convenient under your authority, we ask you in an attentive manner if we can continue supporting you.

They explained that Don Andrés's promise had been circumvented by a local procedure. After the Committee had left, but before Don Andrés took office, Don Trinidad held as assembly in Ticuani to decide the question. According to Don Chucho and his brother, "If the people told us to pay, we are going to pay and pay more than three hundred dollars. But we are not going to pay anything on orders from there [New York]. . . . Only four or five people came, so we did not pay." The assembly was convened in Don Chucho's section of town, where few would vote against him even if they themselves had paid. Hence, despite all the Committee's economic power and its invocation of fairness and sacrifice, in the end the cacique's power and control over local mechanisms of government prevailed. Ticuani may have a transnationalized political system, but it still consists largely of local politics with local power.

This denouement is ironic but offers insights. The cacique's power traditionally is both economic, through his role as a broker to the outside world, and social, through his use of this economic power to develop *compadrazgo* relations. The Committee's economic power is based in New York, well beyond the cacique's immediate influence, and is now much greater than the cacique's in terms of its ability to raise money for public works. But the Committee has no ability to use that economic power to challenge its rival in Ticuani. In addition to threatening to withdraw its economic power, the Committee invoked both the collective responsibility of the religious cargo system and the principle of democratic equality and fairness in demanding that the twenty-two nonpayers pay. But the cacique was able to use his local social base, supported by his still-considerable private economic power, and, ironically, the formally democratic mechanism of an assembly, to deny the Committee the right even to ask that he and his friends should pay.

CONCLUSION

With apologies to the late Tip O'Neill, we can say that all Ticuani politics is local, even if it is also transnational. To a remarkable degree, over more than thirty years, Ticuanenses have successfully negotiated the conflicts, limits, and meanings of membership in the local political community. That even the Committee's critics see its participation as normal and legitimate is evidence of how institutionalized Ticuani transnational life has become. Ticuanense transnational localism is also reflected in and strongly reinforced by the Committee's lack of engagement with American politics and the continued and even deepening engagement with Mexican, Pueblan, and Ticuani politics.[19] Technology facilitates this enduring transnational localism, as does the Mexican state's desire to create a diasporic relationship with migrants in the United States.

One might view this politics as a manifestation of or resistance to global capitalism, or an example of transmigrants transcending the state, but such analyses lose sight of the gritty, fascinating play of local politics. The state, in the form of the *municipio*, is both an object and an actor in this transnationalized local politics. The *municipio* acts, as does the Committee, in a larger context created at least partly by the Mexican central state and the state of Puebla. The *municipio* helps create transnational politics in Ticuani through its thirty-year cooperation with the Committee, even if it is also a vehicle for the interests of the cacique and his friends. Sherri Ortner's concept of "ethnographic refusal" is apposite here. To interpret the actions of the Committee and *municipio* as resistance to domination by global capital would be to dismiss the human motives of the desire for power, of anger and jealousy, and, equally important, the desire to help one's community and be recognized for such sacrifice. These play a role in creating a transnational social reality.

Tracing the evolution of the Committee-*municipio* relationship shows how Ticuani transnational political life accommodates coexisting transnational and local structures of power. While the cacique and his friends prevailed in the matter of their contributions to the water project, the Committee was able to rewrite the rules governing its own participation in Ticuani public life. Its role is now accepted as legitimate by most Ticuanenses, though the forms of that participation are still contested. When I began my fieldwork, the idea that a Committee member might run for office in Ticuani was anathema; now the idea is accepted, albeit with a residency requirement. These contingent relations reflect the different power bases of the Committee, the cacique, and the *municipio*. The cacique and local leaders benefit from local relations of *compadrazgo*, from the influence of their wealth, and from living and being elected in Ticuani. The Committee benefits by obtaining access to the real "tax" base of those Ticuanenses with earnings capacity, by gaining the people's *confianza*, and by helping people to remain linked to their hometown through their communal obligations. In negotiating the terms on which those in New York and Ticuani participate in community governance, Ticuanenses are institutionalizing transnational life on a local level.

4. The Defeat of Don Victorio

Transnationalization, Democratization, and Political Change

"We are all *poblanos* . . . one family, one community united!" said Melquiades Morales Flores, a PRI candidate for governor of Puebla, in a large meeting room of a hotel. He was flanked through the window by the supersized images of Times Square: a twenty-foot-tall woman wearing leopard skin, advertisements for the latest Disney movie, and screeching neon signs. He had come to New York to meet with migrant leaders as part of his ultimately successful gubernatorial campaign in 1998 and to shore up political support in the Mixteca in response to increased electoral competition. In Ticuani, in the same election, victory cheers erupted in Brooklyn at the house of the brother of Don Cuahuatemoc, the upstart teacher who used donations from New York to defeat Don Victorio, the cacique's brother, in the PRI's first primary election for municipal presidents. Both stories show how migration and Mexico's increased democratic competition have transnationalized Mexican politics. The governor fought increased electoral competition in Puebla by taking the fight to New York. Don Cuahuatemoc fought the cacique's monopoly on power by using funds from New York and a new democratic procedure in Mexico.

Don Cuahuatemoc's defeat of Don Victorio in Ticuani's 1999 election offers a lens for analyzing how changes in Mexican politics affect and are affected by the transnational conduct of Ticuani politics.[1] Changes at different levels of politics (local, state, and national) and at different locales (Brooklyn, Mexico City, Ticuani, and Puebla) profoundly affect transnational life. In this case, first the state's and then the dominant political party's actions catalyzed local-level migrant politics in Brooklyn and Ticuani, giving migrants more powerful means of fighting for recognition and respect.

DEMOCRATIZATION AND TRANSNATIONAL POLITICS

Migrants and other Mexican citizens have benefited from Mexico's trend toward democratization and the decentralization of power. The establishment of Mexico's Federal Electoral Institute in 1995 cleaned up elections to the extent that most Mexicans thought that the 2000 elections were fair. Vicente Fox Quesada of the Partido Acción Nacional (PAN) ended the PRI's seventy-one-year monopoly on the presidency; he was elected with strong moral support from migrants and votes from their home communities.

Three specific measures helped catalyze Mexican migrants' transnational politics. First, as part of a Reforma del Estado (reform of the state) in 1996, the PRI was forced by opposition parties to accept a change in the Mexican constitution that would permit Mexican migrants abroad to vote for president. Second, the Federal Electoral Institute issued a report in 1998 saying that implementing this constitutional right was feasible despite objections, especially from the PRI (which defeated the implementing legislation in 1999; it remains unimplemented in 2005). Together, these two measures helped migrants mobilize a great deal of support in Mexico and in the United States for their demands for political participation. Indeed, these demands could no longer be cast as those of migrants asking for special consideration; now they were Mexican citizens asking to exercise an established constitutional right. Third, the PRI changed its processes for selecting internal candidates in response to embarrassing defections, including that of Ricardo Monreal, who left the PRI and defeated its candidate in the solidly PRI state of Zacatecas in 1998.[2] Instead of the party's picking candidates by *dedazo* (literally, a tap of the fingertip), candidates could now demand formal primary elections and use other measures to run for office.[3]

These nationwide changes affected local politics in Puebla, the Mixteca, and Ticuani. As a candidate for governor, Melquiades Morales Flores faced greater competition: one observer described Puebla as "a political laboratory" in which migrants became more important. In the late 1980s and 1990s, the PRI in Puebla lost municipal presidencies to the Partido de la Revolución Democrática (Party of the Democratic Revolution, or PRD), and positions in large cities to the PAN. Moreover, in 1995 the Federal Electoral Institute replaced the PRI in administering elections and sent its personnel to supervise local elections. The PRI's response in the 1998 election was three-pronged: to target some urban areas for reconquest, to strengthen its political support and maximize its vote in solidly PRI areas like the Mixteca, and to democratize its selection process for candidates. In the Mixteca, the strategy included reaching out to migrants in New York. One statewide elected official, in a long conversation over dinner and tequila, described it to me this way: "Imagine if all the heads of households [in New York] who are sending money [to Puebla] call and say, 'Vote for Melquiades!' We will get votes by getting the goodwill of the people here. If we could get each person sending money to include a card saying, 'Vote for Melquiades,' we would win easily."

These changes introduced tensions into the relationship between the cacique and his supporters on the one hand and the Committee and other migrants in New York on the other. The *cacicazgo* of Don Chucho that began in the late 1970s and others like it are locally powerful remnants of the much larger political machine of the Avila Camacho family in Puebla, which included a Mexican president. With the erosion of this machine, the caciques became the main link between the PRI and its base, but the party had to leave them largely free to control local political affairs.[4] Caciques always face the problem of how to deal with new groups making demands. Just as the *avilacamachistas* faced student and worker groups that had emerged from the urbanization of the 1940s to the 1960s and through the liberalization of politics in Mexico City, caciques today face demands from well-funded migrants. The right to demand a primary has profoundly altered politics in the Mixteca, leading to campaigns where none took place before and into which the dollars and opinions of New York Mixtecos flow.

This chapter, like other work I have done, employs and offers a friendly critique of globalist approaches to transnational life, some of which fail to take account of local causal processes.[5] For example, the sociologist John Meyer and his colleagues posit a world culture and society as key in shaping the form and practices of nation-states since World War II. They analyze the influence of global cultural commitments to democracy and to what the sociologist Yasemin Soysal would call the "rights of the modern person."[6] From such a perspective, the Ticuanense story might be seen as simply filling in the details of globalization. After all, commitment to democracy is a central requirement of those demanding change in Ticuani and Mexico and one that created the conditions for the upset of Don Victorio in 1999. Other globalists, such as Saskia Sassen, take a more nuanced approach, analyzing how the role of the state in the global system is changing and emphasizing that the state itself must enact most of the legal changes creating the global system, in the process both freeing capital to pursue profit across borders and increasing sites of intervention in that process.[7] I argue similarly that the movement toward democratization in Mexico creates opportunities for Mexican migrants to intervene, but I stress the importance of national and local systems in understanding how these processes play out. Globalization's broad causality must be refracted through, and is thus changed by, the changes in the Mexican constitution, in Mexican party politics, and in the evolving relationship with older, highly localized systems of power such as *caciquismo* in understanding transnational life.

TICUANI POLITICS BEFORE 1999:
CACIQUISMO, COMPADRAZGO, AND *DEDAZO*

Before 1999, an elite known by the name of the cacique—"los Chuchos"— picked candidates and presidents by *dedazo*. As each three-year municipal term ended, the Chuchos would decide who should be the next PRI candidate, a choice that was tantamount to election. Predictably, each candidate left office wealthier than when he had entered, and his accounts were given scant scrutiny by his successor, who counted on the same courtesy. The *dedazo* was reinforced by *compadrazgo*, the system of godfathership, as described by Don Emiliano (a former migrant with many years of community service in New York and Ticuani): "Chucho put in *don fulano de tal* [Don Anybody] . . . it is pure *apadrinado* [godfathership]." Another said:

> For all of the presidents, who elected the president was them [the
> Chuchos]. . . . When they said that it was *fulano de tal* [anybody], the
> people did not say anything, they [the Chuchos] had already picked
> him. . . . And this year when the pueblo elected him, when they really
> picked the president by voting, there were problems. And before, the
> dinosaurs passed the same bone [the presidency] among them. And
> they even said, we missed Primo, we missed Segundo [the cacique's
> adult sons], that they would be presidents, because they already had
> them "elected."

Describing the Chuchos as dinosaurs places them among the most hardline PRIistas, seen as ready to use continued fraud or other means to keep power. That they were upset that they could not award the presidency to Chucho's sons, who were in line for it but were "missed," suggests the extent to which the Chuchos felt their power had been normalized. Though he would disagree, the cacique described the old system of picking candidates to me in similar terms, saying there was "no vote . . . we just talked to people in a consultation of the base." That Don Chucho invokes consultation to justify this system is understandable, because this is how the PRI conducted business. Indeed, a "consultation of the base" is one of four methods for choosing local candidates recognized by the PRI in its 1998 reform along with primary elections, "customary and traditional methods," and an "electoral council." The PRI is attempting to accommodate a variety of local political realities, including consensual decision making in indigenous communities, continued *dedazo* in *municipios* where there is little challenge to PRI power, and the use of primaries to reinforce the PRI's legitimacy in *municipios* where challenges do exist. The intervention of migrants at the local level through primary elections was not one of the outcomes PRI officials anticipated; but democracy opens up political processes, creating uncertainty and fostering innovation.

Challenges to the Chuchos' monopoly on power were discouraged by the memory of thirty-odd years of political bloodshed before the Chuchos gained power. Although they became wealthier in office, no one was killed in political reprisals during Chucho's *cacicazgo* or even after his candidate's defeat in 1999. Thus the Chuchos have a legitimate reputation for good political stewardship in the Mixteca. Moreover, the lack of formal primary elections made it hard to oppose the Chuchos. In some ranchos, candidates were selected by a show of hands, or by the voters' physically lining up beside their chosen candidate in a public assembly. Since the Chuchos always won, many thought the elections a farce. And, given Ticuani's bloody history, the Chuchos' nonviolent monopoly on power seemed like a good deal.

Chucho maintains that he is not a cacique, although he is commonly referred to as one. "I don't even know what it means to say there is *caciquismo!*" he told me. "I am one of the persons that does not get out in front, I work behind them. . . . I want to serve the pueblo . . . like a humble man, because I serve the most humble people." This response seems in fact to confirm his status as the cacique because he can influence things from behind, without visibility or accountability. Rather than explain why people would call him a cacique, he reiterated that his record of service should not be confused with *caciquismo:* "Several presidents [of Ticuani] invited me to work with them. . . . I did not intervene. Yes, I work [for the pueblo], and I keep my promises, but this is not *caciquismo.* . . . These people who say this are very foolish, with egotism and rancor. I am not a cacique. I work with nobility, humility, honor, and love of the pueblo." Chucho has indeed been asked by each succeeding president to use his wealth and connections outside Ticuani to get projects done. Yet everyone in the town, including his fellow Chuchos, call him the cacique. His refusal to acknowledge the position becomes an exercise of the cacique's power.

The PRI's 1998 candidate selection rules ended the *dedazo*'s monopoly on Mixteca politics and opened the door wider to migrant participation. In Ticuani, the immediate result was that a group of politically active schoolteachers nominated one of their number, Don Cuahuatemoc, to run against the Chuchos' candidate, Don Victorio. They also mobilized Ticuanenses in New York, splitting the New York Committee between backers of the Chuchos and of the teachers.

Tito's Term, 1997–1999

Part of the reason the changes in candidate selection rules had such a large impact on the 1999 election was that the previous president, Tito, had violated what can be called the moral economy of *caciquismo:* the asymmetrical reciprocity that often governs relations between people with unequal power.[8] In Ticuani, the cacique and his presidents implicitly promised not to steal too much from the *municipio* and to provide leaders supporting them—especially in the ranchos—with public resources to distribute. Under Chucho, it also promised no bloodshed. Leaders loyal to the cacique could expect to be rewarded with minor patronage, employment, credit for buying building materials, or favorable rates for exchanging dollars for pesos at Chucho's store.

While a massive peso devaluation in 1994 and 1995 hobbled the Mexican economy and made paying for municipal programs harder, most people also point to Tito's bad administration, arrogance, and disrespect as factors in Don Victorio's defeat. People say he simply stole too much and redistributed too little. One Ticuanense said, "The people lost faith in the Chucho group, because of Tito: because Tito made his ranch bigger, got his truck, . . . lived by card playing and betting. And what did they say? If Victorio gets the nod, it will be the same thing." Don Artemio, a former member of Tito's municipal government who had served as fiscal watchdog, observed that the problem was not that Tito had stolen from the pueblo— everyone did—but that he had done so with hubris and arrogance. "The problem was ostentatiousness, his conduct is what lost it. . . . I feel that his error was not the size of the sin but rather the size of the scandal. He bought new vehicles, constructed . . . this ranch: technical equipment for irrigation, a house for his workers. This is what caught the attention of the people." Working through the numbers with me, Don Artemio estimated that 21 percent of the budget, or nearly US$85,000, had been stolen in the first two years. And, he said, "It got worse in the third year, after I resigned!" Tito's keenest critics allege he stole all the funds from an antipoverty program to buy himself a farm and livestock, and a former worker showed me pictures he had taken of animals that he said were purchased with stolen money. Tito was also seen as inattentive and disrespectful and was accused of taking advantage of most Ticuanenses' lack of education. His robbing the pueblo might have been overlooked, according to Don Artemio, if not for the "bad treatment of our people, he humiliated them." Reportedly, Tito asked them, " 'Why do you come to see me in my house? I will attend to you in the *presidencia*,' this kind of thing. . . . Our people are simple, humble, and he took advantage of that." Telling other Ticuanenses that they could see him only in the formal municipal offices emphasized the president's superior position, thus offending both the constituents' humility and the ethic of equality and reciprocity that is supposed to govern Ticuani's public life.

Tito's graft violated other aspects of Ticuani's moral economy. Not only did he steal too much, but he wasted the money by investing it in unsuccessful businesses. One critic observed that he lived now by "selling milk— the same milk from the cows he stole from the peasants!" In stealing so much, Tito made it impossible for local leaders in the ranchos to keep their promises. The elected representative in one of Ticuani's poorest ranchos told me he actually asked Tito for a "negative receipt . . . give me a letter saying that you did not give me any money so that I can show my people that I am not stealing, because they know I am supposed to get money each month for projects." Furthermore, Tito did a bad job on the projects he did take action on, such as a well that was too shallow and "dried up," like his promises. This rancho leader and others who went begging for their budgets voted against Don Victorio in 1999.

THE NEW RULES AND THE ELECTION OF 1999

The changes in the 1998 candidate-selection rules meant the that the teachers could demand a primary election and that the state of Puebla's PRI organization would send supervisors to ensure the election was fair. This "outside" intervention into the cacique's monopoly made the process and outcome of the election very different from those of previous contested elections. Meche, a young woman active in Ticuani public life, contrasted the 1999 election with that of 1989, when Don Lucio lost to Don Alberto because the Chuchos "would buy votes . . . [and] pressure people." Because no voting credentials were used, the Chuchos could bring in friends from other towns and even migrants to vote for them. In 1989, they broke a tie by doing a recount, in which a "lost" vote was suddenly found. But in 1999, the election was "free, like in the United States."

The primary also gave those in New York a way to participate by giving money. About fifty of Don Cuahuatemoc's supporters in New York contributed some US$1,390 to the primary. This donation enabled his campaign to mobilize a caravan of "twenty-two vehicles" of supporters to visit the ranchos that overwhelmingly supported Don Cuahuatemoc. In previous elections, only the Chuchos had had the money for such caravans, which leaders in the ranchos told me were influential. Hence, migrant donations neutralized the cacique's local advantage of wealth. Don Cuahuatemoc and Don Artemio described how they could gather only about US$10 per outing from their supporters in Mexico, but with money from New York they could "bring people so that the communities [ranchos] would see that I had lots of people, right? If you are a citizen and you see me alone, you are going to say, well, this guy doesn't have anyone to support him, so better I should go with the other guy." Don Artemio added: "It was a psychological impact." Moreover, the return of some of Don Cuahuatemoc's most active supporters from New York brought fresh infusions of cash and gave the impression of overwhelming support, as the Chuchos did not have many returning supporters. Many believed Don Cuahuatemoc would get the Committee's financial support for his projects. Don Chucho also alleges, I think inaccurately, that the Committee itself sent Cuahuatemoc campaign funds.

Bernardo, Don Cuahuatemoc's brother, told of his elation in Brooklyn when "my brother finally called at nine at night . . . and told us he won! . . . I helped in this, and yes, we won!" The vote count showed Cuahuatemoc's strongest support in the agricultural ranchos that had lost out most under Tito and the old regime. (Ticuani's five ranchos vote in two polling places in addition to the *cabecera*, or county seat.) Cuahuatemoc won 79 percent of the vote in one rancho poll and 73 percent in the other. He lost by only eleven votes, or 2 percent, in the *cabecera*, where Victorio's support was strongest. These results represent a strong rejection of Don Tito and the Chuchos (though not a permanent one). Overall, Cuahuatemoc won 61 percent of the vote to Victorio's 39 percent.[9]

To their credit, the Chuchos accepted this outcome peacefully. They did not use force to try to stop Cuahuatemoc from taking office, as I had previously seen done by a defeated team in El Ganado. But they charged Cuahuatemoc's supporters with buying votes, saying, "The Committee from New York sent one doesn't know how many thousands of dollars so they could buy votes . . . three hundred pesos each!" (about US$30). They also argued that Cuahuatemoc had influence with the state of Puebla's PRI and that the Chuchos were penalized for supporting a candidate who opposed the eventual winner, Melquiades Morales Flores. They claimed that the state PRI "sent few ballots where they had few votes, and a lot of ballots where they had a lot of votes. . . . In [one rancho] they had more votes than people! They threatened my people. . . . This was at the state level, because Cuahuatemoc and Artemio worked with Melquiades, and we supported Jose Luis Flores." Interestingly, all of these charges involve Cuahuatemoc's inappropriate use of resources outside the *municipio,* hence outside the cacique's control and not authentically Ticuanense. Don Victorio's defeat marked the beginning of a new era in Ticuani politics.

THE NEW YORK COMMITTEE AND THE 1999 ELECTION

The 1999 municipal elections changed the Committee's place in Ticuani transnational politics too. First, it found itself split between supporters of Don Victorio and Don Cuahuatemoc. A straw poll showed the Committee split sixteen for Don Cuahuatemoc to eleven for Don Victorio. To avoid divisiveness, it decided to remain neutral. Second, supporters of Don Cuahuatemoc mobilized in New York, ending the Committee's monopoly on raising money among or representing Ticuanenses in New York. The Committee also refused to support Don Cuahuatemoc's projects, denying him access to Ticuanense dollars in New York and thus making it impossible to do large-scale projects.

In Ticuani interest focused on Don Emiliano, a founding member of the Committee who had been retired in Ticuani for two years and helped organize the Feast there. Both the Chuchos and the teachers feared that Don Emiliano would offer the Committee's support to the other candidate, or run for office himself. Both sides attempted to recruit him. Don Emiliano's position was complicated by the fact that he lives near the Chuchos, but in his two years back in Ticuani he had found them to be "a monopoly of one team [who] don't want to work cleanly for the pueblo. . . . They want it for their own benefit." Yet Don Emiliano also refused to join Don Cuahuatemoc's team, which included many who had worked with the Committee in New York. He described refusing an invitation to join Cuahuatemoc's campaign:

> I did not accept the position. In two days, here comes Victorio to invite me . . . from the other team. I told Victorio . . . sincerely, that I could not. Why, Emiliano? . . . I gave him some pretext. The next thing, I get a telephone call from Committee friends, and well, we are going to be neutral persons. We want to work for the pueblo. We don't want to get on a team. . . . Please, scratch me off your list if I'm on it. . . . Because I do not want to get in with someone if I see that they are cheating or that things are not right, no? . . . I disentangled myself from the two sides. (Spanish, translated by the author)

The Committee thus negotiated its own internal split by agreeing to remain neutral in the election, thus staying above the corruption they associated with municipal politics. Their neutrality left them free to work, if they chose, with whoever won the election. The Committee also negotiated an agreement from Don Cuahuatemoc's supporters in New York that they would clearly differentiate their activities from the Committee's in public forums. With its neutrality publicly established, the Committee awaited the election results. Their subsequent actions suggest a vested interest in the outcome.

TRANSNATIONAL POLITICS AFTER THE 1999 ELECTION

Democratization—in the form of a PRI primary in Ticuani—opened up ways for Ticuanenses in New York to more effectively aid their allies in Ticuani to challenge the Chuchos' power. It enabled migrants to convert their economic power into political influence in Ticuani and to participate in choosing candidates other than those supported by the Chuchos. It also opened avenues for a younger generation of Ticuanenses to participate in Ticuani politics and thereby disrupted the existing relationship between the Committee and *municipio*.

After the election, the Committee refused to work directly with Don Cuahuatemoc. It described this stance as a continuation of its policy begun during the presidency of Don Andrés, who, one committee member quipped, somehow advanced from not having money "enough even to buy a bicycle" to having a car, a house, and a mistress. The Committee has worked in a "very independent" form on specific projects, such as restoring Ticuani's church, but avoided working with the *municipio* itself.

Don Cuahuatemoc saw the Committee's refusal to work with him as punishment for disrupting its arrangement with the Chuchos. How else, he asked, could one explain why they worked with past presidents whom they did not know, but would not work with him, despite his hard work with the Committee during his years in New York (a point I have heard acknowledged even by his harshest critics)? One reason may be generational: Don Cuahuatemoc's supporters were mainly men aged twenty to fifty, while the Committee consists mainly of men in their forties and older. Don Cuahuatemoc sees their anger at him as proof that Don Manuel, the Committee president, was the New York counterpart to the Ticuani cacique. More forgiving observers describe how the interests of the Committee and the Chuchos were linked in the old system, even if they also competed for influence within that system. The Committee's protestations that it was just waiting to see if Cuahuatemoc was honest conflict with its actions in the previous three transitions—to denounce the old president as corrupt, make stern statements about transparency to the next president, and then work with him. I think the Committee boycotted Don Cuahuatemoc because of its internal differences of opinion and drew back, making the (correct) bet that its collaboration with the Chuchos could resume in 2002.

Don Cuahuatemoc in New York

Despite the lack of support from the Committee, Cuahuatemoc came to New York for several days in October 2000 to meet with Ticuanenses and make direct entreaties for funds. He also hoped to lower expectations for dramatic change among his supporters in New York. He had been advised to make a trip before people returned to Ticuani in January. In an interview, he told me he wanted to "undo the effect of what people are saying about me, about my government. . . . They invited me to come [to New York] to give more details. Because there are people of bad faith, who would give other different versions of the reality."

> RS: What are they saying?
>
> CUAHUATEMOC: That I am a president that is not doing anything, that all my promises, I have not fulfilled. . . . I have been asked to do works that should have been finished by the prior government!

It was surprising that the Committee should refuse to work with him. Both the transparency of the 1999 elections and the earthquake in Puebla during summer 1999 should have mobilized more, not less, support from the Committee.

In contrast to Don Tito's earlier official visit, Don Cuahuatemoc's was described by the Committee member opening the meeting as "not official, but . . . private . . . among his friends." *Friends* here limits the importance of the event by emphasizing its private nature, thus denying Cuahuatemoc the chance to claim he had consulted with the entire Ticuani community in New York. This is ironic because the meeting was attended by about fifty people, both critics and supporters of Cuahuatemoc—more than most Committee meetings. Moreover, unlike Don Tito, Cuahuatemoc came with a clear agenda of planned projects, complete with budgets and videos documenting need. Rather than make impossible promises to end migration by promoting economic development, as Tito had, Cuahuatemoc proposed more modest but feasible plans.

Don Cuahuatemoc emphasized that certain projects—such as repairing earthquake damage to the municipal palace—were seen as luxuries by the state of Puebla and that he would receive no state funds at all for them, especially after his budget was cut following the earthquake. The damage to the municipal palace was detrimental to the pueblo, he said: Ticuanenses and traveling merchants alike had told him it was "ugly" and "an embarrassment." He showed a video of the palace and projected that it would cost about US$3,500 to repair, but he said that his efforts to raise money for any project in Ticuani had netted less than US$10. A second project was to repair the zocalo, which the migrants had first paved nearly thirty years before. He concluded, "I hope that the *compañeros* from New York recognize that we cannot do anything without sufficient money."

The ensuing debate revealed migrants' different positions in Ticuani's transnational politics. Supporters of the Chuchos said Cuahuatemoc did not know how to lobby in the state capital of Puebla, as Chucho had. One Committee member laughed that $3,500 could be an obstacle to Cuahuatemoc, with the following melodic putdown: "Suene tan bonito que es tan poquito" (It sounds so pretty that it is so little). Others criticized "Don Manuel's Committee," asking why they did not consult more with Ticuanenses. Don Manuel and Tomás Maestro countered that few people showed up at their open meetings, and that although they wanted to work "for the good of the pueblo," they would not help here because "the government makes promises but does not keep its promises." In Cuahuatemoc's presence, they publicly repeated their refusal to work with him.

What fascinates me here are the meanings of "private" and "public" in the context of transnationalized Ticuani politics. How is it, I wondered, that the elected president of Ticuani can make only a "private" visit if he comes to New York to do Ticuani's business? I asked Cuahuatemoc, "What would need to happen for [yours] to be an official visit?"

CUAHUATEMOC: If Don Manuel had invited me. Because he has the Committee.

RS: But because Carlos invited you . . .

C: It was private . . . an invitation of those who sympathize with me as a person.

RS: Then Don Manuel's Committee—the people see it, including you, as the public committee of Ticuani. Almost like an organ of the government, here, of the *municipio*, right?

C: I don't take it this way, because they are not under my orders to work. Apart from this, well, Don

> Manuel has to consult the citizens [of Ticuani in
> New York] . . . regarding whether he should con-
> tinue as president. . . . Because it already looks like
> Porfirio Díaz for a long time. . . .
>   I came as president, but I went to meet with all
> those that attended. Yes, but now I lack the support
> of Don Manuel's Committee, and about that I don't
> feel happy. . . .

RS: One thing is very clear, that they are the most im-
     portant Committee here. . . .

C: Yes, yes, yes, yes. . . .

RS: It's only them that can extend an official invitation?
     They speak in the name of the Ticuanenses as a
     people there [in New York]?

C: Yes, but . . . I don't know how they were named,
    only that they are . . . out in front. . . .

RS: As the recently elected president of Ticuani, your
     understanding is that to do an official visit you have
     to wait for the Committee to invite you. You can't
     do your own official visit?

C: No. Because if they are the ones out in front, they
    supposedly control the people. For what would I
    go? . . . to visit my brothers . . . sisters . . . friends.

Cuahuatemoc switches between challenging the legitimacy of the Committee's continued control over access to Ticuanense dollars and public arenas—
for example, comparing Don Manuel to the Mexican dictator Porfirio Díaz,
who ruled from 1876 to 1911—and acknowledging how much he needs the
Committee's help. In the end, he acknowledges the Committee as the de
facto face of the Ticuanenses in New York, without whose support his trip
can be nothing more than a personal visit. This state of affairs shows the extent to which the Committee really does represent an alternative, and to
some degree autonomous, base of municipal authority. In New York, even
the elected president of Ticuani has to acknowledge their power. The slip-
page here in the language of public and private suggests how the institutions
charged with reconciling the increasingly diverging interests of Ticuanenses
in New York and Ticuani have become weak, even as other levels of the state
are intervening in institutionalizing some aspects of transnational life.

THE STATE OF PUEBLA AND ITS DIASPORA

Ticuani's story of rivalry between local caciques and hometown associations
in New York is not unique. Indeed, Puebla state officials report that in 2000,

sixteen of eighteen municipal presidents in the Mixteca were returned migrants. The two largest cities, with fewer migrants, were the exceptions. Five or six of these sixteen won elections that were influenced by funds remitted by migrants in New York. Statewide, migrants participated actively in elections in more than 50 of Puebla's 217 *municipios*.[10] This growing influence of migration on Mixteca politics has engendered both concern and strategic attempts to recognize and organize the support of migrants in New York. Melquiades Morales Flores's first step in campaigning for governor was to visit New York—in stark contrast to his predecessor's neglect of migrants—and then organize a rally of 3,500 political leaders in the Mixteca at which he reported on his trip. He brought with him civic and business leaders from New York, praising them for succeeding there but not losing "their language, their culture, and their values." He pledged to develop the Mixteca and to strengthen ties between Puebla and *poblanos* in New York, noting the need to campaign among them and give them the right to vote from abroad. As governor, he instituted a program whereby funds raised in New York would be matched with double the amount from the state of Puebla. He also created Casa Puebla, a nonprofit organization in New York that provides cultural programs, and held a telethon on the Spanish-language cable TV channel Univision after the September 11 attacks to help people locate their loved ones. Casa Puebla also functions as an informal part of the governor's political apparatus, helping him gain legitimacy at home. Its main benefactor, Jaime Lucero, is a successful Mexican businessman and a naturalized U.S. citizen. He was praised as a migrant leader by President Fox, who attended the opening of Lucero's factory and his son's baptism in Puebla.[11]

Two other significant links between *poblanos* in New York and Puebla merit attention. The first is the PRI federal senator Germán Sierra Sánchez, who has worked on senate committees on migration. His rhetoric stresses that the PRI has "paid the bill" for its past neglect of migrants and is now cultivating relations with them. The second is Mario Riestra, the head of CONOFAM, an acronym for the awkwardly named National Coordinating Council of State-Level Programs for Migrants Abroad. Riestra has organized very successful conferences in Puebla with the explicit goal of strengthening the diaspora, and CONOFAM recently presented a recommendation to the Mexican Congress that twenty of the two thousand regional seats in the federal Chamber of Deputies (roughly equivalent to the United States House of Representatives) should be allocated specifically to migrants. They would attend congressional sessions in Mexico but return to their homes in the United States and their migrant constituents.

The concrete effects of such symbolic support for migrants are still to be determined. Some migrants compare Morales Flores favorably with the previous governor of Puebla, Manuel Bartlett, whom many saw as apathetic toward migrants in general and hostile toward the idea of their participation in *poblano* politics. Indeed, Morales Flores deserves credit for his outreach efforts. Others, however, lament that Morales Flores has not come to New York nearly as frequently as he promised to do while campaigning. I have seen him in New York only two or three times in five years of his six-year term (1999–2004). Moreover, opponents cite a long list of projects discussed with him on which no real action has been taken. These include creating a state-level federation of *poblanos* in New York (similar organizations have existed in California since the 1980s and early 1990s for migrants from various Mexican states); some concrete discussion of the right of migrants to vote from abroad in Puebla state elections (such a law was recently passed in Zacatecas and is under discussion elsewhere); enhanced exchange programs for youths between the Mixteca and New York, including sending teachers to New York to work with *poblano* youths there; programs to help abandoned wives in Mexico to contact their migrant husbands; and even a center for the study of migration in the Mixteca region.

Politicians and state officials are trying hard to position themselves as migrant advocates in Mexico because they see how profoundly migration is changing the Mixteca and how democratization is increasing migrant influence through campaign contributions, running for office, and other means. The larger point here is that the institutions of the state and political parties, even on a local level, matter a great deal in the emergence of the larger forces of transnationalization and globalization. An official who has worked at Casa Puebla and in the Mixteca sees the region "stalling" as too many people leave: those who stay do not work and come to depend on remittances. He also sees the Mixteca undergoing a "transculturation . . . that is not Mexican, but also not American . . . a hybrid culture, a *mestizaje*." He sees dangers in return migrants' strong entry into politics. First, he says, "The opening of the PRI in primary elections opens in the *municipios* a political space in which the economic power of the migrants and this leadership of opinion . . . enables them to generate candidates . . . [but they] do not necessarily know the political and social life of their pueblo and their needs . . . and try to bring the American model of development to their communities." He acknowledges the legitimacy of migrant complaints that their financial contributions to projects were often stolen or administered badly. But he blames the "bad television . . . the Spanish-speaking news [that] makes migrants want to provoke a change, . . . fight corruption." The danger escalates when financial resources from New York support better campaigns, winning more votes in Puebla and disrupting the power arrangements of local caciques. The migrant may become the municipal president, but such an outcome creates not one but "five or six political factions." He continues:

> It is a change with great risk because . . . the cacique [in Puebla] loses power, no? . . . [The migrant] pays for the dance, . . . invites your friends for a beer, no? . . . With strong economic support from your committee [in New York] . . . you return with a new *cacicazgo* . . . a transnational cacique! And we talked about before how the *cacicazgos* in the Mixteca are resolved with bullets, no? There are fights that are going to begin to generate, fights for power. The risk is that the fight turns bloody, no? And that the new caciques will be worse dictators than the old ones.

Several elements of this quote merit comment. First, the speaker notes the effects of the PRI's new primary system. While the system enables migrants to convert their economic power from the United States into political power in the Mixteca, this change poses risks: a divided pueblo, a municipal president from the north who does not really know the town any longer, and the potential for bloody rivalries between transnational and local caciques. He comments specifically on the Ticuani case, with which he is quite familiar, saying that caciques in places like Ticuani "don't have strength because they do not have anyone to dominate. . . . Ticuani is an empty pueblo," but one facing potential conflicts as return migrants enter politics.

Another possible source of conflict between local and transnational leaders is one peculiar to Puebla, the office of the auxiliary president. In some *municipios* in Puebla, the *cabecera* is about the same size as or even smaller in population than some of the communities that belong to it. Such communities elect an "auxiliary" president by popular assembly, without party consideration. According to this informant, a disproportionate number of returned migrants have become auxiliary presidents. Secret balloting in these elections, as opposed to the previous show of hands or assembly voting, has exacerbated the effect of migrant influence. Moreover, in the absence of party funds, migrants' money plays an even stronger role. As a result, a number of the migrant auxiliary presidents are in conflict with the local party and have "economic strength but no social base" in local politics.

CONCLUSION

Don Cuahuatemoc's defeat of Don Victorio and its political aftermath show how Ticuani transnational political life has been catalyzed by migration and democratization in Mexico. Specifically, the PRI's introduction of primary elections in 1998 allowed candidates to emerge outside the *dedazo* of the cacique and his friends and to use funds from New York in mounting a persuasive campaign. Don Cuahuatemoc's upset of the cacique's brother was funded mostly by migrants in New York. The PRI, in turn, would not have changed its candidate selection rules without pressure from opposition parties that resulted in embarrassing PRI defections and losses, and in a constitutional right for migrants to vote (which the PRI has effectively blocked). My analysis traces the sequence of concrete institutional and individual actions by which Ticuani transnational politics has been changed. Consistent with Sassen's analysis, the play between global, local, and national processes is dynamic. Yes, the norms of democratization cited by the sociologist John Meyers and his colleagues as evidence of a world society are at work in Mexican politics writ large, and also through migrants returning from the United States, but these forces must also act through other institutions. The state and the related political institutions of the political parties and of *caciquismo* were key factors. *Caciquismo* is a highly localized, old form of political organization that is contrary to the norms of democratic politics. But in Ticuani, and places like it, the cacique and his allies are able to use democratic mechanisms such as the public voting assembly to consolidate their power and deny any authority at all to the Committee. Other levels of action have also helped produce this outcome, including two decades of migrant lobbying for the right to vote and the growing influence of Mexico's opposition parties, which has forced democratization on the PRI. Finally, place matters. The outcomes of these political contests played out have depended a great deal on Ticuani's location in the Mixteca, with its specific local political customs and history. Such stories would play out differently in other contexts or countries. In the end, these considerations push me away from a strong globalist position to a more contingent analysis that takes greater account of local and national processes in the shaping of transnational political life.

Don Cuahuatemoc's victory also laid bare the dynamics of Ticuani's transnational political system, which emerged over sixty years of migration and thirty years of collaborative public service by the Committee. The PRI's 1998 changes in its internal electoral rules elicited a strong response because the young Turks in New York and Ticuani who backed Don Cuahuatemoc felt that the Chuchos and the Committee had monopolized politics for too long. Similarly, migrants in New York have used Mexico's democratic opening to gain leverage in Mixteca politics, but some fear that they pose the danger of "transnational caciques," using economic power that itself results from decades of migration. This raises the issue of how migrants and their dollars will affect local governance and democracy elsewhere in the migration belt of Mexico. It also raises the danger of a resurgence in political violence. Just as violence increased when the Avila Camacho machine broke down and new centers of power emerged among urban labor, the middle class, and students, the emergence of an organized, well-funded migrant movement from New York posed challenges to local caciques that have prevailed for the last twenty to thirty years.

Democratic institutions may offer adequate mechanisms for managing this conflict. Indeed, although the Chuchos accepted the 1999 election result and then lost the PRI primary again to Don Cuahuatemoc's supporters in 2001, they then employed a new strategy. Claiming that Cuahuatemoc's powerful friends in the capital of Puebla prevented a fair contest, they invited the opposition PAN party into the town and won the municipal presidency back as *panistas* in 2001. Ironically, in this case it was the cacique who went outside the locality to find stronger allies and used this extralocal power, in combination with his still-extant cacique power base, so that his candidate would win the election.

In the next chapter I turn from electoral politics to what can be seen as domestic politics: gender bargains within families.

5. Gender Strategies, Settlement, and Transnational Life in the First Generation

> I am not the only woman; there are a lot . . . [who] always go out alone. I don't have a husband!
>
> > DOÑA TALIA, speaking of her resentment about all the time her husband, Don Gerardo, spends away from his family, including time working for the Committee

> Yes, at times it bothered me. But at the same time, I said, it is good that my husband worries about the pueblo, right?
>
> > DOÑA SELENA, speaking proudly of how she and her family bore the sacrifice of the absence of her husband, Don Emiliano, due to his work for the Committee

These women's diametrically opposed understandings of their husbands' absence while doing Committee work or other public work beg for explanation. Why would Doña Talia and her family come to resent Don Gerardo's absence so intensely, and to see it as a macho self-indulgence, while Doña Selena and her family regard Don Emiliano's absence as necessary for his public service, as a sacrifice accruing honor to him and to them as well?[1] My explanation lies in evolving differences in how the two men and their families think about what the sociologist Arlie Hochschild calls "gender ideology"—what people think men's and women's roles should be— and their "gender strategies" or "gender practices"—how they act on those beliefs.[2] Don Gerardo has hewed tightly to a more traditional gender ideology, eschewing household labor, treating the children as his wife's responsibility, and never involving the family in his public work or his returns to Ticuani. In contrast, Don Emiliano has adopted a more egalitarian gender ideology consistent with the views his wife and children have developed, including a more equal division of labor in the household, involvement of his children in his Committee work, and family trips back to Ticuani. These deeply differing attitudes have yielded very different family lives. The conferring or withholding of honor reflects a judgment by the families on the gender bargains adopted by each man.

94

Understanding the meaning of the men's absence gives us insight into the domestic consequences of Ticuani transnational political life. While the Committee imagines itself present in Ticuani politics despite its physical absence, its members are frequently absent from home: collecting funds for Ticuani public works projects places a heavy burden on them and their families. For several months or even years during a project, Committee members may spend all their weekends collecting funds, meaning that they almost never spend an entire day with their families. Whether families view this absence as positive or negative in turn affects the meaning they give to transnational life and assimilation.

Migration, assimilation, and transnational life challenge dominant forms of relations between men and women and ways of thinking about gender. The sociologists Pierrette Hondagneu-Sotelo and Jacqueline Hagan have shown that in migrating to and working in the United States, women challenge patriarchal constraints, including the unequal division of household labor, and try to renegotiate them.[3] The anthropologist Matthew Gutmann has shown that Mexican men's understanding of manhood has evolved as more men take care of children and do other "women's" work in Mexico. Contemporary Mexican men see themselves as *ni macho ni mandilón* (neither macho nor apron-wearing),[4] and instead try to differentiate themselves from these conflicting images of hyper- or compromised masculinity. The anthropologists Gail Mummert and Jennifer Hirsch have described how younger Mexican women, especially in migrant families, prefer "companionate marriages" (relationships emphasizing egalitarian companionship) to the "marriages of respect" (requiring deference to male authority) of their mothers' generation.[5] Under very different conditions from those considered by these other scholars, I show how Emiliano's and Gerardo's ideas about men's gender roles and the ways they negotiate deals with their partners affect the meaning of transnational life and assimilation for them and their families in New York.

THE MEANING OF ABSENCE

Don Emiliano and Don Gerardo offer what social scientists call a "paired comparison": because their stories run parallel much of the time but then diverge, we can assay the causes of this divergence. Both men have worked hard and steadily in Ticuani public life for more than thirty years in New York. Both describe their central identity as Ticuanense, and both are well known for their public service. Both men have worked extensively with the

Committee, and Don Gerardo has also worked with other Mexican civic groups. Both have worked in restaurants in New York, where their late hours interfered with their ability to spend time with their families but paid good wages that supported a middle-class lifestyle. Both men drank heavily for years, a habit their families identified as a problem. Whereas Don Emiliano came to share this view and stopped, Don Gerardo dismissed it and still drinks heavily on weekends. Similarly, Don Emiliano changed what I call his "ranchero masculinity" during his thirty years in New York, while Don Gerardo has embraced it more strongly there.[6]

Drawing on the pioneering work of the sociologist Robert Connell, I define ranchero masculinity as one hegemonic configuration of gender practices that legitimize men's dominant and women's subordinate position:[7] in this view, men exercise authority, and women obey them. Men sometimes use physical violence to enforce their will; they must be fearless, and even violent, in the face of threats by other men; they are expected to do physically demanding work; and they drink alcohol, especially during religious feasts, as an essential dimension of male friendship. Public space and work belong to men, while private space and domestic work belong to women. By this logic, the wives and children of both Don Gerardo and Don Emiliano were not supposed to attend public events, even a picnic, while the men were collecting for the Committee, though trips to certain "female" public spaces, such as the library or the grocery store, were seen as acceptable because necessary.[8] (Many immigrant men nevertheless feel threatened in public spaces both because of potential conflict with other Mexicans or ethnic groups and because of possible exposure to U.S. immigration authorities).[9] Ironically, it was the more progressive Don Emiliano who returned to Mexico.

An alternative image of masculinity is that of the modern migrant, who retains elements of ranchero masculinity but pragmatically adapts to the new context where his partner must also work, where the state interferes with ranchero prerogatives such as using violence, and where the man then defends such changes in a revised gender ideology. Men who live this alternative masculinity, such as Don Emiliano, participate in an ongoing critique of traditional ranchero masculinity; men who embrace the more macho image, such as Don Gerardo, engage in an ongoing defense of it.

Just as Don Emiliano and Don Gerardo had to renegotiate their notions of masculinity when they came to New York, Doña Talia and Doña Selena had to renegotiate their notions of femininity, engaging with at least four models of migrant womanhood. The first is the hegemonic Ticuani image of the ranchera, a woman who defers to her husband in all things and never shows anger toward him. She focuses her life on child rearing and domestic tasks, depends almost entirely on her husband for economic support, and spends her life in "female" spaces (that is, at home, unless engaged in domestic duties like shopping or caring for children). A ranchera never expresses what the Mexican anthropologist Federico Besserer's informants referred to as "inappropriate sentiments":[10] that is, any lack of respect for men, displayed through anger or disagreement. To express such ideas shows a lack of *vergüenza*, or shame, a primary female virtue. The second model is that of the Ticuani migrant woman who seeks to peacefully accommodate her husband's renegotiation of ranchero masculinity while both adopt new roles. Typically, she works outside the home and takes the lead in dealing with some American institutions, such as schools, while he does some housework and other "women's work." Third, there is the *pionera*, an older Ticuani woman, usually widowed or divorced (or perhaps never married), who lives independently in New York, either raising a family or living alone. The final model is the New York woman, an Americanized vision of independent womanhood who works, supports herself, and does not really need a man but would be prepared to marry one who shares her egalitarian vision. This model, however, resonates more strongly with the second generation than with the first.

Masculinity and femininity are relational concepts that acquire meaning mainly in relation to each other and in relation to other versions of themselves. Don Emiliano and Doña Selena seem to have created a more companionate marriage for themselves, emphasizing the couple's emotional intimacy and friendship while retaining elements of a "respect" marriage. In contrast, Don Gerardo wants a marriage of respect, and Doña Talia wants a companionate marriage.[11] A marriage of respect resonates with ranchero masculinity and ranchera femininity in emphasizing the man's power and honor, the woman's deference and modesty, and the separation of men and women in social space.

Vergüenza, a central element in Mexican female morality, merits more exploration. It is a quality that a woman is said to possess: *ella tiene vergüenza* (she has shame). Its fundamental feature, according to Jack Katz, is "the incapacity for action and a confession to self of moral incompetence in some regard."[12] Shame is clearly distinguished from mere embarrassment, the display of which frames error or other moral failure as situational, and hence not reflective of one's true self. I would argue that in ranchera femininity *vergüenza* is in particular the inability to respond (or at least the willingness *not* to respond) to male anger, the male gaze, or other exercises of male power. Hence, honor requires a woman to feel shame for being female in the presence of males. The ontological basis of ranchera femininity is to defer to men and to lack moral autonomy and competence in relation to men. Rancheras derive honor only from the approval of men. To exhibit sentiments such as anger toward men is to behave shamefully because one has challenged male authority; a woman who has appropriate shame would not be able to respond. For this reason, *vergüenza* fits hand in glove with the emphasis on male privilege and authority in marriages of respect.

These various notions of masculinity and femininity challenge the dominant images of a "crisis of masculinity" and "liberating femininity" in migration research.[13] In this view, men want to return to Mexico, or at least imagine they will return (a phenomenon that the sociologist Luin Goldring beautifully describes as "gendered memory"), because they lose status and power in the United States, whereas women want to stay because they gain authority and establish deeper roots. Powerless migrant men assert largely symbolic power over women to compensate for the loss of their ranchero masculinity.[14]

Among Ticuanense migrants, however, these conditions do not necessarily hold. Although women do more of the work of settlement, such as taking children to the doctor, men also participate. Moreover, men have created institutions, such as the Committee, that give them real power and status. Many men make good money in New York, send children to college, and even buy houses. Hence, they can live successful middle-class lives in New York. Their wives also gain pride and status from being married to men whose sacrifices are recognized by the community and from their own opportunities for service and honor, afforded by their husbands' work.

Moreover, the crisis-of-masculinity view presumes ranchero masculinity to persist in an unchanging, hegemonic form. But what happens when this masculinity must be legitimized—and can therefore be challenged—in the context of competing masculinities and femininities that derive from changes in Mexican society, from migration, and from American society? Such changes affect the relations men and women have with their work, with each other, and with institutions and power. By exploring the ambiguities in such relations, and the evolution of gender bargains and ideologies, I examine the dynamic and constructed character of gender in migrants' lives. In mathematical terms, my analysis attempts to move beyond discerning a reciprocal relationship, in which more American freedom means less traditional patriarchal oppression, to frame the changes as a set of simultaneous equations: things are changing both in Mexico and in the United States, and these changes are related.

This point can be clarified by contrasting my scheme with the images driving other analyses, even in quite insightful work. For example, in describing how first-generation migrant men and women negotiate their relations with their children, the sociologists Min Zhou and Carl Bankston use the metaphor of "straddling the gap," Alejandro Portes and Ruben Rumbaut use that of a "race," and Nazli Kibria adopts that of walking a "family tightrope."[15] All these metaphors portray migrants as attempting to balance the demands of the cultures of the traditional home country and the modern United States. They hope their children will succeed by retaining the virtues of the old culture before they are derailed by American culture. These metaphors do describe much of the reality and the perceived experience of immigrant parents, and I employ them in what follows. But I also focus on how gender roles are being simultaneously renegotiated in Mexico; how both Mexican and American cultures support various and internally inconsistent images of masculinity, femininity, and family life; and how these meanings have simultaneous referents in New York and Ticuani. I thus avoid, in the main, the assumption of a unitary home- or host-society culture.

One insight offered by my approach is that neither first-generation women nor second-generation men or women always prefer American culture, especially when male gender privilege is involved. For example, first-generation women often identify more closely with some aspects of Mexican culture, which they feel values the family more than the American culture that facilitates (or requires) their working outside the home. Similarly, many second-generation men who might be expected to reject Mexican culture as too much like their parents' actually embrace it because it offers them gender privileges that they feel American culture denies them. Moreover, there are larger gaps between generations, and between men and women, on such gendered issues as domestic violence than on such issues as education and upward mobility.

I offer three caveats before beginning. First, although I emphasize the dynamic nature of gender identities and analyze their performance, I stop short of the queer theorist Judith Butler's position that these identities are mainly performative and always in flux, defying categorization and stability. While Butler's position is an important corrective to the antiquated notion of fixed gender roles à la Talcott Parsons in the mid-twentieth century, I see gender identities as being performed in particular institutional and structural contexts that people (here, migrants and their children) help to create and that provide them with greater stability and offer a large, but not infinite, set of possibilities for recombination. To use a molecular

metaphor, recombination of these gender ideologies, practices, and identities creates more stable rather than less stable elements, though with significant potential to recombine further.

Second, the images of masculinity and femininity outlined above all
presume heterosexuality. There is little public acknowledgment of homosexuality among Ticuanenses in either Ticuani or New York. Moreover, in
all my years of research I cannot recall even one reference to any Ticuanenses being lesbians.[16] Two men were said to be gay. The first was Bandolo, who was the frequent subject of jokes between men. Typically, someone would be teased about being "good friends" or "boyfriends" with
Bandolo, or told that Bandolo really missed him while he was in New York.
In fact, I heard about Bandolo by being teased in precisely this way, but I
learned to turn the tables on anyone who seemed headed that way. For example, a Ticuanense man I did not know, who was friends with Committee
members I knew, asked if I knew Bandolo, and from others' responses I
knew he was trying to set me up for a joke. I told him that I did not know
Bandolo, but that he should not worry, I would not steal his boyfriend. This
joke was met with incredulous laughter from those who did not know me
and knowing laughter from those who did. "¡El gringo te chingó!" (The
gringo nailed you!) the men laughed. That I knew about Bandolo, and knew
how to turn the encounter, made me, situationally at least, a fellow Ticuanense sharing in this affirmation of ranchero heterosexuality.

Another case was Yonny, who returned to live in Ticuani and run his
family store after two decades in New York. Yonny was commonly called a
maricón (faggot) behind his back but was addressed with respect in person.
He participated in community affairs for the town and could be counted on
for donations for projects. His status as a store owner and competent man
who fulfilled his public responsibilities meant that his status as a homosexual (an identity I never heard discussed by him or in his presence) was
eclipsed by his status as a competent man. I have seen similar eclipsing of
homosexual status in indigenous communities, where effeminate migrant
men who work hard in community service are treated with respect. When
such a man's homosexuality is discussed in his absence, he is referred to as
a *maricón* (or, sometimes, "homosexual") but a good man who helps in all
the projects: that is, he is okay.

Finally, Don Gerardo's ranchero and Don Emiliano's mixed modern-
ranchero gender strategies are not the only ones by which Committee
members sought to balance their public work and home life. A third
strategy—exit from public life—merits brief mention here. One of the
Committee's former officers ended up leaving the Committee because it

impinged too much on his family obligations. His wife complained about what she saw as excessive absences from family life—all week for work, then most of the weekend for the Committee. His exit from the Committee was a performance of gender and honor. He had told his friends on the Committee privately that he wanted to resign because it was disrupting his family life and his wife was angry. But he did not want to admit this before the whole Committee. To do so would imply that he was not ranchero enough to put his wife in her place and that he had violated the Committee's communal ethic by putting his individual interests first.

The situation was complicated by the ambiguity about which code of masculinity should be used to interpret his withdrawal. I heard comments that his wife "governed" him, that he was not man enough to continue sacrificing for the pueblo, as well as sympathetic assessments of the difficulty of balancing Committee work and family life; and others admitted they also sometimes wanted to withdraw. The Committee was adamant that he must resign in person. One said: "It doesn't matter [what his reasons are for resigning]. Whatever pretext, he has to come and present himself here to resign in front of us." Thus, the Committee denied him an easy exit; they did, however, decide to accept his resignation without subjecting him to a long and potentially shaming discussion. When he finally announced his resignation, he gave vague and mixed reasons including his work obligations as well as his family, thus invoking an external demand consistent with his ranchero masculinity. His reasons were accepted without question, he was thanked warmly for his service, and toasts were made. He and the Committee had negotiated his exit with his masculine honor intact.

Un Ausente Nunca Presente:
An Absent One Never Present

Don Gerardo's wife, Talia, and their children greatly resent his extensive involvement in Ticuani public work. Outside his job he is always working on Mexican civic events, the Committee, or sports leagues. Talia lamented her husband's absence and the lack of time he spends with their children.[17]

> Right now [a Saturday], he went to soccer. . . . I am not the only
> woman; there are a lot . . . [who] always go out alone. I don't have a
> husband! . . . This is why I always go out alone, you see, in the park
> when there are parties, because he does not like parties. . . . My hus-
> band does not say, Let's go, we are going to see the soccer match, I will
> bring the kids, no. He brings his friends . . . and for this I say, Now, on
> Sunday, you should bring them wherever it would be, to the park, to
> the library, to a museum, but no. . . . He always is doing things with

the Committee or drinking or playing. . . . And we fight over this; I say to him, Look, you are always busy with your soccer.

But my kids he never brings to see soccer. . . . In this moment we have a week of not talking to each other, we are mad at him. . . . It's not so much because he is not there with them, but we are fighting because he has his friends, his buddies . . . and because he never gets to know my children. You ask them, see, when he has ever brought them to a park, or when he has brought them even to hang out on the corner—never, not the big one or the littlest one, not anyone. . . . But he believes that the money is everything. "I work like a donkey! I do this, that." I say, "No, the money is not everything! You have to know your children!" I am the one who does what you don't know, . . . to go the school, to the meetings; I have to bring them to the doctor, to the ophthalmologist, . . . to the dentist, . . . to everything! Why?! . . . They interviewed him for the newspaper [workplace newsletter], and . . . he told them, "On my vacation I like to be with my kids," and I said to him, "You are a liar." (Spanish, translated by the author)

These impassioned words depict someone whose domestic life is far from what she wants for herself and her children. More than most migrant couples I know, Don Gerardo and Talia live in separate, gendered spheres. He spends little social time with his family and is always occupied by Mexican male public life. Talia remarks that he never even brings the children "to hang out on the corner." Given the association of "the street" with drinking and trouble, this comment implies that his interest in his children is so weak that he does not even help raise them badly! Ironically, despite his ranchero masculinity and his repeated demands, Talia and her children ignore the sanction against public socializing without the father and go to parties without him. Talia's comments indicate that she has largely rejected ranchera femininity as a model for her own life. She is clearly furious at her husband for refusing to adapt his masculinity to their new surroundings. It is significant that she openly tells him so and shares her feelings with me, a male friend of her husband who is involved with Ticuani public life.

Don Gerardo's absence from his family takes a high toll on family relations. The children are so angry at the father that they urge their mother to leave him, asking what good he brings them. Later in the interview, Talia observes that Mexican women are more long-suffering than Puerto Rican women, who readily leave their partners (she refers to one Puerto Rican friend who has had five husbands), then contrasts her stance with her second-generation daughter's open advocacy of leaving:

My aunt, she says, "You can be screwed in life [*chingada*], but there you are, see?" Because you have to think about your kids. Another man could abuse your kids. You have to put up with a bit, up to a certain limit. No one is obliged to live their whole life tied up, but you see that with my countrymen almost never is there a divorce. You have to put up with this until the end. . . . Now, the new generation is different. Because my daughter says to me, "Mami, why is my father so bad and always not here? Leave him!" But it is not that easy. . . . What crazy man would want me with four kids? (Spanish, translated by the author)

Talia is enacting more than one image of femininity. On the one hand, she feels bound by the requirement of ranchera or Ticuani migrant femininity that a woman stay with her husband even when unhappy. On the other, by rejecting some of her husband's demands—for example, that she enforce his will and not let their daughter date—she seems to be adopting a *pionera* or New York woman position. Then again, by hiding her actions from her husband and staying with him at all, she acknowledges his economic power and seems to act like a traditional Ticuani migrant woman. She later tells me she could not afford the house without his income, which is roughly three times hers. Her only imagined way to escape—to look for another man—is inconsistent with her values and is in any case, she says, hopeless. She is "screwed" but will endure her situation for the sake of the children. Talia's alienation from Don Gerardo extends to her colluding with their daughter to evade his assertion of masculine authority. For example, when he forbade their daughter from having a boyfriend, Talia allowed her to see him and then covered for her when Don Gerardo inquired about the daughter's activities. Talia believes that the children prefer the boyfriend to their father because the boyfriend spends time with them and gives them rides. She also believes, moreover, that Don Gerardo knows it and forbade his daughter from seeing the boyfriend partly out of jealousy.

Talia's public expressions of anger at her husband and her defiance of his proscription on going out in public show that she has rejected the ranchero concept of *vergüenza*. Moreover, she has clearly expressed "inappropriate sentiments" without compunction. In rejecting the ranchera role, she can also reject *vergüenza*. By responding angrily to Don Gerardo's treatment, she has asserted a morally competent feminine self independent of her male partner. She clearly lacks ranchera shame, but her renegotiated moral self feels no shame at this. (That both her male and female relatives support her actions suggests that women have more latitude in gender behavior than is supposed by many scholars of migration.)

Talia continued her criticisms by noting that Don Gerardo returns to Mexico regularly but never takes the family.

He goes [to Mexico] every two years . . . but he does not bring the kids. Because they do not want to go . . . with him, no. . . . I want them to know Mexico because of the people—my husband's mother is very old, and she always faults my husband. . . . "Why don't you bring the children?" And he says he does not bring them because there are animals there and the kids don't eat. . . . But I think that he does not want to bother himself. . . . And they also say: "If my mom goes, I go. If my mom does not go, I don't go." (Spanish, translated by the author)

In Talia's view, Gerardo uses the argument that the children won't eat in Mexico, or might be bitten by scorpions, as an excuse for not taking them. Ticuani has not served for this family, as it has for many, as an important site for second-generation adolescent rituals, such as the Antorcha, the dances, or the procession, which can sometimes bridge the generation gap. In 1998, when this interview was done, the oldest child was nineteen and had never returned to Mexico. Moreover, the words of Talia and her family suggest no benefit to them from Don Gerardo's years of public work in New York and Ticuani. For them, the hours spent away from the family are all just time lost; they believe he simply does not want to spend time with them.

Don Gerardo's role as a provider is one of only two things about him for which Talia has kind words. She qualifies her harsh assessment, seeming even to defend him, or pity him as the victim of a vice he cannot control, when she explains his absence as the result of an alcohol problem and acknowledges that he has progressed at his job and provided well: "He has twenty-five years at his job. . . . He entered as a busboy . . . now he is in charge of a floor. . . . He has a good job there, [but] he goes bad because of the drink. I see him as an alcoholic before anything else; I believe this because he does not stop it, and this is bad" (Spanish, translated by the author). Also to his credit, she says, Gerardo "knows better" than to hit her, unlike some Mexican men.

Overall, Don Gerardo refuses to renegotiate the basic terms of the gender bargain, even in a context where the gender ideologies and bargains of the rest of the family are dramatically different from his. Talia's economic dependence on Don Gerardo, and her expressed belief that one can be "screwed in life" but must endure one's situation, helps preserve the relationship but compromises the quality of their family life. The father has fundamentally different expectations from the rest of the family about their collective life. In this context, it is clear why Don Gerardo's work for Ticuani public life is resented rather than revered as bringing honor to the family; they do not really consider him part of their family.

I was surprised by how openly Talia spoke to me and project researcher Sandra Lara and by the children's vigorous nods of agreement as she complained about Don Gerardo. I had thought such sentiments would be guarded as family secrets, but the material quoted above came out spontaneously, not in response to my questions. Perhaps Talia felt comfortable speaking because she too had known me for years as a friend of Ticuani, or because another woman was there. At any rate, it was clear these were not secrets but open family problems. It was also clear that Don Gerardo's gender ideology and strategy have been rejected by his family. His ranchero masculinity and his separation of home life and public life are among the most pronounced I have seen, approximating the imagined past of fully segregated private and public spaces for women and men in Ticuani. His wife and children clearly want a different gender bargain. Talia, at least, wants him to spend more time with her and the children, in Mexico and in the United States, and to do more domestic work. But Don Gerardo criticizes these positions as too "American," too far from Mexican ways, part of the reason why Mexican youth is going astray in America. The result is an unhappy and conflictive home wherein his public service is seen as a selfish indulgence and abandonment, not a noble sacrifice for the pueblo.

Talia, for her part, steers a course that takes her through various terrains of femininity. Her secret and open disobedience of her husband bumps her out of the ranchera category, but her choice to stay with him despite her unhappiness means she cannot be a pure *pionera* or New York woman. She demands that her husband spend more time with "her" children, to no avail. She also lives a life organized very much as a ranchera life would be: she spends her time mainly with her children and other adult women— though she does not restrict herself to feminine space, as her husband wishes. She is a grudging Ticuani migrant woman who, under different economic circumstances, might become a *pionera*.

Un Ausente Quien Cumpla:
An Absent One Who Keeps His Promises

The harsh meanings ascribed to Don Gerardo's absence contrast markedly with the terms of honor and sacrifice Don Emiliano's family use to describe his public work. While both his wife, Doña Selena, and their children lamented his frequent absences, they came to see them as sacrifices for the pueblo that enhanced his and their own dedication to and status in the community. Don Emiliano's evolution away from a pure ranchero masculinity, his greater involvement in raising his daughters, and their greater involvement with Ticuani resulted in the attribution of very positive meanings to his public work. Moreover, his renegotiation of masculinity involved a renegotiation of the couple's gender bargain and hence of Doña Selena's femininity as well. His greater flexibility made this possible. The end result was a modern migrant masculinity that retains elements of ranchero masculinity but in a form that was adapted to the United States context and not seen as compromising his overall masculinity.

I conducted an interview with Don Emiliano, Doña Selena, and their daughter Mia. The conversational dynamics were interesting.

> RS (TO DOÑA SELENA): I wanted to ask you a question about . . . how you managed all this. Because Don Emiliano went out a lot knocking on doors, right? . . . What it was like when Don Emiliano went out so much for so many years? . . .

> DOÑA SELENA: Yes, at times it bothered me. But at the same time, I said, it is good that my husband worries about the pueblo, right? With all the men who would make a plan and be concerned for the pueblo, because the pueblo had needs, for various things, Robert. So then I said, I hope that the people here in this country will support them, because all the people here have the opportunity to make a weekly wage. I believed that the people will not withhold their cooperation, no? And to do those public works. . . . There were times when it would bother me, no?—Oh God! But to this I grew accustomed. And I did not know if the people would thank them or not. . . .

> DON EMILIANO: I could not think, Robert, only of my marriage or of my wife, no? . . . All of the wives . . . of my fellow Committee members, it was the same reaction. . . . The weekends were the time that we dedicated to go out, and sometimes we could not offer to our wives the chance to go out and drink a cup of coffee. . . . (Spanish, translated by the author)

Doña Selena offers a rationale for Don Emiliano's absence that Talia never advances to excuse Don Gerardo. This contrast underlines how fundamentally different are the gender bargains in the two families. The same behavior by Don Emiliano and Don Gerardo assumes very different meanings. The two men also place differing constructions on the extra burden their absence imposes on their wives. While Don Gerardo sees this burden as part of his wife's womanly duties, one she should accept without complaint, Don Emiliano explicitly recognizes his wife's and his family's sacrifice and acknowledges the extra work his absence has created.

In Don Emiliano's absence, not only did his family miss him, but they were prevented from attending social events without him. Unlike Doña Talia, who defies Don Gerardo and goes out in public without him, Doña Selena and her daughters did not attend public events unescorted, especially not Mexican events, though they could do household errands, such as shopping or going to the library. While the use of public space in Mexico has never been as absolutely gendered as migrants remember—women and children do occupy the streets in Ticuani during school hours, for example—Doña Selena took this prohibition seriously. In observing it, she was enacting a strong version of a Ticuani migrant woman who can work to earn the money needed to live in New York but who sees the value of maintaining some elements of traditional (remembered or imagined) ranchero and ranchera roles. Thus Doña Selena displays a deference to her husband appropriate to a ranchera. Although she admits that his absence bothered her, she makes this response subordinate to the honor accruing to her husband, and by extension to herself and her family, for his sacrifice to the pueblo. Her moral competence as a ranchera is upheld in this relationship with her husband. Despite their daughters' desires to go to the park without their father, this Ticuani immigrant mother enforced her version of femininity as well as her husband's masculinity.

> DOÑA SELENA: This is how it was.... For example, if my husband was not there, I did not go out. I was very accustomed to that if he went out, I went with him.
>
> SANDRA LARA: So then, the weekends when he was out, you would stay in the house?
>
> DON EMILIANO: Yes.
>
> DS: In the house with my children ... looking at movies. . . .
>
> SL: And what did you say to your children?
>
> DS: Well, we are not going out, now we are going to stay home. Yes, then my children said to me: We have homework, well, we are going to the library, and there we would spend the afternoon, we would go eat out, close by, . . . but to another place like that we would not go.

RS: And did they not complain?

DS: No, they did not protest, my children.

RS: Really?

MIA (THE DAUGHTER): We used to get mad, too, that they would not bring us to the park. Our only fun on Saturday and Sunday was Prospect Park, to play volleyball with all our friends. . . .

RS (TO MIA): And you guys did not go . . . ?

M: No, we did not go out of the house, [until] let's say, I think, until Victoria was twenty, twenty-two years old. . . .

DS: Never, never did they walk around on their own, that's the real truth. . . .

RS (TO MIA): So then the sacrifice was from the whole family. And did you understand that it was to make the pueblo better? Or did you only get mad because you could not go out?

M: The real truth is at the beginning [we asked]: Why so much collecting? Why so much collecting? And I believe that at the end I came to understand we made lots of things possible, as my father says, when we saw the water, you know, with the pipeline! Because before when we came back [to Ticuani], oh no! . . . it was a traumatic experience for me because I had become accustomed to bathe at any hour, and I came down here, and it's—You have to bathe between this hour and this hour. . . . And when I came back later and . . . there was a lot of water, then I understood the effort my father had put out, and Don Manuel, and all the Committee. (Spanish, translated by the author)

During the period being discussed these young women were in their mid teens and early twenties, an age at which most American parents let their children go out or travel alone, and even live away at college. Don Emiliano's stance reflects the same kind of ranchero attitude toward adolescence and freedom as Don Gerardo's. Both men forbade their daughters to date until they were in their twenties. But the families' responses were again different. Doña Talia colluded with the daughter to neutralize Don Gerardo's authority and evade the limits he attempted to place on her because the family saw him as having forfeited, by his absence, his right to control their activities. In contrast, Doña Selena shared Don Emiliano's view and enforced it because he shared in carrying family responsibilities and hence was entitled to wield authority. Their daughters internalized this conservative stance, joking proudly that others saw them as old-fashioned *(anticuada)*.

In an interview without their parents a year later, two of Don Emiliano's daughters gave a less tolerant view of their father's absences but still rooted their understanding of it in sacrifice and service. Mia said:

> We used to get really mad. . . . But I guess that's why he's such a respected man. It was a sacrifice for the pueblo, but we didn't get it then. . . . We used to say: Why are you doing it? We're never gonna go back. You don't even have a house! There's no water. . . . But when I came back I saw changes. They were building the school—*that* explains why my father was out all weekend. It made me proud.

This quote shows anger and incomprehension yielding to an awareness of the larger meaning of their father's efforts. When they saw the new school being built, or the water coming out of the new pipes, they understood that through this work their father had become somebody in the Ticuani community. Their pride in their father's standing reflects their close relationship with him and redeems the sacrifice imposed on them by his being always busy with Committee work.

Another reason Don Emiliano came to be honored for his service while Don Gerardo was resented was what Don Emiliano describes as an "evolution" in his gender ideology, starting with his difficulty in wearing an apron while working in a New York restaurant:

> It did not worry me what they said in the pueblo, that Emiliano is frying eggs in New York and is doing the work of a woman. For us, the villagers *[pueblerinos]*, to work in the kitchen is like having your pants pulled down, right? . . . The first time I put the apron on . . . I felt really bad . . . because here [in Ticuani] I worked like a man, leading an ox team, working with material. . . . From here I went and they gave me the white [cook's] uniform, and I could not put the apron on. . . . I felt humiliated, getting screwed where I came to be the one giving it. . . . I could not put the apron on the first time. And I felt that I looked like my pants had fallen down. And after that I changed my ideas and evolved. . . . I said, No, I am here to make dollars. I don't care that my hands are getting burned frying eggs, making soup, because here comes my check! [laughter]. . . . [They called me] henpecked *[mandilón]*, but you know when I reacted? At the end of the week when they paid me. There is where I changed my mind: "Thanks to God, I now have seventy dollars in my first week of work!"

To work in the kitchen, from here was my rotation in life, right? Because I felt ashamed that people from my pueblo knew that I was washing dishes or glasses or sweeping and mopping the floor. . . . I want to say that machismo or ignorance still applies in these pueblos, in the countryside. Yes. After that I evolved in my mentality, I said that . . . I will learn to be a really good cook, [or] at least a good enough one, right? (Spanish, translated by the author)

Don Emiliano used his desire to earn money and the need to provide for his family—also virtues in ranchero masculinity—to rationalize his crossing the line dividing men's and women's work. Earning money in amounts impossible for a peasant in Puebla enabled him to defend his gender identity against both the "machismo and ignorance" of the "villagers" and his own shame.

Unlike Don Gerardo, Don Emiliano was also active in raising his children. He and his wife described how he took care of the girls as babies, and, when they were older, got them off to school in the morning. He sometimes also brought his oldest daughter with him when he was collecting for the Committee. This more egalitarian division of labor engendered resistance from their families in Ticuani. On their first return with their two U.S.-born daughters, Don Emiliano's father objected strenuously to his son's involvement in their daily care:

DE: When I came here, my father totally did not like it. . . . I was bathing the girls in a tub [and] changed them. My wife was making the *gorditas* [fat tortillas] to eat. And my father . . . said, No, son [don't do this]. I said, No, Papa, they are my daughters and my blood. But I had taken note of the first reaction, that I should not do these things. . . .

DS: I was making the breakfast, so, well, I should not go and touch the girls because I was going to have to change a diaper. . . . So I said, Well, help me, take care of the girls while I make breakfast, no? . . . I got on very well with my husband, but . . . my in-laws saw this as weird, they did not like it. They felt that their son, no . . . (Spanish, translated by the author)

Don Emiliano's willingness to do "women's" work shows his evolution toward a masculinity different from that of his father, who, when drunk, still beat his married son. His father also charged that Don Emiliano was being "governed" by his wife, implying that he had forfeited his true masculinity in New York. Don Emiliano's response to his father was not simply to refer to the dollars he earned but was based in valuing a relationship with his daughters that he did not want disrupted by the requirements of a too-macho masculinity. Here again, Don Emiliano rejects hegemonic ranchero masculinity in favor of an emerging masculinity in the Mexican community in New York. His life in New York required him to learn to cook and care for his children while his wife worked, changes he linked with his larger evolution through migration—his "rotation in life"—and his relationship with a new kind of work in the service economy in New York, rather than in agricultural production in Puebla.

> Sincerely, the change [in me] was total. I said to my wife, My father is
> one thing and I am another. You and I are one material, and my father
> is another. He follows his customs, and we are going to follow our
> customs, and we are going to watch as we go. For this we went [to
> New York], to see, to be there. I always thought this was key—to live
> in a super world city, you have to learn something in life. How would
> it do me any good . . . if I went, if one went to spend ten or fifteen
> years there, and I returned the same to my pueblo? Better I never
> went! (Spanish, translated by the author)

Don Emiliano's language indicates how he and Doña Selena jointly decided things, suggesting that he held a less rigid ranchero masculinity even before migration. They decided together to go to New York when they were *novios* (in a committed relationship) but to delay marriage until they could return to Ticuani.[18] Retrospectively, Don Emiliano even includes change as a *goal* of his migration. Don Emiliano's words do not lament lost gender privileges, as most theory would predict, but rather value what he has gained by being in New York. Instead of being *pueblerinos*, he and Doña Selena now think like citizens of a "super world city." Don Emiliano's evolution seems even clearer when we contrast his description of his basically happy marriage and family life with Doña Talia's description of hers. She complains that Gerardo "never gets to know *my* kids" (italics mine), whereas Don Emiliano and Doña Selena use team language to describe their marriage and child rearing.

Doña Selena's notion of femininity matters in this relationship too. In asking him to change the baby's diaper while she cooked, as if it were a natural thing for a father to do for his children, she stepped out of the role of a ranchera, who would in all likelihood have asked another woman but not her husband to do it. Whereas Don Gerardo has tried to impose a marriage of respect on his family while Doña Talia unsuccessfully demands a companionate marriage, Don Emiliano and Doña Selena have renegotiated a type of companionate marriage, one that retains some elements of ranchero masculinity consistent with a respect marriage.

Don Emiliano and Don Gerardo have also adopted fundamentally different stances toward alcohol that reflect different conceptions of masculinity. While both were seen by their families as drinking to excess, Don

112 / *Gender Strategies*

Emiliano eventually gave up drinking because his doctor urged him to and because his family demanded it; and he saw it becoming an issue between them. In contrast, Don Gerardo's family clearly and loudly disapproves of his drinking, but he dismisses their complaints, a stance facilitated by the fact that he drinks mostly while he is out with his male friends at sports events or doing public work. Interestingly, drinking is not as rigidly required a part of ranchero masculinity and male friendship as the talk about it by Ticuanense men and women, and other scholars, might lead one to believe. Although alcohol consumption is normally seen as essential to male rituals, especially among young men, other possibilities exist. Hence, even though most Committee members drank while socializing after the day's collecting was done, it was also accepted that several of these men, including Don Emiliano, did not drink. When the beer and brandy went round, these men were offered soda, without the derisive comments that I have heard in other contexts. The same kind of exception was made for some men in Ticuani and elsewhere in Mexico.

How this exception was negotiated is interesting. It was not the case, as with the male Alcoholics Anonymous members studied by Stanley Brandes in Mexico City,[19] that these men redefined manhood through their refusal to drink and thus avoid the harm drinking would do to their bodies and relationships. Rather, the group was silent on the topic. Respected Committee members had the right not to drink and not to be questioned about it because they had proved themselves by their community service. Don Emiliano renegotiated this dimension of ranchero masculinity, while Don Gerardo used it to justify his alcohol consumption.

My own experience with Ticuani and the Committee and drinking was similar. At first, I experienced pressure to drink more, no matter how much I had drunk already. I would drink one or two cans of beer during a meeting in New York, or at a party in Ticuani, and then politely accept, but not consume, the others I was offered. As I became an honorary member of the Committee and the Ticuani community, the dynamic changed. I would always be offered more beer, but when I signaled that I had had enough, I was not pressed to drink more. At the start of my fieldwork, I reluctantly drank tequila, which I found to be too strong and to cloud my ability to concentrate. But as time went on, I came to enjoy it and brought it to the meetings or dinners and other events. I found it actually helped my fieldwork by enabling me to relax. (I relaxed in many settings doing fieldwork but tried to pay special attention during the meetings.) Partaking of this male friendship ritual also facilitated my friendships. In my experience, multiple models of male friendship and alcohol consumption coexisted at such gatherings: a dominant model required that they go together, but there was also another of moderate consumption and a third of abstention, usually acceptable when the abstainer had earned respect in other ways.

Hence, three factors combined to make Don Emiliano revered for his sacrifice, whereas Don Gerardo was resented for his selfishness. First, and fundamentally, Don Gerardo demanded a strictly gendered division of labor and leisure similar to what he felt had existed in Ticuani before their migration, which included lots of time for sports, drinking, and politics with other men, but little time with his wife or family. And although Don Emiliano also spent too many hours on Ticuani work, and drank a lot, he spent a great deal more time doing the "women's work" of caring for his children and came to see the machismo of the *pueblerinos* as too limiting. Second, as a result of his greater involvement with them, his children and wife came to identify with and embrace the larger public purpose of Don Emiliano's service on the Committee. Third, because Don Emiliano's children spent more time in Ticuani and returned for adolescent rituals, they could see firsthand the results of their father's work and the family's sacrifice. These factors worked synergistically: as Don Emiliano's daughters visited Ticuani for teen rituals, they came to love Ticuani and understand the contribution their father's absences had helped to make in ways that Don Gerardo's children could not. Hence, Don Emiliano's grown children now see his absences as helping the pueblo, while Don Gerardo's children simply encourage their mother to leave their father because he has already largely absented himself from them. The end results for the two men, in terms of the kind of honor and recognition bestowed or withheld by their families, are starkly different. Don Gerardo's sacrifice is barely recognized by his family; his wife acknowledges his progress at his job, but sees him as a loser at home. Don Emiliano is revered at home, and his public honor reflects on his self-sacrificing family as well.

Ironically, given their attitudes toward gender bargains in Ticuani and New York, it was Don Emiliano and Doña Selena who returned to Mexico, while Don Gerardo's family purchased a house in New York. Don Emiliano decided to return to Mexico when the restaurant he worked in closed, his heart condition grew worse, and his doctors told him to find less stressful work. Facing the prospect of less money and equal stress at a new job in New York, Don Emiliano and Doña Selena moved back to Ticuani to build a house and open a store. They still visit New York, and their children and grandchildren, who remained in the United States, visit Ticuani. Their return was not a search for lost gender privilege by Don Emiliano. His wife pushed him to retire to Ticuani for his health, but she has also benefited from the move, as their social status has risen: they have gone from being simple peasants with little education to business owners who also work for the pueblo. Doña Selena volunteers in a charity organization for the poorest residents of Ticuani, and Don Emiliano is heavily involved in planning the yearly Feast. They own a large house overlooking the zocalo and can afford household help. Their return has been a triumph for them, a strong form of social "exit and return with voice."

Don Gerardo, who has chosen to remain in New York, asks why he would want to return to Mexico. He earned more than sixty-five thousand dollars in 1997, owned a house, and had time and money to spend on sports and politics. He has organized a privileged male world for himself. By most outward measures, he has made it as a man and as an immigrant in the United States. He has realized most of the elements of the American dream as it is commonly understood, and he is seen in the community as a successful man.

Contrary to the images of the "crisis of masculinity" and "liberating femininity," both Don Gerardo and Don Emiliano have lived a competent, and uncompromised, masculinity. As migrants, they helped create institutions (the Committee, sports leagues) that helped the pueblo in Mexico and gave them real power in Ticuani and in New York. Moreover, both were able to make good money, provide for their families, and pay for college for their children who wanted to go. Unlike the immigrants depicted in the work of Roger Rouse and Pierrette Hondagneu-Sotelo, they are not undocumented workers fearing to walk openly, and exercising only symbolic power by aggressively asserting patriarchal constraints over their wives and families. Rather, they are legal residents, and exercise power through the institutions they have created, through their economic and occupational success, and in their relations with Ticuani. However, for Don Gerardo this masculine competence is lived in rigid adherence to ranchero masculinity; for Don Emiliano it is achieved through an "evolution" and engagement with other kinds of masculinity. These different definitions of masculinity have yielded different meanings for absence and transnational life for these two families. They have also created different contexts for femininity for Doña Selena and Doña Talia.

Understood using Connell's notion of hegemonic masculinity, Don Gerardo's ranchero masculinity must compete with other, less (or differently) patriarchal visions of masculinity in the United States. His wife and children have not adopted the attitudes necessary to sustain ranchero masculinity in a strong form. Hence, although Don Gerardo lives his ranchero masculinity, he does so largely alone. In contrast, Don Emiliano lives a modified ranchero and modern migrant masculinity, and does so with the support of his wife and children.

Interestingly, the lives of Don Gerardo and his family seem to resonate more with the image of migrants' straddling a cultural gap or balancing on a tightrope than do those of Don Emiliano and his family. The responses of Don Emiliano, Doña Selena, and their children appear to be negotiated settlements to questions of how men and women, parents and children, should act. If they are straddling a gap, they are doing so more or less together, using a set of cultural tools whose choice they have negotiated jointly. Don Gerardo's strategy is clearly at odds with that of the rest of his family, and this division creates both less familial intimacy and a larger cultural gap. It is not, however, strictly a generation gap. Doña Talia sees the world through a lens more like her children's than her husband's. But, being married to Don Gerardo, she must navigate a difficult course between ranchero masculinity and other images of gender.

WOMEN'S PRACTICES OF SETTLEMENT AND TRANSNATIONAL LIFE

Ranchero masculinity and ranchera femininity also frame the experience of settlement and transnational life for first-generation women, but under very different conditions in the United States. Women see changes in relations with their men resulting from women working outside the home and the men doing "women's" work at home and in restaurant kitchens, as Don Emiliano did. These women feel that their men are less "macho" than men in Ticuani. One member of the prayer group commented:

> If we went there to Ticuani, the men would be very *machista*. . . .
> Here, no, because both [man and woman] work. . . . Women in Ticuani
> are very submissive, before they were, but now it's different, even in
> Ticuani . . . [things have changed in New York because] the men work
> in the kitchen in restaurants . . . it's more equal. Before, it hurt them
> to even enter the kitchen. . . . Now, many men have changed. They
> also take the kids to the doctor; my husband works nights, so he always did that . . . men in Mexico wouldn't help, but here, yes. (Spanish, translated by the author)

Such observations reflect the perception that in the United States it is increasingly necessary that both men and women work outside the home, which in turn requires men to work in the home and share in childcare.

In fact, economic and social changes in Mexico are also bringing about changes in relations between men and women there. Nevertheless, first-generation men and women both evaluate their present with respect to an experienced and an imagined rural *poblano* past rooted in ranchero mas-

culinity and ranchera femininity. While discussing changing male and female roles in New York and Ticuani, one woman referred to an old joke between husbands and wives. The wife would ask, upon her husband's return
at the end of the day, "Are you going to beat me first, or should we eat dinner first? Or should we eat first, and you beat me later?" All the women
present laughed, and they repeated the joke to make sure I understood. So
as not to offend them, I offered a small laugh. They told me several times
that this was not how it was today, or with them, but they had grown up
with this joke. Their laughter surprised me because they had just been talking about how much more equal relations between men and women were
today, even in Ticuani.   *reaction* ↓

When I repeated this joke to a group of second-generation youth in their
twenties, including daughters of some of the above women, their reaction
was silence, surprise, and rejection: This is a joke that they told you? It's not
funny. They could not believe that the older women thought it funny either.
The different generational reactions result from two factors. First, the older
women at the meeting all had friends or relatives who had been hit or had
themselves been hit. Making the violence into a joke and placing it in the
"old days" made it easier to deal with. Second, despite changes in gender
roles and ideologies, they still felt attachment to a more traditional view of
the world. They derive satisfaction both from their new status and economic
power in the United States as wage earners and modern women and from
their "traditional" roles as mothers and caregivers (which are also valued in
American society in strong and contradictory ways).[20] Rejecting the humor
in this joke would come too close to rejecting their own histories and the relations with men they know who have been abusive, but whose relationships
are still valued, or men who have changed their behavior.

The second generation, by contrast, has been raised to see such treatment
as unacceptable, even illegal. Indeed, some among the second-generation
group I spoke with had called the police to stop their fathers' abuse of their
mothers. The second generation sees the world differently. They must deal
with these dimensions of their own histories, which they understand as embodying ranchero masculinity and ranchera femininity, while trying to reclaim or embrace some aspects of being "Mexican" on their own terms. On
this issue there is clearly a large cultural gap between the first and second
generations.

Gendered Work in a Prayer Group in New York

This mix of gaining greater freedom but also still needing to engage with
ranchero masculinity and femininity is apparent in the most highly or-

ganized Ticuani women's group, the Prayer Group for Padre Jesús, which contributes to both settlement and transnationalization in ways different from the men's main organization, the Committee. Although it offers women authority, it is still set within a larger, male-run structure. It is common among migrant groups to have some kind of prayer group dedicated to the patron saint of their hometown.[21] The group meets monthly in the same Brooklyn basement as the Committee. Its devotional practices include buying flowers, saying the rosary, and offering special prayers. It began at the suggestion of Don Manuel, the head of the Committee, and the group's status as subordinate to the Committee is clear. When I talked with one of the group's members in 2000, I asked her its name. She first misunderstood and thought I was talking about the Committee, then said that her group had no name, and continued:

> DOÑA FLORENCIA: This is nothing more than that we pray at the end of each month . . . the señoras, we pray to Padre Jesús. Manuel [the Committee president] maintains the list of our countrymen that bring the flowers for Padre Jesús. . . . He is the one who calls them so they bring the flowers.
>
> RS: You [the women] don't call. He is the one who calls?
>
> DF: He calls them because he is the interested party [*el interesado*]. They are the ones from the Committee. . . . [It] is a prayer for Padre Jesús, who helps us and blesses us here where we are [New York]. Because you see how far we are from Him! But we don't forget about Him.

Interestingly, Doña Florencia first thinks that my question refers to the men's Committee, then does not refer to the Prayer Group by the name others use for it, and finally says that Don Manuel is the "interested party" who maintains the list of flower donors. The structure of the meetings reflects the Group's status as subordinate to the Committee. The women sit in front of a large picture of Padre Jesús surrounded by flowers. Informal talk yields to reciting the rosary and offering direct thanks to Padre Jesús or requests for special intercessions. The men, though present, do not usually pray in the meetings. They drink beer, talk, and make jokes or talk politics in the back of the room until the prayers begin, and then stand silently. After the prayers, they eat the meal the women have prepared.

The prayer group aids both settlement and transnationalization. First, it spans the first and second generations. Five or ten Brooklyn-born preteen religion important!

girls say they attend regularly for the camaraderie, to spend time with their mothers, and because they love Padre Jesús. (Indeed, devotion to Padre Jesús has emerged as a surprisingly strong dimension of many second-generation lives in New York.) Second, the basement containing the altar to Padre Jesús has become a semipublic Ticuanense site. "People come by here . . . anyone can use this space," group members tell me, explaining that people come to offer special prayers or organize their own prayer meetings. Third, although the prayer group was created at Don Manuel's behest to (in his words) give Padre Jesús a place in Brooklyn with his people, it also creates a space for female authority and power and gives its members public roles in a Ticuani-oriented institution in New York. Group members regularly serve as sponsors *(mayordomas)* for the Feast of Padre Jesús in January, helping to organize the flowers and the party after Mass. The group also offers a way for them to express their own devotion to Padre Jesús and their identity as Ticuanense women.

This mix of subordination, public honor, and women's authority in Ticuani public life, local and transnational, is illustrated by Doña Paz, the wife of Don Manuel. Doña Paz runs the prayer meetings, leads prayers, and is recognized in the community as someone with authority. When she learned that my researchers and I wanted to interview second-generation youths, she took me from table to table at the party for Padre Jesús, asking women if we could interview their teenaged children, and everyone quickly volunteered their telephone numbers. Yet when I asked Doña Paz for an interview, she responded, like other women, that it would depend on her husband. Her public role was clearly subordinate to her role as a wife, and she did not contest that subordination. Her silent perseverance in the face of the challenges his actions pressed on her was the very embodiment of the long-suffering ranchera; she never publicly expressed any "inappropriate sentiments," such as anger, disappointment, or impatience.

Doña Paz's faithful service to her sacrificing husband confers on her honor and moral virtue among Ticuanenses. For example, she and the other wives of the Committee members were strongly praised (in their absence) by their husbands in a speech by Don Manuel in Ticuani during the inauguration of the potable water system in 1993. He thanked all the wives of the Committee members

> for their patience they have with us. To abandon our children on Saturday, Sunday, instead of going out . . . with our wives, they sacrifice, getting up as if it were another work day to prepare us something to eat because they know that when we leave, we will go from nine in the morning going house to house, and we don't know what time we

will return. And I believe that it is not only my wife [but] the wives of [all] members of the Committee that merit this recognition.

Despite the fact that she was absent from this and most other events in Don Manuel's public life, honor accrues to Doña Paz by her husband's acknowledgment. Indeed, the stoic Committee president's voice cracked with emotion when speaking of his wife's sacrifice.

Such public praise reinforces Doña Paz's position as a leader in the group and community and resonates with her own understanding of a woman's role. She explained that the job of a woman and wife was to always, always be there for the husband, no matter what: always cook his food, make sure he has a well-ironed shirt when he goes out, and be sure that he knows you will be there, waiting, when he gets home. To wait, cook, and clean for your husband is also to serve Ticuani. For Doña Paz these sentiments were not simple statements in an interview; they were expressed in everyday conversation, and she lived her life by them. In doing so, she manifested, more strongly than most Ticuanense women, traditional *ranchera* virtues of shame and deference.

Even if only in a male-dominated context, the prayer group creates a space for women's authority and leadership in Ticuani public life. It creates a formal institution dedicated to a traditionally female domain, religion, in which women are in charge. The existence of the group testifies to the importance of this "women's" work and world in Ticuanense life, and in the process helps to maintain Ticuani traditions in the first and, to a lesser extent, second generations. Moreover, the group concretely expresses a permanent Ticuanense presence in New York and a desire to create institutions to preserve special dimensions of Ticuani culture.

The different attitudes of Doña Paz and Doña Florencia show contrasting forms of renegotiated femininity in public life. Doña Paz emphasizes her duty to stick by her man in all circumstances. In contrast, Doña Florencia is almost a pure *pionera*. For decades she has lived apart from her common-law husband and has raised her children alone. She owns a house in Ticuani and conducts herself, as some Ticuanenses observed, "like a man": she expresses her opinions openly and even contradicts men, and does not give their objections much currency. She drinks beer in public without trying to hide it. She is a woman who has reached a certain age (about sixty), has no man in her life to shame by her conduct, and hence can break conventions without great penalty. Yet in the prayer group, she adopts a position much closer to the deferential *ranchera* or Ticuani migrant woman, ceding authority to Don Manuel; the job of the women is just to pray to Padre Jesús. The world of the Committee is a public, male one linked in people's minds directly to the male-dominated space of electoral and other public politics in Ticuani, to which the prayer group can be seen as mainly an appendage.

Returning to Ticuani

First-generation men and women visit Ticuani for vacation and emotional replenishment.[22] They escape the pressures of life in New York and take a long drink of *ticuanensidad* (Ticuaniness) and *mexicanidad* (Mexicanness) at their source. Ticuanenses contrast the pace of life in New York with that in Mexico, saying: "New York is a place to work, but Ticuani is a place to live." In the small courtyard of his house in Ticuani, Tomás Maestro plays with his three-year-old son and tells me that although the work of the Committee and the political issues do matter, what really matters is time to sit in the sun, eat some good food, and play with his son. As he and I spend the afternoon trading stories about our three-year-old boys and kicking a ball around with his, I have to agree.

Returning to Ticuani places migrants and their children in a complex field of social interactions, which is intensified by unaccustomed propinquity. Gossip that runs through the Ticuanense community in a week by telephone or personal meetings in New York spreads almost instantaneously in Ticuani, as people see each other constantly. Returning for the Feast is like attending a two-week, nonstop party, engendering the sense that one is being observed and evaluated by others all the time. This sustained intensity causes returnees to experience a sense of what I call "accelerated social time," which makes relatively short stays in Ticuani feel like long periods. This phenomenon helps explain how and why Ticuani occupies such an important place in the social world of many in the second generation too.[23]

The migrants' ritual of returning to check on their houses in Ticuani embodies enduring links with the town and implies the ability to go home permanently or visit as one wishes. While most Ticuanenses and their children stay in these houses only for a few weeks or months every year or two, their visits stir up vivid memories of the Ticuani of their youth. Increasing numbers of the earliest migrants, first-generation men and women, are inheriting houses. Women migrants who have divorced or been abandoned are maintaining their houses in Ticuani and bringing their children and grandchildren back with them on extended visits. One woman migrant told me that maintaining her house in Ticuani was crucial because she never knew what would happen in the United States. Though she had applied for U.S. citizenship, having the house in Ticuani made her feel safe. If need be, she could return to live there off her Social Security benefits and a very small pension.

Women tend to stay longer in Ticuani than their male counterparts, one or two months to the men's one or two weeks. Many of these women have retired from a garment workers' union and receive a pension and Social Security benefits. Many now work as unpaid daycare providers for their own adult children in New York, often living in the same apartment or building. During the winter and summer, they take their grandchildren to Ticuani to enjoy the greater freedom and open space, offering them both a different quality of life and a chance for the third generation to learn Ticuani religious and civic traditions.

As in New York, men and women visiting Ticuani have different spheres of activity.[24] Men organize public rituals, while women participate in religious observances; they often rise for the 5 A.M. Mass, *las Mañanitas*, celebrated every day of the Feast. At public events women cook and serve the food while men do the organizational work, serve the beer and soda, and break down the tables afterward. This division of labor persists among the second generation. However, the border between the public male and private female worlds is porous. Although returning men do tend to drink and hang out in the street at night, there is a great deal of family time in Ticuani. By my estimate, many such men spend at least half their time with their families doing nothing in particular or enjoying Ticuani's traditions (cockfights, rodeos, and so on), even while attending to public Ticuanense business. Similarly, women do most of the childcare in Ticuani, but men share in it. And this responsibility is diluted by the omnipresent extended family and the greater security parents feel for their children in Ticuani.

Finally, Ticuani allows a relaxation of family bargains over issues such as drinking. Tomás Maestro at first resisted but ultimately accepted the deal his family negotiated with him in New York. He can drink heavily on the weekends if he is in their house with his friends; if he is out, he must be more careful. He cannot drink on weekdays. But in Ticuani, where every day is like a weekend, he can get drunk with his friends every night if he wants to. Yet he does not; rather, he chooses to stay home some nights with his wife and children.

CONCLUSION

These histories of first-generation Ticuanenses offer several insights into the negotiation of gender bargains and ideologies in transnational life.

First, such bargains and ideologies are always context-dependent. The image of the crisis of masculinity, of disempowered men imposing hard gender bargains on their women and yearning to return to Mexico, fails to explain the situation of many Ticuanenses. A good number of Ticuanense men have succeeded economically and created institutions linked with Ticuani premised not on return there but rather on permanent settlement in New York and continued engagement with Ticuani. Rather than lose power and their links with home, they demonstrate newly created power and sustained links to a hometown to which most have no intention of returning permanently.

Though Ticuanense men may have been raised on a macho, ranchero masculinity, they can change, both in New York and in Ticuani. Just as working Ticuanense women often renegotiate their gender bargains in the United States, men too can rethink their gender ideologies. This process is aided by raising U.S.-born children, especially girls, whose gender ideologies tend to be more egalitarian than macho. Yet it would be facile to posit a dichotomy by which Mexico is seen as macho and the United States as egalitarian. While gender relations tend to become more egalitarian in the United States, they are tending in the same direction in Mexico.[25] And U.S. culture offers its own models of male privilege and female subordination. Moreover, while migration accelerates the negotiation of gender bargains, there are parts of the old gender bargain that many Ticuanense men and women wish to preserve. For example, many Ticuanense women revel in their newfound earning power and the ability to express "inappropriate sentiments" such as anger, but they also value mothering and staying home with their kids as well as pleasing their husbands. Their reality is more complex than the images of a unitary Mexican or American culture. Thus femininity, too, is renegotiated to accommodate, reject, or relate in other ways to New York and to their men's renegotiation of masculinity.

Men tend to participate more in transnational public life than women do, while women tend to do more of the everyday settlement work in New York, especially things like enrolling children in school, and private transnational life, such as caregiving for the third generation. Settlement activities can increase women's power and autonomy in the United States,[26] while public, transnational activities tend to create institutions that reproduce or create arenas over which men have power, both in Ticuani and among Ticuanenses in New York.

6. "In Ticuani, He Goes Crazy"

The Second Generation Renegotiates Gender

The gender negotiations of the first generation must seem easy to their children. For the first generation, ranchero masculinity is still a dominant ideology, even if other gender practices coexist with it. But the second generation negotiates gender in three contexts: various hegemonic and non-hegemonic "Mexican" and "American" notions of masculinity and femininity, nagging generational questions of ethnic authenticity and nostalgia, and an immigrant narrative of upward mobility that they experience as an "immigrant bargain" with their parents. Hence, second-generation Mexican American boys must figure out how to become Mexican American men while trying to fit the hegemonic images of the macho ranchero, the white middle-class man, the striving immigrant, and other Mexican and American stereotypes, while also redeeming their parents' sacrifice in coming to the United States by succeeding in school and at work. Similarly, second-generation Mexican American girls must figure out how to become Mexican American women while engaging the images of the deferential ranchera, the autonomous and pioneering female migrant, and the second-generation New York career woman, and doing well in school, taking care of the men in their parents' home, and marrying good men and having careers and children. If this is exhausting to read, imagine living it![1]

Transnational life offers a clear view of second-generation Mexican American gender ideologies, bargains, and practices because it is a site in which they are challenged and renegotiated, and through which members of the second generation seek to authenticate or legitimize their Mexican-ness. I was able to observe at length the relationship of Julia and Toño, the son of Tomás Maestro, *novios* in their mid-twenties who grew up in New York and regularly returned together to Ticuani. (Although the word *novios* is translated as meaning simply a boyfriend-girlfriend couple, in

Spanish it implies that the couple will eventually get married, though it does not connote a formal engagement.) They visited friends and relatives, went to parties, and reconnected with Mexico, but they also used their return in other ways. While Toño attempted to reclaim the lost Mexican gender privilege that he felt his father had in Ticuani, Julia attempted to recover dimensions of Mexican culture and "authenticate" herself while retaining her autonomy. Their respective pursuits of their ethnic and gender projects sometimes put them in conflict, and this conflict reveals how each one thinks and lives gender. I have known Toño for more than ten years, and I met Julia when she and Toño first began dating seriously. My research team, especially Sara Guerrero-Rippberger and I, followed their return to Ticuani for three consecutive years, from 1999 to 2001. We spent time with them and their friends and families in New York and interviewed both of them several times, thus observing them both from their early courtship until their breakup more than four years later. I examine how their relationships with each other, their families, and others were affected by their return to Ticuani, thus tracing how gender is lived in, and structures, transnational life.

Ranchero masculinity still thrives in the imaginations and lives of young men like Toño, but it coexists and sometimes competes with the hegemonic masculinity of the white middle-class career man and with three other notions of masculinity—the hardworking immigrant, the American rapper, and the Mexican gangster, or *pandillero*—each of which can be dominant in a particular context. These masculinities are also refracted through ethnicity. Hence, many young men like Toño, who was born in Ticuani but moved to New York at age ten (technically making him of the 1.5 generation in my definition), feel they have been made to forfeit the privileges they would have enjoyed had they been born in or stayed in Mexico, where they imagine ranchero masculinity to reign unchallenged. Yet they also feel drawn to "white" middle-class masculinity, wherein a man acquires postsecondary education and a career—meaning a "clean job" in an office—and makes decisions jointly with his wife on the presumption of gender equality. Moreover, their second-generation girlfriends and wives largely reject ranchero masculinity and the family life based on it. Finally, American rapper and Mexican *pandillero* masculinity resonate a great deal with many youths. Both are what Robert Connell would call "marginalized" hypermasculinized stances arising from exclusion by society. Both prize aggressiveness, power, money, and the potential use of violence as means to dominate both men and women. But both also defend an ethnic masculinity these young men feel has been violated. They feel they are denied the chance to realize the American dream and middle-class masculinity, to be somebody, and instead are seen as being nobody. The image of the hardworking immigrant—the New York alternative and close cousin to the ranchero—who legitimizes his masculinity through his enduring capacity to work and sacrifice thus upholds their Mexicanness but is a less attractive option for these young men because it lacks the second-generation narrative of upward mobility. In Ticuani, however, enacting ranchero masculinity places Toño squarely in the center of Ticuani's hegemonic, though not exclusive or unchallenged, masculinity.

Second-generation women face similar complexities. While they are almost uniformly told not to be rancheras—women who defer to their husbands in all things and content themselves with child rearing and housework—they are still expected to do the lion's share of the domestic work, as daughters and as wives, and not to assert themselves in ways that create rancor at home. They are simultaneously expected, and expect themselves, to get a postsecondary education and pursue a career that will enable them to demand equality in their relations with their future husbands or to be independent from them in the event of a bad match.[2] The first image is that of the hegemonic second-generation Ticuanense woman, and the second that of the hegemonic New York woman. These sometimes incompatible images can be partly reconciled in the image of *la pionera* (the pioneer), a working immigrant woman autonomously making her way in a man's world, bucking the system when necessary. This nonhegemonic image offers a strong role model for these young women.

The impossibility of fully realizing all the dimensions of these different images of masculinity and femininity is not unique to Mexican or second-generation culture. Indeed, the psychologists Daniel Kindlon and Michael Thompson, in *Raising Cain: Protecting the Emotional Life of Boys* (1999), and Carol Gilligan, in *The Birth of Pleasure* (2002), note how dominant images of masculinity demand that white middle-class boys appear invulnerable and stoic, even during their most vulnerable developmental phases, when such a stance is unhealthy.[3] Similarly, Mary Pipher, in *Reviving Ophelia* (1995), writes that the demands of middle-class white femininity—that girls simultaneously be competent adults, make relationships work, and not offend anyone or complain—are impossible to always achieve.[4]

What makes second-generation migrants' gender practices different from imagined middle-class white ones is that they are negotiated as part of the "immigrant bargain" with parents.[5] "Bargain" describes the expectation that sacrifice by the parents will be redeemed and validated through the children's achievement. While such a bargain occurs in most families,

immigrant and nonimmigrant, the life-defining sacrifices of migration convert it into an urgent tale of moral worth or failure. Especially in cases
where the second-generation youth's success is uncertain, parents often
tell their children, effectively, "We sacrificed our homeland, struggled with
English, and lived in fear of the Migra [the immigration authorities] so you
would have a better life in New York. All we ask in return is that you succeed in school and at work." Second-generation success validates parental
sacrifice, but failure incurs a burden of shame: "You have it so easy, you are
a U.S. citizen and speak English, and you cannot even do well in school and
get a career." Parents and children both ask: "What was all this sacrifice for,
if the children end up doing the same work as the parents?" The children
understand the implication that their parents, who overcame long odds,
would have done better, and they judge themselves harshly.

This bargain elicits three main responses from the second generation,
which resonate strongly with the work of Marcelo and Carola Suarez-
Orozco: some try harder, some withdraw, and some reject this narrative and
come to feel that their parents' expectations fail to take account of their
children's difficulties and greatly exceed their ability to help the children
live up to them.[6]

The immigrant bargain orients my analysis somewhat differently from
research using the cultural gap or family tightrope as central metaphors.[7]
Rather than positing a balancing of old, traditional with new, modern cultures, my perspective recognizes that the cultures of the countries of origin
and destination are themselves both evolving and internally inconsistent.
Moreover, gender frames how one engages these cultures. Toño, as we will
see, embraces the old, traditional ranchero image of masculinity in an attempt to enjoy the privileges he believes it should offer him and that American middle-class masculinity and femininity deny him. He also uses dimensions of *pandillero* and rapper culture. He must balance his assertions
of such gender privilege with the need to uphold his part of the immigrant
bargain and prove himself as an upwardly mobile second-generation youth.

"TWO KINDS OF MEXICANS"

"Me and Toño are two kinds of Mexicans," says Julia in contrasting Toño's
macho, traditional ideas with her more equal vision of their relationship. Ticuani is charged terrain for the two of them when they visit because they both presume that Ticuani norms will approximate the macho
ranchero ideal. For example, Toño attempts to control his sisters' and girl-

friend's movements to such an extent, and is so prone to fighting, that Magda sums up his return by simply saying, "In Ticuani, he goes crazy." Returning to Ticuani enables Toño to make demands on Julia and his sisters in a context where he believes others will expect them to obey him, while they feel they must transgress local norms to demonstrate their autonomy. These gender negotiations take on added weight because return has become a key ritual in second-generation adolescence. In this context, examining Toño and Julia's relationship offers a strategic research site for gaining what one might call "relational leverage" into gender: because masculinity and femininity are defined relative to each other (or to other forms of themselves), closely examining an evolving relationship can give us insight into the broader process of negotiating gender.

Toño's macho stance toward his sisters (and Julia) is not the only option available. Indeed, my study team followed other older brother–younger sister pairs with very different gender dynamics. In one case, Teresa wanted to spend all her time in Ticuani with her boyfriend, who lives there and whom she had been seeing during vacations for two years, despite her parents' disapproval. One night, Teresa stayed out past her curfew. When she wandered away with her boyfriend from her group of friends, which included her brother, Leo, others in the zocalo began to comment. A friend of Leo's who lives in Ticuani urged him, "Yell at her about this, if you want to," implying that Leo had the right and responsibility to confront her for aberrant behavior. Leo refused, responding, "She can take care of herself." Leo's refusal to criticize his sister and his assertion of her competence and autonomy stand at odds with Toño's belief that controlling his sisters and girlfriend is his right and responsibility. The ranchero masculinity and moral framework inhering in the friend's invitation for Leo to criticize Teresa's behavior is the same one that Toño attempts to mobilize in his renegotiation of his gender bargain with Julia and also with his sisters.[8]

Julia and Toño met in a traditionally Mexican way, when he attended her *quinceñera*, or "sweet fifteen," party in Brooklyn, and he was stereotypically macho in pursuing her. He got into a fight at her party, apologizing profusely the next day and attempting to court her. She expressed scant interest at first, but eventually relented, and they became *novios*. Toño then broke it off because she seemed unenthusiastic. Several years later, they met on the subway, and their attraction became more mutual. Though Julia commented that "he's not my ideal of a perfect man . . . Toño's the opposite: skinny, no eyebrows or facial hair, and short,"[9] they were dating exclusively. Through 2002 they seemed likely to marry, which was what their families expected from a serious relationship.

Julia sees Toño as more traditionally Mexican and herself as more Americanized, a view consistent with their individual and family histories. When Toño came to the United States at age ten, he spoke no English. He was first placed in a special-education class (because of a lack of classes for Spanish speakers) but moved quickly into bilingual and then into all English-language classes. His family's gender dynamics were more traditional, Mexican, and macho than those of Julia's family. His parents, Tomás and Xochitl, eloped and married as teenagers, and Xochitl left school. Tomás, who was a teacher in Mexico, keenly felt his loss of status and power when he became a busboy in New York. He told me: "[In Mexico] I was accustomed to being in charge. [In New York] I felt inferior. And here they were in charge of me. . . . I felt bad, bad, totally inferior." Now that he has learned more English and been promoted at his job, he feels better.

Tomás Maestro asserts traditional "Mexican" male privilege in his relations with his wife and daughters: "In the house, the man is the law." He outlines the hierarchy in the household: "It is an authority not due to *machismo*, it is an authority idiosyncratic to Mexican culture: where there is a man and a woman, the man is the law. And after the man comes the wife, and after her the oldest son." For Tomás, as for Toño, this male authority is part of being Mexican; ethnicity, gender, and power are intertwined.

Interestingly, Tomás does not demand that his daughters enact this model in their own relationships with men. He says that he hopes they will follow his and Xochitl's example but that he suspects they will want more egalitarian relationships with their husbands. That will make sense, given that they have their own careers and think differently because of growing up in the United States.[10] This change can be interpreted simply as a result of migration to the United States. But older Mexican men, and especially women, also want more egalitarian relations for their young-adult children. Jennifer Hirsch and Gail Mummert see this change as part and parcel of the modernization of gender relations in Mexico, born of economic and other changes in society. While such changes are also fostered by the "modernizing" journey of migration to New York, there is a more overt conflict—between the requirements of the family's gender ideology and that of second-generation mobility—inherent in that migration. Tomás and his daughters see their upward mobility as trumping the ranchero gender model that would require deference from them. In fact, Tomás undercuts this gender ideology when he uses the accomplishments of Magda, Toño's younger sister, to pressure Toño to improve his lackluster performance at school. Moreover, Toño's jobs in college have not paid as well as Magda's or Julia's, though he did graduate in 2001 with a business degree and computer training. If Toño's role in the family were defined mainly by his lack of educational or job success in comparison with his sisters, then his privileged position as the eldest son would be eroded. Without his father's support in upholding this gender ideology, Toño risks losing it. Here the definition of the generation gap is contingent both on Toño's performance as an upwardly mobile second-generation male and on Tomás's willingness to privilege gender ideology over second-generation ideology.

Magda intuitively understands Toño's precarious position and attempts to push him to work harder and do better in school. In 2001, Toño was having a hard time finding a job, which for her has never been a problem.

> MAGDA: I can't tell my brother . . . You are doing good, we are happy for you . . . because I feel he needs a bit more. I don't . . . compliment him, 'cause I feel he needs to do more. I feel I am in competition with my brother, at least from his side.
>
> RS: Do you feel competitive with him too?
>
> M: Yeah, basically, but I am not even trying to do that, you know? I get job offerings like every day. . . . Do I look like I need a job? *(laughs)*

Her stronger position with regard to the immigrant bargain translates into greater privileges, such as being allowed to travel without family to Ticuani and, even against her parents' wishes, to another place in Mexico.

Toño, for his part, joins his father in chiding Magda for being lazy, for not cleaning the house, and especially for not learning to cook, something her family tells her that her husband will expect her to do. Their message to her, she says, is " 'cause I am a woman, [I] have to follow that role." The family sometimes discusses and laughs at Magda's ineptitude at cooking: by her own reporting, their mother has tried to teach both daughters, but both have failed to learn. But both also fail to see it as a necessary skill, telling their mother they will order food in if they come home from work late and do not feel like cooking. Magda's friends even call her a "feminist" because she does not know how to cook, and she sees herself "as more Americanist, since Mexicans do know how to cook, every girl knows how to cook except me." The family invokes ranchera femininity (which resonates with more traditional American culture as well), which casts cooking as women's work and a skill men require in a potential mate. The issue of Toño's learning to cook was not raised in this discussion.

Xochitl has alternatively worked in factories and stayed home to care for the children. While she usually stays silent when her husband asserts his authority, she asserts herself, within limits, in other ways. She was present when I was interviewing Tomás and occasionally participated. While she prepared food for Tomás and me, Tomás expounded on male authority. When he said, "Inside the house, the man is the law," Xochitl laughed out loud, covering her mouth with her hand, but kept preparing the food. And while she rarely challenges him openly when he asserts authority over their daughters, she secretly encourages them to resist him when they disagree.[11] Hence, while Xochitl conforms, in the main, to the model of a ranchera wife, she sometimes departs from it.

Several months later I interviewed Xochitl and her two daughters while Tomás and Toño were out of the house and asked her why she had not contradicted Tomás in front of me, when her laughter so clearly expressed her disagreement. She told me, "When I want to say something to him, I say it, that is, . . . when he is saying things he should not say, I do not say it to him in front of the people because I don't like to lack respect for him or for the people, because I don't like to . . . be arguing about foolishness, because I will tell him this is foolishness. . . . And I don't like to be fighting. . . . I don't like to yell." She also told me later that after I had left, she did challenge Tomás on his remarks. This knowledge makes her performance when I was there even more skilled: her laugh was a stage whisper, clearly registering her disapproval of Tomás's assertion of privilege, but she continued to cook, staying on the periphery of the conversation while her husband held forth at the table. Xochitl showed both her modern migrant woman's disagreement with her husband and an appropriate ranchera demeanor.

Tomás played the encounter with equal skill, passing over her laugh, which he surely heard, without remark. By not commenting on it, he also upheld their gender bargain. During our interview, in which I had hoped they would both participate, I asked Xochitl questions to draw her into the interview. She responded sometimes by saying that she thought "the same as him," nodding to Tomás, and sometimes expressing her own opinion. But no matter how hard I tried, the conversation never became truly three-way. The dynamic kept returning to that of a conversation between two males, Tomás and me, with myself mainly in the role of listener and questioner.

Julia's household was very different. Her mother assumed adult responsibilities after her own father died when she was young in Mexico, and she never adopted the role of subservient wife and mother with her husband, whom she ended up divorcing. Julia described her mother's influence to Sara Guerrero-Rippberger in 1999:

> I admire my mother a lot for that. . . . She's very independent, too, for
> a woman who . . . was born out there [Ticuani], . . . because some of

them from her age group seem more, I don't know, not so independent. . . . Not that they're dependent on a man, but they will do whatever the husband said; basically, they will follow the husband's rules.
And my mother, she never went for that. Like she did her part, her
thing, and my father did other things. And you know, she told him,
"Don't expect for you to come home and me have everything ready on
the table, 'cause I work, too, just like you do." And I see that other
Mexican mothers—they're like, "Oh, my God, my husband is coming,
I gotta get the food ready." And my mother was never like that. And I
think that's why I told myself that I would never be like that either. I
mean, I'm not saying that I would never give—I'll take care of my
house, and I'll cook dinner, if my husband is good, you know, he provides for me, you know, good, caring. I don't see why not. But I don't
expect him to tell me, "When I come back, it has to be ready." . . . If I
work like he does, he has no right to learn [expect] to have it ready.

Julia sees her mother as a model of an autonomous, pioneer migrant
woman who has pursued her dreams without letting the gender norms of
her youth force her into a life she did not want. Julia does not reject domestic life—she says she will cook "if my husband is good"—but wants
womanhood on her own terms, embracing things she values but not being
forced by a man to do so. Julia says she did not grow up "Mexican": she
spoke both languages at home, but her English is much better than her
Spanish; she cannot tolerate spicy Mexican food; her family does not always eat together; and she prefers American music like R&B to traditional
Mexican ranchero or *cumbia* music. She is embarrassed when Toño howls
along loudly in a traditional *grito* (shout) to Mexican ranchero music and
dislikes the convention in dancing *cumbia* that the girl always follows: "His
rhythm, his steps, and how he wants her to turn. . . . But it's always like
that, the girl has to follow the guy." And she even "had to learn how to act
around Toño's family, how to be polite and greet each one of them."[12] Despite rocky periods in her teens, she did well in school, and in her early
twenties she was seen by her family as successful, working at a well-paid
job as a medical secretary while attending college. Here the image of a cultural or generational gap could be transformed (just this once) into a military or football analogy: Julia's mother has created a gap in the gender line
by living as a *pionera*, and Julia has followed her through the breach.

In other ways, Julia and Toño had similar panethnic adolescences. Both
had Puerto Rican and Black friends in elementary and middle school. Their
friendship circles became more Mexican through adolescence and in early
adulthood, a process coinciding with their evolving relationship and returns
to Ticuani. Both also emerged from what they describe as "crazy" periods in

their mid-teens without major mishap. Toño had hung out with a panethnic crew (gang) that included Puerto Ricans and Blacks at school during the week and with an all-Mexican gang on the weekends. He left the gangs after being shot at and after an ultimatum by his father to leave the gang or leave the family. His father offered him a trip to Mexico if he made the right choice and did better in school. He improved his grades and went to Mexico for several weeks over winter break. Before he and Julia began dating, he fell in love with a girl in Ticuani and saw a different way to be Mexican as he hung out with the Ticuani youth, who were all studying to be professionals. It changed his life: "I started doing better in school, and realizing about a lot of things, you know, go to college, have a degree, you know," and he began to think that Mexicans in New York needed "more Mexican professionals." He also feels he became somebody in Ticuani: people there are glad when he returns. "Since then I like been going back once [per year] . . . like everybody in the town, the young people, the young crowd, knows me now. When I go, they're like, 'He's back.' " Even his sister Magda acknowledges that Toño is somebody bigger in Ticuani than in New York: "The fact that he knows a lot of people over there, I guess it makes him feel recognized . . . like, wow, someone really knows what I am doing."

Much as Toño asserted different identities through membership in Mexican, and Black, and Puerto Rican crews, he adopted both a traditional ranchero masculinity and the hypermasculinized image of rappers such as Puff Daddy (Sean Combs) and Biggie Smalls, who was shot and killed in 1997, shortly before our interview. He idolized Smalls, he told me, because of "the words he used to say in his songs, the way he used to be, he used to talk . . . he was like a major—womanizer, you know. He used to have all the women, all the money—everybody used to envy him. That's why I believe he got shot. . . . He was like a Selena, he was a like Selena for us, the guys." His idolization of these two rappers is in fact consistent with some aspects of a macho, Mexican ranchero culture. Both project images of violence, fearlessness, and power and enjoy the company of many women. In simultaneously thinking of himself as a Mexican macho, a Ticuani ranchero, and a thuglike rapper, Toño has adopted some of the most hypermasculinized images in Mexican and American culture. Interestingly, though he expressed admiration for the Mexican American actor James Edward Olmos, he did not discuss a Mexican male role model. Moreover, he identified Biggie Smalls as his role model as a "Selena for us, for the guys," referring to the female Mexican American pop singer.

For Julia, trips to Ticuani had less immediate and dramatic effects, but they did engage her with a set of Mexican practices, such as preparing food with her female relatives and participating in adolescent rituals such as the Grand Dance. These rituals heightened her sense of being Mexican, which was affirmed when others treated her as Mexican. When Julia expressed the feeling that she was not as Mexican as others, Meche, her friend from Ticuani, told her, "You are more Mexican than a cactus!" This increased involvement with a Mexican world in New York and Ticuani also coincided with renegotiating her place in her house in New York, getting her mother to acknowledge and appreciate how much housework she did for the family. Both Toño's and Julia's social worlds have become increasingly Mexican through their adolescence and courtship. Now in their mid-twenties, they hang out mainly with their cousins and other relatives and go to family parties, though Julia still has a fair number of non-Mexican friends. While Toño's life has always been more Mexican than Julia's, together they became more involved in Mexican activities, including trips to Ticuani.

Machismo and Female Autonomy and Labor in Ticuani

Toño and Julia participate in a transnational life that creates both harmony and conflict in their gender bargain. Julia attempts to renew her connection with Mexico in ways that respect her autonomy. She enjoys working with her grandmother in preparing religious feasts and attending *las Mañanitas*. She also permits Toño more authority over her than she allows in New York. Yet she also resists some gender practices, and this resistance sometimes places her in conflict with Toño, who uses Ticuani to live a certain image of ranchero masculinity. Toño embraces these more traditional gender roles because they enable him to be Mexican in a different way than he is in New York, including having a relationship with his girlfriend that is more like that between his parents. In 1997 he told me it was good that relations between men and women "are more equal than they used to be" and that even "girls back in Ticuani and Puebla want their rights and careers . . . they go to Puebla to study," but that now men could not control relationships as he thought they should. He referred approvingly to his parents' relationship, saying his father "keeps my mother in check. . . . I would love that . . . with my future wife." In Ticuani, Toño expects and asks Julia to do what he sees as traditional Mexican women's work, things he would not usually ask of her and she would not usually do. Julia and his sisters report he acts more macho in Ticuani than in New York.

In embracing this macho image, Toño presumes authority over his girlfriend and sisters in public and expects them to take care of him at home. He provokes conflict with other young men, drinks a lot, and spends time with older male migrants, including his father, of whom he speaks with great respect as his *jefe* (boss or leader), a slang term for father. Sara Guer-rero-Rippberger notes that Toño said being Ticuanense was about " 'wear-ing a cowboy hat, getting drunk every night—like a true Ticuanense. What Ticuanense doesn't like to drink?' . . . listening to Ranchera music and Ay-yah-yahhhhhing! at the dance."[13]

The changes in Toño's behavior are clear to anyone who knows him. He becomes involved in many more conflicts in Ticuani, and Julia says she "hates the ways guys act when they come here [Ticuani] to drink. . . . They act 'macho,' then act stupid, then end up fighting." His sister agreed but noted that their father's presence there partly counteracts these tendencies. She told me: "My father has totally [sic] control of him when he's around. When he's not, I don't know. . . . When will he grow up? Over here [in New York], he's calm. Like my father said, he can have all the fun in his life in Ticuani. . . . He's crazy over there." By enacting this ranchero masculinity, Toño is also authenticating his Mexicanness and expressing his essential *ticuanensidad*, thus co-constructing ethnicity and gender.

Toño's performance of masculinity is made more urgent by the immi-grant bargain, which is different for him and for his sister Magda. During 2000, Tomás and Xochitl refused to give Toño, who was in his mid-twenties and, like most of his peers, still living at home, permission to go to Ticuani alone. They told him that it would not be safe for him to go because his habit of hanging out on the street drinking put him at risk when there were *pandilleros* in Ticuani. Xochitl described their talk: "[We said] he cannot go alone, . . . so that we could keep a close eye on him so that nothing happens." In contrast, Magda went to a friend's wedding in Mexico alone, despite her father's forbidding it. She had "begged him" for a month, but he said that she could go only with another family member. "He said that just because I have my money, that doesn't mean that I can do whatever I want." Ac-cording to her sister, her father had insisted that "as long as she lives under his roof, she has to abide by his rules." But in the end, Magda simply pur-chased the tickets using money she earned. Although Xochitl had sup-ported Tomás's blocking of Toño's solo journey to Ticuani, she spoke to Tomás privately on Magda's behalf: "I told him that she is already grown, that she behaves well in the house, that she has a right to go on vacation." In the end Tomás had to relent.

Toño's heightened displays of masculinity also result from the nonstop party atmosphere in Ticuani during the Feast. There are parties or dances literally every night, but the same kind of dense social interaction that takes place in large Mexican parties in New York is intensified in Ticuani because everyone is there night after night, so that *broncas* (problems) and *chisme* (gossip) that might evolve over months in New York evolve over a few days. Hence, Ticuani offers Toño a stage on which to create an entire play, so to speak, about his masculinity during the week of the Feast. Conflicts that might lie dormant or die in New York because of lack of contact between the parties are more likely to escalate. In Ticuani, too, since everyone sees the initial conflict, those involved feel greater pressure to save face or seek revenge.

Gendered Roles and Expectations in Ticuani and New York

In New York, Julia's and Toño's lives are connected but largely autonomous. Both of them live with their parents, and they spend little time together because they both work and attend college. Thus, for example, they do not negotiate the division of household tasks. In Ticuani, the scope of potentially gendered labor involving Julia and Toño together expands significantly. Julia, like other returning young women, helps older women relatives by doing housework, such as preparing meals and a special "hangover soup" called *guashmole* for Toño and other male returnees who often eat at her house. The social fields in which they move also differ in Ticuani. In New York, they attend family or Mexican parties, in a more "Mexican" style of courtship, but the two also spend time alone in a more "American," companionate dating style. In Ticuani, they spend a much lower portion of their free time alone together; instead they spend time with the "American" clique of second-generation returnees or the "Mexican" clique of first-generation migrants and Ticuani residents. This separation in their socialization supports Toño's ranchero gender ideology, giving him lots of time to spend hanging out and drinking with his male friends.

On a typical day in Ticuani, Julia gets up early, helps her grandmother or aunt, and spends time with her girlfriends and sister and sometimes with Toño relaxing, going shopping in Puebla, or visiting a local pool. In the evening, she might spend some time with Toño in the zocalo, hang out with her friends there or at a party until midnight or a little later, and then go home. Toño's day begins and ends later. He gets up at noon or later and might go the zocalo and to Feast events, such as the rodeo, and then spend time with Julia. When leaving to hang out with the men, he might shake a finger and admonish Julia to be good and not to get into trouble.[14] Toño hangs out more than other 1.5- or second-generation youth with young men living in Ticuani. For example, he goes away overnight to run the Antorcha and hang out with the older Ticuani men organizing the event. He is also more warmly greeted by older men from Ticuani than are most other young returnees, and might drink with some of them all night, coming home early in the morning. In one case, he stayed at the local bar, which only admits men, until well past dawn, when his aunt dragged him home. He regularly gets into confrontations, including fistfights, spurring constant fear among Julia and his family that he could be hurt or killed.

In New York, Julia and Toño live a fairly "American" life. Although she dislikes the traditional role Toño attempts to force her into, she does not reject entirely the compromises required by her relationship with what she calls a "real Mexican." This stance is clear in response to Sara Guerrero-Rippberger's question "How would Toño characterize you?"

> Oh, he always tells me, "Oh, you should just be [her brother], and he should be Julia." . . . He says that I try to be like the man. I said, "What do you mean, like the man?" He said, "You used to go to karate school, you thinks you could do it all, you have such an attitude, you're such a hard-head, and you're too independent, and I hate it!" That's exactly what he tell me. . . . Well, . . . I'll tell him: "How about this? That's exactly what I'm gonna do, and if you don't like it, too bad—that's what I'm doing. I'm just letting you know." He hates that [chuckles]. . . . I don't act a certain way when I'm around him. I mean, yeah, you do have to act a certain way around family, you know, but at the same time it doesn't mean that I'm gonna change completely, like, "Oh, okay, I'll do whatever you want."

Julia is struggling to maintain her independence in a relationship with a man who expects deference. Her New York woman struggles to accommodate his Ticuani ranchero. She resists his attempts to control her directly but compromises and "acts a certain way" around his family. Indeed, Toño attempts to use this family context to try to make Julia behave as he thinks women should, to make her display an appropriate sense of ranchera shame. But she keeps refusing him, not only by not responding but by openly rejecting his demands. For example, when with his family, he wants her not to drink, and to openly show her devotion to him, behavior she sees as reflecting his notion of a traditional Mexican woman:

> When I'm with him, and he's, say, with a bunch of family, he has to tell me, "Uh, come and walk next to me and hold my hand." And I'm like, "If I don't want to, I don't have to hold your hand." And he's like, "Yes, you do, because you're *my* woman." So I feel like, What am I, property to you? No, if I want to hold your hand, I'll hold your hand. . . . Sometimes we get in a lot of disagreements because of that. . . . Oh, like once I got really upset because he told me, it was a birthday party and . . . I was having a couple of drinks, and he said, "Oh, don't drink that much, or don't hold that bottle, it doesn't look right on a woman." So I really got upset, and I said, "No, if I want to

drink, there's nothing wrong with that, I'll drink. And I don't care who sees me, and what people think about me." And he said, "Oh, there you go again." . . . So we get into problems because of that sometimes. And I feel that sometimes I can't see myself in a future with him, 'cause he's so old-fashioned in a way. And . . . he talks marriage, which I don't. And I said that, well, if you want that, you have a long way to go, and if you do, I tell him that everything's gonna be fifty-fifty—meaning the bills, cleaning, changing diapers, whatever it takes. I said just because, you know . . . your mother was . . . how you see your family, but I will never, . . . never live like that. And at first it was hard for him to accept it, but then he finally said okay. 'Cause nothing was changing my mind. And so I guess in that sense he is . . . like a Mexican—not just Mexican, but I think Hispanic men in general. It's like a macho thing—Oh, my woman has to do this and do that for me. . . . They say it nicely, but I tell him, "No, you know, if you want it that bad, you get up, and you have hands, so go and serve yourself your own soda."[15]

Yet despite these conflicts and Julia's protestations that she does not see a future with him, three years later, in 2002, she seemed even more committed to working through the imperfections in their relationship.

In Ticuani these differences manifest themselves in conflict as well as in assertions of gender privilege by Toño that Julia does not contest. She not only does his laundry and meals but also arranges her other responsibilities so that she can do so. Sara Guerrero-Rippberger described one scene this way:

On the morning of the 25th [the Feast day], [Julia's sister] and I went early, at 6:00 A.M., to [her aunt's] house to help prepare the food. Julia met us later, because she had to wait to make the boys' breakfast [Toño and his cousin]. The night before, Julia told me Toño had told her, "Don't go to help out your Tia before you serve us breakfast." Julia agreed, as if she took relish in the idea. . . . It turned out that the boys didn't want to eat that early, so Julia met us at her aunt's house soon after we got there. Later, while Julia was scrubbing her brother's and Toño's dirty socks, they woke up, and Toño called to Julia, "Serve us to eat, babe." "Oh," she said, and quickly got up to prepare their lunch.[16]

Hence, in Ticuani Julia often accedes to Toño's demands that she adopt the traditional woman's role that she otherwise rejects. Once she even went to his house to wash his clothes because "he doesn't have anyone else to do it for him." In doing such work, and in thinking about it this way, Julia moves closer to embracing, for that time, a deference to male authority and what Toño would see as an appropriate sense of shame.

Toño sees his role in Ticuani as increasing not his gender privilege but his male responsibilities. For example, when two male friends failed to meet him to help escort Julia, her sister, and Sara Guerrero-Rippberger to Puebla from the Mexico City airport late at night, he felt a special responsibility and burden. He said, "I don't like this. I'm the only guy—with three girls. I don't like to travel like this, with all girls. Now I'm responsible." When Julia rolled her eyes and asked what the problem was, he said, "Oh, yeah, right, you're gonna protect us. I'm responsible." Toño not only feels responsible but also resents the fact that the women for whom he feels responsible do not respect his authority. His worry was not wholly misplaced. As it turned out, the other young men who were supposed to have met them had been robbed at gunpoint within half an hour of arriving in Mexico City. While Toño's perception of threat was valid, his gender logic does not hold: the other car had three men in it, but they were still robbed. (Of course, he may have worried about the risk of rape or abduction, which would be less likely if the group included only men.) At any rate, Toño clearly felt he alone was responsible for keeping the three "girls" safe, and if anything had happened to them, he would have been seen as having failed to protect them.

Even in her more deferential role in Ticuani, Julia does not acquiesce in all Toño's attempts to assert masculine privilege. She reacted angrily to the many fights he got into while drinking. One morning, when she came to his house to clean, he sought sympathy, saying his lip hurt from getting punched the night before. She chided him for drinking and fighting, telling him "that if he came to have a good time, then have a good time and relax, but if he came here to do stupid things like get drunk, get macho, and start fights, then he should leave or 'take it like a man'"[17] and not complain. In 2000, on one of their last nights in Ticuani, Toño and Julia went to the *gallos* (cockfights). Julia spent the time with returning second-generation youths, including her sister, other friends, and Sara Guerrero-Rippberger. Toño hung out most of the night with Ticuani-born men but periodically went to see how she was. I moved among the various groups. During the last few cockfights, Toño told me he had been betting on every fight and had lost more than US$150. My field notes record the following exchange: "Running out of money to bet on the *gallos*, Toño turned to Julia and said, 'You got my back, right?' to which she responded, 'What?!' impatiently. They spoke more, and Julia ended the conversation by saying loudly to him, 'Don't ask me for money for *los gallos*. If you lose your money and don't have any more, that's your problem!' He turned away sullenly from her without saying anything and went back to the hangout with the guys he was drinking with."

Julia thus limited the extent to which she would cooperate in Toño's attempts to live out an entitled, ranchero masculinity. She refused to play the woman who supports her man no matter what. First she tells him that as a macho, he must not complain about his lip; if he cannot take a punch, he should avoid fights or go back to New York. She deftly limits his demand for sympathy from an unconditionally supporting girlfriend or wife by invoking the image of a real macho, who would not complain about his lip. She also refuses to lend him money to bet more on the *gallos,* again invoking the image of a macho ranchero who would not need to ask his woman for money because he would win, or have more money to bet. She was not interested in helping him live the image of the hard-drinking, hard-betting macho; she herself works hard and spends prudently. In both cases, she successfully set limits on his demands.

MASCULINE DISPLAYS

Toño's gender ideology led him to explosive confrontations with both men and women, especially about control over and responsibility for the women in his life. These issues invoked powerful emotions of jealousy, empowerment, and tests of a man's true *mexicanidad* or *ticuanensidad.* One incident in January 2000 is notable for the way a trivial incident yielded dramatic jealousy. Toño spends a lot of time in Ticuani talking to girls whom he introduces as his "cousins," thus dismissing the possibility of romantic entanglement. Julia asked her friends if they thought Toño was having an affair; though many thought she had grounds to be angry, she did not publicly confront him. Toño, however, reacted with fury to a similar suggestion about Julia. She had gone with her sister and some girlfriends to Puebla to buy some souvenirs. While she was away, the brother of one of the young women, a mutual friend, teased Toño that Julia had gone to Puebla with three guys whom she was supposed to have met the night before while Toño was off "with his boys." On their return, Toño immediately and angrily confronted Julia, screaming, "Where were you? Who were you with? I know what you were doing!" The resolution was described by Sara Guerrero-Rippberger:

> Julia calmed Toño down, and they talked it out in the other room. I was surprised that the end result was not that Julia got mad at Toño for being so stupid, but that she calmed him down and then stayed with him to hang out for the rest of the evening (or at least the beginning, until he went to hang out with the guys), almost to prove to him that she really wanted to be with him. When Julia and Toño came out of the room from talking, [Julia's sister] and I asked her if she

wanted to join us in the Centro while we waited for Toño to get ready. Julia said, "Nah," and then Toño, smiling, said proudly, "She's staying right here with me while I get ready."

By placating Toño in such a situation, Julia seems to conform to the traditional, ranchera role of supporting her man at all times and disallowing anger—that most "inappropriate sentiment"—at being unjustly accused. Toño's jealously possessive behavior without real cause fits a ranchero masculinity.

Other performances of masculinity involve controlling women's access to public space and their relations with "inappropriate" men, which also implicate Toño's relations with these men and imbue these encounters with even more masculine charge. One such encounter happened early in the morning of January 26, 2000, as revelers left the Grand Dance. This is a rarified time because the revelers move from an area of heavy police and adult presence outside the dance down the road to the zocalo, where there is less adult supervision. Add alcohol, and the mix becomes volatile. When Toño saw his sister Magda getting a ride with a *pandillero,* he became angry. She told him to back off and later described the scene to me in this way: "He screamed, '¡Pendeja! [Asshole!] Go home!' . . . But [the *cholo,* or gang member] thought it was at him, so they got into a pushing match. . . . I told him [the *cholo*], 'You misunderstood,' so he went back [to his car]. . . . The next day the guy apologized to me and my brother. . . . Neither one of them remembered what happened, because they were drunk." The brewing fight was quickly broken up by older men, who told Toño, "Don't be an asshole. Those guys carry guns," as they pulled him away. Both men were still angry as they separated but allowed the older, adult men to calm them down, preventing the dispute from escalating.

In another example, Toño wanted his sisters to go straight home after the last night of the *gallos,* at dawn, because he did not think they should be out that late. They ignored him until he finally yelled repeatedly and loudly at them in the zocalo: "Go home!" to which his younger sister, Marisol, responded, "Shut up, shut up, shut up!" This infuriated him, and he yelled a threat to his other sister, Magda, who yelled back so that everyone in the zocalo could hear, "Oh, really? Then why don't you come over here and hit me?" He responded sullenly and yanked Julia roughly by the arm, saying, "Julia, let's go home." Julia glared at him but went, while his sisters stayed with their friends. When he got to Julia's house, he knocked loudly on the windows of her grandmother's house, alarming her so much that she forbade Julia to leave the house again. Toño's father Tomás Maestro watched all these events from a distance, following his son and Julia back to her house, then following Toño, again at a distance, back to the zocalo.[18]

This incident was witnessed by four members of my research team and followed up closely by Sara Guerrero-Rippberger and me. Each actor interpreted the events differently in the service of different gender ideologies and projects. Toño saw his demand that Magda leave the car as his attempt to keep her safe, thus fulfilling his masculine ranchero responsibility and also protecting the family's honor. He told her getting a ride with the *pandillero* did not look good. Yet Magda felt no danger, as she had known these young men since childhood and had been hanging out having fun independently all week.

Magda's view was almost the opposite. She told me and Sara separately that she had purposely stayed in the zocalo after Toño's confrontations in order to watch out for him. She described her position to me this way: "I would never leave until my brother went to sleep. The whole house [family] would monitor him. . . . My dad didn't go to the dance on the twenty-fifth because of a swollen leg. I woke him up" to bring him to the zocalo. She said, and Xochitl confirms, that in New York her father calls from his job to check up on Toño, asking both Toño and his sisters how he is behaving. Tomás told me, "I got up at five in the morning to keep an eye on my son" in Ticuani, saying that he wanted to let Toño have his freedom and his fun in Ticuani but not endanger himself. Hence even as Toño saw himself as taking up his male responsibilities by protecting his sisters and his girlfriend, he was the object of a family collusion to safeguard him from the dangers of his own ranchero masculinity. In Magda's words, his entire family is "on alert" to protect him from himself.

This group protection of macho young men was noted among others we observed both within families and within friendship groups of youths. Fascinatingly, there are simultaneous gender dynamics: while Toño asserts male power by claiming the authority to send his sisters home, they not only refuse him but are collaborating with his parents in an exercise by the whole family to keep him safe from his masculinity. Toño's family and girlfriend both indulge his desire to assert masculine power but treat him as a child by secretly protecting him from himself. To my knowledge, family members did not tell him about these efforts, even though his parents had told him that they would not let him go to Ticuani alone.

Julia's interpretation of these events shows the compromises in her gender bargain in Ticuani. She was angry at Toño for treating her badly in front of her friends (including members of our research team, especially Sara). She told Sara she went home with Toño not because she felt she should obey him but because of Toño's father: she "felt ashamed that he would think bad things of her if she didn't stop drinking and leave the party when Toño told her to," a shame that intensified because Tomás "wouldn't even look at her" but followed them the whole way home at a distance. Toño's skillful amplification of the perceived risks to Julia's person and honor combined with Tomás's silence to make her feel such shame that she was unable to defy Toño. My later conversations with Tomás indicate that he was trying not to meddle but still to keep his son out of trouble, as I watched him do again in 2001. He saw himself as exercising vigilance from a distance. He would have intervened if the situation had escalated physically, with Julia or with others, but, short of that, he saw the episode as an issue between the couple. When a member of the research team asked Julia the next day if she had felt safe allowing Toño to walk her home under these circumstances, she laughed off the question.

After dropping Julia at home, Toño returned to the zocalo, walking past his father and pointing his finger at him, saying, "Go home!" quickly and directly, an unusual challenge. Tomás let the slight go, but continued to be vigilant as Toño rejoined his male friends, eating tacos, drinking beer, and joking around in the zocalo past sunrise. Interestingly, Toño was attempting to enforce a code of conduct for his sisters that was stricter and more traditional than the one their father enforced. Tomás Maestro's passiveness in the matter seems to suggest he found nothing wrong with his daughters' being there so early in the morning but did not entirely disagree with his son's attempts to control them, either. Hence, Tomás also seems to vacillate between different gender ideologies and practices. With his wife, he practices a stronger form of ranchero masculinity than he does with his daughters, whose relationship is negotiated within a second-generation narrative of upward mobility. With his son, he supports a shared ranchero masculinity while exhorting Toño to take the narrative of mobility more seriously.

The interpretation of these events by Julia's Ticuani friends offers insight into local gender ideologies and the difficult situation they create for Julia. Meche expressed anger that Toño had treated Julia this way and shock that she had allowed him to do so. She added, "And he doesn't even let her go out with her friends!? This is not the way to treat your girlfriend, because she is not your wife." Her sister echoed, "This is not the way to treat your girlfriend, she's not your wife!" and then added, "You shouldn't treat your wife this way either, but it's different." This clearly implies that Toño overstepped the limit. They also expected that as an independent New Yorker, educated, and working at a professional job, Julia should have been able to negotiate a more egalitarian relationship with her boyfriend. And although people apparently expected her to become Toño's obedient wife, they would be disappointed in her if she did, because they also expected her to become an independent, autonomous, New York woman—what Sara Guerrero-Rippberger insightfully calls a "New Ticuanense."[19] Julia is in a catch-22: she is too independent for a ranchera but not independent enough for a New York woman.

For Toño, these conflicts were ideal opportunities to display ranchero masculinity. First, he defended "his" women's honor by attempting to get them to "go home . . . for their own good," thereby discharging his responsibility as an older brother. In his view, an authoritarian and possessive tone toward his women is justified by their resistance to the authority he possesses by virtue of his responsibility to take care of them. Second, he not only asserts authority over women but does so by getting into a violent, if aborted, conflict with someone dangerous, a *pandillero*. He later further asserted his masculinity by fighting with a *pandillero* who had asked for Julia's telephone number. He thus showed that, though small in size, he had "heart"—the courage to fight anyone who disrespected him, his girlfriend, or his sisters. His courage—and Julia's anger at his recklessness—appeared even greater afterward, when members of the gang spray-painted their gang symbol on Julia's grandmother's house. Moreover, Toño fought while drinking a lot of alcohol, "like a real Ticuanense," whose behavior can run to excess during the Feast, just as Ticuani "blood" is seen by older men to run hot in politics. Toño was thus not only displaying behavior appropriate to a man and older brother but also affirming his authenticity as a Ticuanense and a Mexican.

Gender Performance and Other Young Men

Toño also negotiated his gender role through a set of conflicts over who "lowers their eyes" to whom—or, as Jack Katz frames it, which men command respect and generate fear and dread in others.[20] During the Feast in 2001, Toño became involved in a conflict between his group of cousins, the Zavalas, and another group, the Buendias. He involved himself in some fights and was also present at a tense set of negotiations between the leaders of the two groups on the last night of the Feast. The negotiations were held inside the tent housing the cockfights and ended in the early hours of the morning. Emerging onto the street after the danger of conflict had passed, Toño told me without irony that "I'm just a thug . . . living a thug life," with his hands splayed out in rapper fashion, with the inner and outer fingers of his hands pointing out at different angles. I immediately thought of his interview in 1997, when he told me of his admiration of the rappers

Puffy Combs and Biggie Smalls. Involvement in these confrontations and negotiations gave Toño a sense of being strong and dangerous, a man to be reckoned with—someone ignored at one's peril. While significant differences exist between ranchero masculinity and rapper masculinity—for example, the latter emphasizes money much more—they are similar in imagining power over women, fearlessness in response to challenges from other men, and willingness to use violence to defend one's honor if someone else "lacks respect."

These encounters also clearly illustrate the accelerated and intensified nature of such confrontations set in Ticuani transnational life. The Buendia and the Zavala youths were almost all born or raised in New York and had developed rules of engagement for their adolescent conflicts based both in New York and in the kinship networks that their migrant parents had brought with them. They also resonate with the ranchero political violence illustrated in earlier chapters of this book. Being back in Ticuani for two weeks speeds up the evolutionary cycle of conflicts, as events develop by the hour and involve others. I return to this incident and related dynamics in later chapters.

CONCLUSION

The second generation renegotiates their gender bargains and strategies in different physical and relational contexts in New York and Ticuani. Julia embraces Mexican rituals on her own terms, but must do so through negotiation with a boyfriend who wants to be more traditionally "Mexican" and who pressures her to act more deferentially in Ticuani. His pressures resonate with a powerful gendered memory in Ticuani of a macho, ranchero past lost to migration. In his negotiations with Julia, Toño also invokes images of the rapper who fears no one and who gets all the girls—a player. Ticuani offers a kind of secular sacred space for renegotiating gender bargains and ideologies.[21] It creates "accelerated social time" by bringing into close, extended, intensive social contact people whose social interactions usually occur over longer periods in dispersed locales. The intensity and stakes of these interactions are fueled by the urgency of asserting adolescent identity and the reauthenticating function that Ticuani has assumed in the lives of many young returnees.

Ticuani is a key site for practicing and developing gender strategy, one in which young men can exhibit a hypervigorous, macho ranchero masculinity. They can enjoy the traditional customs like the rodeo or *gallos* and drink or get into confrontations with other men. Returning *pandilleros* have heightened both the danger and the appeal of such conflicts. Young men like Toño see the *pandilleros* as posing a danger to women's honor and offering a chance to demonstrate their own honor and heart by refusing to shrink from conflict with them.

Ticuani's gender reality approximates the images of masculinity that some, like Toño, believe their fathers enjoy and that offers them relief from the need to compete with more economically or educationally successful siblings or peers. Ironically, Toño, as a college graduate, is educationally way ahead of most of his male peers. But his sisters have done better at living out the immigrant narrative of upward mobility. Toño uses the setting of Ticuani to prove his masculinity and renegotiate his gender bargain with Julia. He simultaneously invokes the images of the Mexican macho and the fearless rapper: he can imagine himself a cousin to both the revolutionary Emiliano Zapata and to Puffy Combs and Biggie Smalls, who fear no man and get "all the women" and "all the money."

Julia's return to Ticuani causes conflict with her New York gender strategy. Although in New York her gender ideology is not unproblematic, conflicts there are not irreconcilable. In Ticuani, her conduct is always making someone unhappy. In this setting Toño sees her as too independent for a Mexican woman, but her friends from Ticuani see her as too accommodating for a New York woman. When she is with Toño's family, she feels pressure to become a more submissive (that is, "Mexican") woman, to attend to Toño's needs and hide her inappropriate sentiments. Her taking care of Toño, which she does because she loves him, becomes blurred with the pressure of the conflicting expectations of her peers and her family and by Toño's leverage of such expectations. She thus goes along with his demands—for example, going home when Toño aggressively insists—that directly contradict her imagined future as an independent, New York woman and inheritor of her mother's very "un-Mexican" autonomy.

Julia negotiated Toño's demands more easily in one-on-one situations not involving his family. One example is her rejection of his request for more money to bet on the cockfights. But she gave in to his demands and tolerated his irrational accusations of jealousy. She also clearly felt pressured to submit to him in the presence of his family, especially his father, whose silence she interpreted as an endorsement of the same ranchero masculinity. Yet Toño's family was not a united front imposing such a gender bargain on her. She had bonded quite closely with his two sisters and his mother, who supported each other's independence and rejected Toño's harsher gender ideology. When Julia and Toño eventually broke up, the three women in his family all felt they had lost one of their number. My speculation is that in addition to feeling pressured by Toño's father, Julia was attempting to find ways to make the relationship work by accommodating Toño when she did not want to. The loving relations she had with his family made her try harder, but she came to resent and react against these compromises.

Transnational life is structured in part by these renegotiations of gender bargains, drawing on various Mexican and American gender idioms. Julia and Toño's renegotiation of their gender bargains is interesting and complex because they both use Ticuani to authenticate their Mexicanness but must also engage the gender notions they have learned in New York. Moreover, in the early-morning confrontations in the zocalo, Toño pursues a more macho masculinity with his sisters in Ticuani than his father does precisely because Ticuani is so important for demonstrating his masculinity. His rage when his sisters and girlfriend defy him reflects his fear that his male authority is not respected. He exploits the Ticuani context to enforce his gender bargain on Julia and send her home in silent, shamed, protesting compliance to a gender norm she resents and rejects.

Transnational life is also structured by the interaction between the second-generation narrative of upward mobility and the various competing gender ideologies. Hence, Tomás Maestro asserts tighter control over his son in New York, giving him more freedom to "have his fun" in Mexico, but also implies that his son's lack of effort toward educational and professional success imperils the male authority to which his status as the oldest son entitles him.

Finally, the modeling and renegotiation of gender roles by Julia and Toño and their parents both resonate and clash with the images of the migrant family walking a tightrope or "straddling the gap."[22] Xochitl and Tomás live as a fairly traditional Mexican couple, and she continues to defer to his authority even in New York. She does not work outside the home and use that economic power to renegotiate power relations with her husband, the situation literature posits as the impetus to renegotiation. But neither is she always subservient; indeed, she openly laughs at him, though without an overt challenge.

These metaphors are of no help in interpreting Julia's mother's gender mentorship, though they shed some light on Julia's experience. Julia's mother is not attempting to straddle traditional and modern ways; she has struck out on her own. But Julia attempts to embrace aspects of her "Mexican" culture in Ticuani while trying to preserve her autonomy. Similarly, Toño is not railing against the strictures of Mexican culture in favor of a freer American culture. Rather, he seeks to use dimensions of Mexican ranchero culture to alter the more Americanized gender bargain that Julia has struck with him.

7. "Padre Jesús, Protect Me"

Adolescence, Religion, and Social Location

"In New York, you don't fit in because you're Mexican. In Ticuani, you don't belong because you're not Mexican enough." This remark by Willie, a twenty-two-year-old college student who works in the finance industry, captures some of the complexity facing second- and 1.5-generation Ticuanenses returning to Ticuani. While many in the second generation dream of returning to Ticuani, they are not always welcomed as *hijos y hijas ausentes* (absent sons and daughters) as their parents are. While most Ticuanenses receive them with open arms, a few see them as "tourists"; *presumidos* (arrogant or conceited ones); *pochos*, who do not belong fully in either place; "New Yorkers"; or, most pejoratively, "New Yorguenses," a Spanglish term amalgamating "Ticuanenses" and "New Yorkers" that implicitly disputes their claim to *ticuanensidad*. These ambiguities create curious tensions in second-generation experiences of Ticuani and transnational life. Having been told all their lives that they are Mexicans and Ticuanenses, and having participated in Ticuani rituals with Ticuani friends they have known since childhood, these returnees are understandably disconcerted when treated like outsiders. While tensions are usually managed well by both sides, this selective withholding or granting of recognition of authenticity by those in Ticuani is often met by assertions of superiority and modernity by the returnees. After all, their parents left Ticuani because it could not offer them a living, and everyone in Ticuani seems to go, or want to go, to New York, the worldly metropolis.

Despite such tensions, return to Ticuani and participation in its religious rituals bridges gaps between the second generation's various social worlds.

Return transnationalizes adolescence by affecting relations with parents, with ethnic and racial identity, and with God, whose presence, they say, is easier to feel in Ticuani. Running the Antorcha, for example, demonstrates one's authenticity as a Ticuanense and can help positively define Mexicanness as an ethnic and not a racial identity, one thus associated with positive rather than negative assimilation. Such participation also helps create common ground between the second generation and their immigrant parents in lives that are riven by generational, educational, cultural, and other rifts. The "embodied experience" of these rituals produces physical and emotional feelings that the parents and children can share and remember later, but which do not require them to talk explicitly about the things that divide them.[1] Parents are more lenient with their children in Ticuani because they feel it is safer than New York; this relaxed attitude leads to both greater freedom and easier relations between teens and their parents, in contrast to what many teens describe as a virtual lockdown in New York. Finally, these returning youths feel closer to God in Ticuani, which they feel also makes them more authentically Ticuanense. Hence, participation in religious rituals transnationalizes adolescence, helps in negotiating ethnic and racial identity, and makes God a more palpable part of second-generation lives. Building on the analysis in chapter 6 of how the second generation renegotiates gender in a transnational context, this chapter describes why and how their participation in religious rituals facilitates the transnationalization of adolescence.

Three psychological and sociological insights guide my examination of the transnationalization of second-generation adolescence. First, I follow most contemporary psychologists and sociologists who posit adolescence not as a time of inherent Sturm und Drang, of conflict and withdrawal from parents, but rather as a time of transitions with uncertain outcomes. From this perspective, adolescence is a time when teens have difficult choices to make, choices with long-term consequences they know they will have to live with. In this view, adolescents want more freedom but also want parents and other adults to be "around the corner when they need you" in making choices about peer groups, schooling, work, or romance.[2] Second, and relatedly, psychologists have found that parenting practices, and subsequent parent-teen relations, change based on the kind of neighborhood a family lives in.[3] As Frank Furstenberg and his colleagues argue, it is not adolescence itself that produces successful or unsuccessful outcomes, but the fit between teens' needs and their environments. In areas seen as dangerous, parenting practices are stricter and more conflictive relationships ensue, whereas areas perceived as safer promote better teen self-image, autonomy, and parent-teen relations. The effects of bad neighborhoods are greatest for youths of precisely the ages discussed here.[4] Third, in psychoanalytic terms, Ricardo Ainslie argues that adolescence represents a second individuation from the parents, through which teens learn to be adult members of a larger community. This process involves testing parental limits and can be difficult or dangerous under conditions of migration, poverty, or high risk, such as exposure to crime.[5] Return to Ticuani fosters adolescent individuation and mutual parent-teen understanding through religious rituals and embodied practices. It also enables parents to offer what they see as a different, better-fitting environment to their children, at least temporarily.[6]

TICUANI RELIGIOUS RITUALS

The religious rituals in which the second generation participates have themselves been transnationalized, adapting elements of Ticuani's indigenous past to its migrant present. Devotion to Padre Jesús is widespread among Ticuanenses and, to a surprising degree, their second-generation children in New York. Religious practice and belief help create and sustain transnational life. The physical icon of Padre Jesús of Ticuani is a nearly life-sized statue of Jesus carrying the cross, which came to reside in Ticuani in the mid-1800s when pilgrims going from Oaxaca to Mexico City stopped to rest overnight. On their departure the next day, they could not lift the icon. Ticuanenses took this as a sign that Padre Jesús had chosen Ticuani as his home. Devotion to Padrecito is devotion to Ticuani itself, enacted in public and private practices in the United States and Mexico. Public devotional practices range from Masses to large events held in his honor in the United States or in Mexico that require months of preparation. The most important private practice is the internal dialogue these youths carry on with Padre Jesús in both extreme and quotidian circumstances. For example, while driving around making deliveries for his family's business, New York–born Nacho told me he had to go to Ticuani this winter because he had "promised Padre Jesús" that he would do a *promesa*. Marisol, a high-school student also born in New York, told me she regularly prayed to Padre Jesús when leaving the house or before taking a test. Teenaged Ticuanense girls in New York sometimes grow their hair to donate it for the weaving of wigs for the many statues of Padrecito. They say they do this both "for my mother" and "for Padre Jesús." Thus a 150-year-old Mexican religious icon may be adorned with permed, bleached hair grown in Brooklyn.[7]

FIGURES 5 AND 6.   Icon of Padre Jesús adorned with permed hair grown by a New York–born Ticuani girl as a *promesa*, 2000, front and back views.

The Feast of Padre Jesús runs for eleven days, spanning two weekends, in late January. The observances are both religious and secular. Religious observances consist of various Masses in honor of Padre Jesús, the most important being the Mass that welcomes home the youths who run in the Antorcha in the middle of the week. There are also several processions, large and small, in honor of Padre Jesús. The smaller processions travel around a particular section of town and involve only local residents; these take an hour or so. The larger ones circle the entire town, involve the whole town population, and take five to six hours. In addition, there are parties every night, some open to all, some private, and a series of public events and amusements. These include amusement-park rides and one of my favorite events, the rodeo: both of these move like a traveling circus from town to town to celebrate local feasts. The biggest secular event is the Grand Dance, which arguably draws the greatest number of attendees, including many from surrounding towns. Typically, a well-known regional band is hired to attract a large crowd, and the success of the Feast is evaluated partly by such events. In fact, the success of the Feast is invested with such importance in conversation that it seems to be understood as a reflection on the health and image of the Ticuani community itself.

The organization of the Feast has been changed by migration. The death in the 1980s of the man who had been *mayordomo,* or grand marshal, of the Feast for twenty years led Don Chucho, the municipal president at the time, to open the position to others, including New York migrants, who were demanding inclusion. Now the honor of being *mayordomo* or *mayordoma* increasingly goes to New Yorkers, or their Ticuani relatives, who can pay the rising costs associated with the position. As first-generation migrants reach middle age, they have more time and money to devote to such pursuits and can travel to Ticuani more easily. Returning migrants want the Feast to be "bigger and bigger," as one Ticuani leader put, and the *mayordomo/mayordoma* now spends a year coordinating the myriad activities of the Feast Council. Having spent a decade in New York, Don Chucho knew that the New Yorkers could raise more money. He also hoped to satisfy their growing demands for inclusion in Ticuani-oriented activities.

The Antorcha, the torch run for Padre Jesús, takes the form of a religious pilgrimage *(peregrinación)* and is perhaps Ticuani's most important ritual of reincorporation.[8] Don Manuel, the Committee president, reports that Ticuani's first Antorcha, in 1963, resulted from the rivalry with El Ganado. (Ticuani's runners traveled through the cold night to the start of their relay legs on the back of a flatbed truck; the richer Ganaderos rented a bus.) Starting with about twenty runners, the event grew to about one hundred in the

FIGURE 7.   After thirty-six hours on the road, runners in the Antorcha climb the last arduous steps to Ticuani's church for the Mass for Padre Jesús, 2000.

late 1980s. Since the early 1990s more than two hundred have run, half of whom are returning first- or second-generation migrants.

The Antorcha itself is transnationally organized. Ticuanenses in New York print and sell tickets, advertise the Antorcha, and donate the runners' T-shirts, which are printed in a Ticuanense-owned Brooklyn factory and carried to Ticuani in duffel bags by returnees. In Ticuani, the teachers rent buses, secure permits, supervise runners, and settle the accounts with those in New York.

Technology facilitates this transnational organization, with videotapes being used to include the absent donors and organizers in the event. For example, the teachers in Ticuani videotape each step of the Antorcha, from leaving Ticuani to the Mass in Mexico City's Cathedral to the Virgin, to the triumphant return to Ticuani thirty hours later. They periodically pause while the tape is running to tell the runners to remember the Ticuanenses in New York on their pilgrimage because the migrants have remembered Ticuani by making T-shirts, holding a raffle, and sending money to make it all possible. These acknowledgments help generate goodwill in New York and encourage the runners to think of migrants in New York as Ticuanenses whose sacrifice deserves recognition. In New York, Ticuanenses watch the tapes and the acknowledgments appreciatively. During the screening of these often long videos, they joke and drink but quiet down when the teachers in Ticuani acknowledge the Committee's sacrifice, for example. Hearing one such acknowledgment, a Committee leader said, "He did it," and the others nodded. Satisfied that their identity as Ticuanenses had been affirmed, they resumed drinking and laughing.

Since the early 1990s, Ticuanenses have been enthusiastically recreating the rituals of the Feast of Padre Jesús, with the explicit intent, on the part of the older Ticuanenses, of cultivating Ticuanense identity among their children. Many felt that, due to extensive outmigration, young people were losing their links with Ticuani's past. The movement's origin can be traced to the making of a short documentary video depicting Ticuani's indigenous past by a small group of teachers in Ticuani and migrants from New York, including Leobardo, who organized the first Antorcha in New York.

The producers gathered a group of Ticuani youths to hike in the predawn chill into the mountains surrounding Ticuani to perform for the video. It shows these youths in native dress and includes a voiceover and interviews; dozens of copies were sold in Ticuani and New York, and they circulated widely. The longest interview is with an old man, Don Camilo, who was said to be the last person alive who knew how to play the song for the Dance of the Tecuanis. The dance and its accompanying song are critical because they provide the music to which people dance as they parade energetically through Ticuani's streets, or around the basement of the church in New York where they hold the celebration of the Feast. Don Camilo lamented about what would happen once he died: would the song, the expression of Ticuani's past, be lost? Moved by these questions, the migrants and teachers organized to have Don Camilo teach a youth in Ticuani how to play the song. When he later migrated to New York, he taught the song to others.

The fear of children's losing their Ticuani roots has been a prime motivation for these recuperations of old traditions and their importation to New York. One migrant involved in this effort remarked to me that "these are our children, and they do not even know what the Dance of the Tecuanis is about." Teaching them the dance was, he thought, a good way to preserve Ticuani identity. While most second-generation youths may not know both versions of the story behind the dance (one involving peasants overcoming nature by killing the jaguar, the other involving mockery of the Spaniards), they have some sense of the background and enjoy the dance, some also performing it with their parents. I have seen the same parents dance with their children over the course of several years.

After the video, the next step was the organization of the first Feast of Padre Jesús, including a Mass and an Antorcha, in New York in 1997. The Mass was attended by more than 1,500 people, leading the priest, whose church is not usually packed to standing room only, to wipe tears from his eyes and apologize for not having opened the choir loft. In later years, Ticuanenses in New York paid to fly Ticuani's priest to New York so that he could celebrate the Feast there the weekend before it was done in Ticuani.

In Ticuani the Antorcha is especially important because it is a pilgrimage in which the town's youths dedicate themselves to their patron saint and to God. Hence it was an emotional event for older Ticuanenses to see more than two hundred Ticuanense youths, many born in New York as well as resident there, running in sweatshirts bearing the image of Padre Jesús. The first Antorcha was a run through Brooklyn to a church in downtown Manhattan. The Antorcha continues to draw more than two hundred runners, mostly youths, along with some hardy adults.

Since 2000, the Antorcha has been run from a church in downtown Manhattan to a church in central Brooklyn, where the priest has been very supportive of the Mexican community, especially the Ticuanenses in his parish. Perhaps the most important development was the installation in January 2005 of a life-sized replica of the icon of Padre Jesús in an alcove in the front of this church, the realization of a long-anticipated project to build and bring to New York a copy of the Ticuanenses' beloved Padrecito (paid for completely by Ticuanenses in New York). The priest's making permanent space for Padre Jesús gives the Ticuanenses a sacred space that is also geographical and recognizes, at least at the parish level, the growing importance of Mexicans in the Catholic church in New York. Although it is too early to tell what effect the statue will have on Ticuanense life in New York, the response at the 2005 Mass and party for Padre Jesús was emotional, with many tears shed and prayers and donations offered to Padrecito. Leobardo told me that bringing Padrecito to Brooklyn was, first, a "spiritual fulfillment for the Ticuanenses." Second, it was "for our children, that they will say in some future day, 'Look what they left us, what they did for us.'" Finally, it was a source of comfort for undocumented Ticuanenses who cannot return to Ticuani to see Padre Jesús, including one woman who told Leobardo she had not seen him in fifteen years. Leobardo also said with satisfaction that an acquaintance who did not go to church before now goes, "to see Padre Jesús." "Those," Leobardo said, "are the results."

FIGURE 8.   Ticuanense youths gather in Manhattan to begin the New York Antorcha on a frigid January day, 2004.

FIGURE 9.   Ticuanense youths running over the Manhattan Bridge toward Brooklyn in the New York Antorcha for Padre Jesús, 2004.

FIGURE 10.   Ticuani youth performing *la loba* (the wolf) in the Dance of the Tecuanis, 2004.

FIGURE 11.   An informant for this book and her son at the Feast of Padre Jesús, New York, 2004.

FIGURE 12. Full-sized replica of statue of Padre Jesús, paid for by Ticuanenses in New York, installed in a Brooklyn church, January 2005. In the background is a picture of the original in Ticuani.

MEXICANNESS IN NEW YORK AND TICUANI

Denying Ticuani and Mexican Authenticity

Although Ticuani rituals are increasingly being practiced in New York, return to Ticuani is still a central part of many second-generation youths' adolescence. These second-generation returnees to Ticuani face a two-faceted struggle over Mexican authenticity and the terms of American assimilation. The return to Ticuani helps some to positively define their Mexicanness, but it also forces them to confront the feeling that they are, in Willie's words, "not Mexican enough." They simultaneously feel embraced and judged, included and alienated. Many Ticuanenses in Ticuani believe migrants' children do not love the town as "real" Ticuanenses do, that they are too Americanized in their display of wealth, and that they have negatively affected Ticuani youth. Don Andrés says of those born in New York:

> They have another culture, they see Ticuani differently, do not love it as the adults [migrant parents] do, no? It's logical because they were born there and feel themselves to be Americans. . . . [Our] youths are very given to imitation of certain youths who do not live here perma-

nently. . . . Those *chavos* [guys] . . . come with their gold chains this
thick [holds fingers an inch apart] that they do not use there, yes, they
only use them when they come here. They show them pictures of
trips, the ocean . . . then the *chavos* follow illusions and want to be
part of that crowd, no?

Don Andrés criticizes the vanity of the returning second-generation in
noting, and I think exaggerating, the thickness of their gold chains, whose
meaning to returnees he does not understand, having never been a migrant. The chains are not mere ostentation; they represent prosperity and
a modern, urban lifestyle. But his remarks underscore the belief among
adult Ticuanenses that returning migrants have negatively changed youth
culture in Ticuani. One Ticuani native in her mid-twenties, who has long-
established friendships with returning second-generationers, is uncomfortable with the contrast between their apparent ease and her own family's difficult financial situation. Indeed, many Ticuanense locals, especially
those living in hard economic circumstances, seem irked by the fact that
those from New York take for granted their ability to come and go as they
please, while residents are stuck in a precarious situation through no fault
of their own.[9] This is an expression of the New Yorkers' power that they do
not themselves recognize. Ana is a college student who lives in Ticuani but
has many returnee friends. When I asked her, "Is there a certain type of
conflict or bad understanding between the New Yorkers that come back and
the youth and other Ticuanenses that live here all year?" she responded:

> Look, it's not a conflict. It depends on what group of youths you are
> talking about . . . because if you see the group of youths we go with
> [gives names], to the contrary, you feel happy and that you are really
> being friends with them. . . . But . . . the gangs come from the United
> States—and there are people in Ticuani that probably belong to a
> gang. . . . Another conflict is . . . youths here who because they were in
> New York . . . the Polo and that Nautica—and how they put on airs to
> you! fucking conceited people! Instead of coming to be with your
> people, they come here—how they try to step on others!—and then
> you say to them: Your parents are washing dishes, they are doing
> work for others! And they come here and believe themselves to be
> kings! These are the conflicts. (Spanish, translated by the author)

This eloquent and painful passage traces one native Ticuanense youth's negotiation of the second-generation reentry in Ticuani. Ana's college career
in Mexico, interrupted frequently by financial difficulties, contrasts with
what she sees as the easy life of the second-generation returnees in Ticuani;
she never sees their own struggles trying to make ends meet as college
students in New York. In fact, Ana is good friends with many second-

generation returnees and will likely join them in New York once she has finished college. This reality, and the fact that simplicity and humility are prized among real Ticuanenses, makes the arrogance she sees in many second-generation returnees more intolerable. Her perception of arrogance, and the second generation's feeling misjudged, are two sides of a coin of cultural misunderstanding. They illustrate how belonging and alienation coexist in this transnational context.

The Feast observances can bring such tensions to a head. For example, Ticuanenses in New York raised less money than anticipated in their raffle for the Antorcha in 1992, requiring a consultation with the teachers in Ticuani and the imposition of an entry fee of Mex$50,000 (about US$18) instead of Mex$20,000 (about US$7) as originally announced. Returning runners who had sold raffle tickets in New York, or bought extras, felt unfairly treated at being asked to pay again. This issue broke open among a mixed group of Ticuani and New York men standing in the zocalo late at night drinking beer. Some from New York implied that the shortfall arose from embezzlement by the teachers and threatened to "tell the *chavos grandes* [big guys]" in New York. But Anibal, a Ticuanense college student living in the city of Puebla who had been in New York and attended Antorcha committee meetings there, said the extra fee had been approved in New York. Those from New York said that it made sense to organize the Antorcha in New York because the money was there, but that Ticuanenses should acknowledge their sacrifice. Others said angrily that they should not have to pay anything at all, because they had put their labor and money into the raffle, a greater sacrifice than the paltry fifty-thousand-peso fee. They argued that they should be admitted for free.

Suddenly, Eduardo, who lives permanently in Ticuani but had worked in New York, lashed out at Carlos, one of the New Yorkers: "Where do you live, anyway? You live in New York and you just come down here for the Antorcha. But the Antorcha is from *here!* From *here!* It's in Ticuani, not New York! If we wanted to, we could make our own Antorcha, with just money from here. We don't need you in New York." He said that if Carlos did not trust the teachers, he should confront them about the issue instead of just gossiping. Anibal rejected Eduardo's criticism of Carlos, saying: "He has a right [to say this] because he is a Ticuanense." Anibal repeated this phrase several times, trying to assert control and defuse the argument. He also attacked Eduardo: "We are talking in confidence, and you are acting like a child. Don't be that way, or we will not be able to talk in confidence in front of you. We will be distrustful." Eduardo ceased raving and repeated his statements more calmly. In turn, the New Yorkers asked whether the

Antorcha could be held with only money from Ticuani. Maybe, they said, but it was clearly done better with New York money. They pointed to the marked increase in the number of runners over recent years made possible by increased funding from and participation by New Yorkers.

This dispute resonates with larger issues of membership and authenticity in Ticuani transnational life. New Yorkers assert belonging and membership by demanding recognition of their efforts and the necessity of their support. Eduardo reminds them that their economic power cannot buy their place in Ticuani, and, if used unwisely, could even endanger it. By drawing this line, he also deflects the truth he learned from his six years in New York: the Antorcha needs New York support.

Ticuanenses have also asserted social sovereignty by refusing in recent years to invite New York girls to compete to be the Queen of the Mass *(la Reina de la Misa)*, who officiates at Feast events and makes a speech to Antorcha runners at the Mass. Excluding New Yorkers from 1999 to 2003 departed from the practice of the late 1980s and 1990s, during which time several New York girls won. Those in Ticuani admit that local Ticuani girls did not want to compete with New York girls, whom they saw as preferred by local men. A male official who assists with the event told me, "You know, all the work and dust" in Ticuani make local girls less attractive and that New York girls know how to dress, walk, and talk better. When Alicia from Brooklyn (Juana's younger sister) was chosen as queen in 1998, local Ticuani girls complained that her physical beauty and "New York look" put them at a disadvantage.

I heard similar comments on work and dust from others, reflecting a broader notion that New York girls are more beautiful, glamorous, and sexual than local girls. Originally organized through the church to promote cultural pride, the competition has become one in which physical beauty is the primary criterion. Physical appearance and poise in front of a crowd are key to winning, which organizers say hurts "the local girls, [who] feel shame" *(vergüenza)* at exhibiting themselves in front of others. *Vergüenza*, a central element of *ranchera* femininity, underpins a woman's deference to her husband and other men in her life.

Alicia, widely regarded as very beautiful, does not look down or avoid eye contact with men, as do most local girls. Her beauty, "look," and self-confidence won her the competition but also drew criticism. The following year, she returned to Ticuani to crown her successor. On that occasion she offended onlookers by refusing invitations to dance with drunken men and dancing with someone else, instead of sitting out that dance and pretending she was tired, thus sparing the rejected man any implication that she did not want to dance with him. She made jokes about this as a group of us walked her home that night. She even refused to dance with the drunken male organizer who had commented on the local girls' "work and dust" problem. He screamed at her: "I am going to tell on you! [As queen] you are supposed to dance with everybody! Everybody!"

I intervened in this situation by offering the man a drink. I came over, stood next to him, and offered to buy him a beer. He relented and came away with me. This was the only response I could think of. I wanted to stop what I saw as angry abuse of a teenager, but directly intervening would have been unwise, both because he was intoxicated and because it would have been seen as acting beyond my place. Offering him a drink was an act of apparent male friendship that drew him away from Alicia. I had been standing right in the area when he began to yell at her and waited for others to intervene, but no one did. The others in the area were mostly youths in their teens or twenties; older men probably could not hear the man, though he was screaming, because of the very loud music. Hence it seemed that if I did not act in some way, Alicia was going to be left to deal with him alone.

It is precisely the *presence* of shame, this most appropriate ranchera emotion, in local girls that makes them less attractive to local men in the context of this pageant, but it is Alicia's *lack* of shame that outrages the event organizer who wants to dance with her. If the sociologist Jack Katz is right in saying that one goal of street masculinity is to generate fear and dread in other men, we can say that one goal of ranchero masculinity is to generate shame and deference in women. Alicia's autonomy in dealing with such men no doubt strengthened the hand of locals who wanted New York girls excluded. Yet, despite her poise, she later told me she had "wanted to cry" when he screamed at her. At the time, she did experience some form of shame: because she did not know how to respond to him, she simply sat, face frozen in a half smile, eyes focused in the distance, and waited for the next dance. Though she was from New York, she was still a teenage girl and he was still a grown, inebriated man.

Denying the Denial of Authenticity

The returning second generation not only assert that their sacrifice gives them the right to be seen as Ticuanenses in Ticuani but also unapologetically claim to be authentic New York Mexicans—*New York* modifies *Mexican*. Indeed, they argue that they are more Mexican because they have been raised in New York and then chosen to live as Mexicans there. The exchange below begins with my asking: "What do you guys think about . . . people who live in Ticuani who say, *'Aquí vienen los turistas* [here come the tourist] *ticuanenses'?"* Jericho had not heard this criticism before.

> JERICHO: Well, . . . it kinda pisses me off, you know, 'cause I know
> where I came from, I know where my roots are, so I
> don't need you to be telling me that I'm a tourist, you
> know. I'm Mexican. . . . Okay, yeah, I grew [up] in New
> York, I was born in New York, but my background is
> from Ticuani. . . . I didn't forget about the traditions and
> stuff. . . .
>
> NAPOLEON: Just because I was [born] in here doesn't make me any
> less Mexican than you. You should be glad I'm going
> over there 'cause that shows that I'm proud . . . I'm Mex-
> ican . . . not ashamed of my country. . . . I feel more Mex-
> ican than American . . . even though I was born here—
> I'm as much American as any American—but if anybody
> asks me about a flag . . . I'll first put up my Mexican flag
> [rather] than American.
>
> J: That's the way I grew up also . . . you believe in our flag,
> being of Mexican background, eating mole, tortillas, you
> know, *adobo.* Of course, I didn't grow up eating ham-
> burgers and pizzas and hot dogs . . . it goes all the way
> back [to] . . . how your parents raised you up.

That Jericho does not know that returnees are referred to as tourists reflects how much of Ticuani's social world is closed to these young men, even if they are also embraced sincerely by Ticuanenses. The comment brings out feelings of alienation and resentment at how Ticuanenses qualify their be-longing. In response, Jericho and Napoleon assert their authentic Mexican-ness, linking it defiantly and positively with their New York life. Being Mexican does not mean they must live in Mexico but rather that they eat Mexican food, know Mexican traditions, and are proud to be Mexican in New York. Such efforts give them a special claim on Mexicanness. I con-tinued by asking about the relationship they have with Ticuani-residing boys who "give you guys hard looks":

> J: I think Ticuanenses from over there have this kinda of stereotyp-
> ing thing, that they saying, Oh, look at him. . . . He was born over
> there, he's wearing all that nice clothes and everything, so . . .
> they give you hard looks because they're thinking . . . you're so
> full of yourself. . . . That pisses me off. . . . Just because I'm wear-
> ing one-hundred-dollar sneakers and a seven-hundred-dollar
> gold chain, don't judge me. They thinking that you all *que ya te
> crees tanto . . . tu eres de Nueva York, ya sabes hablar inglés y*

todo eso [you think you are all that, you are from New York, you know how to speak English, and all that]. But I don't buy it.

RS: So what do you think they think of someone wearing a seven-hundred-dollar gold chain and hundred-dollar sneakers? . . .

J: I think they think they're very conceited . . . that they're much more better than they are. . . . I'm wearing a seven-hundred-dollar gold chain. . . . I mean, yeah, yeah, I got a gold chain, I'm gonna wear it, but I'm not gonna show it off and flash it in front of people.

RS: So what does it mean to you to wear your . . . sneakers and . . . chain when you go down there?

J: Oh, it doesn't really mean anything, it's just my attire that I wear every day, so why I'm gonna change because I'm in Ticuani? . . . Even though I am Mexican, I was born in New York, so you know I was raised . . . with the style and everything, the hairdo. But I'm not gonna change just because I'm in Ticuani. I know I'm Mexican, yeah, I act Mexican every day.

Though I did not mention Don Andrés's remark about gold chains to Jericho, he seemed defensive about his. The consistency between the beliefs of native Ticuanenses and the perceptions by second-generation returnees that they are seen as arrogant show-offs was remarkable. Moreover, while second-generation returnees deny the native Ticuanenses the power to deny their claims of Mexican authenticity, they also refuse to acknowledge any special meaning in their wearing of expensive sneakers and gold chains. In Jericho's view his attire—gold chain, sneakers, baggy pants— needs no explanation, suggesting it is not a claim of modernity and superiority of the kind he sometimes makes in other contexts. Rather, it is authentically Mexican—New York Mexican. Hence, Jericho is demanding recognition of his version of Mexican authenticity. He concludes defiantly and affirmatively that he would not change his appearance in Ticuani. His position reflects an emerging, transnationalized youth culture forged between New York and Ticuani.

TICUANI AND MEXICAN IDENTITY IN NEW YORK

Second-generation participation in transnational life not only makes a claim to be authentically Ticuanense, it also disputes negative social locations and images in New York. Such practices deny the image of Mexicans as vulnerable, uneducated, and undocumented and differentiates them from Puerto Ricans and Blacks, whom Mexicans quickly perceive to be at the bottom of New York's economic, social, and racial hierarchies. Many embrace, though some dispute, Mexican claims of superiority to these other groups. Others attempt to use these new definitions of Mexicanness to improve their own lives. These embraces of Mexican superiority show how race plays an important role in defining an upwardly mobile assimilation; like much of American life, then, even these positive outcomes are tainted by racism.

The image of Mexicans as powerless and victimized in New York was strong from the late 1980s to mid-1990s, when they first became a visible group and received attention in the mainstream and Spanish-language media. Perhaps the most enduring image was that of Don Sixto Santiago Morales, a Mexican flower vendor who died of a heart attack after being assaulted by Puerto Rican and Dominican youths who stole his flowers and money on Fathers' Day 1991, when he had risen early to go to work. Don Sixto represented the nobility and vulnerability many Mexicans felt: We work very hard, but others prey on us, and no one protects us. Intense media coverage and ineffective attempts by the Mexican consulate to mobilize second-generation help for the vendors reinforced the image of Mexican powerlessness. Members of the Ticuani Youth Group (described in the next section) told me they disliked the fact that flower vendors were the only media images of Mexicans; they wanted images of Mexican professionals. Some youths had dissociated from being Mexican. Juana told me she "did not want to be Mexican" as a child and would silently nod when people asked if she was Puerto Rican. For her, being Mexican meant sharing the vulnerability and backwardness she saw in her parents.

> I had a bad image [of Mexicans]. . . . When I was small . . . one day Immigration took my father . . . and we had to like run out of the house . . . and I hated that. . . . Why we have to go through this? I was small, but I realized what was going on. And I used to hear people outside, they even do it today. . . . Oh, Immigration is coming for you. . . . That's why I was like, I'm not Mexican. I'm something else. I just did not say I was Mexican in school. I was like embarrassed to say I was Mexican—'cause they were short little people, and they dressed funny sometimes.

While others I spoke to had less dramatic stories and more pride in being Mexican as children, many told of a struggle to maintain a positive image of Mexicanness in the face of insults. For example, students, flower vendors, and friends have told me that strangers would invectively shout "Mexico!" at them on the street. The widespread practice of using "Mexico" as a generic form of address or insult to unknown persons tightens the link between Mexicanness, vulnerability, and lack of social power in New York.

One response to this vulnerability is to embrace the immigrant analogy, which asserts that immigrants are different from and superior to Black Americans. This view—we may not be much, but at least we are better than Blacks—has guided immigrants' imagining of their place in the United States social order since the 1840s.[10] In New York the often phenotypically similar Puerto Ricans are lumped with Blacks in the most racialized, stigmatized category.[11] Many first- and second-generation Mexicans assert their superiority over these other groups, with whom they share schools, neighborhoods, and parks, thus claiming an identity as good, "ethnic" immigrants as opposed to bad, "racialized" minorities, though some dissent.[12] Embracing this position of superiority offers a basis for an ethnically segmented upward mobility. It also does what Michelle Lamont calls the "boundary work" from which the relational categories of white and Black derive meaning. Here, Ticuanenses seek to draw racialized moral maps that differentiate them from "less desirable" minorities, just as Lamont's white American interviewees did with Blacks, and white French men did with Muslim immigrant men in France.[13]

The Organization to Defend the Race (ODR) and the Ticuani Youth Group

This dynamic of racialization expresses itself clearly in two otherwise quite dissimilar organizations: the Ticuani Youth Group and the Organization to Defend the Race (Organización de la Defensa de la Raza, or ODR), one of the first Mexican gangs in New York. The Youth Group organized sports tournaments to raise money to refurbish a chapel in Ticuani, while ODR patrolled the streets looking to avenge violence against Mexicans. Yet both also tried to create "good," nonracialized social locations for Mexicans in New York.

According to some founders and early members, ODR was founded in 1985 to "defend the Hispanic Race" against Blacks and Puerto Ricans, and less often Dominicans, who preyed on them. Puerto Rican and Black minors in gangs often assaulted Mexicans walking alone or in small groups, and, say ODR members, the police never prosecuted them. Abraham, a founder of both ODR and the TYG, said the obvious solution was to form Mexican gangs.

> Drugged-out people, *boricuas* (Puerto Ricans), and Blacks, that if you don't give them money, they hit you . . . they shout[ed] "Mexico—

[unsaid word]!" . . . Only together could we do something. . . . That they respect us. . . . They laughed at all my countrymen. . . . If a Mexican bought a six-pack of beer, they would want to take it from him. They are all so abusive because they think [Mexicans] are humble. . . . We found one countryman *[paisano]* that they were taking his clothes off him. . . . It was for things like this that we started our own thing. (Spanish, translated by the author)

This image of Mexicans as easy prey is universal in oral histories of gang members and other Mexican youths from that time, as are shame and anger at being humiliated for being Mexican. When I asked Abraham what he left unsaid in the above answer, he told me, "Things that I do not want to say" because they are too offensive. Moreover, ODR's definition of the Raza Hispana resonates with the immigrant analogy and New York's racial hierarchies by including Mexicans, Central Americans, South Americans, and Puerto Ricans born on the island, and excluding Blacks and Puerto Ricans born in the United States. ODR's view clearly distinguishes good ethnic Mexican immigrants and bad racial minorities.

When fully elaborated, this message also has subtexts. First, African Americans and Puerto Ricans are lazy: despite being U.S. citizens and speaking English, they are all on welfare or unemployed. Second, they are prone to vices such as drugs or crime. Third, they are morally unfit; and their women get pregnant without marrying. While such expressions inevitably include formulaic disclaimers about knowing good Puerto Ricans or Blacks, these are always exceptions. In contrast, Mexicans work hard and prosper without English or even a visa; they do not take drugs or commit crimes; and Mexican women do not go out alone and get pregnant (or, if they do, at least the men marry them).

The emergence of Mexican gangs in New York has challenged the dichotomy of the good immigrant/bad native minority. Indeed, ODR broke up after some members were jailed for assaults on another Mexican gang. Such actions visibly puzzled and worried Committee members such as Don Manuel and Don Emiliano, who exclaimed: "Mexicans fighting Mexicans! If they are going to fight anyone, they should fight the Puerto Ricans and Blacks who have been abusing us all these years!" That Mexican gangs were mainly fighting other Mexicans made no sense in the Committee members' understanding of what it means to be Mexican in New York.

The Ticuani Youth Group was formed at roughly the time ODR was breaking up. It had thirty members, of whom about six were U.S.-born Mexican Americans, about fifteen teen migrants, and about nine 1.5-generation youths, born in Mexico but raised from the age of ten or younger in the

United States, attending U.S. schools. The Youth Group also distinguished between Mexicans and native minorities. While watching a volleyball tournament the Youth Group had organized, its president, Abraham, said to me: "Blacks and Puerto Ricans, they have all kinds of problems: drugs, crime, teen pregnancy, disobedience to their parents, girls walking alone at night. . . . Now, look at this group," he went on, pointing to the Ticuanenses. "Do you think that the Puerto Ricans and Blacks have this kind of community? No, they do not, and this is their problem." The Ticuani Youth Group and this tournament were, for him, evidence of Mexicans' superior culture, which enabled them to resist the vices to which Blacks and Puerto Ricans fall prey.

Such prevention was part of the mission of the Youth Group and a way that Padre Jesús protected Mexicans even in New York City. I followed up this point several times, including in a 1997 interview, when I asked Abraham to explain his point that the problems of Blacks and Puerto Ricans stemmed from having a different type of culture from Mexicans.

> ABRAHAM: To live this life, Robert, one needs morals. Morals, culture, and you need this call from your people—you need an example to advance—or else who are you going to learn from? I, thank God, with my parents, they have put me in good ways. . . .
>
> RS: Blacks and Puerto Ricans . . . this is what they lack?
>
> A: They do not have the culture. Their parents have not inculcated it [into] them. . . . I remember my great-grandfather and great-grandmother taught me the same ideas. They always taught me to be honest, to work, and to live well. And this is the mentality for many peoples in Latin America, for many peoples, not just Mexico. (Spanish, translated by the author)

Several elements in this narrative recur in other discussions of first-, 1.5-, and second-generation participation in transnational life. Both ODR and the Youth Group respond to threats posed by New York to their Mexicanness and to their well-being, and to the negative perceptions that they felt motivated their attackers—the belief that Mexicans were powerless. Both also see cultural or physical exposure to Blacks and Puerto Ricans as dangerous and try to "inoculate" Mexicans against the threat by celebrating Mexican religion and culture, thus expressing a belief in ethnically segmented assimilation. And Abraham also juxtaposes Mexican virtue with minority vice by invoking the Raza Hispana, saying this hardworking mentality was found in "many peoples in Latin America," again excluding

Puerto Ricans and Blacks. These positions were repeated by many other second- and 1.5-generation youth I spoke to. Juana, a Brooklyn-born member of the Youth Group, in a separate interview, agreed with Abraham's cultural explanation of why Mexicans do better.

> I think so, very much. Even though we're here, and we're taught certain things, like, you know, sex is very open. . . . But at home, we still have those same values. . . . American girls are so natural about it, they move out with their boyfriends, and that's still their boyfriend, it's not their husband. . . . In a Mexican family, you move out with your boyfriend, he's your husband, 'cause you sleep with him. . . . We've had girls getting pregnant, . . . but it's not taken so lightly. . . . I see Puerto Rican girls and it's just like . . . pregnancy after pregnancy. They either get an abortion or just get on welfare. . . . When I was smaller, we had meat on the table but maybe once or twice [a week], but we never went on welfare. It's a matter of pride. Puerto Ricans have gotten a lot Americanized . . . and we [Mexicans] still have strong values from over there.

Further evidence of the second generation's wanting to distance themselves from the Black and Puerto Rican "other" comes in Juana's response to my question about why she is embracing Mexican traditions so strongly in her teen years, becoming, by her account, more "traditional" than even her own mother:

> JUANA: We have to keep ourselves that way, you know. Not so much that we close our minds to what's outside, but enough to keep . . . our values in perspective, like, "Don't get pregnant, don't do drugs."
>
> RS: And what would happen if you guys weren't so traditional? What's the danger?
>
> J: Then we would be just like everybody else. . . . Like those talk shows that your mother sleeps with your sister's husband, just junk. . . . I don't know how those people grew up in their houses.

Juana broadens her analysis of the sources of danger to Mexicans and Mexican Americans to include the degeneracy of American popular culture. Mexican values, which guard against such a breakdown of morality, must be jealously guarded. This worry clearly resonates with Juana's earlier feeling that being Mexican means being short and powerless and "dress[ing] funny." Such fears about social location often underpin a Mexican belief in superiority over Blacks and Puerto Ricans in New York.

Not all in the Ticuani Youth Group accepted this racialization. Indeed, in a separate interview, Nora, a U.S.-born Youth Group member, responds to a question about how the Ticuani Youth Group made Mexicans different from Puerto Ricans.

> RS: Do you think that Mexicans try to define themselves by not being Black and not being Puerto Rican? Is that part of what it means to be Mexican in New York?
>
> NORA: I think so. . . . They actually think that we're better than the Puerto Ricans and Blacks because the Puerto Ricans rob and . . . the Blacks rob. . . . But they . . . do the same things. Why do they have to have a gang? Supposedly that's only Blacks and Puerto Ricans. . . . And why do they have to go around drinking "forties," the big bottles of beer? . . . I think they wanna make themselves look better. . . . I mean, they're hardworking people, but . . . they believe they're supe-rior . . . 'cause they work for whatever money . . . [while] Blacks and Puerto Ricans . . . won't work for whatever. . . . [But U.S.-born Mexicans] also make sure they get paid what they're supposed to get paid.

Nora's insight confirms that Mexicans and Mexican Americans see them-selves as better than Blacks and Puerto Ricans, but she debunks the proofs offered of this superiority. She rejects the racializing logic of the immigrant analogy through her observations of how assimilation in the United States is changing Mexicans in New York, saying, "I think everybody's the same."

Redefining Mexicanness in Ticuani

Going back to Ticuani helps redefine Mexicanness, giving second-gen-eration returnees a deeper understanding of Mexican culture. This changed meaning of ethnicity in turn helps returnees in a key task of adolescence: choosing peer groups that will nurture and not destroy their future possi-bilities.[14]

By his mid-teens, Toño saw Mexican and native minorities as having very similar lives and, in his experience, good relations. Of himself and his Mexican friends, he said: "We thought we were part of Blacks and Puerto Ricans. We spoke like them, dress like them, act like them," and, he said, failed like them, thinking that "only whites" were "smart" and "got ahead." He became involved in both a Mexican gang and a mixed gang of Black immigrants, Puerto Ricans, and Mexicans. His parents sent him to Mexico in part to break his connection with gang culture. Reflecting on how returning to Ticuani had affected him, he said: "It was a different kind of knowledge . . . a different crowd—more mature. . . . I came back feeling more mature." Being Mexican to Toño came to mean earning respect with-out fighting for it. He now assesses his life in the gang like this: "Yeah, I was like . . . at the bottom. . . . I had no life; I considered myself a bum. Just hang out on the streets, doing nothing." Toño's identification with Blacks and Puerto Ricans and his gang involvement were linked with a pessimistic outlook on life and a negative conception of Mexican identity. Going to Ticuani helped him revise its meaning from being a bum to being a young man studying for a profession.

After returning from Mexico, Toño left his old friends and began cultivating friendships with more upwardly mobile Mexicans in college. His social life centered on his family and steady girlfriend. He graduated from college in 2002. His return to Ticuani helped change his life in enduring, positive ways. It was not a magic bullet: his parents' intervention and his own fear—"I was scared to die"—were also important. But the practices through which he changed were largely provided by Ticuani's repertoire of religious and adolescent rituals, which gave him the chance to experience an alternative kind of Mexicanness linked to personal and professional growth. He also said that being out of the gang's social world for a while made it easier to stay out when he returned to Brooklyn.

Juana's Mexicanness and life trajectory also changed through her visits to Ticuani and work in the Ticuani Youth Group. From denying her Mexican identity as a girl, she hung out with a Mexican gang in her early teens. She cut school to be with her boyfriend, a member of a gang whose violence made her nervous. Her life changed at the age of fifteen, "when I came here" to Ticuani and felt like "I found my people." She describes realizing that being Mexican does not have to mean being a "short, ugly Indian" but could be about the "respect" that people in Ticuani demonstrate. She said that the Youth Group "took me away from a lot of bad stuff. . . . I was hanging out in gangs. . . . I came [to Ticuani] for a week. . . . I found people like me." Moreover, she said, Youth Group members had jobs, went to college, and seemed to have positive lives ahead of them; there was one member whom she particularly admired. She said, "I saw people doing something. And I saw that she had her money. And I wanted that for me and for my kids, that life would be easier." After her first Ticuani trip, Juana spent less time with gang friends and more with the Youth Group, attended school regularly, and graduated. She came to describe the gang as a bunch of "lost little kids"—mainly teen migrants—and preferred the company of "people like me" who promoted education as the Mexican way.

Juana has since graduated from college and works in a responsible job. Both her life and Toño's were changed not just by returning to Ticuani but by crossing symbolic and social borders, using the religious and adolescent rituals of Ticuani to change the meaning of their Mexicanness.

ADOLESCENT LIFE, RITUALS, AND PARENTING

Whereas many second-generation migrants describe life in New York as being "trapped," "in jail," "in a cage," or "on lockdown," and the City as being "dangerous" and "pressured," of Ticuani they say: "I feel closer to God," "You are safe," "You let go of all your problems," and, most emphatically, "Ticuani means freedom." These different experiences are partly functional: Ticuani is a place for vacation and leisure, New York a place for school and work. But conditions and choices in the two places also differ starkly. In New York, most second-generation Ticuanenses live in crowded apartments and have parents who work long hours for little money. They live in neighborhoods and go to schools where being Mexican must be explained and may provoke a violent reaction, especially for young men. Many girls are on complete lockdown, meaning that outside school hours they may not leave home without an older relative. They are what they call *muchachas de la casa* or "inside-the-house girls," or what Carola Suarez-Orozco calls *las encerradas* (shut-ins).[15] Second-generation complaints about confinement are not just the metaphorical laments of rebellious teenagers but rather reflect the real and imagined dangers they and their parents perceive New York to hold.

By contrast, in Ticuani (at least until the late 1990s, when gang members became publicly visible), the second generation could, as a rule, walk without fear of confrontation and felt that Ticuani was physically and culturally theirs. While their Mexicanness is sometimes contested, they do not have to explain it or feel that it makes them vulnerable as it does in New York. Rather, Ticuani offers practices and conditions that make possible an alternative experience of adolescence, Mexican ethnicity, gender, relations with parents, and class. Second-generation returnees enter Ticuani at the top of its social hierarchy, using their U.S. dollars to participate in rituals and wearing the U.S.-style clothing that marks Ticuani's elite. Their houses in Ticuani, often large, beautiful, and spacious compared to their cramped apartments in New York, are surrounded by stark, expansive natural beauty instead of a cramped urban landscape. Finally, they have safe public spaces in Ticuani—both exterior space, such as the zocalo, and ample private, interior space, such as houses and yards—which they do not have in New York, spaces that profoundly affect the kinds of adolescent rituals possible. For example, in Ticuani, young people can spend the whole night in the zocalo with friends or drink and dance at a party. In New York, Mexicans control little public space and few institutions, and staying out all night to look at stars, as they might in Ticuani, is not safe. The control of geographical space in Ticuani makes possible a more confident performance of masculinity and femininity, understood as an authentication of *mexicanidad* and *ticuanensidad*, than is possible in New York.

THE SOCIAL WORLD OF
TICUANENSE YOUTH IN NEW YORK

The confluence of the dangers of adolescence in New York and the relative freedom of Ticuani make Ticuani the primary social world for many second-generation migrants, especially girls. Parents loosen their parenting practices while their children are in Ticuani, and teens are also offered an expanded repertoire of rituals and practices for negotiating adolescence. Parents feel they can safely give their children more freedom in Ticuani, letting them go out without a curfew and unchaperoned. Many parents, in fact, send their teenaged children on vacation to Ticuani without them, leaving a group of teens under the loose charge of their Ticuani grandparents or an adult from New York. No wonder second-generation returnees associate Ticuani with freedom.

Linda, the fifteen-year-old Brooklyn girl whose dreamlike experience of being in Ticuani is quoted in the opening paragraphs of this book, contrasted her degrees of freedom in Ticuani and New York this way:

LINDA: Like here [New York], I can't go out. If I go out, it has to be with a family member or brother. If not, I can't go out. My mom doesn't let me go out with my friends. . . . Like, go hang out. Go bowling, you know.

RS: You can't go bowling without your brother?

L: No, I can go, but my cousin needs to go with me . . . a cousin . . . that my mom knows.

RS: So if you had a girlfriend that you want to go out with that's not a cousin, your mom won't let you go out?

L: Yeah.

RS: And down there?

L: Down there I can go out. 'Cause my parents don't go to Mexico. . . . Like this year they sent me with my brother, it was like all the teenagers, no parents. Only one aunt went. We used to get home at like two or three in the morning. . . . Yeah, we used to go see the *gallos*.

For many second-generation returnees, these conditions produce a social world in which Ticuani looms large. Indeed, many returnees wait all year to go to Ticuani, and keep their Ticuani friends as mainstays at least through young adulthood. One reason for Ticuani's predominance is that it places one within an extended-cousin network that constitutes a pool of friends acceptable to one's parents. A map of Linda's social world would include her neighborhood, apartment, and some cousins' apartments in Brooklyn, and then Ticuani. It would resemble the famous *New Yorker* magazine cover from the 1970s showing the view from its office windows, with Tenth Avenue and Manhattan looming large, the Midwest lacking distinguishing features, and Los Angeles and points beyond sketched in lightly. On Linda's map, her house and her cousins' houses would loom large, with only Ticuani at a similar height, and the rest of the world flat and featureless. She describes this world below, in an interview in which Griscelda Perez participates:

> RS: [Do] you see your friends, all the people you hang out with in Ticuani, when you're up here?
>
> L: No, not up here. We don't see them here. . . . No, I don't see them. Just over there. . . .
>
> GP: Why don't you get to see your friends here?
>
> L: 'Cause here they all live mad far. You have to go through the expressway to go see them, and they live, some of them live on like Forty-second Street and Tenth Avenue [in Manhattan]. So, you know, right here I don't go out, so I don't get to see them. And my brother gets to see them 'cause they go to parties. When my brother goes to parties, sometimes they go. That's life. . . .
>
> RS: So if you got to go to *sonido* parties, you would get to see all those people, too, but you can't see them because—
>
> L: —some of them live in Manhattan, that's why.

Although Linda characterizes a twenty-five-minute subway ride to her friends and cousins as "mad far," she never mentions, in hours of interviews and ethnography, how geographically far away Ticuani is. In her transnationalized world, Ticuani is socially closer to Brooklyn than midtown Manhattan.

Gendered Freedoms and Parenting

In all the brother-sister couples interviewed and followed for this study, boys were given greater freedom at a younger age in New York than girls were. Linda's perception of her parents' gendered rules was confirmed by her father, Bernardo, who came home during an interview Griscelda Perez and I were doing with her. I had known Bernardo for a decade, and he joined the conversation. We discussed how his son Bennie disliked school while his daughter liked it, and general differences between boys and girls, including who gets to go out and at what age. After saying girls are more "tranquil" and boys more "raging with their parents," and that both must ask permission to go out, he continued:

> BERNARDO: The men say, I am leaving now, asking permission in the same instant they leave. And the women, no, because they ask permission and we say no—well, at least that is how it is . . . up to the present, we have never let her [Linda] go to a party by herself. No.
>
> RS: Her, no. But Bennie?
>
> B: Yes. And at the same age that she is now, he was going to parties by himself.
>
> RS: And didn't you both worry about him the way you would worry about her? *(Bernardo shakes his head.)* Is it something else? Is it different?
>
> B: It's a little different. It is simply that the worry one always has is of the fights that they do in the club or street between the Mexicans themselves. (Spanish, translated by the author)

When Griscelda Perez asked about this "double standard," and Linda said she thought it was unfair, Bernardo stressed that gangs made these parties dangerous. I asked about the apparent contradiction between Bernardo's saying gangs made parties dangerous and letting Bennie but not Linda go.

> RS: Let me ask you—if the fights are more from the *pandillas*, from the guys, well, if the guy goes [to the party] and there is a fight, although the guy is not in a gang, maybe the people are going to involve him . . . but maybe a *pandilla* is not going to attack a woman. Well, then, how is it that you both worried more for her than for him, at the same age? . . . It looks like the danger would be greater for the man than for the woman, right? . . .
>
> B *(laughs):* That this is the truth. But it is that the man always takes care of himself, and the woman—she also can do it. . . . But, you see, because the woman is the "weaker sex," one worries more about the woman, as a father, see. (Spanish, translated by the author)

After her father left, Linda supplied the unsaid piece of his argument—that parents will not let girls go out by themselves for fear that they will get pregnant. The whole exchange offers insights into how gender structures

Linda's life in New York.[16] Bernardo openly accepted Griscelda Perez's description of his rules as a "double standard," and when confronted with an alternative analysis—that parties posed a greater danger for young men because of gangs—he acknowledged this as "the truth." But he defended his parenting practices by falling back on biology and designating women as the "weaker sex." Linda openly disagreed with him. These gender rules make return to Ticuani a bigger mountain in girls' social topography.

Napoleon and Ceydi, also siblings, had similar gender rules. Although Napoleon is four years younger than Ceydi, their parents permitted him in his early teens to hang out on the street until ten o'clock or even midnight, while Ceydi could not leave the house unless accompanied by her brother, and only when there was no school the next day. Ceydi was so rarely seen that the neighbors did not know her:

> NAPOLEON: She was allowed to come out in the summer, but only if I came out. . . . My mom would say, "Yo, keep an eye on her." . . . I got older, like thirteen or fourteen, [and] . . . the new people would move to the neighborhood, they'd be like, "Who's that?" . . . They wouldn't even know that was my sister.
>
> CEYDI: They wouldn't even know I live on the block.
>
> SARA GUERRERO-RIPPBERGER: Wow—'cause you were inside most of the time?
>
> C: Yup. Another excuse for me to come out was my little brother, when he was born. I'd be like: "Yeah, I'm going to take him outside." That was the only way I would be able to come out. . . . I was locked down. I was on serious lock. I was on serious lock.

Lockdown was an expression widely used among the second generation, especially among girls, consciously evoking prison. Ceydi's second-class standing meant that she had to answer to her younger brother when out of the house. He told other boys on the block not to talk to her and told her to go home if she drew attention from boys he did not like. Her parents reinforced his authority. Indeed, Napoleon was being taught to enforce and Ceydi to obey a Brooklyn version of ranchero and ranchera gender roles. In this context, it makes sense that Ticuani becomes so important in the lives of girls like Ceydi.

Given that the perception of danger reinforces harsher parenting practices in New York, going to Ticuani is like temporarily moving to a better neighborhood: it allows parents to ease up on their teens and teens, especially girls, to experience themselves as competent and autonomous, a very different experience of adolescence. In answer to my question about what it feels like to go to Ticuani, Linda responded: "I like it 'cause over there you can do anything. Go out, and your parents won't tell you anything. But here you go out, 'Where are you going? Who are you going with? What time are you coming back?' Over there you just hang out with your cousins, your friends, and they don't say nothing to you. You come home at the time that you want. That's why." Many other second-generation youth, especially girls, echoed this sentiment. In 1992, Juana, then seventeen, told me that her parents were able to treat her more like an adult in Ticuani:

> You know, my parents weren't afraid of me going alone. It was . . . so much trust. Not so much on me . . . [but] they were sure that nothing was gonna happen to me. See, they had that security. And here [in New York], you're even at your house and your mother has to call you to see if everything's fine. And over there, all the doors [are] open, you just walk out. . . . [In New York], you knew you weren't safe. Even now you're not safe to be on the train, at whatever time, even in daytime.

Juana, too, felt safer in Ticuani. She described how it felt on her first independent visit: "It was quiet. It was calm. . . . If you would get home at three o'clock in the morning, like, you didn't risk yourself, that something would happen. It was like more freedom. Without anybody telling you, you could do anything you want, anytime you want." This feeling of being competent, powerful, and autonomous in the world has positive effects on parent-teen relations and on adolescents' general development. The second individuation that Ainslie posits as essential adolescent work seems possible in Ticuani in ways that it is not in New York.

Parents and grandparents also told me they are more permissive in Ticuani than New York. Doña Maria, a pioneer Ticuanense migrant who cares for her fourteen-year-old granddaughter and her younger siblings while their parents work, described the difference:

> DOÑA MARIA: Here [in Ticuani], the kids enjoy themselves more, they have more liberty, they don't work because they come when they are on vacation. . . . There . . . they are

closed in, the poor things, . . . always locked up tight, and I am also inside the house. . . .

RS: And do you see it as dangerous there, and here, no?

DM: Well, there is danger here, too . . . but it is more dangerous there. There, they might take them away, rape them—here too there is this, but very little. . . . Here they can go out until midnight. . . . So I give them a chance to go out. . . . The girls have come home at midnight and one in the morning.

RS: And did you not worry?

DM: Yes, I worried, because they are big girls now, I don't like them walking around at night. But, afterwards, nothing had happened to them. And she knows how to take care of herself.

The language that Doña Maria uses to describe second-generation life in New York echoes the expressions that teenagers themselves use—being on "serious lockdown" seems quite akin to being "locked up tight" (*encerrado con llave*, or "locked in with a key"), a restriction she also feels herself, being always "inside" in New York. She lists serious dangers—being kidnapped or raped—immediately when the theme comes up, as if she regularly worries about these issues in New York. Contrasting how adolescent girls are treated in New York and Ticuani offers insight. Linda, Ceydi, and many others are treated by their families as the "weaker sex," unable to take care of themselves in New York. Yet Doña Maria says that her granddaughter knows "how to take care of herself" in Ticuani. Differential gender rules are certainly not suspended there, but the restrictions placed on girls are looser. Such feelings of empowerment and freedom anchor second-generation girls' desires to go to Ticuani and participate in its rituals and power the imagination of transnational adolescence.

Despite the attraction of returning to Ticuani, most adolescents see their visits as limited in time and scope. Ticuani is a vacation spot where they see friends and reconnect with Mexican roots, but only a minority stay for more than a month at a time. This group includes a small but growing number of second-generation youth who have been sent back to Ticuani against their will by their parents or have moved back with them, and even a few who have lobbied their parents to return. About 6 percent of students attending Ticuani's middle school in 2000 were born in the United States. Young men use Ticuani to hide out for months at a time from gang troubles in New York, or they return to seek employment with relatives there to "calm" them, giving them a safe space in which to mature. But members of the Ticuani Youth Group who told me in the early 1990s they wanted to return to Ticuani to do service have not done so. And most returnees intend to stay only for a few weeks, especially once they are in college and working. Linda said her limit for Ticuani lasted about as long as the other New Yorkers were there:

> A week or two weeks, I go, that's it. I can't last a month. . . . This year . . . the Feast finished like February third, so that was the last party and I went to it, and then I had to stay there for three more days, and I was bored. 'Cause there's nobody in the *centro*, everybody's home. And I used to hang out with my cousin, but she had to go home early, . . . at nine, and then I used to hang out in my uncle's pizzeria . . . 'til they closed.

In addition to boredom, Linda notes Ticuani's sanitary conditions, lack of water, and different eating habits as obstacles to longer stays. She described her daily fight with her grandmother over the enormous breakfasts she cooked for Linda. She contrasted the "bagel and coffee" she eats in New York with the "fried beef with tortillas . . . too much food" her grandmother urges her to eat.

PROMESAS:
EMBODIED PRACTICES BRIDGING
TRANSNATIONAL AND GENERATION GAPS

Ticuani offers another powerful ritual that helps second-generation migrants share meaningful experiences with their parents and transnationalize their adolescence: the *promesa*. This is a promise to perform certain acts to demonstrate devotion or gratitude to Padre Jesús or the Virgin Mary for intervention on some issue. *Promesas* usually involve physical acts, like running a race, growing one's hair for a Padre Jesús statue, or walking in a procession. Because they are physical, social, and spiritual at the same time, they offer a particularly rich site for investigating how emotions work and how the self is reformed in social and corporeal processes. I analyze in two steps how *promesas* figure in second-generation transnational life. First, they offer what the sociologist Maren Klawiter calls an "embodied experience" or an "embodied practice": because they involve the body as well as the mind and soul, and repeating the act rekindles the associated feelings. In addition, I refit the neurologist Oliver Sacks's work on physical self-perception to the social realm as "social proprioception" to describe how one jointly experiences one's own body and emotions in relation to other people and to particular places. I also draw on Maurice Merleau-Ponty's insight that we need to see others seeing us in order to experience awareness of our own bodies. Jack Katz illustrates this by pointing out that our perceptions of ourselves in funhouse mirrors only become compelling and viscerally funny when we see others seeing us view our distorted reflection.[17] Merleau-Ponty thus captures the necessarily social dimension to our corporeal experience of emotions and self.[18]

The embodied nature of the *promesa* resonates with advice from Blaise Pascal: "Kneel down, move your lips in prayer, and you will believe."[19] Participating in physical rituals in Ticuani makes second-generation Ticuanenses feel closer to God and enacts their surprising degree of devotion not just to God but specifically to Padre Jesús. Some *promesas,* such as the Antorcha, also require long-term, sustained attention or absence from parents. Hence, *promesas* can both promote an adolescent's feelings of competence and autonomy and foster love of the same traditions the parents learned. Moreover, *promesas* create shared, meaningful experiences that do not require parents and their second-generation teens to explicitly talk about their relationship. It is this shared involvement in the activity that enables each party to experience himself or herself in a deeply authentic way that depends on the other's physical presence. These dynamics are aptly illustrated by the cases of Napoleon, Ceydi, and Jericho.[20] Ceydi described how she and her mother have always had a certain distance in their relationship, resulting partly from their long separations caused by Ceydi's mother's work, until she changed jobs when Ceydi was eight years old.

> Just the other day, my mom, she sat down with me and . . . she just stared. And she says, "You know what I've been thinking lately? . . . That I was never really there for you when you were younger . . . until like age eight years old." She would come home late, like at six o'clock. . . . [Sometimes] she wouldn't even pay attention to us 'cause she would have to cook . . . she would just like eat, sleep, watch some TV, and . . . make us go to sleep like at nine o'clock . . . that's it. . . . I didn't have a bad childhood, but . . . I just had to grow by myself. . . . Like nobody was there . . . to help me do my homework.

This passage, which describes the painful time bind most working parents confront, made me cringe at the prospect that my own sons might feel this way some day. The situation is worse for immigrant or other low-income parents, who have less control over their working hours and must work longer hours because they earn so little.[21] Ceydi's comments provide a backdrop for appreciating the shared experience *promesas* make possible.

Doing a *promesa* enabled Ceydi and her mother to share something important. In a pattern seen with others—which bears out Pascal—Ceydi initially did the *promesa* as a favor for her mother, but was surprised by how

FIGURE 13.   Procession in honor of Padre Jesús, Ticuani, winter 2000.

much she got out of it. She and her mother walked several hours together in a religious procession. She describes her mother's reaction:

CEYDI: Like she was just happy that I was helping her out . . . proud that you follow the religion. . . . [Making my mom happy] brought me satisfaction too. 'Cause it's important to me that you being in like, *que estes bien con tus papas, portado* [that you are okay with your parents].

RS: At the beginning of the interview, talking about how you feel like you grew up a lot by yourself—was this a way of like trying to put those problems behind and like make a link with your mom?

C: That's something that I talk [about] with God—because some people don't realize that we really never had a good relationship because her point of views till this day sometimes conflict with mine. . . . [The *promesa*] was like two forces uniting, you know, to be good with one. . . . It's powerful. It's something you can't explain. . . .

RS: Do you and your mom ever talk about the *promesa*?

C: No. . . . She was just happy with me. She just like smiled.

RS: Like she didn't say much, but you knew by the way she looked at you?

C: I knew, mm hmm.

The *promesa* did not produce an entirely new relationship between Ceydi and her mother. Although Ceydi told me that she only felt "a little bit" closer to her mother, she described her satisfaction at making her mother happy, feeling she was okay with her parents, and continuing in their Ticuani customs. This bonding is unlikely to have occurred in the absence of the *promesa* in which she and her mother could both participate. That they never spoke about it afterward only heightens the importance of this connection having been made in a context where they had a readymade script and a sustained physical task to perform and did not have to verbally negotiate the difficulties of their relationship. Such corporeal, social experiences of bonding with others are powerful and sustaining, as recent work on emotions and participation in social movements has shown.[22] Such rewards offer another reason why transnational life is compelling to many in the second generation.

Ceydi also described at length how doing the *promesa* and being in Ticuani changed her relationship with God. She now feels she is more open to God in Ticuani, that she and God can hear each other better there than in New York. When I asked her if she felt close to God doing the *promesa,* she answered:

CEYDI: It was . . . like, wow, I'm actually doing a *promesa.* . . . You feel very wonderful and emotional inside. . . . It's like a one-on-one encounter with God at the same time. Not everyone, I think, gets the opportunity to do a *promesa* like that. . . .

RS: God hears you better down there?

C: It's easier there. . . . Over there, the whole thing about the church is way stronger. . . . Like just looking at him, Padre Jesús . . . I start to cry. It's hard for me not to cry because I think about . . . people that I've lost . . . that I wish I would've gotten to . . . say the last goodbye. . . . It's just a feeling of . . . things that you cannot talk about to someone else, you could talk to it with God, you could just let it all out.

RS: So . . . there's nothing separating you from God when you're on the *promesa* in Ticuani. . . . And in New York is it like there's stuff between you and God, things get in the way?

C: Things get in the way. . . . Sometimes I think you're so busy that you don't even have time even to think about God. . . . And I'm not justifying that. I don't go to church . . . as often as most people do.

For Ceydi, doing the *promesa* led to a spiritual encounter—her first ever, she told me—which contrasted starkly with her cluttered life in New York. She feels in Ticuani that God really listens to her. Hence returning to Ticuani deepens her relationship not only with her mother but also with God. The *promesas* in Ticuani provide the rituals that allowed these relationships to deepen and to be experienced socially and corporeally in ways that are not normally possible in New York. The busyness of life in New York, the lack of rituals possessing the requisite emotional and spiritual power, and the lack of uncontestedly Mexican geographical and social space all militate against these youths' having a profound experience with the same kind of authentic, Mexican self. Moreover, the depth of feeling these youths report in their *promesas* is compelling. And the ritual of *promesas* offers second-generation returnees concrete ways through which their adolescence, including their relationship with their parents, is made easier and is practiced transnationally.

Both Jericho and Napoleon have done *promesas* "for Padre Jesús" and "for my mom," which have involved running the Antorcha or carrying religious objects in the procession—heavy statues, crosses, and the twenty-pound flowerpots that adorn the altar. In this exchange, Napoleon says first that he thinks in *promesas* "our parents are showing us a way to give back to God."

> I had mad fun doing it, even though the flowerpot was pretty heavy and it was bothering me. . . . It felt good 'cause . . . people look at you like, damn! . . . I can't believe he's carrying that. . . . And you finally take it down . . . you feel relieved, like, yeah, I gave something back to God. . . . I think it would not have looked good if I would've not have carried it . . . what kind of son do you have? So I . . . wanted to show that . . . I'm not just . . . one of those kids who just don't want to do nothing. . . . My uncle [asked], "You want me to carry that for you?" And I'm like, no . . . it's okay, I could carry it by myself. . . . Then my mom looked at me . . . she's like, "You don't need help." I'm like, "No, I don't need help."

Napoleon struggles with the flowerpot but revels in the perception of his physical struggle by others, especially his mother, and their evaluation of his moral competence, even victory, at performing this act for God. Merleau-Ponty could almost have written Napoleon's account himself.

My own reflections on embodied experience and social proprioception reflect my in-between status as a fictive Ticuanense and an American ethnographer. My experience changed over time as I came to feel like, and by many to be seen as, an honorary Ticuanense. When I first ran in the Antorcha, I participated with wide-eyed interest, and everyone vigilantly noted my reactions at each stage. I was hyperaware of being watched, and I felt I had to put on a face that conveyed both curiosity and appreciation of

FIGURE 14. Young men carry the heavy icon of Padre Jesús in the six-hour procession through Ticuani, winter 2000.

the privilege of sharing in these rituals. This feeling changed both over time and in particular situations. During my first long visit for the Feast of Padre Jesús, in 1990, I was asked by a returnee migrant to drive her ailing father in his car behind a particular religious procession for Padrecito. I was glad to help and reciprocate in some way for the many kindnesses the family had shown me, but I had no idea why this procession was such a big deal. I committed the gaffe of referring to the statue of Padre Jesús as *la muñeca grande* (the big doll) instead of *el icón* (the icon), eliciting a smile and then a loud, snorting laugh from my migrant host. But when I was asked ten years later by Don Emiliano to walk with him, carrying a large cross, in the same procession, I knew and felt deeply what an honor I was being given. My sense of belonging came in part from this knowledge but also from the way that people looked at me. I knew that Don Emiliano and I were friends and that I belonged there because he wanted me to be there. And while some faces registered surprise at seeing a gringo in the procession, there were many who smiled quietly or waved at me, knowing exactly why it made sense for me to be there.

Another example involves particular contexts. The Antorcha from Mexico City back to Ticuani takes about thirty-six hours, and it is run in relays. A runner steps off the bus to take the torch, runs a stage of the relay, and awaits pickup by the second bus. The wait, sometimes more than half an hour, can seem long during the wee hours of the night. As I awaited pickup one night, I heard Napoleon yelling ahead of me. A pack of loose dogs from a nearby village were barking and threatening him. I ran to catch up to him, while other friends ran back to meet him. Together we yelled and threw rocks at the marauding dogs, who retreated; we also moved on lest they regroup.

This experience offered a particularly intense, adrenaline-fueled camaraderie that made me a part of this adolescent group in a way that would not otherwise have been possible. I experienced myself as part of the group. After fending off the dogs, Napoleon and I were able to have several long, private talks, ranging across topics from school to love to Ticuani. A series of such dramatic experiences of joint belonging, in combination with more quotidian interactions and conversational interviews, yielded a more intimate emotional context. I seemed to my informants and felt to myself like a person who belonged in and with Ticuanense youth, even if I was not formally one of them.

CONCLUSION

This chapter describes the interaction of religious rituals, adolescent processes, and second-generation contested belonging in New York and Ticuani. Ticuani religious practices provide adolescent rituals for returnees that help them to negotiate their feelings of belonging and alienation in Ticuani, their social locations as ethnic immigrants and racial minorities in New York City, and engagement with New York's segmented assimilation process. The site and practices Ticuani offers help the second generation negotiate key adolescent tasks more easily than they can in New York. These rituals facilitate a less conflictive "second individuation," more teen autonomy, and better parent-teen relations because parents and teens perceive Ticuani as safer than New York and parents can relax some of their rules. The cases of Juana and Toño also demonstrate how return and ritual can help foster positive choices in another key adolescent task, choosing among peer groups. Finally, sharing "embodied practices" such as *promesas* helps immigrant parents and their second-generation children transcend the rifts of education, culture, and other differences that divide them, without the need to speak directly of these divides.

A final lesson of this chapter is that place matters. Ticuani is the site of a more liberated experience of adolescence, of feeling closer to God, of feeling the power and pleasure of cultural and physical possession of a space closely linked to one's dearest identities. Ticuani offers the second generation both a way to live outside their New York limits and a world of possibilities as they become immersed in a social milieu where everyone else also sees themselves as Mexican and all are dedicated to celebrating Padre Jesús. Ticuani has become a sacred site to these adolescents. Their experience of growing up is shaped in part by religious practices. Their relationship with God is an essential part of their experience of being Ticuanense. These considerations help explain why return to Ticuani is so compelling for the second generation, and why and how adolescence has become transnationalized.

8. "I'll Go Back Next Year"

Transnational Life across the Life Course

Over time, I noticed changes in my informants' attitudes toward Ticuani and the frequency of their visits. Meeting Alicia in Ticuani in 1999 as she crowned her successor as Queen of the Mass was quite a surprise, given how much she had hated Ticuani five years earlier. At that time she had told me she was uncomfortable there because her Spanish was not good and she missed eating at McDonald's, though she did enjoy Ticuani parties. Born and raised in Brooklyn, Alicia had gone from disliking even going to Ticuani to seeking and gaining the highest honor it can bestow on a young woman. At the same time, I noticed that Alicia's sister Juana and her Ticuani Youth Group friends were returning to Ticuani less frequently and for shorter periods than they had in the early 1990s: jobs, children, spouses, and other adult responsibilities inhibited their ability to go. And some pioneer migrants, especially women such as Doña Maria, were now returning more frequently and for longer periods and taking their third-generation grandchildren. After retirement they had more freedom to return and had assumed child-care responsibilities for their grandchildren. I noted these changes partly because changes in my own life—getting my first job as a professor and the birth of my children—had also limited my ability to travel. I realized that as I was watching the Ticuanenses and their children grow up and grow older, I was doing so myself.[1]

The common thread in these stories is something that social scientists call the life course. Life-course studies analyze the social meaning of passage through life stages, from birth through childhood, adolescence, young adulthood, adulthood, old age, and death. Some studies focus on how historical events such as war or the Great Depression affect the whole life course, whereas others examine the social causes and effects of specific personal transitions, such as marriage.[2] Here I analyze how life-course transitions affect the practices and meanings of transnational life.[3] First, I tell Alicia's story to illustrate how the passage into adolescence leads some youths to participate more in Ticuani life and to make it a key part of their identity. Second, I use the examples of Juana and the Ticuani Youth Group to analyze how the passage into young and early adulthood changed their participation in transnational life.[4] Third, I examine how the transition of pioneer migrants into retirement and the passing of their children into full adulthood has brought these grandchildren back to Ticuani with their pioneer grandmothers. Examining the effect of life-course changes on transnational life requires assessment of settlement conditions in New York, including the limited incomes and day-care options of many second-generation parents. Finally, I reflect on possibilities for and limits on creating a lasting local-level transnational life.

THE REINA, ADOLESCENCE, AND MEXICAN IDENTITY

Alicia's story illustrates how transnational life evolves over the life course and how this evolution can be bound up with other processes, such as racial and ethnic identity formation. A long line of research, from Erik Erikson in the 1950s and 1960s to Marcelo and Carola Suarez-Orozco today, documents the strong need during adolescence for a secure ethnic identity that also locates one's social position.[5] Ticuani has become a site for adolescent rituals confirming authentic Mexican identity, especially for adolescents who are becoming increasingly aware of the racial and ethnic challenges they face in New York. Ticuani's adolescent rituals provided Alicia a vehicle by which to change from being a "lockdown girl" in New York to being the Queen of the Mass in Ticuani.

After Alicia handed over her crown to her successor in Ticuani in 1999, I interviewed her at home in Brooklyn. When asked why she did not like Mexico before, she said she was a "lockdown girl" there before becoming the Reina. She could go out only with her older sister, who would not take her because she felt Alicia was too young to go to parties. Being old enough to become Reina meant she could attend key adolescent social functions that Ticuani provides in abundance.

> RS: So when you were thirteen—at your sister's interview—you didn't like Mexico?
>
> ALICIA: I guess because I was younger, I was more with my parents. My sister didn't want me out [with her] because she was older, and I really had to be stuck there with my parents. And

I guess once I got older, like she started taking me out, and I
started going to Mexican parties, and it was fun. . . . [And] I
didn't like the food, the hot foods. My mother don't usually
cook Mexican food because me and my sister would hardly
eat it. But now, I guess we learned more. We're older. . . .

RS: Before you were the Reina and you went to Mexican parties,
how did you feel?

A: I was bored. . . . And then my sister was teaching me to dance
cumbia, so that also changed.

Being invited to compete and then being chosen as Reina was "a big thing"
for Alicia. She had seen her cousin compete and "loved the idea" of being
Reina because all the Ticuanenses in Ticuani and New York know who the
Reina is. It allowed her to socialize with the girls from Ticuani and become
more involved in events there. She recalled that it was the "tenth anniver-
sary [of the pageant] and they wanted girls from New York to compete. But
there was a problem . . . so it was only me and my cousin from New York"
and ten girls from Ticuani. Her recollections show how her participation
made her feel more Ticuanense and gave her a place there but also raised
issues of how "New York" she felt there. She felt honored to compete to be
the Reina but also something of an outsider:

I remember once my cousin . . . competed for it. I always wanted to
[also]. . . . So when they told me [I was invited to participate], I was
like, "Yeah." . . . It was real fun because we're from here and we got
to socialize more with girls from over there. So, we got to know
them. . . . I wanted to know what it felt like to be in a little pageant,
and just to have fun. I didn't really go to win, 'cause, you know, the
girls from over there had more rights to win than we did. 'Cause we
were born here. . . . They're more involved with Ticuani than we are.
We live here, [so] any activity that [we] would have to be invited [to],
it's hard for us to go because I had school. And they were born over
there.

While she says that the local girls had "more rights" to be Reina because
they are from Ticuani, later she also says she is "just as" Ticuanense as they
are, but "also New York." She went on in the interview to describe what
being Reina meant, linking it with her growing up.

RS: What did it mean to you to be Reina?

A: It meant a lot. I was born here and then to have the chance to be
Reina—it's big. . . . I got to meet more people. . . . I think that
kinda changed the way I am. Before I was way shy. . . . [Being the
Reina,] I got more involved with the girls and . . . It's something I

wanted to do when I was younger. Everyone knows who the Reina is. Every year they come back—

RS: Did you think what would it be like to have everyone think, "Alicia is the Reina"?

A: Yeah, it was fun. I loved the idea. . . .

RS: And do you feel like part of this was like a way of growing up or something?

A: Yeah, I think it was. . . . It changed . . . who I was. . . . I used to hate being shy. . . . [Being Reina,] I realized where I came from, that I loved being Mexican. That I was proud. . . . [Before] I wasn't really into it, as I am now. I was younger. . . . Back then I didn't like going to Mexican parties, and over there you like feel the music, you know? . . . You just get there and you're happy to be there, and it's just a good feeling to feel. I mean, that's where your parents are born, that's who you are.

RS: Do you feel like there's no other place where you're as much yourself as when you're there?

A: No, . . . 'cause when you're over there, it's not like being here. Here you have to rush . . . your routine. . . . Over there, you're on vacation. That's where you're from. . . . Over there, to whoever, you probably don't know them and you could say good morning, *buenas noches, buenas tardes.* . . . And here, you talk to a stranger, it's like you're gonna do something to them. Here I don't have time to go to church. Over there . . . you get there, you feel everything. You feel closer to God. You feel more Mexican. . . . [My parents] were proud to know I was born here and that I didn't really like Mexico, and then to say I wanted to be the Reina and then, you know [be chosen]—I remember my mother, that the next day she wanted to go tell my grandfather. And he was proud.

Alicia's experience of being the Reina eased her passage into and through adolescence. It helped her to overcome her shyness and fear of being rejected, enabling her to be more social in Ticuani and New York. Afterward she enjoyed going to Mexican parties in New York, which had "bored" her before. These changes were steps in becoming an adolescent. Her Ticuani coming-of-age narrative is reinforced by the positive response from her family. The pride expressed by her mother and her grandfather make her feel more authentically Mexican. This pride and recognition also led to greater adult privileges. After she was crowned Reina, her parents did not give her a curfew in Ticuani, and they allowed her to go out without her sister in New York. Hence, Ticuani's adolescent rituals, especially the

Reina pageant, became important parts of Alicia's adolescent experience and narrative. Ticuani pulled her into its adolescent rituals, fostering a more intimate link with Mexico and ushering her from a shy, preteen existence into a more socially active adolescent one.

THE TICUANI YOUTH GROUP

If Alicia's passage through adolescence made Ticuani more important to her, the passage into early adulthood for her older sister Juana and other members of the Ticuani Youth Group had more complicated effects. Scholars such as Frank Furstenberg and Jeffrey Arnett have identified a new phase in the life course: "early adulthood," usually placed at ages eighteen to twenty-five and distinguished from adolescence and from full adulthood. Early adults typically have achieved some of the milestones of adulthood, such as finishing their education, living independently from their parents, and working full-time, but not others, such as marrying and having children. Although some members of the Ticuani Youth Group move more quickly through early adulthood than others, their entry into that phase of life set off changes in how they relate to Ticuani and transnational life. We can think of the Youth Group as an adolescent invention that endured but changed irrevocably in early adulthood. This point becomes clearer from an examination of the Youth Group's history.

Juana and her friends thought of the Ticuani Youth Group as their version of the adult men's Ticuani Solidarity Committee. During its heyday in the early 1990s, the Youth Group raised money for public works in Ticuani. Its members spoke openly and enthusiastically about their dreams of going back to Ticuani to work. Carolina, for example, was studying nursing and dreamed of going back to work on public-health projects; Juana dreamed in a similarly public-spirited though less specific way. The Youth Group was their attempt to form a second-generation transnational institution. They ultimately failed to realize their larger dream, mainly because early adulthood changed their priorities. But the group did support the establishment of long-term connections to Ticuani and helped cement primary friendships, with return to Ticuani a key shared activity.

The Youth Group became part of its members' coming-of-age story and helped them with two kinds of assimilation work as they moved from adolescence into early adulthood. It first did "racialization work" in helping them differentiate themselves from Blacks and Puerto Ricans. Relatedly, it did "generational work" by showing their parents that they were keeping the immigrant bargain and justifying by their own success the parents' sac-

rifice in leaving home. To the Youth Group, this bargain meant being successful in work and school, keeping up Ticuani and family customs, and
demonstrating that they were not like other Mexicans who were choosing
"the wrong path." They also engaged with racialization when they attempted to create, through such events as sports tournaments and parties,
safe Mexican spaces in which second-generation Mexicans could learn
Mexican ways, in contrast to what they saw as the unsafe spaces and ways
of Puerto Ricans and Blacks. Youth Group members showed their devotion
to Padre Jesús and Ticuani by raising almost twenty thousand dollars between 1991 and 1993 for fixing a chapel dedicated to Padre Jesús and for the
kindergarten in Ticuani. Abraham described the group's purpose to me in a
1997 interview in New York:

> More than anything, the group was to try to support the pueblo [Ti-
> cuani]. By contributing a little bit, so that the older people would no-
> tice that we young people had our eyes open. That we wanted to do
> something for our pueblo. That we had desire. Because we are all Ti-
> cuani citizens, it does not matter if you were born here. (Spanish,
> translated by the author)

Youth Group members went farther educationally and professionally than
most of their peers, all either continuing with their education—many earning associate's degrees, some bachelor's degrees, and one a master's degree—or doing well at work, some opening their own businesses. Such success became important during the later 1990s, when the fates of increasing
numbers of Mexicans looked bleaker than they had before. Juana explained
her rationale for belonging to the group in terms that resonate with the
immigrant bargain and with distancing herself from her less successful
counterparts:

> You're young, you can do it; you should take advantage of this . . .
> your parents worked so hard, why should you go in the wrong
> path? . . . A lot [of] . . . our generation, instead of taking . . . educa-
> tion—[they] get married, have kids, and stop going to school. And it's
> the same circle over and over, and we're never gonna get out of
> that . . . we haven't probably gotten to where we wish we were, but
> we've gone a lot further . . . and I think we should be proud. . . . We all
> have decent jobs, we all work—comfortably . . . not in factories like
> our parents . . . we can travel. . . . That's what they wanted . . . what
> they worked so hard for, so we wouldn't do the same thing. . . . I did
> okay.

Later in the same interview, I asked Juana and Eliana (Mia's sister, another
daughter of Don Emiliano and Doña Selena) what the immigrant bargain
represented for them; what was their understanding of the "deal" with

their parents? Juana answered, about her parents: "I guess they've never asked anything from us. But just to go to school, you know, and that was it. . . . Like my mother used to tell me, 'Finish school, get yourself something that, whatever happens to you, you'll be able to take care of yourself, to get a job. Then after that, you could marry.'" Eliana described it more simply: "To get an education for us. To be able to survive." These are apt descriptions of how Youth Group members fulfilled various aspects of the immigrant bargain. The group helped them to achieve their educational goals and created a context in which they could talk explicitly about upward mobility and link it with their parents' sacrifice. Through it they could prove that they had taken the right path.[6] Membership in the group also showed that they had not lost their essential *ticuanensidad*, because they also worked and sacrificed for the pueblo and revered Padre Jesús, whom they credited with the group's successes.

The Shrinking of the Ticuani Youth Group: The View from 2002

Ten years later, the Youth Group has not become the enduring transnational institution some had hoped. Although its members will not say it is actually dead, they have not organized an event in years and are too busy to revive it. Members and their contemporaries return less frequently to Ticuani now, making a trip every several years instead of one or more per year, as before. Yet they still participate in transnational life, and the group plays a role in it. And the cohort, or "class" of teens, coming behind them have also begun to enter into a transnationalized adolescence, for the same reasons.

Why and how did the Ticuani Youth Group lose steam? One reason its members give was the relationship with the men's Committee, which wanted the group to function as a Committee auxiliary, under its authority. For example, the group balked when the Committee asked them to do a census of all Ticuanenses in New York, which they felt "had nothing to do with anything!" They felt the Committee members did not understand the time constraints they faced as youths who "had their own business or were in the university or had a profession." They also believed people would treat them badly when they went to their houses seeking information, according to Abraham. Another fear, especially keen among the teen migrants, or "-1.5ers," who were born in the United States but grew up partly in Ticuani, was that working with the Committee would involve them in what they saw as Ticuani's corrupt, undemocratic, and violent politics. With their futures looking bright in the United States, why enter into that? Speaking before the 1998 election (which broke the tight link between the *municipio* and the Committee), a Youth Group member described how he thought the Committee and the municipal authorities were "working together" and the problems this created for cooperation with the group:

> They collect the cooperations here and send the money there. . . . What they do, only they know. They . . . never include anyone, including the people in Ticuani. . . . We want democracy on a world level, and in Ticuani . . . there is no vote. . . . Five or six people decide who will be president. . . . We would not work . . . with the president of Ticuani. We were definitely apart . . . neutral. . . . With no one. (Spanish, translated by the author)

Group members distinguished between their unwillingness to work with the Committee and *municipio* and their eagerness to work for the pueblo "very independently."

Group members also saw the Committee as "very *machista*." They contrasted the progressive structure of their organization with the macho structure of the Committee—all men, with the same president throughout its history. They also saw the departure of Marla Lanita—the only woman to serve in a responsible position on the Committee, as treasurer—as a macho expulsion of a woman who had tried to be independent, though she herself refuses to characterize it this way. Several members of the group described their relations with the Committee in a 2001 interview:

> They're older men and they think different. . . . Don Manuel, he didn't think we were capable. It [the Committee] was mostly men, and we [the group] were mostly women. . . . They were always opposing our ideas. Marla Lanita—they pushed her out because she was a woman. *Ellos son muy poco liberal.* [They are not very liberal.] Don Manuel didn't even let Eliana [the Youth Group's female president] finish her sentences! . . . Yeah, he would finish her sentences! . . . We had too much respect. But my father woulda smacked me for disrespecting an older man. The Committee is very *machista*. . . . We had a woman and a man president. . . . We all had very strong attitudes. . . . But *no dejamos dominar por el hombre* [we did not let the men dominate].

The group also fell victim to life-course changes as its members grew older and became weighed down by adult responsibilities. It was formed when most of its members were in or just out of college, in their late teens to mid-twenties. Most have since married and had children; a number have jobs with inflexible hours and demanding time commitments. These changes have focused their lives more on marriage, raising children, and working in New York. In 2001, group members described the group's loss of momentum this way:

> At first, every Saturday or Sunday we had meetings, and we'd plan
> events for the summer. For two years. Then the group started to disin-
> tegrate. Two people married outside Ticuani. . . . It was harder to get
> together than when we were all single. . . . Gradually, less people came
> to the meetings. . . . We all said, even when we get married and have
> children, we won't stop coming. . . . But people started leaving the
> group. Ana married someone from another pueblo, and since you
> usually follow your husband's group, they were gone.

These problems reflect conflicts between the elements of adolescent transnational life and those of adulthood, settlement, and assimilation. The as-
pirations, lack of time, and autonomous ambition in the second generation
that enabled them to keep the immigrant bargain with their parents con-
flicted with the demands of their previous level of transnational activity.
The New York Committee has not institutionalized and reproduced itself
across generations; it has neither drawn large numbers of the second generation in nor worked out other ways to cooperate with them. And the New
York focus of Youth Group members makes Ticuani less central in their
imagination of their futures. Most are coming to see it as a place mainly for
vacation and ethnic renewal.

The changing gender bargains in the second generation limit the extent
to which the Committee can serve as a model for the Youth Group. While
most of the first-generation wives of Committee members work, most also
take nearly complete responsibility for domestic duties, freeing up the men
to do Ticuani public service. But most second-generation women have
renegotiated this division of labor, and many second-generation men want
change too, with the result that most are unwilling to sacrifice as much
time for Ticuani as their parents did. The women, in particular, do not feel
that they also serve by staying home and waiting. Neither is honor among
Ticuanenses as powerful a motivation for many in the second generation,
because Ticuani itself occupies so much less of their imagined future.
Hence, assimilation and transnationalization can work in complementary
ways, as shown by the greater interest and ability of upwardly mobile
second-generationers to participate in transnational life, but they can also
conflict, with the goal of upward mobility allowing this group less time and
inclination for transnational life.

Lasting Effects of the Ticuani Youth Group and Other Second-Generation Return

That adult obligations consume much of the time formerly dedicated to the
Youth Group does not prevent its former members from participating in

transnational life in other ways. Many second-generationers who are now married, with children and jobs, still return to Ticuani to experience the closeness to God, to see their relatives, and for special events, such as baptizing a child. The devotion to Padre Jesús that emerges in adolescence among many persists into young adulthood. Eliana, who endured a very difficult pregnancy, had promised Padre Jesús that she would baptize her child in Ticuani if he was healthy. She described her experience:

> I made a promise to Padre Jesús that if everything would be fine, I would do Xavier's christening again [in Ticuani]. . . . Also, when we come back here we feel a lot closer to God . . . the first thing you do when you come, you thank God that you're here. It's just—like going to church in New York is a lot different. . . . I was concerned that maybe Xavier would be disabled, because that was one of the risks [of the medications]. The doctor . . . even suggested . . . an abortion. . . . I was like, I'm gonna have the baby, and I'm just gonna pray to Padrecito, and hopefully everything will be fine. And that's when I promised that I would bring Xavier [to Ticuani].

When she was blessed with a healthy child, the entire family and many friends traveled to Ticuani for Xavier's baptism. Although a baptism is not an event that recurs, as was Eliana's adolescent return, it helped cement her own and her son's and her family's links with Ticuani.

Many friendships that developed in the Youth Group have remained central to the friends' lives. This is partly due to the intensity of the experiences the members shared in Ticuani and partly because they shared them as teenagers, when such identity-affirming friendships become especially compelling. Juana observes: "I got really good friendships out of it. These are still my main friends. Carolina's mother called me her *mugre*. . . . I see her [Carolina] almost every day." Their friendship was characterized by activities suggesting a close extended family: "I mean, we see them, like if we're ready to go out, we'll see them, or like I said, when they cook [a meal for everyone] in their house, we'll see them, or when there's a birthday, we all get together. We still pass Christmas together. Yeah, over Christmas, we all get together, and stuff like that." Calling Juana Carolina's *mugre* was a gentle way of teasing her about how close the friends were; *mugre* is the Spanish word for the dirt under one's fingernails. This emergence of primary, enduring friendship groups has been seen, with similar dynamics, in studies of the effects of Jewish and Protestant religious camps and programs on the enduring importance of religion and ethnicity in participants' lives, and anecdotally in the effects of Jewish summer camps in the Catskills.[7]

Ticuani also offers young adults the chance to see friends they do not see often in New York because their lives are now so busy. Young adults can return each year to Ticuani and know they will find friends; they may even have a small reunion. Now twenty-six years old, employed full-time, and living with her boyfriend, Juana described her feelings about Ticuani after a three-year absence in a 2001 interview there: "It means a lot . . . to come back. . . . For three years, I used to see all my people come back, and I would stay [in New York], and that felt horrible. But now, I'm ecstatic. That night that I flew here, I didn't want to stop [in] Puebla [or] Mexico [City]. I came straight from the airport." Juana did not have these intense emotional attachments to Ticuani and Mexican friends as a child but rather formed them by participation in Ticuani's adolescent rituals and the Ticuani Youth Group.

Young adult returnees play important roles in the adolescent rituals of their younger relatives who return to Ticuani. Carolina teaches local girls who wish to participate in Ticuani's beauty pageant to walk in the appropriate way, put on their makeup, and speak in public, offering an older New York woman's reassurance. Single men and women return to Ticuani to meet prospective mates. And most returnees derive great satisfaction from participating in the religious and civic rituals and ceremonies for Padrecito.

RETIREMENT AND THE TRANSNATIONALIZATION OF CHILD CARE

Just as adult responsibilities have affected early adults' relationships with Ticuani, older people find that their changing situations, and those of their grown children, have altered their transnational life. These circumstances in turn create the transnational life of the third generation. Retired pioneer women in New York become the primary caregivers for their U.S.-born grandchildren and bring them back to Ticuani for extended periods. Some pioneer migrants retire to live in Ticuani, and their second-generation children leave the grandchildren with them for periods of time. The links between these three generations are forged both in the conditions of life in New York and the evolving links with Ticuani and Mexico, partly determined by migrants' movement through the life course.

During the 1990s, many pioneer migrant women retired with small pensions from the garment workers' union or other unions to which they had belonged, and, as naturalized U.S. citizens, began receiving Social Security or Supplemental Security Income. Like Doña Maria, Doña Florencia is retired and cares for her grandchildren full-time while her adult children spend long hours at work and study. Often, second-generation adult children take over a cheap apartment lease the pioneer parents have held for many years, or the two generations purchase a home together. Having grandparents take care of the children enables the family to save on child-care expenses. Moreover, parents feel that their children are safer and better taken care of by their own parents than by strangers in institutional day care.[8] And since grandmothers are thereby relieved of the need to spend much of their limited income on rent, they can afford to travel to Ticuani more often.

This arrangement supports evolving relationships with Ticuani that are also driven by the first generation's life-course changes. Many of these retired pioneers spend a couple of months at a time in Ticuani, especially in the winter, when they and their grandchildren would be stuck indoors in New York. Moreover, many of them have inherited houses in Ticuani from their deceased parents or other relatives, and hence must return to Ticuani to maintain the property, which they see as vital to their future security. Doña Florencia inherited a house that she says she keeps for her children and herself. She now has a tenant who lives in an outbuilding on the property, keeps an eye on things, and turns the light on for her when she comes to Ticuani. In an interview in New York, she told me why she goes back despite no longer having relatives in Ticuani:

> This is your own property. We are not going to sell it. . . . Having all the children there, one goes to relax a little, one in one's own house. Here, the weather does me harm—asthma—and I go to my house [in Ticuani]. And there one does not pay rent. . . . It is not just for me, but rather that all my children go to rest . . . in August, in January, well, they have somewhere to go, their house. (Spanish, translated by the author)

Doña Florencia sees owning a house—her "own property"—as giving emotional security, a good vacation spot, and also, she later commented, refuge from the uncertain environment in the United States. This conversation took place in 1997, the year after Congress had greatly restricted immigrants' access to a variety of services and benefits, including Social Security, unemployment insurance, and Supplemental Security Income. As a result, Doña Florencia told me, she was applying for U.S. citizenship, because "I am not going to let them take that Social Security away from me."[9] She saw her house in Ticuani as a safety net: if she became unable to survive in New York, she would move back to Ticuani. She also enjoys enhanced status by living in her Ticuani house without paying rent. Eco-

nomically successful families in New York often build huge houses in Ticuani not only so that returning grandparents and their third-generation
charges can live in a more spacious and less stressful environment than in
New York, but to provide tangible proof of their hard work and virtue in
New York.

In New York, Doña Maria lives with her daughter and son-in-law, who
entrust her with the care of their five children, aged five to fourteen (in
2001). Both parents leave for work very early and get back after dinner. She
described their schedules this way:

> He leaves . . . at five in the morning. . . . The mother leaves at seven-
> thirty. . . . The whole day . . . they are with me, the kids. And I take
> care of them . . . I get them up and ready and fed, and they don't want
> to go, but . . . they go to school. . . . At three the little one finishes and
> the big ones come, and they are with me all afternoon. And I give
> them something to eat, if there is anything. (Spanish, translated by
> the author)

Commenting on taking the children to Ticuani, she notes that the fourteen-year-old wants to have her *quinceñera*, or "sweet fifteen" party, there:

> DOÑA MARIA: [The five-year-old] has come four or five times [to
> Ticuani]. . . . She was two months the first time I
> brought her; she was really little. I brought her bottle,
> her medicine, her carrier, and her stroller. . . .
>
> RS: How are you teaching them the customs of here? . . .
>
> DM: I explain to them all the customs, and the food . . . and
> they eat. I teach them how to make the sauce, how to
> use *chile*, but only a little. Not too rich, but they eat
> their *tapas*, their tacos. . . . And [the big ones,] they
> went on the Antorcha. . . . For this, they come too be-
> cause they like the pueblo, the Feast, the customs. And
> [the fourteen-year-old] told me, "I want to marry a
> Ticuanense." . . . She is going to celebrate her *quin-
> ceñera* party here. (Spanish, translated by the author)

Doña Maria spends a month or two in Ticuani during the winter and two
months in the summer. She finds life easier and better for her and the
grandchildren in Ticuani, commenting that in New York the children are
closed up in the house ("the poor things" from chapter 7), while in Ticuani
they can run around freely. Moreover, in New York, the family lives in a
small apartment in a walk-up building down the street from the elementary school the children attend. The apartment's four rooms are not enough
for eight people, though they are always full of the good smells of Doña

Maria's cooking and the noise of the children's play or the (too-loud) television. In Mexico, they live in two houses—Doña Maria's own house, which she inherited from her parents, and the new house her daughter and son-in-law have built next door. Her house is a now-standard construction, a one-floor cinderblock house with four large rooms laid out in an L shape. It has a large yard, about thirty by seventy yards, where chickens, pigs, and other animals range and in which the children are free to run, dig, and otherwise enjoy themselves or to take naps in the hammock strung under the large tree in the middle of the yard. Outside their house is a walking path that leads in one direction to the church and in the other to the zocalo. There is no traffic. The new house, which sits only a few yards from hers in the same yard, is a state-of-the-art returning migrant house. It has two floors, a pitched roof (unlike the old cinderblock houses), and darkened glass windows on the upper floors to keep out the heat.[10] The children have three or four bedrooms to themselves instead of one bedroom and the living room, as in New York, and there is a large kitchen with modern appliances and an adult sitting room with sliding glass doors that open into the yard. Air conditioning is planned.

Doña Maria also described how the children learn about Ticuani customs and religious practices, such as devotions to Padre Jesús and the Antorcha. I saw them participate in a variety of religious processions and Masses, as well as attend secular activities, such as the dances and the rodeo, and the amusements (such as video games, carnival rides, and table soccer) that come to town during the Feast. In my conversations with them, they seemed to be thoroughly acquainted with and eager to participate in all these activities.

Although it is most common for grandmothers to bring preschoolers to Ticuani, older children also visit. Doña Monica's oldest grandchild, Nestor, a high school senior in New York, brought his seventeen-year-old girlfriend to live with his family for two and a half months in Ticuani in the middle of his senior year. Interestingly, they were treated not as errant teens but rather as a young couple. The girlfriend's mother approved of the trip, and Doña Monica spoke of Nestor and Marlena, who was Puerto Rican, as if they were already married and Marlena was part of the family. The couple, who had been together for three years at that point, participated in many Ticuani rituals together, and she was warmly received.

Bringing grandchildren to Ticuani for long periods of time results directly from the converging life-course changes of the first-generation pioneers and their second-generation children. The latter need time to work and study and hence need help in taking care of their children. The former

FIGURE 15.   Luxurious two-story house, Ticuani, 2004. Note the images of Jesus and Mary in the second-story windows.

have the time to travel and the freedom to live in a place that offers them and their grandchildren more freedom and safety than they have in New York.

Some third-generation children spend longer periods in Ticuani with resident grandparents or other relatives. Xavier, the five-year-old son of Youth Group members Eliana and Lazaro and the grandson of Don Emiliano and Doña Selena, is one of these. After Eliana's hard pregnancy, Xavier had some health problems. Even after these cleared up, he was seen to be "too skinny" and was sent to live for several months with his grandparents in Ticuani to "fatten him up" on a Mexican diet. They believed eating more meat would strengthen him. Since then he has visited Ticuani at least once a year, and he sometimes goes with an aunt but without his parents. Second-generation parents may send their children on extended visits for a variety of reasons: to improve their health, to teach them Mexican and Ticuani culture, to keep a *promesa* to Padre Jesús, or to enable a parent to finish schooling in New York. Parents are most likely to send children on long visits if they lived in Ticuani for a time during their own youth.[11]

The conversation below shows how Ticuani has become a regular, normal part of Xavier's experience.

ELIANA: I told him, "Xavier, we're going to Mexico *para el 25 de enero* [for the twenty-fifth of January]," and he's jumping like, "Oh, Mommy, I want to go *a la procesión* [in the procession]—I wanna dance *como los Tecuanis* [like the Tecuanis]." . . . He's following our culture—that's another, a new generation. Hopefully he'll get to come when he's older. . . . That's my hope, but . . . I'm gonna let Xavier live his life. . . . Of course, I will always lead him to the right stuff. . . .

RS: Twenty years from now, what do you want his life to be, in relation to this place?

E: I want him to be educated, have a good degree, a good career. . . . To Ticuani—to keep our traditions, to do something for his pueblo—not his pueblo, but his family's pueblo. . . . He's growing up with that idea that ever since he was born, he's been coming to Ticuani, especially for the *fiesta de Padre Jesús*. . . . He loves it, he lives it. Do you know how many times he watches his christening? He's like, "Wow, Mami, that was in Ticuani, with Padre Jesús," and you know, he's really happy about that. Yeah, he remembers.

RS: And how often does he watch the tape?

E: Every weekend, two times. . . . He loves it, he just loves it. . . . One thing that he must do, on the twenty-fifth, he must come with me on the procession and walk all the way to the church. . . . He knows that's one of the main things we came here for.

That Xavier walks in the procession extends his mother's promise to Padre Jesús during her difficult pregnancy. This procession is a six-hour walk at night through and around the town, with many people carrying heavy candles, crosses, or other objects of worship. The men take turns carrying the heavy icon of Padre Jesús on his throne, encased in glass. I have twice walked in this procession with Xavier, Eliana, and their family, and he does indeed seem to be excited about and devoted to Padre Jesús. (I carried him on my back for part of the procession not because he complained, but because I missed my own son.) He also talks about Padre Jesús in New York. For him, spending time in Ticuani is as natural as it is for any small child to visit his grandparents and other relatives. It seems likely that for Xavier and others like him, Ticuani will always be a second home. Even if he does not continue to go, Ticuani has already strongly influenced how he thinks of himself and about what being Mexican means. If he does return regularly, Ticuanense transnational life may persist into the fourth generation.

Victoria, Eliana's sister, has embarked on another transnational child-rearing strategy quite similar to the one her own parents used. She has left her two young children with her parents in Ticuani while she finishes her master's degree in New York. As things were, she could not make enough money to pay for both day care and her schooling, leaving her the painful choice between finishing her degree and keeping her children with her. She felt a great deal of pressure from her family to finish the degree, as it would be a symbol of the family's success. Indeed, Don Emiliano expressed disappointment that she had had children before finishing her degree, even confessing in one extreme moment that he felt his daughter had betrayed and made fools of her parents by doing this. Her parents' offer to take care of the children and their emotional investment in her success, combined with her own desire to finish the degree and her exhaustion at trying to do it all, convinced her to leave her two children in Ticuani until she finished.

CONTEXTS FOR COMPARISON

These stories document how three life-course transitions—from childhood to adolescence, from adolescence to early adulthood, and from middle age to retirement—affect transnational life. Return to Ticuani and participation in its rituals have different meaning at different stages in life. Many children use Ticuani and its safe space and rituals to help them forge a positive Mexican identity in adolescence. As adolescents pass into adulthood, they participate less actively in transnational life, both because they have settled many of the adolescent identity questions that animated their earlier participation and because of the demands of jobs and children. Yet most still return to Ticuani and maintain the close friendships forged through Ticuani. And as pioneer migrants, especially women, retire, they are free to spend more time in Ticuani and often bring along the third generation, for whom they are primary caregivers. In Ticuani the children enjoy more open space and freedom, and they learn Ticuani religious and civic customs, including the devotion to Padrecito that can persist through life. Ticuani is not just a family story passed down through generations, as are so many Americans' links with their ancestral lands, but rather a lived experience.

I raise two questions to provide comparative context, to which I will return in the book's conclusion. The first concerns enduring effects of participation in transnational life. I have documented some effects over the course of fifteen years, but longer-term effects are probable. One source of comparison is the Jewish summer camps that brought up to a million Jewish children from the New York area into the Catskills each summer from the postwar period to the early 1970s, as documented by the sociologist Phil Brown.[12] Another is the National Conference of Synagogue Youth (NCSY), created by the Union of Orthodox Jewish Congregations in America in 1959 as a way of stemming the exodus of young people from Orthodox Judaism. According to my former Barnard College colleague, the late Nathalie Friedman, the techniques and practices of this organization included youth camps in Israel, weekend-long observations of the Sabbath called *shabbaton*, and organized prayer meetings. Special efforts focused on the high school and college years, which were seen as "make or break" years for shaping Jewish identity and practice. Results of the NCSY efforts included increased religious observance in adulthood and marriage between observant Jews.[13] The long-term effect of the *shabbaton* was heightened, especially for those attending public schools, by the high level of activity,[14] the company of friends, and opportunity to move into leadership positions working with younger adolescents.

Similarly, those reflecting on their Catskills experiences report that their annual summer-camp experience there was an important part of their journey into young adulthood. Former camper Alan Stamm relates how his time in the Catskills camps affected him and his generation:

> Without articulating it, we took meaningful steps . . . toward discovering what we enjoyed, what we did well, who we were, what we might like to be when we grew up. We got to test ourselves in the security and relative freedom of an alternative world without homework, music lessons, assigned reading . . . and other strictures. . . . But we'd carry the values—honesty, respect, teamwork, love of family—that were reinforced as we put on musicals, competed in color wars, listened to Sholem Alecheim morality tales and learned lifelong lessons. We value our camp months as a clear, dramatic transition time from adolescence to young adulthood and who we have become now. More than school, the concentrated and intense eight-week crucible was the first place we thrived, explored, experimented and maybe rebelled a tiny bit outside the nest. Such a bargain our folks got for the price.[15]

This quote evokes the continuing emotional importance of the writer's Catskills experiences in middle age and beyond and captures the same notions of belonging and adolescent transition expressed by second-generation Ticuanenses. The summer camps and NCSY experiences resonate with those of returning children of Ticuanense migrants. The eight-week camp sessions correspond roughly to the annual sojourn of many returning Ticuanense youths. Ticuanense youths also participate in an intense set of rituals, religious and communal, with returning friends. Judg-

ing by the NCSY data, the company of friends should make more enduring the influence of Ticuani on their identity. The metaphor of a "crucible"
that helped shape the writer's transition from adolescence to adulthood is
an apt one and is perfectly pitched to my argument. The extent to which
the returnees enjoy the Antorcha and related events is evidence that something important is happening, and, by the participants' own reckoning, it
involves their coming of age as Mexicans both in New York and, in key
ways, in Ticuani.

Comparing (not equating) these Jewish and Ticuani experiences is instructive. While I doubt that the New York area will ever send a million
teenagers back to Mexico every summer, with more than twenty million
Mexicans and Mexican Americans in the United States, it seems quite
likely that at least a million Mexicans go back to their own or their parents'
communities of origin every year or two. Even assuming that Ticuani exerts a stronger influence than most, such return must affect identity and
promote some transnational practices. A growing literature documents
similar transnational practices by migrants from most migrant *municipios*
in Mexico. With more than 600 hometown associations registered with the
Mexican government in the late 1990s—prima facie evidence of transnational activity—and about 2,200 *municipios* in all of Mexico (some of
which have more than one hometown association), transnational life seems
widespread. Although it probably does not include all migrants, that it includes many in the second generation seems hard to dispute. Moreover,
given that the transnationally active tend to also be most active in public
life in the United States—in politics, business, and even gangs—even limited participation can have significant effects. In New York City, for example, there were more than 300,000 Mexicans in 2000, over half of whom
were under age twenty-five. Taking a pessimistic view, even if only 5 percent are transnationally active, that means 7,500 youths. And the likelihood is that more than 20 percent of second-generation Ticuanenses participate in transnational life, and perhaps more.

A second issue is whether transnational life itself persists over time and
generations. The failure to institutionalize the Ticuani Youth Group reflects
the second generation's imagination of their futures mainly in New York
and not in Ticuani, the demands of their assimilated lives in New York,
and the Committee's failure to involve younger people. Hence settlement
and transnationalization often work at cross-purposes among young
adults, though they reinforce each other among adolescents. Yet the issue
is complex, and the forms and functions of transnational life vary by contexts of reception, the quality and frequency of transnational life, and his-

torical epoch. The sociologist Cecilia Menjívar argues that obstacles to movement, poverty, and being indigenous result in few return visits by second-generation Guatemalans in the United States. As a consequence, the chances are greatly reduced that they will maintain ties to their parents' home country.[16] When I compared local-level Swedish transnational life from the 1850s to the 1930s with that of Ticuani today, I found that second-generation Swedes lived more "Swedish" lives—speaking Swedish in school and in public, marrying other Swedes, and living in mainly Swedish communities—than Ticuanenses in New York live "Mexican" lives.[17] But second-generation Swedes had almost no transnational activity (such as travel to the home country or sending remittances) even when their parents did, whereas second-generation Ticuanenses had transnational activity their Swedish counterparts could not have imagined. Similarly, a study of Italian migrants shows a great deal of second-generation immersion in Italian enclaves in the United States, and a great deal of first-generation return to Italy, but not a great deal of documented second-generation return or other active transnational life.[18]

Other cases, less well known, show important second- and later-generation transnational life. Prior to World War I, Polish migrants pursued exile politics, with Nationalist, Communist, civil, and even religious organizations lobbying to have the international community restore Poland's territory and sovereignty. During World War I, Polish nationalist organizations intensified this lobbying campaign. Poles in the United States even organized the Polish "Kosciusko Army" on American soil (but under French auspices), for which some 38,000 U.S.-born Polish Americans volunteered and some 22,000 served (out of a total force of 90,000 in the Polish army). These Polish Americans accounted for half of Poland's casualties in the war, and many others later fought in the Polish-Soviet war of 1920.[19] That Polish Americans volunteered to fight and die for Poland in such numbers shows the importance of second- and later-generation diasporic links.[20] Similarly, during the 1990s, second- or later-generation children of immigrants have returned from the United States to the Balkans to fight in its wars and to former Soviet states such as Estonia to participate in its politics.[21]

CONCLUSION

Forms of transnational involvement change with the life course, attenuating and intensifying at different stages. Among Ticuanenses, the prospects for third-generation transnational life are still uncertain. The extent to which it will continue to matter to individuals will depend on many factors, including level of outmigration from places like Ticuani, relative levels of development in the home and host countries, the extent to which the Mexican government and Mexican American organizations create diasporic links with the Mexican American population, and the reaction of the United States government and others to such links.

9. Defending Your Name

The Roots and Transnationalization of Mexican Gangs

When I returned to Ticuani in August 1998, for the first time in more than five years, the first thing I noticed was the gang graffiti. The pleasure of striding through Ticuani's dry midday heat and being greeted by friends was disrupted by my surprise at the graffiti and the *cholo*, or "gangster," dress and haircuts of many local youths. Ticuanense locals told me how the gangs had changed Ticuani, especially during the Feast in January. Violence had increased: according to local leaders, gang members had killed a local taxi driver, and some had gone to jail. Even though *pandillas* had become a pervasive influence among Mexican youths in New York during the mid-1990s, I had come, like most Ticuanenses, to see Ticuani as a refuge from the pressures of life in New York. Now those pressures were being exported back to Ticuani.

The emergence of *pandillerismo* in transnational life is not an aberration but a logical outgrowth of the migration and assimilation processes in which migrants and their children are embedded. In this chapter, I trace how and why Mexican gangs formed in New York and what their effect has been in Ticuani. Drawing on observations of and stories from gang members and other youth, I show how gang activity has resulted from changes in the migration process itself, including the migration of male teenagers and their assimilation in New York. Here I focus on how elements of the assimilation process—the immigrant bargain, gender bargains, and coming of age—fit together in lives that are turning out to be fundamentally different from those of the non–gang members discussed thus far. For example, adolescence is fundamentally different for teen migrants than for second-generation migrants. I also show how the creation and use of Mexican public space in New York has gone hand in hand with gang formation and the validation of *pandilla* Mexicanness and masculinity. Finally, I consider cultural assimilation pressure from the media, examining how American movies about Mexican gangs have served as models for how to be Mexican in New York. Hence I examine here the darker sides of transnational life and the bleaker narratives gang members and others use to understand them. I pursue these issues transnationally, showing how the deep transformations resulting from migration have created fertile ground for gang recruitment in Ticuani and indeed throughout Mexico.

I use the terms *cholo* and *pandillero* interchangeably, and would translate them roughly as "gang member," "gangster," or "homeboy." A *pandilla* or *banda* is a gang. *Pandillerismo* involves both "real gangs" and "crews."[1] (There is no Spanish equivalent of *crew;* these groups use the English term.) Crews are groups of adolescent boys who hang around on their street corners and give themselves a name in order to "be somebody," but they do not usually engage in serious violence or crime and usually grow out of the crew as they enter adulthood. A crew's name is often not known by "real" gangs, even those nearby, because crews are not important enough to fight. Gangs, in contrast, engage in serious violence and crime; many of their members stay in the gang as adults; and they are known to other gangs and have alliances and disputes with them. Gang members are required to use violence to defend their brothers against attack or disrespect and are subject to the leader's discipline and command. Crews often affiliate themselves with a gang, with some crew members later becoming gang members.[2] Most Ticuanense teen migrants and 1.5- or second-generation youth involved with *pandillerismo* are in crews and do not engage in serious criminal activity. Yet the practice and regular threat of such violence has become a social reality in Ticuani and New York and has had a disproportionate effect on Ticuani public life.

TRANSNATIONAL GANGS IN HISTORICAL, THEORETICAL, AND COMPARATIVE PERSPECTIVE

That gang members return to Mexico from the United States is not new. In the late 1970s and early 1980s the Mexican anthropologist Gustavo Lopez Castro found that *cholos* who had migrated to the United States and joined gangs there were returning to Gomez Farias, Michoacán, and importing their gangs, while teens who had joined gangs in the northern Mexican city of Monterrey migrated to the United States for "adventure" during the 1990s, exporting their gangs from Mexico.[3] In Ticuani, in the late 1980s and early 1990s, gang members returned to visit their families or "chill out"—that is, get away from trouble in New York. Ticuani seemed to cool them down more than they seemed to heat it up. But by the late 1990s, Ticuani youth culture had been profoundly influenced by returned *pandilleros*. The gangs opened a cultural gap between local youths who saw themselves as *cholos* and the "regulars," as nongang youth sometimes call themselves.

Nonmigrant youths from poorer families or poorer ranchos in Ticuani are especially likely to adopt *cholo* ways: wearing very baggy jeans worn low; sporting "fade" haircuts (with short hair on top and shaved hair below) and even having gang letters shaved into their hair; and cruising around the town center in cars. Such relatively harmless changes were also noted by Lopez Castro. More serious consequences in Puebla include drug abuse and increasing violence. At dances or other large social events, gang conflicts are now frequent and range from arguments to "fights that end in knives, even guns," says Don Pepe, president of the neighboring *municipio* of El Baile, which also has gangs. In Puebla, the problem became so serious that the regional paper, *La Jornada de Oriente,* sent a reporter to New York to investigate gangs in 1999. The state of Puebla also began assigning a special task force of the State Judicial Police to public security issues, focusing especially on *pandillas* during municipal feasts in the Mixteca. Three killings in Ticuani were attributed by townspeople to *pandilleros*. All used the same weapons and methods, and all were committed while the victim was drunk and alone late at night. Some *pandilleros* are in jail for these crimes, but others fled back to the United States. Such random criminal violence is otherwise relatively rare in the Mixteca. Interestingly, the *cholos'* violence was openly and indeed passionately discussed by Ticuanenses, while non-*pandilla* violence, including killings, that took place the same year was not discussed at all. Gang violence is apparently ascribed a particular moral meaning.

Evidence suggests that the transnationalization of gangs is widespread and likely to grow in Mexico and elsewhere in the Western Hemisphere. Migration itself fosters the growth of gangs. As I discuss later, many teen migrants and U.S.-born youths return alone to Mexico to live largely unsupervised, but with dollars in hand and enhanced social status. Moreover, an increasing number of U.S.-born youths are returning to live in Ticuani long-term or permanently; this group constitutes about 6 percent of Ticuani school-aged children and the largest group of foreigners in Mexico outside Mexico City.[4] In addition, increasing numbers of migrants come from urban areas and have previous gang experience, thus exporting their gangs to the United States, and then experience gang hostility from other ethnic groups or from other Mexicans in the United States. Finally, the U.S. policy of deporting all aliens convicted of crimes, begun in 1996 and accelerated after September 11, 2001, has ironically catalyzed the transnationalization of criminal activity, including gang activity, in El Salvador, Belize, Jamaica, the Dominican Republic, and other countries because these states lack the means to deal with such crime.[5] Deported gangsters continue their activities in their countries of origin while maintaining their links to partners in the United States, and many later return to the United States as undocumented immigrants. Salvadoran researchers have documented the role deportations have played in expanding and changing gang activity in El Salvador.[6]

While the U.S.-born second generation incorporates Ticuani communal practices as adolescent rituals, teen migrants have experienced what amounts to an abrupt modernization of their adolescence as a result of changes in migration patterns. Family reunification and related migration, and harsher border control, fostered a boom in teen migration and a tendency toward long-term settlement. In Mexico this group would have experienced only a short adolescence before becoming workers, a phenomenon that the sociologist Glen Elder Jr. says is typical of less industrialized societies and earlier American history.[7] Through migration they were jerked out of this familiar pattern of coming of age and dropped into an extended, urban, assimilative adolescence in New York, in which being Mexican invited ethnically motivated aggression by other groups, especially Puerto Ricans. Although there have always been some early-teen migrants, the huge increase in their number during the mid-1990s meant that their adolescence *as a group* was no longer a quick transition, largely accomplished by migration itself. Hence, instead of migrating in order to work, as most earlier migrants had, and becoming adults in the process, adolescent gang members during the 1990s began to report that they went for *la'ventura* (adventure).[8] This longer transition was unclear to them and had to be made in English, with little effective guidance from adults.[9] This difficult context of reception led many, though not most, teen migrants into an oppositional subculture. It is not the racialized, native subculture of some Black and Puerto Rican youth that they entered, as segmented assimilation theory might predict, but rather a teen migrant subculture in which ethnic pride coexists with suspicion toward U.S. institutions and a sense that the migrants are better than native minorities. Whether such attitudes will ultimately lead to a "rainbow underclass," as Portes and his colleagues suggest, I am not sure. There are subcultures emerging among Mexican second-generation and teen migrants that could avoid this fate.

My discussion of gangs here draws on and critiques three perspectives on gangs. First, a long line of research, beginning with Frederick Thrasher's classic book, *The Gang: A Study of 1313 Gangs in Chicago* (1927), emphasizes how immigrant gangs emerge out of the disorganization of immigrant communities.[10] James Diego Vigil reprises and extends this view by showing how enduring marginalization prevents later generations from escaping gangs, which fill social voids. A second line of research focuses on gang-community relations, arguing that gangs are organic parts of the communities, a sign of organization rather than of social entropy. Finally, a third perspective sees American-style street gangs spreading to Europe and as far as New Zealand because of the globalization of the economy and the media, which exports a homogeneous, Americanized image of gang culture. My own research shows social disorganization that creates a need for new institutions of belonging and settlement, which gangs meet, as Vigil and others argue. But these gangs do not exist entirely apart from the rest of the community, as the image of filling a void suggests; like the work of Sudhir Venkatesh and Martín Sánchez Jankowski, my research indicates that most gang members, and certainly crew members, also have other roles within their communities.[11] Finally, rather than simply invoke the abstract notion of globalization to explain the spread of gangs to Mexico, I trace in detail their formation in New York and exportation to the Mixteca, creating a gang world that is local but transnational.

MEXICAN GANGS IN NEW YORK

Pandillerismo in New York grows in part out of changes in migration and assimilation. Changes in immigration laws in the United States, including the 1986 amnesty and subsequent measures, have made return more difficult and contributed to the tripling of the city's Mexican population to 300,000 between 1990 and 2000. Legalization of undocumented parents in the late 1980s set off a boom in family reunification during the early to mid-1990s. Indeed, as discussed in chapter 2, the average annual number of legally admitted Mexican immigrants under age twenty-five arriving in New York increased from 183 in 1990–91 to 567 in 1992–94 and 360 in 1995–99. I believe these age-group demographics roughly reflect the much larger influx of undocumented entrants. This influx put more teen Mexicans into New York's schools, parks, and neighborhoods and transformed their experience of adolescence. Puerto Ricans and Blacks in the same neighborhoods or schools as these teen migrants often picked on them, feeling that their space had been invaded. According to my Mexican informants, these groups took advantage of the Mexicans' small stature, often undocumented status, recent arrival, and lack of organized resistance. (In an ironic dynamic explained below, such violence by Puerto Ricans against Mexicans indirectly fosters Mexican-on-Mexican violence.) Those migrating legally for family reunification came at a younger age, about twelve instead of eighteen; their undocumented friends followed, contributing to an exodus of teens from the Mixteca during the 1990s. Their extended urban adolescence made the gangs an important institution of reception, protection, and adjustment in what they perceived as a dangerous and discriminatory New York.[12]

The immigrant bargain makes more demands on teen migrants who go to New York to join their families than on their second-generation counterparts, who have grown up in New York. Because teen migrants are going to live with parents, sometimes for the first time, they have very high expectations. They know their migrant parents as what Peggy Levitt calls "fairy godparents," who dispense gifts and money from New York when they visit.[13] Life with their parents is literally a party because it happens only during holidays. Once arrived in New York, many teens find a cruel duplication of their experience in Mexico: because their parents work long hours, they almost never see them. The parents, who often have little education, are ill-equipped to offer their children concrete help in meeting their expectations of academic and work success in New York.

Moreover, because the family is unaccustomed to living together, all become frustrated at the effort family life requires. They may have expected reunification to solve rather than create problems. The exodus from the Mixteca during the mid-1990s dovetailed unfortunately with a difficult emotional dynamic. The psychologist Ceres Artico has shown that adolescents left behind by migrant parents come to understand their parents' absence either as abandonment or as heroic sacrifice, depending on how constant the parents are in sending support and how the child's caregivers discuss the absence. As many children left Ticuani at younger ages to be reunited with their parents during the 1990s, those who stayed behind had more reason to feel abandoned, even if they were left only because their parents could not legally bring them to the United States; this resentment came with them to New York. Gang members often tell of difficult relations with parents, which reinforce their feelings of being abandoned by their parents even as they gratefully acknowledge their parents' sacrifice.

Two other factors promoting gang formation are public space and the media. The creation of safe "Mexican" spaces for these teen migrants becomes a difficult issue, especially for boys, many of whom (unlike their sisters) are allowed to stay out until late at night. Through the 1990s Mexicans did not have physical possession of neighborhoods, so they created a hypermasculinized Mexican space by "steppin' up" to (confronting) other Mexicans in dance halls, parks, neighborhoods, and schools. Two American movies about Mexican gangs, *American Me* and *Blood In, Blood Out*, released in 1992, have served as templates for how to be Mexican in New York. *American Me*, for example, resonates powerfully with male youths (in or out of gangs) because the Mexican characters in the movie go from being powerless to powerful in the face of white and Black gangs.[14]

In sum, *pandillas* provide a social structure of belonging that youth want and need, but that their parents cannot readily provide.[15] These young men need help in school, in adapting to their new world, and in becoming Mexican men in a context where their manhood seems everywhere challenged or compromised. The *pandillas* provide a way of both rejecting and fulfilling parental and societal expectations. In the gang they are men who command respect and fear; outside it they often reject the other means of achieving manhood that seem impossible to them, such as school, a good job, or a career. The late Robert Merton would have characterized these *pandilleros* as innovators: lacking the conventional means to success, they innovate and pursue alternative pathways to achieve success, with a minority using violence and crime.[16]

Tiene Que Unir para Defenderse:
You Have to Unite to Protect Yourself

Talking in a restaurant in Ticuani through a long, hot afternoon in 2001, three O.G.s (original gangsters) of the Mixtecos Locos (Crazy Mixtecos) related to me the same foundational story I have heard about other gangs since the late 1980s. The story involves gangs composed mainly of U.S.-born second-generation members, those with a mixture of teen migrants and second-generationers, and those newly formed by teen migrants. Over four years of visits to Ticuani, I had come to know these three leaders of the Mixtecos Locos, one of the two or three biggest Mexican gangs in New York City, by participating in events such as the Antorcha, hanging out in the zocalo, and playing pool. Knowing we were doing interviews with other youths, Horacio, Dionisio, and Homero offered to tell their story to Griscelda Perez and me.

Mexican gangs in New York formed, they say, because Mexicans had to defend themselves against violence by Puerto Rican and Black youths in the public schools, parks, and subways. While ethnic conflict in American cities is not new, it helped to create a large number of Mexican gangs within five or six years in the 1990s. The members claimed it was not really possible to protect oneself if alone, and I asked them to tell more about why they felt that way. The themes of challenged, compromised, and demonstrated masculinity thread their way through the narrative, mainly one of ethnic antagonism with Puerto Ricans.

> HORACIO: When I came there, the Puerto Ricans assaulted me all the time, and assaulted my friends. . . . Now, no . . . it's not that they come upon a Mexican in the street and they are going to rob him—now, no! . . . Everything has changed. . . . This is [why] the Mexican people began to unite and to protect themselves with the Blacks, and the Puerto Ricans, not all of them, but to me they have done it . . . [taking] our crosses, the chains, everything. . . . They would use these words: "Give me the money, Mexico! Give me the money!" . . .

> HOMERO: Now, if we are on the block and they come by, it is not like it used to be before, that they insulted you—eh! . . . Now, we don't walk with our heads bowed *[cabeza agachada]*, because now we have a little bit of reputation, you know? . . . Respect. . . . [Before] we did not look them in the eye. Like they are doing now, right? . . . Before, they said "Mexico! Go back to your country!" . . .

> RS: And what did you say? . . .

> HOMERO: One only walked along. (Spanish, translated by the author)

Humiliation by the other groups made these young men feel like *putos*—punks or faggots. Psychologists such as James Gilligan and sociologists such as Elijah Anderson, Ruth Horowitz, and Jack Katz have documented how such deep shame provokes violence among young men, leading them to be hypersensitive to suggestions of disrespect and to enjoy generating dread and fear in response to such perceived slights.[17] When Horacio, Dionisio, and Homero spoke of walking with their eyes lowered, we could hear the shame in their voices; when they spoke about the respect they now get, we could hear the satisfaction. This transformation illuminates why resistance to Puerto Ricans has become central to the narrative of Mexican gang formation in New York. Dionisio describes the change in how Puerto Ricans treat them on the street. Instead of assaulting Mexicans as before, he says, "Now they say hi to us," as if it were just a normal, everyday interaction.

This narration of their feelings engages my arguments about embodied emotion, social proprioception, and shame as a key emotion in gendered experience. Walking along with one's head bowed is a physical expression of shame and manifests quite clearly the inability to respond to insult. Failing to respond with the "heart" that *cholo* masculinity requires is an exhibition of moral incompetence, to borrow again from Katz. It places these Mexican *cholos* in an ontologically feminine relation to the more powerful Puerto Ricans, just as a ranchera wife would defer to her husband. But, Dionisio and his friends tell us, things are different now. Puerto Ricans bow their heads to the Mexicans, conceding masculine power, or they show respect, and simply say hello.

It is also not accidental that Homero emphasizes that the Mixtecos Locos don't walk with their heads bowed any more, and no longer fear to "look people in the eye." It is in the experience of walking together that they experience themselves as powerful, both through their relations with each other and with other groups. In being seen by each other and by the other group as powerful, they experience themselves as physically strong men whose masculine honor is embodied in their dangerous reputations. Their reputation empowers them to expiate their gender shame and to walk as men, in a group with other men, in a world of men.

That Mexicans were the targets of violence by other groups was no illusion. Cesar, one of the Puerto Rican crack dealers in Philippe Bourgois's 1995 book *In Search of Respect*, describes Mexicans as easy to pick on: "Them Mexican people get drunk like real crazy man. Everybody be ripping them off; they easy prey 'cause they illegal, most of them. . . . Everybody takes Mexicans like a joke. It's a little crime wave. Mexicans be fucked up with crime in New York. That's like the new thing to do."[18] I spent a night talking to and walking around with Cesar, along with Bourgois and his other main informant, Primo, who both described in detail how they targeted Mexicans. They and others told me that youths also waited outside bars where Mexicans drank, mugging them when they left, especially on Friday—payday. That some, like Cesar, understood their oppression of Mexicans as a consequence of both their undocumented status and their Mexicanness makes compelling and reasonable the Mexican teen migrants' desire to organize gangs of their own to defend themselves. Ironically, however, most Mexican gang violence now targets other Mexicans.

I also heard many reports of Mexicans being targeted through my volunteer work with Mexican flower vendors in the late 1980s and early 1990s. The vendors protested that the police unfairly enforced laws about vending without a license, even imprisoning the vendors, while failing to protect them from robbery, assault, and even homicide. Indeed, I knew men and women who left for work in the morning, were arrested for selling flowers and jailed for lacking identification documents, but could not contact their families because they had no phone. I was told many times that Puerto Rican, and sometimes Black and Dominican, youths targeted Mexican flower vendors because they carried cash and were alone. Don Sixto Santiago Morales, mentioned previously, was one such victim. One vendor with whom I spent a lot of time was attacked several times by Puerto Rican youths—more than once by the same group, he said—and hospitalized. The youths yelled, "¡Vete, México!" (Get out, Mexico!) as they beat him. Once I was riding on the subway with a group of flower vendors taking their shopping carts of flowers back uptown after a day's work. A young Black man approached one of the vendors and, in English, demanded flowers. As they usually did, the vendors all looked to me to translate, as did the young man. I translated his demand and the vendor's refusal. He became angry and more insistent, raising his voice. My appeal that the vendors made little money and needed to feed their kids in Mexico only made him angrier. To defuse the tension, I told the young man that these vendors were "not worth his trouble"—he was stronger and bigger, they would be afraid, and they did not even speak English! With this, he nodded to me, smiled, and gave me a hearty handshake. My reading of this response (which is only that; I did not try to follow up) was that he had seen the Mexicans as easy targets, but his interaction with me had provided the recognition of his superiority that he had been seeking.

The theme of ethnically inspired victimization provides a justification for the violence described by Mexican gang members: Mexicans fight to demand respect from others who oppress them. The two stories below, told by Mexican high school gang members, have the same moral elements. Francisco describes his response to seeing his cousin beaten up by a mostly African American gang I call the Knights. His cousin did not speak much English and was new to New York. Francisco speaks with his friend Enrique and Augustín Vecino, a Columbia student researcher on the project.

> They took money from him . . . [gesturing as if talking to perpetrators]. Yo, when you took my cousin's money—I'm goin' right there. I got my bats. I was lookin' out for them. I knew who they was. . . . They picked on him. That's why I got suspended too. 'Cause they beat him up. In my school . . . They told me, my friends, they beat up your cousin in school. I ran over there, and I saw him all fucked up. His black eye. He's blue. He was fucked up! They sent him to the hospital. . . . Yeah, like they hit him from all angles. I was pissed. . . .

> That's what the police report said—all angles. . . . So I just saw the kids and I [gestures as if swinging a baseball bat]—this is for him!

Such direct, immediate retribution differs drastically from the days described by the Mixtecos Locos when "one only walked along." Picking up a bat and beating someone who has beaten up your greenhorn cousin—despite the fact that your victim belongs to a bigger gang—shows "heart" and projects an image of fearlessness and violence appropriate to a tough, unquestionably masculine *pandillero*. Francisco also saw the retribution as righteous, an emotion he relived in the interview as he swung his imaginary bat. Francisco was then thrown out of this school and placed in another school with many Knights. After the first day, he decided, "I'm risking my life," and refused to return. He eventually transferred to a school with few Knights and formed his own Mexican gang there, "for protection."

In the second example, again Mexicans defend a friend against the aggression of the African American Knights. Lorencio describes the action:

> We were in a fight against the Knights, all the Mexicans. Francisco went straight up to a Knight and said, "If you gonna hit me, do it now!" and he [the Knight] didn't do nothin'. In the whole school, there are like seven hundred Knights—is that a lot? . . . It was in front of the dean's office, and nothing happened. Then in the lunch room, Rogelio got beat up by Knights. . . . But then we . . . beat up the security guard who had held Rogelio while the other guy hit him, . . . with bandannas on our faces.

This narration is also rich in *pandillero* masculinity in the context of ethnic conflict. The David and Goliath image is invoked: five or six Mexicans fight members of a gang of seven hundred. By asking me rhetorically if seven hundred is a lot, Lorencio implies that no number of them would truly scare him. However, the confrontation took place in front of the dean's office, where a fight would have been broken up, and when they sought retribution for the attack on Rogelio, they attacked not one of the "hundreds" of available Knights, but rather the security guard they felt had unfairly intervened. I was surprised that they attacked a school official, though I suspect they anticipated less severe consequences from it than from taking on the Knights. The underlying message of the tales is the same: If you mess with a Mexican these days, you will pay. The time of messing with the "illegals" in a "mini crime wave," as Cesar put it, is over.

Teen Migration and the Growth in Gangs

If ethnic antagonism catalyzed the surge in Mexican gangs in New York during the 1990s, the growth in teen migration contributed to it. Growing numbers of teen migrants boosted the size of the gangs and their propensity for violence. This trend shows gangs forming among youths who are, technically, first-generation migrants, and not second-generation, U.S.-born children, as many theories of gang culture and assimilation presume. Nacho, a Brooklyn-born man in his mid-twenties who had been in the Brooklyn Rancheros, a large, influential gang since the late 1980s, expands on his earlier statement that Mexican gangs changed during the mid 1990s as many new immigrants joined. He had gone to school or grown up with most of the longtime members.

> NACHO: The Brooklyn Rancheros started with a lot of people that were born here. . . . Then . . . the Brooklyn Rancheros got big. A lot of people from Mexico just started coming, and they were so afraid of not fitting in that they would just come in through some other little gang. . . . And that's when they were mentally: "I could be in this country and everybody could be afraid of me." . . .
>
> RS: So it started with a lot of U.S.-born guys, and then it grew really big all of a sudden when you had this huge influx of new, young Mexican immigrants?
>
> N: Young Mexican immigrants, yeah. . . . They would come freshman year [of high school], the age range at that time is like fourteen to sixteen or seventeen. . . . A lot of them would go to school, but the majority would start working.

Nacho's account accords perfectly with the trend of family reunification based in the amnesty of the 1986 Immigration Reform and Control Act. After obtaining temporary residency in 1987 or 1988, an eligible adult male immigrant would have obtained permanent residency or even citizenship by the mid-1990s, entitling him to petition to bring his family to the United States. The huge influx of children of migrants from the Mixteca by the mid-1990s added to the surge in gang activity.

Gangs came to function as an institution of migrant reception and recruitment. U.S.-born gang members recruited their own relatives in Mexico to join the gangs. Pedro, a past leader in the Brooklyn Rancheros when Nacho was a member, described to me how the gangs appealed to teen migrants and estimated what percentage of the gang was born in Mexico or the United States.

> It's half and half. . . . They got no family when they come from Mexico to over here, so they don't got no other choice [but] to be hanging out with these guys. That's like a second family to them. Drinking at each other's house, get drunk; next day, they wake up, do the same thing. . . . The two guys that started the Brooklyn Rancheros . . . were

born here but . . . started recruiting members that were coming from
Mexico from the same family. . . . Yeah, they were coming from Mexico, they spread gossip that they were one of the most powerful
gangs. And the guys liked the idea, they wanted to be part of it.

While gangs have served as institutions of reception elsewhere, including
California, the speed and scale on which they did so in the mid-1990s in
New York is noteworthy. Pedro's analysis of how he and other teenage
newcomers sought a way to fit in echoes Nacho's account, again comparing
the gang's role to the family's:

Maybe where you lived there was a couple of guys that belonged to
the gangs . . . and if you wanted to go chill out, you could go chill out
over there . . . and you start drinking, and you see these people aren't
that bad. Next week comes and you want to go again, and then next
thing you know . . . after your job, you start going straight over there,
you find all your friends and then you start drinking. Then, it's like,
Yo, let's go to a party. . . . And, everything else, it just starts coming
into form, then bam—you're in a gang. You have fights with them already, you have done everything, and that's that—you consider
them . . . like your first, I don't know, like your parents.

While Nacho talked about the gang's family function, Lazario, in a group
interview with Nacho and other gang members, linked the growth in gangs
to the increased numbers of teens migrating without their parents. "The
majority . . . [are] teenagers . . . old enough to support themselves," who live
with "my brother . . . my sister, or my aunt, whatever. They have a place to
land over here." They make friends at parties; drinking is a key part of gang
life. Lazario stayed away from such parties to avoid being "stepped up to"
or recruited there. His account makes clear that young migrants depend for
most of their social support on other teens, often new acquaintances. The
gangs offer places where they can feel they belong.

Some independent teens have formed their own gangs. Donal, a youth
who was born in the United States but raised in Puebla, started Los Abandonados, composed almost entirely of teen migrants, in 1998. He purposely
recruited teen migrants so that he would have more "soldiers" and be
stronger. Comparing the gang to a family, he told Sara Guerrero-
Rippberger that he sent for more soldiers because "it's like the kids, like
there is the main head, and—what I order, they do. So they call themselves
soldiers, because it's like, um. . . . If some problems comes, right, see—*ellos
se meten po' mí, vez?* [they jump in for me, see?]" Donal also claims he
told his immigrant "soldiers" to be proud that they were Mexican, because
he saw many U.S.-born Mexicans making newcomers feel ashamed or
inferior.

The apparent speed, ease, and lack of awareness with which these youths become gang members suggest that their adolescent need for social structures of belonging is being addressed by gangs and not by other institutions. Teens being incorporated into New York under such conditions lack a "compelling project," something larger than themselves to which they can dedicate their energies.[19] Metaphors of family recur in these gang narratives because they capture the sense of belonging these young men apparently seek and because peer groups become especially important referents during adolescence. While the experience of needing to belong is especially intense among teen migrants, it is also present among the U.S.-born second generation and leads to quick friendships forged in arenas lacking adult supervision. Gang parties involving heavy drinking both heighten the danger of violence and illustrate the hypermasculine *cholo* image, which becomes the most compelling model of masculinity for teen migrants. The working-immigrant model (*gente trabajador*, as gang members describe them) does not seem worth their time, and the model of the upwardly mobile second generation model seems impossible to emulate. The power over others that gang membership conveys is seductive.[20]

Teen Migration and the Growth in Violence

The surge in teen migration has catalyzed two forms of tension among and within Mexican gangs. First, the membership of some established and influential gangs like the Brooklyn Rancheros has changed from being mainly U.S.-born to mainly teen migrants. And scores of new crews and gangs composed mostly of teen migrants have emerged, many of which attempt to prove their mettle by confronting the older, better-established Mexican American gangs. A second type of conflict is based on age. Because teen migrants do not respect the authority of the older gang members, often U.S.-born, rivalries and tensions have arisen within gangs or between teen-migrant and Mexican American gangs. Teen-migrant gangsters have told me they resent U.S.-born Mexican Americans' attitude of superiority toward recent migrants. One confrontation between an older gang, with mainly U.S.-born members, and a newer, mainly teen migrant gang cost one youth his life in a stabbing outside a New York City high school we followed in 2000. Pedro, drawing on his own experience as a leader in the Brooklyn Rancheros, described the problem:

> PEDRO: Before . . . there were young kids, but they respected the old leaders. . . . If they tried to pick a fight, they had to go to the leaders first. . . . Now they don't talk to the leader no

more . . . they just go, grab the gun, and do what they gotta
do. . . .

RS: Who are most ready to shoot? . . .

P: The immigrants [are] most ready, . . . they know the
system . . . that if you're a young kid and you shoot somebody, you ain't going to serve that much time. . . . They try to
prove themselves that they're *chingones* [badasses], too . . .
you're the man . . . then the word is going to spread out to
other gangs: Yo, *el mero* [big guy], that *cabron* [asshole] right
there is *uno de los meros chingones* [one of the big bad-
asses], . . . be on the lookout for him. They try to keep a high
profile. . . . They be like, Now I got respect. . . . I'm one of the
meros meros. . . . They proud of it.

The teen migrants want to show that they no longer have to defer to gang
leaders. They also exploit their youth in confronting older gang members.
Many of the O.G.s now in their late twenties are more reluctant to use violence because they are legally adults; many have criminal records already
and thus might face long jail sentences for subsequent offenses. In contrast,
teen migrants know that they will be tried as minors if apprehended or believe they will be able to escape to Mexico if they need to. Ironically, their
youth enables them to assert a harsher version of *pandillero* masculinity
than older gang members.

A group of Mexican- and U.S.-born friends, including Nacho, discussed
these issues in a full-day group interview in 1999 with Sara Guerrero-
Rippberger and me. Some were former gang members; some had never
been in gangs but knew of them through experiences in school, at *sonidos*,
and in their neighborhoods. They described the gangsters as younger
now—thirteen or fourteen, as opposed to seventeen or older before—and
said that previous gangsters were more "mature." Because "they were
grown" when facing a potential conflict, they would evaluate it more seriously: "And they be like, no, *sabes que?* [You know what?] *Eso no vale
la pena.* [This is not worth it.] . . . Whatever. They kinda like thought about
it more." They saw these young gangsters as more violent: "Now it's
like they find you in the street, and alone, and guys is coming that you
don't get along with, that's it, you dead, right there. . . . They'll kill you."
Napoleon summed it up: "This isn't the '80s or anything like that. Gangs
are different—sixteen-year-old kids killing other kids—they know how to
use a gun. You got little kids killing people." In a later interview, Nacho expanded on his belief that teen migrants act more violently to try and prove
they are tougher than other gang members. He answered my question

about why teen migrants are "so caught up in trying to prove how bad they are":

> I have no idea. Before it was just like to get respect from everybody to yourself, just to show . . . I have enough balls as you do. . . . I started hanging out with the Brooklyn Rancheros 'cause I wanted to prove to everyone that I was strong as them. It's totally different now. Now they're kids, already in gangs—you don't even know how to clean your dumb ass, right, and you want to be in a gang already. It's just stupid. [Before] it was like seventeen to maybe twenty to twenty-two [years old]. Already, older people . . . thinking . . . there was not as much violence before . . . it was just pure fistfights. You know—I can fuck you up if you can fuck me up. And now it's like stabbing, now more guns than before. . . . And now it's like these little kids have a knife, they think they're so bad. . . . And, you know, older people really fought with their fists and with their minds. If they think there was a bad situation in front of them, then they wouldn't fight.

Nacho voices a general perception of a move away from the earlier period's fistfights and rare stabbings to quicker, more deadly violence. While my field notes, recollections, and interviews with gang members from the early 1990s show that there were stabbings, shootings, and deaths ten years ago, too, they were more unusual, and most fights were between "crews" rather than long-term, highly organized gangs. Interestingly, Nacho seems perplexed by the level and intensity of violence, a reaction that I suspect reflects both the trend toward more violence and his own stance on and distance from it. No longer involved in gangs, Nacho recognizes and fears the increased violence. His response reflects a trend also documented in the Hallway Hangars, a white crew studied by the urbanist Jay McLeod: although gang violence increased over time, its members feared its effects more as they grew older.[21] Hence, even if the image of gangs fighting only with fists and honor seems somewhat self-serving, it does reflect gang life in the late 1980s more closely than today's. Moreover, in the earlier period there were many fewer gangs and less higher-level organization and alliances among them.

Creating Masculine Mexican Space and Gang Space

The creation of more Mexican public space by young men was another key factor in Mexican gang formation. In the 1980s and early 1990s, as Mexican immigrants confronted the real problem of not having any geographical space populated mainly by Mexicans, Mexican space was created in several ways.[22] First, several "little Mexicos" emerged, neighborhoods with notable concentrations, though not majorities, of Mexican residents. As Gerald Suttles observed in the early 1960s, a neighborhood or area within one does not need to be all "Mexican," "Italian," or "Greek" to be understood to belong to that group; the control of public space and adolescent notions of ethnic territory matter more. Accordingly, during the 1990s gang members told me of their gang's controlling an ever-larger territory. However, in contrast to Suttles's analysis, this was mainly understood to mean controlling it against other Mexican gangs. Their dominance over this geographical space was meant primarily to secure their place in a Mexican hierarchy. In the absence of some active conflict, as might happen with Puerto Rican youths, other groups could call their own a larger area within which the Mexicans claimed their turf, without the Mexicans seeking confrontation to establish dominance. This was most obvious in neighborhoods that the Mexican youths told me were controlled by adult Italian men, who they believed were in the Mafia, and the youths linked to them. Here, the Italians and Mexicans coexisted in parallel space. But for Mexican youth, turf controlled by a particular gang was a kind of no-fly zone for Mexicans in, or who might be suspected to be in, other gangs. Controlling such geographical space became increasingly important among Mexican gangs during the 1990s.[23]

During the 1990s, several other kinds of Mexican space were also created, enabling "street socialization": Mexican crews and gangs could use these spaces to meet, socialize, and challenge each other and Mexicans who were not in gangs.[24] This kind of space brings into propinquity people who normally do not interact at length. I differentiate again between geographical space (physical territory); social space created by the relations between people, places, and institutions; and emergent space, that is, temporary ownership of geographic space, such as a park, dance club, or conference hall, when it is in use by a specific group. Such spaces make possible many more iterations of social interactions than are normally possible, thus creating a sense of "accelerated" social time.

A second form of emergent space can be described as a kind of parallel Mexican social universe. As I walked around a high school with a teenage boy who was considering joining a gang, I learned how he saw this geographic space: which parts of the school and which students he had to avoid, which routes he had to use to travel home, and which high schools he had to avoid because of rival gangs. None of this social topography was visible to his teachers or to most other students; he wore no gang colors and did not tell non-Mexicans in the school about his relationship with the gang. The Mexican gang world he inhabited, and which presented special dangers to him, existed inside and outside the school and could be mapped, but it was largely invisible to others. Some scholars refer to multiple social worlds as being "stacked" in geographical space.[25] I dislike the stacking metaphor, which implies that these worlds do not occupy the same physical space. The metaphor of a parallel universe more accurately conveys the simultaneous existence of Mexican and non-Mexican social spaces. At the same time, the control over these Mexican spaces is an attempt by Mexican youths to express their dominant position in a Mexican hierarchy.

Public schools are important places for gangs to form and grow. Candido describes how ethnic antagonisms push Mexicans to form gangs, and how violence escalates from lower-intensity ethnic conflict at school to more severe Mexican-on-Mexican violence outside it. He responds to Sandra Lara's question "How did you get involved with these gangs?"

> It stems from my patriotism. . . . [Before] I was in Mexico I wasn't around a lot of Mexicans, just my cousins and my family, but not other Mexicans. [I] hung out with . . . Puerto Ricans, African Americans, in Graves [High School]. There were a lot of Mexicans, but I wouldn't speak to them until I started hanging out with one or two, then a little chain formed, and I started meeting others. . . . Then I noticed a lot of them were getting picked on by other ethnic groups . . . and that would get me mad, not only me, of course, them too . . . we were young, maybe fifteen or sixteen years old . . . and we said, No . . . we shouldn't take this. If we're together, they won't do nothing to us, and this formed a group, but in high school it's not called a group, we just call it a gang, and it became that. We had confrontations, some people left, some stayed, some were suspended, some got hurt. . . . After a while we had a reputation, and then other [Mexican] gangs start to look at you. You get along with some and not others. There are a lot of Mexican gangs out there. As you grow you move into the bigger circle, not just a little high school gang. You move into a bigger street gang.

Candido summarizes a story I have heard many times. The gang's rationale shifts from ethnic self-defense inside the school to more intense, intraethnic conflict. This process has been helped along by the confluence of the teen-migrant influx, the propensity for violence among adolescent males, and the "funneling" that occurs in the New York City school system as students progress from elementary to middle to high schools. This funneling concentrates an otherwise quite dispersed Mexican population. Hence, for many Puerto Ricans, high school provided their first school encounter with large numbers of the Mexicans they felt were invading their neighborhoods. Similarly, many Mexicans told me high school was the first time they had attended a school with large numbers of other Mexicans and thus saw the possibility of defending themselves collectively from attacks by students from other ethnic groups. Moreover, the poorest and least compliant Mexican students are those most likely to be funneled into a high school within their neighborhood or school "zone"; the effect is to concentrate the students who are likely to join gangs.[26] Mexican gangs can also form in schools with few Mexicans, as, for example, when students like Francisco allied with larger Mexican gangs outside that school to "have their back." For the increasing number of teen migrants who entered high school during the 1990s, a primary dimension of their resocialization and assimilation pressures was ethnic and intraethnic conflict. One can easily imagine how teen migrants would understand their lives as dangerous, humiliating, and requiring collective self-defense.

Within the schools, gangs operate in specific ways. If no gang "owns" a school, rival gangs compete to control it. A gang that owns a school must constantly guard its turf. Both dominant and competing gangs must recruit new members through friendship or "contextual coercion." New Mexican friendship groups form in school from the enlarged Mexican population, and non–gang members sometimes join gang members in cutting class, doing "hookey jams" (parties held while cutting school), and general "hangin'." Such friends may "hang with" a gang and be in its social orbit but not be "down" with it, meaning they are not initiated members. Contextual coercion occurs when Mexican gang members attending a school "step up" to any other Mexican they see and ask them, "¿Con quién andas?" (Who do you hang with?) to determine their gang affiliation, if any. If they do not accept a student's denial of being with any gang, a warning, a suspicious glance, or a chase and beating may ensue.

Because students are constantly stepping up to others and risking conflict each time, Mexican students feel that they must either be able to avoid such situations or affiliate with or join a gang so that "someone has their back." Federico told me that he wanted to join the Vaqueros Feos (Ugly Cowboys) because their rivals had already stepped up to him, assuming he was a member because of his friendships; so he was going to join to be safer and to "be something." During the three years I knew him, Federico went from being an honors student to being a high school dropout who in fact did join, and then leave, a gang. Part of the reason he left school was that his friends, most of whom eventually were in or hung with the gang, told him that "college was not for Mexicans" and that anyone who told him otherwise was humiliating him. Despite the presence of another set of friends, largely college-bound women, and myself (a white, married professor in his thirties) telling him he too could go to college, I think he ended up leaving high school because he felt that he could better defend himself and his masculinity with the gang than with his college-bound friends.

Gang recruitment and confrontation also occur outside or in transit to and from school. Younger gangs attempting to establish themselves often target particular high schools, hanging out in front of them to step up to anyone who looks Mexican. The curious result has been that some Mexican youths who don't "look Mexican" get a "pass" and are left alone, while others who "really look Mexican" are stepped up to constantly. Noe, a former crew member who has relatives in gangs, explains how Mexicans are identified: by their accents, baggy dress, and fade haircuts. In addition, there is what I call a "racial science of the street" that gang members use in attempting to identify other Mexicans who may be in gangs. Noe described it in an e-mail message:

> The main targets of "stepping up to" are Mexicans. No other groups are pursued unless there is some sort of history with other groups or they are competing for the territory of their 'hood. . . . And it is not difficult distinguishing Mexicans from any other group, except for Guatemalans and Ecuadorans. However, there are distinguishable differences that prevent Mexicans from making a mistake. For example, Ecuadorians and Guatemalans both are of lighter complexion and have more of an indigenous look to them. They have higher cheekbones and longer faces, whereas Mexicans have rounder heads, are darker complexion and tend to be shorter.

Some Mexican youths have told me that they don't get stepped up to because they "look Dominican" or "look Ecuadoran." Step-ups thus often target many Mexicans who are not in gangs but simply dress according to the current fashion for boys. Some told me that my easy-fit Gap jeans were "mad tight" and "crazy tight" and laughed at them; dressing like me would be unthinkable for any self-respecting Mexican youth. I was worse than recently arrived migrants! Step-ups also pass over a significant number of Mexicans who don't "look" Mexican because they appear too indigenous or too light-skinned or have "longer faces," in Noe's words. This description suggests that the borders between the *cholo* world and the regular world are porous and not always easily seen. A young man who dresses the wrong way or is seen the wrong way can suddenly find himself thrown into a gang confrontation.

Mexican parties also offer gangs the chance to confront other gangs and affirm themselves. Mexican parties include *sonidos*, or Mexican DJ parties, usually held in rented clubs, and baptisms and "sweet fifteen" parties. DJs travel throughout New York's five boroughs and northern New Jersey for *sonidos,* and particular gangs often travel with them. Some DJs travel between Mexico and New York, staging parties for friends and relatives, including gang members, on both sides of the border. *Sonidos* offer the chance to affirm identity and challenge other gangs by, for example, sending "shout-outs," greetings or messages announced by the DJ to the crowd. They can run the gamut from cheers to direct provocations of other gangs, present or not. Many *sonideros* (DJs) focus their music on links with Mexico. They also send nongang shout-outs from people in Mexico to people in New York, and to Mexico from New York.[27] The *sonido* is thus a charged atmosphere: teen migrants are highly nostalgic about Mexico and also feel they must be on guard against aggression by other Mexican gangs. Many at the parties are consuming alcohol, and some are using drugs.

Gang conflict at these events can be ignited by someone "giving you hard looks," "dissing" you, "bumping" you on the dance floor, or talking to your girlfriend or sister. These confrontational tactics are also used in school and at other social events. They carry the potential for future consequences, making daily life fraught with anxiety, excitement, and real danger. Mexican baptisms and weddings held in New York often continue, in modified form, the Mexican tradition of inviting the entire village to a day-long party. In New York, families rent halls and circulate information about the party through their friends. But gangs crash these parties, and conflicts can ensue, often with disastrous consequences. Nine-year-old Melenny Melendez was accidentally killed in 2002 as she walked home from a baptism party at her church in the Bronx. The fear of such violence has led to partygivers posting bouncers at the door and checking guests for weapons.

Sonidos bring into close proximity a large number of Mexican youths whose dispersal normally diminishes the chances for conflict. Such concentration facilitates intense social interaction and the sense of accelerated social time and its concomitant, a constituted Mexican space, similar to that in Ticuani during the Feast. The possibility of "bumps," "disses," and responses grows exponentially in a *sonido* or similar setting with the potential to quickly involve large numbers of people, especially gang members. Three conditions make *sonidos* a kind of proving ground for Mexican youths: they are infused with ethnic nostalgia, small conflicts have the potential to explode into epic battles, and they are highly visible: any such conflict will be seen by one's friends and enemies. This last condition makes the experience of fighting compelling.

Technology also facilitates confrontation. One summer day I stopped by Federico's house when he was watching a video of a recent party. As he watched, he practiced making up shout-outs that proclaimed in rhyme the many ways in which his gang was better than a rival. He stopped the tape periodically and went close to the screen to discern the facial features of people he thought were gang members. At one point he identified someone he believed I knew and asked me what gang he belonged to. I told him, despite his insistence, that the tape was too blurry for me to make out the face. He explained to me that gang members would exchange tapes of Mexican parties and *sonidos,* scouring them to identify other gang members. Thus they would know gang members by sight even if they had never met them, even if they had never been in the United States. A similar logic was, I think, at work in an incident reported in the news in 2001, in which Mexican gang members shot other, apparently nongang, youths who had been videotaping themselves coming home on the subway from a family party. I suspect that the gang members saw this act as video espionage.

American Movies and Mexican Gangs: Life Imitates Art

The 1992 movies *American Me* (Universal Studios) and *Blood In, Blood Out* (Hollywood Pictures) fostered the gang surge by providing what Clifford Geertz would call a "model of" and a "model for" reality.[28] Although *American Me* in particular seems like an attempt by its director, James Edward Olmos, to shock the public into action through realist depiction—the film was shot on location in a California prison—the film was used differently by young Mexicans on the East Coast. These movies offer Mexican young men an alternative narrative by which to understand their own experience and a moral framework for evaluation and action. I finally watched them because they kept coming up in conversations and were even offered as answers to my questions about why gangs in New York were growing so much. A former Brooklyn Ranchero said that when these films came out, "se enlocuran la gente" (the people went crazy). Gang members and other Mexican young men bought the videos and watched them repeatedly.

In *American Me,* Santana, a Mexican American youth in California, is put in a juvenile detention facility for petty crimes and then kills an older boy who rapes him. He "gets respect" but is also put into an adult prison. In prison he builds a Mexican gang, La M, or Mexican Mafia, which demands respect from the Black and white gangs inside the prison that have victimized Mexicans; the new gang even muscles its way into the drug trade controlled by the other groups. Meanwhile, Santana's ex-girlfriend's brother dies of an overdose, and Santana comes to see the gang and drugs as destructive. He "loses heart," loses his faith in the gang, thus breaking its code never to show weakness. His childhood friend and the gang's co-founder then has him killed in prison.

Mexican viewers of this film, gang members and non–gang members alike, find Santana a compelling character because he and the other Mexican gangsters demand and get respect from more powerful whites and Blacks. I asked Pedro to tell me "the story of *American Me*." He starts by telling me that "*American Me* is . . . about gang membership":

> PEDRO: The way that *American Me* started, that's how it really happens. They [are] young teenagers, they want to represent *el barrio*, but it went beyond that 'cause they get locked up. . . . To me they had to prove themselves that Mexicans had power also, not only the gringos, the *morenos* [Blacks]. . . . I liked the way they stood up for each other and started forming their own gang in there. That they were controlling . . . half of the jail. . . . Rarely you could hear of Mexicans out here in New York to do stuff like that. In LA, it's . . . a different story. . . . Santana, I really admire him . . . because he grew up without the love of his father. . . . He just had his boyhood friends, and they just grew up being somebody, and he spent only most of his teenage years locked up. When he came out . . . he started seeing life, how it was going on, and reflect . . . he was trying to change his life around. . . .

> RS: [Was Santana] a model for . . . what Mexicans in New York could be? Did you see your future?

> P: I think I did, yeah. I was comparing myself to that person and saying, you know, bam, it got to the point sometimes that I would like to be like him, be like that gang—all powerful, never, never go down, *los putos* [faggots]. . . . It really inspired us, and we were like, Yeah, *Simón!*[29] . . . everybody started talking about the movie, saying: Yeah, that's how we should represent.

Pedro eloquently relates the standard story of *American Me*. Santana inspires because he forced Blacks and whites to respect Mexicans, empowering Mexicans to take control of part of the prison and then the drug trade. But Pedro also relates to Santana in surprising ways, noting the absence of the father and Santana's dependence on his friends to back him up. Indeed, Santana's situation resonates with many teen migrants and their U.S.-born counterparts whose families are unable, for many reasons, to give them the kind of support they need. They feel keenly that, despite their parents' hard struggle, they have been let down by the people and institutions in their lives.

Later in this interview with Pedro and two friends, we talked more about why they watched the movie so many times and talked about it so much. Their answers here and elsewhere always came back to the question of power: Santana inspired them because he took power where he and his people had been powerless. Pedro not only links Mexican gang growth to the powerlessness of Mexicans in New York but also explains why Mexicans mainly fight other Mexicans. I asked Pedro if he and the Brooklyn Rancheros felt that "being Mexican in New York, there was no way to be powerful? Is that why . . . that film was so important to you?" He answered:

PEDRO: In New York, us Mexicans, we're not powerful, all right. . . . We were trying to be powerful back then, but . . . not fighting white people, black people, or Puerto Ricans, we were fighting between our own. . . . We would not defend our own *raza*, we just fight them, we got to defend our barrio. Honestly, we did felt sometimes that we were powerful enough to stand up to Puerto Ricans or whites or Blacks . . . [but in a fight] nobody woulda stood up to them. They would run away . . . unless they had a gun. . . . It's a different thing from LA. . . . In LA . . . the Mexicans, they don't give two fucks. . . . They go and fight. . . .

RS: So . . . everybody liked the movie [because] these Mexicans never backed down . . . and being Mexican in New York, you feel like you had to back down?

P: Exactly . . . you feel stupid, you don't feel like you got respect, 'cause if you're running away from Puerto Ricans, or Blacks or whites, or anybody . . . you consider yourself a *puto*, and . . . word goes out—they like, Nah, the Brooklyn Rancheros, they scared. . . . I heard they got beef with some *morenos, boricuas* [Puerto Ricans], and they don't go up to them niggas. They just fight between the *raza*. They *putos*. . . . That was . . . destroying the image of the Brooklyn Rancheros.

Pedro went on to describe how the Brooklyn Rancheros members had backed down from several confrontations with a large Puerto Rican gang, which I call the Jíbaros Nobles, which he described as "not even a gang, it's a nation . . . they got like ten thousand members." This need to back down— and the shame of feeling like a *puto*—contrasts markedly with the power and pride one feels from demanding respect by using or threatening to use violence to respond to affronts. He also added that the problem was that although the Mexicans gather to go cruising as a gang, they were not always there in force in most neighborhoods the way the Puerto Ricans were. The

Jíbaros Nobles could field large numbers of members in almost any neighborhood. According to Pedro, if you had "beef" in your neighborhood, "your boys are gonna run away . . . but you stay in that neighborhood . . . the Puerto Ricans recognize you, they gonna beat the crap out of you or kill you." The result is that Mexican gangs mainly fight other Mexican gangs "to get respect between other gangs." When they cannot fight Goliath, they fight other Davids. In any of these scenarios, the price is high. You pay either with a beating from Puerto Ricans or other Mexican gangs, or with the loss of self-respect for running away. It is a hard life.

Interestingly, when Pedro criticizes the Brooklyn Rancheros for fighting other Mexicans to prove their power, he does not say instead that Mexicans should become powerful through work, education, politics, or business. His comments resonate with those of others we interviewed: while they all acknowledged that education helped people get ahead, and wanted their younger cousins to stay in school instead of joining the gangs, they still felt it offered no alternative for them. They continued to seek power by demanding respect from everyone, even larger Puerto Rican or Black gangs. Pedro's explanation of *American Me* differs from that of other gang members in its insights about Santana. But he shares their view of the world as hostile, a place where you need someone to "have your back."

Pedro's attitude to intraethnic violence is contradictory. He berates himself for fighting his own *raza* instead of defending Mexicans against a stronger foe. But he then affirmatively notes that his gang must "defend our barrio" against the real threat of other Mexicans. His remarks convey both the pride he experiences in violently defending his barrio, thereby defending his masculinity, and the shame of being a member of an ethnic group that must fight itself, instead of other stronger groups, to prove its mettle. In psychological terms, these contradictory emotions create the constant potential for violence among *cholos:* one feels shame for being weaker than Puerto Ricans, and so one fights a more manageable enemy to expiate this shame, generate fear and respect, and gain glory by defeating other street warriors. This impetus is strengthened because shame is, in the ranchero worldview, a feminine emotion, and thus emasculating. Pedro feels that backing down brands him as a *puto.*

I am *not* saying that Mexicans have a constant potential for violence. Rather, I am saying that gang members I know view the world as constantly and simultaneously threatening to their *cholo* version of Mexicanness and masculinity.

One Mexican, Froilan, who had joined a primarily Puerto Rican gang, told us he joined it because Mexicans were always "playin'," fighting each other, with lots of little kids, young immigrants, who were too crazy. Below, he relates how Puerto Ricans had humiliated his cousin, a member of the formidable Mixtecos Locos:

> So my cousin was talking to me, right, . . . pushin' me like that [demonstrates easy push]. Just playin'. . . . 'Til my Jíbaros Nobles . . . ran up . . . "What's the problem over here?" My cousin was like, "Why the fuck you getting into this?" . . . So Jíbaros Nobles got mad. "Mixteco Loco, pick on somebody that you can pick on. You know what I sayin'? Or we'll kick your ass right now." . . . I was like, "Nah, that's my cousin. Leave him alone." He told my cousin, "You lucky that's your cousin." . . . So, I'm like—that's fucked up 'cause they put a Mixteco Loco down like that!

Froilan joined the Jíbaros Nobles because he felt they were powerful and fought not other Puerto Ricans but Blacks, whom he said he did not like because they had jumped him when he was younger. He contrasted the power of the Puerto Rican gangs with the weakness of the Mexican gangs in New York, pointing out that even members of one of the biggest, baddest Mexican gangs backed down when confronted by the Jíbaros Nobles. His remark, "That's fucked up 'cause they put a Mixteco Loco down like that!" means that Froilan expects more from the large Mexican gang.

This ethnic conflict holds great potential danger. As the Mexican population grows, if ethnic violence against them by Puerto Ricans continues, it will strengthen the Mixteco Loco rationale for forming Mexican gangs, and New York City could face a great deal more ethnic violence. This is not a necessary outcome, and steps can be taken to avoid it.

MEXICAN ROOTS AND MANIFESTATIONS
OF *PANDILLERISMO*

In Mexico, the boom in *pandillerismo* and its effects on transnational life started with the youth exodus from Ticuani in the early to mid-1990s and their incorporation into New York in difficult conditions. Three trends have exacerbated the problem: the voluntary return to Ticuani of gang members who have had troubles in New York; the practice of New York parents' sending errant teens, especially boys, home to Ticuani; and the changed social structure into which these teens are reintegrated, including the weakened means of social control and the cachet that returnees have among Ticuani youth. Changes resulting from migration, in combination with pressures of assimilation, work to transnationalize gangs that formed first in New York.

A review of sixteen in-depth interviews with current or former gang or crew members showed that all had at least returned to their parents' hometown and that more than half had used the town as an important site for gang or crew activity. While escaping the consequences of gang activity in New York, they could recruit new gang members in Ticuani and later bring them back to New York. Sometimes transnational gang activity stems incidentally from being in Ticuani: members of different crews meet in Ticuani and then establish a friendship in New York. That our sample showed no Ticuanense males involved in gangs who are completely uninvolved with transnational life reflects Ticuani's growing importance as a site for New York gang activity.[30]

These return trips have been both voluntary, as when youths seek temporary refuge in Ticuani, and involuntary, when their parents send them back. Below, Brooklyn-born Pedro describes how he started a chapter of the Brooklyn Rancheros in Ticuani's neighboring town of El Ganado in the mid-1990s and then recruited local youths in both towns. Gangs spread to El Ganado and Ticuani at roughly the same time, fueled by gang rivalry in New York. Each gang now controls territory in Brooklyn and Queens as well as the Mixteca.

> There was no gangs in El Ganado until '94; that's when . . . I went back with my cousin. . . . I had to leave here [New York] 'cause we had one or two problems with the police. . . . Me and him went to Mexico, but before we left from New York, we were already really into the gang. . . . He took some beads that we always used to carry around, the colors of Mexico, and we started sporting them over there. And same thing, they recruited us here, we started recruiting people out there. . . . We started telling young kids, . . . Belong to the Brooklyn Rancheros . . . in New York, we powerful, lot of people respect us. . . . We could try to form our own clique right here, our own chapter. And the kids over there, they liked the idea. . . . We started making them beads, and they started wearing it. . . . We had about twenty members with us that year. . . . We used to go to *bailes* [dances] like a whole mob, and we stand there and just send shout-outs for the Brooklyn Rancheros, and it was all good. . . . When [my cousin] came back . . . he says, Yo, the guys, they say they proud of us 'cause we created our own chapter and still defending our name. Well, that's cool, yeah.

The first purposeful transnationalization of gang activity in Ticuani and El Ganado, then, was not by returning teen migrants, but by U.S.-born gang members hiding out in Mexico. These returned Brooklyn Rancheros encountered fertile ground for gang recruitment. Pedro stresses how the Brooklyn Rancheros controlled youth space in El Ganado. They could go as a "whole mob," identifiable by their beads, to all the dances and send shout-outs without challenge. To recruit new members, Pedro used the Brooklyn Rancheros' reputation in New York, implying that migrating Ticuani

FIGURE 16. Gang graffiti: gang names crossed out and replaced with others, Ticuani, 2004.

FIGURE 17. Gang names spray-painted on wall, Ticuani, 2000.

youth could become powerful by joining. This prospect appealed especially to poorer youths in Ticuani and to those left behind by migrant parents. The Brooklyn Rancheros held both geographical space, by controlling the zocalo and other public areas in El Ganado, and the emergent social spaces, by controlling the parties. The Rancheros held this power unchallenged until the Mixtecos Locos also came to Ticuani.

A second scenario for return involves mainly teen migrants, as well as some U.S.-born children, who are sent to Ticuani because of their parents' marital problems or divorce. Others are sent because they show signs of getting into trouble and need to learn to *portarse bien* (behave properly). Sometimes such measures preempt greater gang involvement in New York, or even reverse it and cause a significant change in a young man's life, as for Toño. Others sent back to Ticuani have actually deepened their gang involvement. Fifteen-year-old Victorino was hanging with a crew and beginning to cut school and drink in Brooklyn when his father finished their house in Ticuani and sent the family back to live there. "My father sent me back because he thinks I was in a gang. I was only in a crew," Victorino told me. His return to Ticuani has had mixed results: he is doing much better in school, but he has become active in a local gang chapter in Ticuani and seems likely to return to New York more involved in gang life than when he left. One current gang member who had migrated to the United States as a child with his parents was sent back as a teenager. He said: "I was behaving badly, and my parents sent me back to Ticuani." But he declared that when he turned eighteen in few months, he would go back alone, which would be easy because he had legal residency.

Donal, born in New York, was sent back to Puebla when his parents separated, and he lived in Mexico from age thirteen to sixteen. He later founded a gang in New York and used his contacts in Mexico to reinforce the gang's transnational structure. His experience of feeling out of place, away from his parents—who stayed in the United States—and hanging out with the gang members and friends in Ticuani and another town in the Mixteca region (he lived with family in both places) embedded him more firmly in gang life. Interviewed in his early twenties, he describes being sent back. He tells Sara Guerrero-Rippberger of finishing junior high school in Puebla and founding Los Abandonados. She asks him, "What did you do every day? Like, what was your life like there?"

> DONAL: It was *nadamas estuve yo jugando, na'mas puro—echando puro desmadre.* [It was nothing more than, I was there messin' around, nuttin' but—just fucking around.]

SGR: How did it feel . . . to go back? . . . You hadn't really been there before [age] thirteen, right?

D: Yeah . . . To me it was like, it was like another world, *pues* [well]. . . . It was, ummmm, *como aqui en la ciuda'*, right, *no me adapte, pues. ¿No es lo mismo, como cuando, este, te— me, te cria, vez? ¿Si?* [Like here in the city, right, well, I didn't adapt. It's not the same, like, how when, this, you—me, you were raised, see? Yes?] But yeah, I didn't feel like I was home. . . .

SGR: Okay. And what did it mean to you to go back . . . seeing where your parents grew up?

D: Nuttin'.

SGR: Nothing? How come?

D: Because, because I wasn't—because I didn't even want to go.

For Donal, being sent back to Ticuani had several negative effects. He was sent back alone and felt out of place, "in another world," and abandoned by his parents. His stuttering remark that "I didn't even want to go" sounds very much like the frightened child he must have been. The feud was so fierce between his parents that he did not see his mother for six years, until he returned to New York as an adult to live with her, and he now has only a sporadic relationship with his father. Departing from the normal pattern, he reports no gang involvement before returning to Mexico; once there, however, he became involved with a large, local gang at his school. He was sent back to New York because his aunt's family feared him and his influence on his two younger brothers, who were also living with the aunt but not involved in gangs. By Donal's account, "Nobody could control me down there."

Back in New York, Los Abandonados is a fast-growing, new immigrant gang whose young members often fight more established gangs with many native-born members. It has chapters in Queens, New Jersey, and several towns in the Mixteca, from which it actively recruits. Donal's transnational gang grows directly from his and others' negative migration and assimilation experiences in New York and Ticuani. His "soldiers" are so poor that several sleep on the floor in his mother's living room.

PARENTAL MEMORY AND MISUNDERSTANDING

The migrant parents who send their second-generation or teen migrant children back to Ticuani often misunderstand the consequences. They expect that in Ticuani troubled children will learn respect and become more Mexican, which will help them succeed. But the choice can be disastrous. The returnee often does not know Ticuani or speak Spanish well. He does not fear and respect his grandparents as his parents expect him to, and they lack the strength and understanding needed to deal with him. In effect, the parents send their children back to the Ticuani of their memory, which no longer exists: a pueblo where men have the authority, a tight social structure controls behavior, and everyone is poor and works in agriculture. Ticuani is now a shadow of its former self, with its lopsided population of old people and children dependent on remittances, a disproportionately small number of men, and a small but influential population of disaffected returned youth with disposable income, increased social status, and little effective supervision. Parents send their troubled teens to a place with weaker mechanisms of social control than they had in New York, within which the teens are seen by local Ticuani youth as being very cool because they are New Yorkers. Local adults see returning teenagers as proof of the corrupting influence of American culture. The result is a transnational disaster.

Don Andrés's eloquent description of the problem resonates with Pedro's account. Pedro may in fact be one of the youths to whom Don Andrés refers. Explaining the influence of *pandillas*, he observes that many of the youths in the town live with the grandparents or other relatives, or "even live alone":

> Their grandparents . . . do not have sufficient energy or . . . sufficient strength to raise and teach a grandson. . . . The [local] child . . . falls in the hands of these guys [*cholos*] . . . they tell them, "You know what? Join up with us. We are the law, 100 percent, with us you will be different." . . . And just with them saying this, the child joins themselves fully to them. . . . It is easy to recruit here, with these adolescents . . . because they are alone here, and because they have the illusion that they will also be big like them, no? To carry guns or dance well, to have lots of chicks [*chavas*]. . . . The parents [are] sending money to them. . . . [But] this is bad because . . . it is enough [money] that they . . . can go to the dances, drink beer, smoke. . . . There is no one to guide them. . . . Now, the guys who come here from there . . . those that stay here, or those that they send from there to here, are the lost causes over there . . . with penal histories in the United States . . . that they are looking for them to seek justice, that take refuge here in Ticuani. . . . The two guys that armed a gang of more than twenty youths . . . killed the taxi driver. This was something real. Two that came back from there to here [and] . . . organized a gang. (Spanish, translated by the author)

A local Ticuani mother comments that returned migrant children live "semi-independently"—meaning they care for themselves at a younger age, with less adult accountability—or completely independently, meaning accountable to no one. Serious consequences have resulted, including at least three deaths in Ticuani.

Ticuani cannot handle these social problems in the way its emigrants imagine it can. Migration has depleted Ticuani of the social structures that in the past would have prevented youth gangs, while also investing *pandillas* with greater prestige and honor. These problems are worst during the annual Feast, when many migrants return to participate in the town's communal rituals, alcohol flows plentifully, and life is different. Octavio Paz's classic essay about the role of the feasts in Mexican national life describes how during the feast, social mores loosen, creating possibilities for love, death, and redemption in the same dangerous instant.[31] In the Mixteca today, local authorities attempting to use normal mechanisms of social control, such as talking to the parents or relatives of the youths, are often rebuffed. Don Pepe of El Baile, which has more gang members than Ticuani, reports that locals want him to control the youths, their parents want them left alone to have fun, and the youths want freedom. The returning migrant youths say to him, "In the United States we have liberty, the police respect us—why in our own country do we have to behave ourselves? . . . We have come here to enjoy ourselves!" When he approaches the parents, they agree that the child is now harder to control but also ask for lenience: "Since he went to New York, he does not want to obey us. . . . But you're not going to put him in jail, because he will leave soon. . . . Why did you pick up my kid?" Meanwhile, locals fault him for permitting such disorder.

Pandillas also prosper because the municipal infrastructure is especially strained during the Feast. Local police are typically campesinos with very little education or police training, almost like sheriffs' deputies in the Old West in the United States. They do not understand the *pandilleros*. Their main qualifications are that they carry shotguns and carbines; their main activities are apprehending drunks and other obstreperous persons and confiscating weapons. They sometimes throw drunks or belligerents in jail to sleep it off. Their social status can make it hard to enforce the law against the wealthy and influential. And they work only part-time, usually days, so that the town is often left without police protection. One Ticuani president commented: "I have police only five or six hours a day, they cannot cover the whole town. When something happens over there, there is no one to cover over here." Ticuani's inability to handle serious crime showed in Don

Andrés's answer when I asked what he thought of the widespread belief that the *pandilleros* had killed someone in 2000:

DON ANDRÉS: It's possible, . . . [but] there is no information that proves this killing. . . . Well, they found the wounds on his front and his back . . . on his face, without his watch [or] jacket, which all indicate that he was beaten, no? This was not . . . an accident, that he had fallen because he was drunk, no? This possibility is discounted, but there is no witness. We have to be formal to be able to accuse them. Of course, they are investigating. . . .

RS: Are they doing a forensic analysis?

DA: No . . . in a more superficial manner—he [the municipal president] is pursuing it via his office, and the Judicial [state police] are intervening. They are seeing who was with him before. (Spanish, translated by the author)

I also asked the president about the investigation: Had people been interviewed? Had the suspects been interviewed, or had their houses and clothing been searched or confiscated? Nothing could be done until witnesses came forward. Eventually, in each case, those involved bragged about it while drunk and were jailed in Mexico or fled to the United States.

The situation after the 2000 murder was summed up by Napoleon, the second-generation returnee who had had conflicts with the *pandilleros* during that Feast: "The people here are mad scared. They are mad petrified about the *pandilleros*. . . . It's easier to kill someone here than in New York because the police are not that well-trained and because at night there is no one around to see anything."

Yet Ticuani did exercise more social control after the January 2000 murder, and no such crimes occurred during the 2001 or 2002 feasts. The state of Puebla formed a twenty-five member unit of the State Judicial Police that focuses on public safety issues, including gangs in the Mixteca. This unit, based about forty minutes away from Ticuani, showed up in Ticuani to investigate the 2000 murder while we were there. But the unit's territory is huge, and it did not come to Ticuani for least ten days after the murder. I do not know the unit's overall effect in the region. Moreover, strengthening the police's ability to apprehend criminals should not be the only response to this phenomenon, and cannot be successful on its own.

Local Ticuanenses also considered enacting vigilante justice. Some of the older men in the town, including returning migrants, told me they would not hesitate to shoot the *pandilleros* if confronted by them. One angrily described how younger relatives had been harassed by the *pandilleros,* then said, "I am capable of defending myself," while patting the gun tucked inside his belt. A mutual friend told me that several young campesinos unhappy with the *pandilleros'* effects on the pueblo had decided that if such problems continued, "they would have to kill four of them to calm down the pueblo." While I did not try to verify this story, the town's history of political bloodshed makes it plausible. However, as of mid-2004, this plan had not been acted on and had probably been abandoned.

CONCLUSION

Transnational *pandillerismo* in Ticuani, like other dimensions of transnational life examined in this book, grows out of the processes of migration and assimilation. Just as conditions of incorporation in New York have given rise to *pandillas* there, so the changes in social structure resulting from migration have made Ticuani into a fertile field for returning *pandilleros* to recruit. Just as parents' long working hours in New York and their children's search for positive meaning for Mexican ethnicity and gender have led some to become *pandilleros* there, so the lopsided population, lack of social control, high status of New Yorkers, and glamour of gang violence have given *pandilleros* an influence beyond their numbers in Ticuani. Yet even with its depleted capacity for social control, Ticuani has managed to quell some of the most serious consequences of returning *cholos,* though not the larger changes in youth culture that they have helped bring about.

The defense of masculine, Mexican space in a context where Mexican young men, especially, feel threatened has amplified the *pandillero* influence in New York. Teen migrants in particular are likely to seek solace in the kinds of social settings that facilitate gang life, such as *sonidos* and other Mexican parties. These youths are part of the larger Mexican community but are in danger of becoming an enduring oppositional subculture, as they are in Los Angeles, akin to but different from the "rainbow underclass" predicted by segmented assimilation theory. This chapter contributes to our understanding of transnational life and of gangs by explaining the boom in gangs in New York during the 1990s as a result of changes in larger patterns of migration. Teen migrants' negative experience of adolescence, as the result of an accelerated migration and harsh assimilation, leads them to want to "defend their name" in New York and Ticuani. Ethnic victimization by Puerto Ricans and others meshes unfortunately with the *cholo* narrative expressed in movies such as *American Me*. Rather than explain these processes by invoking an "invisible hand" of globalization, I trace out how pressures of assimilation and migration combine in New York and the Mixteca to transnationalize gang life. The next chapter focuses on how the presence of *pandilleros* affects the experience of return to Ticuani.

10.   Returning to a Changed Ticuani

Why you gotta mess up a good place?
MAGDA, angry at how *pandilleros* have changed Ticuani for her

We feel here [Ticuani] the same way as when we arrive there. The people don't want us.
DIONISIO, a Mixteco Loco

The quotes from Magda and Dionisio capture two sides of the experience of return to a Ticuani that has changed because of the presence of *pandilleros*. Magda's view is widely shared by her friends, a mixed group of U.S.-born second and 1.5-generation "regulars," non–gang members whose regular return to Ticuani with their families makes them feel at home there. They describe what it means to be Mexican by saying, "We're just normal" or "We're regular." "Preppies" are a second social group to which no one admits belonging but for which everyone expresses firm dislike. Preppies think they are better than others, and are usually seen as being more American and less Mexican. Although some youths admitted to dressing preppy, none named themselves as such. *Cholos* or *pandilleros* are the only group who self-identify using the name by which others identify them, which is linked to a distinctive style of life, dress, and behavior. Regular, *cholo*, and preppy are what the sociologist Elijah Anderson would call "folk" categories, terms that the people under study themselves use and understand.[1]

In examining the effects of *pandillerismo* on the experience of return to Ticuani, I take a second pass through the concepts of embodied experience and social proprioception discussed in previous chapters, and I also draw on the sociologist Arlie Hochschild's concept of "emotional labor,"[2] which describes how people become alienated from themselves by the need to present an inauthentic emotional self. Whereas Hochschild examined how airline stewardesses must subordinate their real feelings in order to present the image of someone eager to please passengers, I analyze how the presence of *pandilleros* requires returning regulars to don their New York selves in Ticuani, a practice that feels inauthentic to them there. They report that their sense of being at ease in Ticuani has been disrupted by the *cholos,* and as a result they must feel and behave differently there. I then turn from the social psychology of the changed experience to documenting the dynamics of social distance and respect between *cholos,* regulars, and Ticuani locals, invoking the sociologist Erving Goffman's work on stigma management. This section focuses mainly on social interaction between groups. Finally, I turn to the *cholos'* feelings of belonging and alienation in Ticuani. The same social distancing mechanisms that regulars employ as self-protection are experienced by *cholos* as exclusion and racial discrimination. And, not surprisingly, *cholos* frame their experience as a darker narrative than that of regulars, casting migration from Mexico and incorporation and assimilation in the United States as dangerous and requiring a forceful response to preserve one's dignity. In explicating these themes, I pay special attention to how adolescence and masculinity are negotiated in public Mexican space and to the strategic use of racialization.

As elsewhere in this book, *cholo* and *pandilleros* are interchangeable terms referring to those who identify and are identified by others as gang members. *Cholos* can also be returnees, whom I normally refer to as returning *cholos. Wannabe* normally refers to a current or aspiring member of the Ticuani chapter of a New York gang, or a teen migrant in New York, who wants to be a real gang member. A *regular* is a non-*cholo* returnee, usually a second-generation migrant whose family returns often and who hence has a sense of ownership of Ticuani. Some regulars also belong to crews in New York, and some belonged to gangs when they were younger but are no longer active members. Even the few regulars I knew who were in gangs in New York were not, it seemed, in deep enough to be publicly identified as gang members. They did not have conspicuous tattoos, dress very "baggy," or get into fights in Ticuani on the basis of their gang membership. Hence, although they may have hung with or even been down with a gang in New York, their other identities were more prominent in Ticuani. The Mixtecos Locos, especially the leaders whose actions we follow here, were almost always publicly identified by their tattoos, dress, and outsider status as gang members first and foremost. Yet this identity receded in importance for at least one of them after he married a local Ticuani woman.

CHOLOS AND SOCIAL CHANGE IN TICUANI

Understanding the evolving experience of return for regulars requires close attention to how the *cholos* have disrupted the functioning of their transnationalized adolescence. Ticuani has generally offered returning youths a safe site for adolescent rituals and a sense of ethnic ownership, in contrast to New York, where their own and their parents' fears inhibit feelings of freedom and belonging. The emergence of *cholos* as a permanent feature of Ticuani life, especially during the Feast, has changed this experience. The disruption has been magnified because these groupings reflect power divisions in Ticuani. As a group, regulars tend to be educationally or economically successful second- and 1.5-generation youths whose main friends in Ticuani are its higher-status, more affluent youths. Returning *cholos* tend to be less educationally or economically successful teen migrants (along with some 1.5- or second-generation youths) whose main friends in Ticuani are from the poorer families in town and the surrounding ranchos. In general, *cholos* have lower social status in Ticuani than regulars and tend to be blamed for trouble there.[3]

My researchers and I observed social dynamics among returning youths over four consecutive years of the Feast, from 1999 to 2002. We hung out mainly with the regulars we knew in New York, including those whose voices we have heard already: Magda, Toño, Julia, Napoleon, Jericho, Juana, and Linda. But we also developed relationships with *cholos*, interviewed them, and observed dynamics between *cholos* and regulars in various settings. Contradictory patterns of *cholo* engagement in Ticuani emerged. First, *cholos* came back to participate in the same events as regulars—dances, parties, religious events, and even *promesas*. However, their participation in and behavior at these events changed the feel of the events for regulars and demonstrated the *cholos'* desire to dominate. Second, while the *cholos* became more visible and "looked for beef" more aggressively in Ticuani in 1999 and 2000, in 2001 and 2002 they had a more normalized, if still strained, relationship with others. In 2000, *cholos* threatened violence if the son of the municipal president did not pay for their tacos and threatened to kill the taco vendor if he did not serve them first. Yet in 2002 this same president presided at the civil wedding of a *cholo* leader to a young local woman. This evolution softened but did not erase the social difference between regulars and *cholos*.

The social friction does not extend to younger children, who do not express much concern about the *cholos*. While some preteens had been stepped up to in New York, in Ticuani they were not out late enough at night in the zocalo or at the events where problems started.

COMPROMISED FREEDOM

The physical presence of the *cholos* in Ticuani changes the regulars' experience of themselves in Ticuani (in relation to a place) and in the presence of other regulars (their social proprioception). Below, Ceydi and Napoleon describe themselves as freed from the kind of emotional labor they must do every day in New York. They explain how Ticuani represents freedom, a frequent theme in their conversations.

> CEYDI: You could stay out as late as you want. You won't have to be locked up in your house, . . . [and] you have somewhere to go [the zocalo]. . . . [In New York], where am I gonna go? . . .
>
> NAPOLEON: I just love Ticuani. . . . You just think about the memories over there, and you be like crying. . . . Oh, if I could go back. . . . January this year was the best for me. . . . Over there [in Ticuani], you don't have to worry about . . . if you go into this neighborhood, they gonna say something to you. . . . Over there . . . you know where people at, they know you, they know your family, and you feel so relieved. . . . Once we get over here, you feel depressed. You feel like locked up. . . .
>
> RS: It means like complete freedom to be . . . what?
>
> N: To be who you wanna be, to be the person that you really are, not tryin' to be someone that you not. . . . Over here, you walk with somebody and right away—oh, there's gonna be problems. . . .
>
> C: It's like a image you gotta keep up when you here [New York]. . . . I can release all my stress over there. There's more nature. And I like to learn about my culture. It's exciting to learn beyond what you're expected [to]. My race [Mexicans] just settles for the same thing. They don't try to do more. Going to Ticuani gives me the courage to continue to educate myself. . . . Don't settle. . . . In Ticuani, you can let out all your griefs—sadness, happiness—you just looking at Padre Jesús and it's hard not to cry.

Napoleon and Ceydi describe several kinds of emotional labor from which they are free in Ticuani. Freedom from this emotional labor offers them a more authentic experience of themselves. The safe space of the zocalo allows parents to ease restrictions and youths to feel ownership of Ticuani and its adolescent rituals. This security contrasts sharply with the anxiety New York provokes among both parents and youths. In Ticuani, one need not worry about going into the wrong neighborhood, or getting into trouble with peers for walking with the wrong person. Returnees also feel like they are somebody on Ticuani's social map: people know them and their families.

In New York, Ceydi and Napoleon say, they must project an image that will stop others from confronting them; this emotional labor becomes part of their physical and emotional experience of themselves. In Ticuani they are freed from the need to dissociate themselves from their feelings. Napoleon's observation that in Ticuani you are free to be "the person that you really are" is connected with his saying that people will comment or confront you even about who you walk with in New York. Ceydi also says that in New York there is an "image you gotta keep up." Her remark recalls Merleau-Ponty's point that we realize our true selves in relation to others. Ceydi and Napoleon experience their true identities in relation to positive images of Mexicanness in Ticuani rather than often-negative ones in New York. In Ticuani, they can let their guard down, turn off their emotional image projectors. This freedom opens possibilities for what I call "embodied experiences of belonging" in Ticuani that do not exist in New York.

Emotional Labor and Social Proprioception: Regulars' Experience of *Pandillero Return*

Just as Ticuani's religious rituals create a context for returning regulars to feel linked to their parents through embodied experience, the social changes in the Ticuani context alter the regulars' experience of themselves. Moreover, these changes affect all the processes involved in transnational adolescence, including perceptions of masculinity and femininity. Below, Napoleon and Ceydi discuss how the *cholos* have changed Ticuani for them.

> NAPOLEON: Now over there is starting to get like over here. . . . Somebody's gonna say something to you. . . . Jus' like over here. . . .
>
> CEYDI: Don't just walk around so confident—ain't nobody gonna step up to me.
>
> N: Like always expect the unexpected. . . . Always think—like the way I always do every time I come out or anything like that [in New York]—if they come up to me, I know what to do—jus' not say nuttin', jus' walk away. . . . Now over there you have to walk with the same image that you walk with here. . . . Now suddenly people looking at you over there like you're a stranger, you know? . . . They look at you very bad. . . . They wanna start wit' you. They wanna pick a fight. . . .
>
> RS: What's different with these gang guys down there than before those gang guys were there?

N: Now they step up to me. Jus' like you think about over here, when you go to a party, go to another neighborhood, you gotta think the same over there. . . .

C: You gotta use the same mentality that you walk with here . . . over there. . . . I'ma look out for myself. Protect yourself, make sure you're safe. Make sure that nobody . . . disrespects you, too. . . .

RS: Before . . . nobody would try to disrespect you?

N: Before you didn't even have to think about it.

This long exchange shows how the social proprioception and embodied experience of returning regulars are being affected by the *cholos*, and the emotional labor the change forces them to do. While Ticuani required some emotional work before—such as negotiating their Mexicanness with Ticuani natives who call them "tourists"—that work was not nearly as hard, and they did not feel as threatened, either physically or emotionally. Napoleon says that now you "gotta think the same" in Ticuani as you do in New York. Wherever you go—"to a party" or another neighborhood— you must watch for danger and disrespect. Such pervasively changed feelings affect the transnationalized adolescence of second-generation Ticuanenses and their experience of social proprioception.

Young second-generation men like Napoleon have become foils for native Ticuanenses who want to assert their masculinity by stepping up to returning New Yorkers. Local teenagers are often quite poor, many have been left behind by their migrant fathers, and their dress clearly identifies their local origins and their poverty. Napoleon made fun of these youths in a later conversation by saying that they wore "Air chanclas" or "Air huaraches." Instead of the expensive Nike Air sneakers worn by those from New York, these locals wear either huaraches (peasant sandals adorned with goat hide) or *chanclas* (flip-flops). Napoleon's joke cruelly and deftly juxtaposed a symbol of his power and modernity as a New Yorker with the local boys' envy and poverty.

These local youths experience their masculinity as further compromised because they are labeled as wannabes by both returning second-generation youths and the leaders of the gangs in New York to which the locals have pledged their allegiance in Ticuani. Horacio commented: "Those guys are wannabes. . . . If I brought them to Brooklyn, they would cry." In this context, returning second-generation youths, with their designer sneakers, fashionable clothes, and gold chains, present an image of modernity and power that becomes a ready target against which locals can prove their manhood. According to Napoleon, the *pandilleros* first influence local youths, who then challenge returning second-generation young men like him. Locals "look up to" *pandilleros* from New York and think that "I gotta show him that I could do the same things like him." This has "made things worse" for Napoleon and other second-generation returnees because "kids got more words over there, they got more disrespectful. . . . I don't like it. . . . They get smart wit' you. . . . They get mad smart." His words echo those of both Don Andrés, the former Ticuani president, and Pedro, the returning gang member.

Napoleon was stepped up to more than other second-generation returnees because he is physically small and does not back down, and because his girlfriend, Marqueza, was with him in Ticuani. Confronting Napoleon was a perfect way for local wannabes to prove themselves: they could count on him to rise to their bait, he had a girlfriend other young men desired, and he was not physically intimidating. Yet he was from New York and thus possessed a power denied many of these locals: the power to leave Ticuani to go north when he wanted.[4] Napoleon recounted a specific example in which local wannabes linked to the Mixtecos Locos had whistled at his girlfriend as they walked together in Ticuani:

NAPOLEON: I was in the bus [station in Ticuani] one time. . . . They started whistling at my girl. . . . And I'm like: Who you whistling at? I'm like: *¿Quién estan chiflando?* And then they just looked at me: *Pues a tu vieja* [Well, at your old lady]. And that's when I got mad. . . . They were like sixteen, seventeen. Around that age. They were gang guys. . . . Horacio's friends, but the small kids . . .

RS: Were they wannabe guys? . . .

N: That's a perfect word for it. They were the kids from the *pueblitos,* trying to be jus' like the ones from New York. . . . Tryin' to dress like them, act like them, tryin' to do things like them. . . . They like, This kid's from New York, let me get smart wit' him. Show how good I am. . . . Yo, I stepped up to a kid from New York. I show me like, mad big.

CEYDI: They be like, *No el güey, no hizo nada* [The dumb ox, he didn't do anything].

Napoleon's story clearly shows that New York gangs hold a privileged social position in Ticuani, with many local youths wanting to become "real" gang members. Returning "kids from New York" like Napoleon are used as the measure against which the wannabes test themselves. These tensions resonate with the social differences between the local higher-status youth, linked to the upwardly mobile New Yorkers, and the lower-status "kids from the *pueblitos,*" who are often linked to returning gang members or less successful migrants. These tensions are driven by the importance of manhood, class, and authentic Mexicanness among adolescents. For example, the term *el güey,* used by Ceydi, echoes the language men in the Mixteca would use in establishing relations of *confianza* (deep trust) or of dominance. In this context, *güey* implies that Napoleon is incapable of defending himself either because he is literally dumb as an ox or because he fears physical attack. A real Mexican ranchero would defend himself verbally, without fearing the physical attack his words might elicit. Hence, Napoleon felt he had no choice but to protect his masculinity by yelling back at them—especially in front of his girlfriend in Ticuani, a place where events take on heightened meaning.

I felt a surprising sympathy with Napoleon as a result of a confrontational experience of my own. In 2002 I went back to Ticuani for Homero's wedding. The night before the religious ceremony, I walked with him as he paraded with his friends and relatives, according to custom, to his fiancée's house for the brief civil ceremony. At the party, I worked the beer and softdrink detail with the other men. I met a number of the local gang members, young adolescents to whom I was introduced as a friend of Homero's. Later in the evening, one of these youths sat down, somewhat drunk, and began to talk to me. He was very friendly at first, but then became more aggressive. He asked me repeatedly, "You understand me?" a question often implying that the speaker will *make* you understand if you disagree. He seemed to be trying to find in my conversation some form of disrespect for him, for Ticuani, or for Mexico that would give him a pretext for attacking me, verbally or otherwise. For example, he asked me if I liked Ticuani, "even though" I was from New York, and his manner suggested he suspected I did not. I answered that I really liked Ticuani, had come back for years. I named some adult Ticuanense friends, including Homero, saying they treated me like another brother or son.

Although I was able to defuse this situation, I realized that it would have been very hard for someone like Napoleon to extricate himself peacefully without being humiliated. That this youth apparently sought an argument that would give him a pretext for feeling insulted and then to attack, verbally or otherwise, in the context and with the person he did, is notable. We were in the middle of the wedding of a leader in his gang, and he was trying to provoke someone who was, by most markers, a full adult, and physically much bigger than he was. He had seen me talking and laughing with Homero and with adults there, including the municipal president, who performed the ceremony. Though I was regularly addressed as *joven* (a form of address to an unknown young man) into my early thirties, such was, alas, no longer the case. At the time of this incident, I was thirty-eight years old, had a little gray hair around my temples, was six feet tall, weighed about 185 pounds, and was more than twenty years older than my interlocutor, who, I later was told, was fifteen or sixteen. The encounter was sometimes tense, and I felt myself getting angry at this young man but also getting nervous about what he might do.

The encounter was instructive in how such dynamics of confrontation can work and how much emotional labor they require.[5] My anger at this youth's attempts to twist something I said into an insult disrupted my enjoyment of the event and the flow I was experiencing.[6] I was pleased to be attending Homero's wedding, and he seemed pleased to have my company as we marched together. We spent a lot of time talking on the long walk and later, even though I gave him several chances to excuse himself. He told me how his life had gone since we had last spoken, with many positive changes, including his engagement and marriage. I was also pleased to be back in Ticuani and to experience myself as *el gringo* who is friends with many Ticuanenses, from the municipal president to the returning gangster. I resented this youth's challenges because they threatened to reclassify me as a disrespectful "outsider." Of course I *was* still an outsider, even when experiencing this flow. My sense of myself as a person who had a real place in Ticuani was disrupted by this youth, and I had to stop enjoying myself and get to work on defusing this potentially serious situation. In so doing, I had to do the emotional work of denying outwardly that I was angry.

My experience also offers insight into social proprioception and disrupted social relations. I knew that the situation was getting more serious when the other people at the table, all second-generation returnees or local Ticuanenses, turned away from the young man and me to disengage themselves from the confrontation. They also stopped making eye contact with me. I realized I was caught in the processes of avoidance and social distancing that I had observed around *cholos*. But I also knew that my companions were listening and that they would help me if things really did get out of hand. When the youth finally left, the people at the table turned themselves back squarely toward me and asked, "What was up with him?" This question marked the end of the altercation and my passage back into "regular" social space. Observing their reactions heightened my own perceptions of the risk of the situation and the social distancing and isolation of the *cholos*.

RESPONSES BY THE SECOND GENERATION AND TICUANI FRIENDS TO *PANDILLERISMO* IN TICUANI

Returning second-generation regulars and their Ticuani friends usually avoided confrontations with *cholos* in three ways. They associated with grown men, especially "retired" gang members, who could command the respect of the *cholos* without fighting. They also exercised practices of social deference or distance when they could not avoid contact with *cholos*, or they avoided the *cholos* altogether by staying out of spaces where they might encounter them or by leaving when the *cholos* arrived. However, some returning regulars and their Ticuani friends refused to yield to the *cholos*, instead "looking back" at the *cholos'* "hard looks" and even fighting. These practices helped create the sense of accelerated social time discussed earlier and demonstrated various forms of masculinity and belonging.

Avoiding Conflict by Any Means Necessary

The regulars' methods for negotiating their relations with *cholos* evoke Erving Goffman's classic analysis of stigma, with a curious power inversion. According to Goffman, stigmatized people lack the power to contest their stigma, and so must settle for managing a hard reality. They manage their stigma by, for example, "passing" as members of the nonstigmatized group and trying to restrain the flow of discrediting information. Returned *cholos* may be stigmatized by the larger U.S. and Ticuani societies, but they also have power and social cachet, especially among poorer Ticuanense youths, which they use to fight that stigma. Coming from New York, they are seen as modern; being in a gang, they are seen to embody a dangerous masculinity. However, while most regulars fear the *cholos*, the regulars understand their own power. They can and do withhold recognition and acceptance, a denial the *cholos* feel keenly. Nevertheless, the *cholos* project a tough image and an alternative narrative of migration and return. They also gain some legitimacy because their harsher narrative of migration resonates with the hard life experiences of many Ticuani youths in a way that the standard, positive narrative of migration does not. While Ticuani youths, especially those left behind or brought back against their will, want to migrate, they also recognize that migration entails problems from which the *cholos* promise protection, and suffering, of which the *cholo* narrative offers validation because it does not cast them as responsible for their failure to prosper. Hence, the alternative project of the *cholos* not only rejects the risk of a judgment of failure for those who are not conventionally successful according to the immigrant narrative, but also offers them an alternative, self-empowered rhetoric. The *cholos* have the threat of force and macho honor but lack the social standing they both crave and reject: they both contest this stigma and try to manage it. The *cholos* must perform the emotional labor of appearing to eschew the social acceptance they desire and challenging any who might seem to deny it to them.

The regulars' first strategy was to associate with older men who could command respect from the *cholos* without fighting. One of these was Pepe, aged about thirty, who told me he was one of the "original gangsters" in the Brooklyn Rancheros during the 1980s and 1990s. He left the gang, joined the military, married, and had children. In 2000 he returned to Ticuani for a vacation. Although he and others told me he was no longer active in the gang, he saw *cholos* in the sports leagues he still played in. Pepe told me that *cholos* "give me respect" as a former O.G. He also still had a well-deserved reputation for being tough and unpredictable when he felt disrespected. In Ticuani, younger regulars used him as a safe base, seeking him out after *cholos* appeared but before problems occurred. Pepe told me the *cholos* would not bother him, his family, or his friends if he was with them or had been seen with them.

A second strategy among the regulars was to avoid any social contact with *cholos*, even when close proximity was unavoidable, as at dances. Most returning New York girls would not dance with *cholos;* many *cholos* did not dance at all, simply staying to one side, drinking and watching. Tellingly, when my research team members spoke with *cholos,* our regular group friends did not make eye contact with us, speak to us, or stand near us. They warned us not to believe anything the *cholos* said because "son mentirosos" (they are liars) and to avoid them and the danger they posed. Although we often did avoid them, we still managed to develop relationships with some of them. Griscelda Perez's field notes and paper for this project describe this effort:

> In Ticuani, some of our informants urged [us] to leave parties or places where we were just hanging out whenever gangs came onto the scene. However, this was only in instances where it was towards the end of the night and there weren't as many people around. Their whole attitudes were just leave and don't ask any questions. When Joy saw that they approached me, she couldn't believe that I was talking to them. She asked me not to introduce her, because she didn't like the Mixtecos Locos and she didn't want to know them either. On another occasion, Lazario immediately cut off his conversation and moved away when he saw one of the gang members was approaching me.[7]

We later learned that Joy had been chased by Mixtecos Locos in Brooklyn. Other, older adult men and women warned their adolescent children not to interact with the *pandilleros* and not to confront them because they were dangerous.

I had similar experiences when speaking with *cholos*. In one case, I sat in the zocalo speaking with Dionisio, who had been living in Ticuani for several months. As we talked, more than fifteen returning or local youths I knew walked by, but only two openly said hello, and only one, who also knew Dionisio, actually stopped to talk. Yet, during the following days, several of these same youths made comments about my conversation with Dionisio: although they had kept their distance, they had heard what he said. He had been telling me that he had been shot by a friend in his gang but had not pressed charges with the police because his friend was drunk and was getting married the following week. The youths who had passed by without saying hello had been listening closely; they could not believe that he was talking about this incident so openly in the zocalo or that he had let it pass. They said: "Letting your friend shoot you goes way too far; he's crazy." Others who had not spoken to me at the time later warned me to be careful.

These interactions require two forms of emotional labor by regulars and result in particular kinds of social proprioception. Regulars first must hide their fear of the *cholos*, which they enact through New York–style avoidance tactics, by avoiding eye contact and holding their bodies with a forced casualness. But they also perform the emotional labor of enacting their anger and their social power in a "hidden" way by treating the *cholos* as socially invisible, avoiding or ignoring them. Hence the friends who walked past me in the zocalo while talking to Dionisio had the embodied experience of attentive listening joined with profound social disengagement in a place where they were used to having their senses heightened and being fully socially engaged.

The zocalo is a place where returning regulars feel a special sense of belonging, and walking around it is an important physical and emotional expression of this ownership and belonging (as exemplified in Linda's amazement that her presence there was real and not a dream). The layout of the zocalo facilitates social interaction, both that which affirms others by engaging with them and that which negates them by ignoring them.[8] It has a large exterior path ringed by benches; at the center is a small snack kiosk linked to the outer rectangle by several small paths. As people walk around the exterior rectangle, or along the paths leading to the kiosk, they stop and talk to people sitting on the benches or the low walls of the paths, which

FIGURE 18.   Ticuani's zocalo, 2004. The layout of the zocalo, with its many paths, creates multiple, dense webs of social interaction as people walk around and through it.

often double as seats. In addition, the zocalo is bordered on one side by the road and on the others by the market, the municipal palace, and an open area that holds arcades and video games during the Feast. As one walks around the zocalo, then, one walks through Ticuani's various social worlds: one might first encounter a group of returned adult men talking with their local counterparts, then a group of local schoolchildren, then a group of second-generation regulars talking with their Ticuani friends, then *cholos*, all at very close quarters. No wonder Ceydi and Napoleon feel that they have to walk and act in the "same way" as they do in New York. By having to project their New York toughness, they lose their previous, prized sense of physical and emotional ease in the zocalo.

The third social strategy of the regulars was to move on when *pandilleros* approached or asserted their presence. This avoidance strategy became a sort of minuet as the Feast wore on. The wedding of a New York–born Ticuanense woman and her Mexico City husband became the site of a tense encounter between regulars and *cholos*.[9] Weddings are usually public events in small Mexican towns, and everyone can attend and eat. This wedding reception was held in the basketball court on Ticuani's main road, and after dinner guests began dancing there. The *cholos* showed up and began throwing hard looks at Napoleon and asking the women in our group to dance. Most declined, with one telling them they were being too rude to dance with. Seeing the tension brewing, Jericho, the oldest male in the group, told the others that he was going to go the *gallos* (cockfights) and that they should all come with him, which they did. I was already there and learned of this encounter when the group arrived. Napoleon started to tell me about wanting to throw hard looks back at the *cholos*, but leaving when Jericho told him to. Hearing us talk, Jericho broke in and said to Napoleon: "I told you, 'Don't be stupid, 'cause if there's trouble, I won't be there.'" In a joint interview back in New York, I asked Napoleon and Jericho to tell me their understanding of these events.

> JERICHO: I was getting worried that . . . they were gonna start with my cousin Napoleon . . . [he] was telling me that those guys kept looking at him, so I was like, Listen, let's go. . . . But . . . because a certain song came on, they all wanted to go back to the party. But I decided, No, you already told me that guys were lookin' at you all hard . . . so *we leaving*. . . . Napoleon wanted to go back, and I was like, Listen, if you want to go back, go back, but I won't be there if anything bad happens. . . .
>
> RS: Yeah, tell me how you came to make that decision. . . .
>
> J: I was thinking that if something would happen to my cousins, then the blame would be on me. My aunts and uncles would blame me for everything, knowing that I'm the older cousin, I should take more responsibility, watching over them . . . making sure that they get home . . . nice and safe. So that whole thing popped into my head, and honestly, I'm not a person that likes to look for trouble, so whenever I see trouble I try to avoid it. So I was trying to get Napoleon . . . to avoid the trouble as well.

This story clearly illustrates the regulars' strategy of placing social and physical distance between themselves and the *cholos*. Jericho also exercised a specific masculine, familiar authority and responsibility in what the group saw as a dangerous situation. He was fulfilling his obligation as the oldest cousin to ensure the group's safety. That they all followed his lead suggests their common perception of the danger and acknowledgment of his authority. On the other side of the interaction, the regulars' actions would have confirmed to the *cholos* that they themselves are powerful and the others are *presumido*. These are the two sides of the minuet described above.

Jericho's choice embodies an avoidance masculinity or long-view masculinity with respect to the *cholos*, choosing to avoid trouble even if it means losing face. Jericho's leadership constrained Napoleon's ability to pursue his own, more macho form of masculinity, wherein such challenges must be rebuffed if one is to avoid being labeled a *puto*. If Napoleon had thought that Jericho "had his back" and would defend him in a fight, the encounter would have developed very differently. Where Jericho saw a problem to avoid, Napoleon saw a challenge to respond to. In a follow-up conversation, their comments displayed their different views of masculinity, but each also curiously embraced some of the other's view, as Jericho does here:

> RS: I asked Napoleon what it meant to be a man . . . in that situation. He repeated the same thing: "If you're gonna be lookin' hard at me, you might jus' as well step up to me, because it doesn't matter if I'm short, I'm not gonna let you push me around by looking hard at me." What was your understanding of what being a man meant in that situation?
>
> JERICHO: Being a man is jus' trying to avoid it. You could get stabbed on hard, . . . but you can avoid it and live to see the next day. 'Cause you never know. If my cousin Napoleon or anybody else walked up to those guys and then they do something bad . . . like stab you or shoot you, that's it. You gonna get dropped jus' because you looked at me hard? Nah, I'd rather jus' avoid it and then live to see the new, the next day. That's why I told my cousin, "Listen, let's leave. . . ."
>
> RS: You're not less of a man 'cause you said let's walk away?
>
> J: No . . . 'Cause I don't need to prove myself, step up to you, and say, "Why you lookin' at me hard? Look at me hard, why don't you do something?" I don't feel that's appropriate.

Jericho's long view sees his masculinity as being upheld in his exercise of both authority and discretion; in this way he keeps an implicit bargain with his adult relatives and his own future. By steering everyone away from danger, he honors his responsibility to his older and younger relatives and exercises a mechanism of social control. He upholds his masculinity through a less confrontational stance that many would see as being a *puto*—indeed, others from his group later criticized him, telling me he should have had Napoleon's back—but that he views as keeping everyone safe for the long haul and allowing him to seek success, manhood, and other goals elsewhere: in schooling, fulfilling parental expectations, and avoiding unnecessary conflict. He even describes such confrontations as "inappropriate," showing his sense that mature men neither give nor respond to hard looks, especially when the risks are so great. Yet even within this alternative masculinity, Jericho sometimes embraces a more macho line. He challenges the imaginary *cholos:* "Why don't you do something?" instead of just "lookin' at me hard." I have heard Jericho say other, similar things when commenting on *cholo* aggression, though his actions have always been in line with his long-term masculinity. I think the more macho narrative is so dominant among adolescent men that Jericho has to signal to his audience, and perhaps to himself, that his forbearing version of masculinity has its limits and could permit him to respond in a macho way, at least rhetorically, if pushed too far.

Napoleon's stronger reactions were moderated by the presence of Jericho and his female cousins, whom he felt he would endanger if he fought. His first reaction was to defend his masculinity by throwing hard looks back at the *cholos.* During my later interview with both men, I asked Napoleon to tell me his version of these events.

> When I would be dancing, they keep looking at me, so I told Jericho, . . . Yo, they keep lookin' at me . . . like they wanted to do something. . . . I was mad. . . . Don't look at me if you're not going to do something. . . . At that time I was just like, "Let's leave," because my cousin was with us, two of my cousins and another girl, it was more girls than guys. We was like, Yes, we should leave to avoid it. I don't want my cousin to get in the middle of it, so I listened to him [Jericho], and we left. I wanted to go back 'cause they were gonna think I was scared. . . . But you know what? . . . That's how I left, too [the same way as Jericho]. . . . I have nothing to prove, he's [Jericho's] right, so let's just leave. So we left, and I didn't think about it twice till we got to the *gallos,* when I told him—Yo, those niggas were looking at me hard . . . it wasn't just that day they looked at me hard. It was that whole week. . . . If I would be with my ex [girlfriend], they would say something to her. If I would be walking by myself, they would say something to me.

That Napoleon does not actually confront the *cholos* shows him managing the situation in a way that prevents escalation but reinforces the larger system of meaning. By commenting on the *cholos'* inaction, he shows that he understands by what Elijah Anderson calls the "code of the street" and Jack Katz calls the "generation of dread."[10] In his telling of the incident, he has faced down the *cholos* by painting them as *putos* who throw hard looks but do not back them up with action. By not lowering his eyes, Napoleon defends his honor. He experiences himself, physically and emotionally, as a strong, honorable man in front of his friends. Such dynamics, however, always carry the risk that someone will miscalculate or misperceive and that an attack will follow.

As happened here, tension is often defused by the intervention of older men or young women, or by the young male principals' thoughts for their own safety. Napoleon withdraws because he must protect his female cousins and Jericho, whom he views as older but as less tough and street-smart than he. He does not want to fight if there are more "girls than guys" or only with Jericho, who, he says, will not know what to do. Instead Napoleon adopts Jericho's definition of masculinity by saying that he does not have to prove himself. Judging from similar dynamics in other situations, I think these young men sometimes seek out conflicts when they know that their friends or relatives will intervene to stop them. If they are with women, then their withdrawal from conflict takes the form of being responsible for their women. If they are with other men, then they see it as having listened to masculine advice or shown sufficient force to intimidate the other side. Jericho's version of masculinity sometimes wins out over the more macho form, persuading even an aggressive youth like Napoleon. But Napoleon has a hard time maintaining that perspective: in this case, once he went back to the *gallos,* he feared being seen as a *puto,* and he tried to enlist Pepe's support to go back and confront the *cholos.*

Napoleon's flip-flopping between a macho and a long-view masculinity also shows the emotional labor of attempting to sort out how he "really" feels and how this leads to a sense of himself in conflict. He feels angry that the *cholos* are staring at him but must deny that anger, along with the shame of feeling like a *puto,* and justify his leaving as the decision of a mature man. When he first told me of this encounter, he showed physical signs of stress: the muscles in his neck tightened as he spoke, and his face was flushed.

Napoleon's physical expression of these emotional dynamics differs depending on whether the *cholos* are present. In their presence, Napoleon returns their hard looks, but not for long, then seeks confirmation and backup from his friends. When he is away from the *cholos* and recounting his experience to friends, his anger is emphatically expressed. He gesticulates wildly and angrily, and then turns to an imaginary *cholo* and yells at him: "Yo, why you lookin' at me if you ain't gonna say something?" He seems to enjoy the physical sensation of this kinetic expression of his anger and his masculinity.[11]

Two things seem clear from Napoleon's narration and physical responses to these encounters. First, his attitude toward conflict is variable: he leans toward the ranchero and *cholo* masculinities but cannot maintain that view that in opposition to Jericho's long-view masculinity. Second, his experience of himself—his social proprioception—is profoundly different as he tries on these two different versions of masculinity.

Steppin' Up or Steppin' Back

Other encounters with *cholos* became violent, or nearly so, when regulars responded to *cholo* provocations. Most cases involved actual or perceived insults, which regulars responded to in kind, though two involved *cholos* asking other youths' girlfriends for their phone numbers or a dance. All the violent confrontations involved drinking. In the serious cases, families of the non-*pandilla* youth intervened to end the conflict. When Napoleon confronted a larger El Ganado–born young man who had asked Napoleon's girlfriend for her phone number, two friends were present: Lazario, who advocated calm, and a larger, tougher cousin with a reputation, who visibly "had his back." Napoleon's rival was a wannabe who hangs with a local chapter of the Mixtecos Locos. Lazario saw Napoleon's actions as rash and dangerous; Jericho's cousins took a car to search for Napoleon so he would not "get jumped." Later he returned to see his girlfriend Marqueza and other female friends pouring away all the remaining alcohol to stop him from drinking more and becoming even more aggressive. Marqueza screamed: "I'ma let you drink but not get crazy." He screamed back but, he later said, "accepted it because I knew she was right." Napoleon's confrontation proved his authentic Ticuani ranchero masculinity. He proved his fearlessness in front of his girlfriend and his male cousins and friends, who then supported and protected him. Acknowledging the frequent link between drinking and fighting in Ticuani masculinity, he accepted his girlfriend's emptying out the liquor.

Toño also had several confrontations with *cholos* over his girlfriend, some of which led to fights that were broken up by relatives and friends. Tensions persisted for a week and always involved alcohol. It was not clear whether people fought because drinking made them aggressive or got drunk in order to stoke their urge to fight. It was clear that women and other relatives monitored the alcohol intake of the young men to prevent confrontations from becoming too violent; it was also clear that the men were trying to prove themselves to be macho in front of women and other men. Such fights usually occurred at parties, so that the largest emergent Mexican community could witness the men's defense of their manhood but would also intervene before things went too far. Relatives of these warring regulars thought aggressive responses to the *cholos* were "dumb."

Who Blinks First?

Toño's conflicts with the Mixtecos Locos took on an added gravity in 2001 as part of a conflict between larger groups. In chapter 6, I briefly discuss the conflict between the Buendias, the Zavalas, and the Mixtecos Locos over who should "lower their eyes" to whom. Both the Buendias and the Zavalas had been coming down to Ticuani since childhood and felt Ticuani was theirs, but their sharing of the space had grown strained. Adding the *cholos* to the mix escalated tensions, leading to repeated contests over who would blink first. In one case, two of the Zavalas were stepped up to at a party by some Mixtecos Locos, who issued a respectful warning—"You guys ain't punks. You don't put your face down to nobody. Yo, this all our area. This is our town. We don't want no problems"—and showed their guns. "They were all strapped," said Erving Zavala, who said he and his cousin were unimpressed but did not want a fight: "We got guns down here too. But I hate violence." He said the Mixtecos Locos thought Ticuani was their town and that the Feast was like a week-long Mexican party, with everyone stepping up to everyone else. In stepping up to so many, the Mixtecos Locos engaged the local ranchero use of violence to defend their honor. Another Zavala also told me he was unimpressed with *cholo* guns and that his father had taught him how to use a gun: "We've got guns too. My father told me, 'The gun is in the house. Don't be afraid to use it if you need it.'" The brewing conflict was over whose town Ticuani really was and how far each side would go to claim it. Interestingly, the Mixtecos Locos often called their antagonists "Puerto Ricans," even though they were all born in Ticuani or of Ticuanense parents. Each side presented itself as a reluctant participant in the potential conflict: they simply came down to have a good time, but "those guys" were messing with them. This sentiment ultimately won out and prevented a serious conflict.

During the dance in 2001, a Zavala was confronted by a Mixteco Loco, and a fight involving more than a dozen people ensued. The next day, I hung out in the zocalo for several hours with six Zavalas and a sense of foreboding. At one point, about twenty local Mixtecos Locos walked by, giving these six hard looks. Later, a Zavala walked up to us and asked: "So, this shit squashed, or what?" "Squashing" a conflict means agreeing that no fight is needed to settle the issues, that the two sides have either made peace or agreed not to pursue it. His cousin answered, "I don't know. Guess we'll see tonight." Those with friends on the other side looked for opportunities to talk to them one on one, laying the groundwork for the conflict to be squashed. Tensions escalated at the *gallos* that night but were defused. My field notes describe this:

The *bronca* [problem] from last night continued but did not erupt into the violence that it might have. For about two hours, I watched while [Zavalas and Mixtecos Locos were] talking things through in the tent covering the *palenque de gallos* [cockfight arena]. It was a perfect metaphor. Toño was closely involved, or tried to be, and things got very tense at times. It was kind of eerie, actually: standing in the crowd watching the *gallos* fight, with the music blaring at times, while I looked on and saw others looking on too—Tomás Maestro [Toño's father] was looking on nervously. In the end, the boys worked it out, they squashed it.

The situation was indeed tense. Leaders of the two sides stood toe to toe, sometimes leaning on each other's shoulders, jabbing their fingers in each other's faces to make their points. While they were not yelling, they spoke animatedly, and all were drinking. Violence did not ensue for several reasons. First, neither side really wanted it. They seemed to be feeling each other out. Second, each side was well-represented, so neither had the superior strength that would make violence an easy solution. Third, armed police were present because of the gambling, money, and drinking at the cockfights. Fourth, adult men present promised to intervene if necessary but encouraged the young men to work things out peacefully. One young politician declined Toño's request for help in negotiating or fighting, joking that "I am in it when the fights and stabs come" but telling him not to be stupid, to work it out without fighting. His remarks assured Toño of support if it was needed but also gave him permission to avoid a fight without loss of reputation or masculinity. Finally, these young leaders skillfully emphasized their common need for respect from each other and agreed not to give past offenses importance in the current context, a concession that Ruth Horowitz argues is key in conflict resolution.[12] This agreement was expressed in the equal physical and emotional stances of the parties in the negotiation—for example, in the way they leaned on each other while negotiating—and meant that no one was made to feel shame by their conclusion to the interaction.

These negotiations at the *gallos* enabled particular emotional and physical experiences and performances. A casual observer might have seen the conflicting groups as one large group of friends enjoying a spirited talk during the male ritual of betting on the *gallos*. Although they made confrontational gestures, they also nodded their heads vigorously in agreement when they spoke of the need for mutual respect. They smiled, laughed, and got more drinks for each other. They looked each other directly in the eye. The leaders were definitely enjoying negotiating the terms of respect and accommodation with legitimate interlocutors. (My field notes inadvertently capture this spirit by saying that "the boys" squashed it, as if the stakes were no higher than in a friendly baseball game.) There was definitely a sense of performance in these gestures and interactions. The laying of hands on shoulders and the leaning on each other embodied a recognized masculinity. These young men perceived and presented themselves as true rancheros and *cholos* whose competent negotiation of their interests with worthy rivals made them feel powerful.

These encounters clearly illustrate how transnationalization has accelerated and intensified such masculine conflicts, set simultaneously in Ticuani and the transnational life it anchors. The Buendia and Zavala youths were almost all born or raised in New York and had acquired their rules of engagement from their adolescent conflicts there. Yet these conflicts and their rules are also based in the kinship networks of their migrant parents and thus resonate with the rules for ranchero masculinity encoded in Ticuani's history. The conflict between the Buendia and Zavala youths is a less intense version of the bloody rivalries that have long afflicted Ticuani public life. One can easily imagine these youth feeling "hot" Ticuani blood running through their veins, quickened by alcohol. The transnational dimension, however, is new. The experience of accelerated social time and intensified social meaning that accompany return speed up the cycle of social conflicts. Each day, each hour, can give rise to a new version of the conflict, which mutates to involve other participants in new ways.

"LA GENTE NO NOS QUIERE": THE PEOPLE DO NOT WANT US

The experiences of returning *cholos* and regulars are different but related. While regulars feel they sometimes do not fit in because they are not Mexican enough, *cholos* feel unwelcome despite having been born in Mexico. Both feel their standing in Ticuani is contested. *Cholos'* stories of return dovetail with those regulars tell about them; for example, *cholos* correctly perceive that people fear them and blame them for problems. The regulars' experience of compromised freedom and social distance in Ticuani is experienced by the *cholos* as the assertion of ownership of Ticuani and their social exclusion by second-generationers who think that they are "Mexican, but better." Moreover, the narrative by which the *cholos* have framed their lives conflicts with the immigrant narrative by which the first generation and most of their U.S.-born children live theirs. These conflicting narratives combine with actions of *cholos*, regulars, and the adult world in New

York and Ticuani to create among the *cholos* a sharp sense of social exclusion and resentment.

One way this exclusion manifests itself for *cholos* is through targeted police scrutiny, which, from the perspective of Ticuani locals, is simply an attempt to reassert social control. Horacio, Homero, and Dionisio told me that people feared them because they "think that we are criminals, right? The only thing is that the police are giving it to us." Most of the *cholos* who lived in Ticuani for more than a few weeks were thrown in jail, or at least detained, for disorderly conduct or being drunk. While many Ticuanenses are jailed for drunkenness and released once they dry out, the police and municipal authorities told me their policy was to confront *cholos* more aggressively if trouble seemed likely. They did this partly for public safety and partly to force the *cholos* to respect their authority and their masculinity. They also wanted to punish the *cholos* for their ostentatious displays of wealth, as happened on one of the last nights of the Feast in 2001. As everyone was leaving the *gallos* around 2:30 A.M., three *cholos* walked up the main road back to their house. Several shots were heard, and the dozen or more police present at the *gallos* scrambled with their shotguns and carbines into a pickup truck and headed in the direction of the shots. About twenty minutes later I saw four or five police officers literally riding shotgun in an open red BMW, followed by the police pickup, in which sat Horacio, who owned the car, surrounded by police. "This doesn't look good," I said to a friend. However, the police who had confiscated the car soon returned and told me that when they had gone to investigate the shots, the *cholos* had sprayed beer at them. Angry, the police chased the *cholos,* apprehending and jailing one; two escaped and were hiding in the hills. "They have to respect us," one policeman told me. "That was a lack of respect!" Yet Horacio appeared less than an hour later in the zocalo and sat down to drink with friends. He told me the police were "messing" with him, adding sarcastically that "that was the only time those guys have ever ridden in a Beemer in their lives." Here, he asserts his migrant's modernity and economic power, but he also admits that he is vulnerable. While he has something the police cannot even dream of—a red Beemer—they can still "mess" with him. Peace between *cholos* and the police prevailed for the rest of the night, and the car was returned to him. The shots themselves were not considered a problem, so long as no one was hurt; in Ticuani every responsible man is entitled to carry a gun. Once the police had punished the *cholos* for their lack of respect, no further action was necessary.

On another occasion, in 2000, police intervened when several Mixtecos Locos (including Horacio) cursed the mother of the municipal president as he went by, using very strong words: "¡Chinga tu madre!" (Fuck your mother!). He responded by bringing the police back with him and telling them to put the *cholos* in jail until they learned respect. According to one second-generation participant, the conflict included not only the police but also adult men, local youths, and returned youths from New York.

> My uncle, being president, he felt that they should have more respect for him. So he made a U-turn back to where the police officers were and then he asked the *comandante* [the sergeant], . . . "No, arrestame todos de la mesa de ahi." [Arrest all those at that table for me.] . . . We all got out the car, and my uncle stepped up to one of the guys . . . at the table and he asked him, "¿Que dijiste? ¿Que dijiste?" [What did you say?] and then the guy said, "No, yo no dije nada" [I didn't say anything.] . . . they don't have no respect . . . the guy was in jail for three days.

The various narrations of these events I have heard from the president, his second-generation relatives, and Horacio all present it as a conflict over respect among men: "That's the whole thing, that they don't have no respect." Indeed, Horacio told me that he was surprised by the president and impressed by the guts it took to throw him and his companions in jail. He knew he had gone too far in cursing the president's mother, and the president had used his power to enforce local codes of masculine honor. The president understood the incident as forcing the *cholos* to respect Ticuani and Mexican ways: they might say whatever they liked in New York, but in Ticuani such behavior would land them in jail. To the *cholos*, the incident shows them as standing alone against the rest of Ticuani male society: Ticuani men, native and second-generation youths, and the police all confront them to defend the honor of the president's mother. And this second-generation observer frames the confrontation using *cholo* language: the president "steps up" to the *cholos*. The *cholos* were subjected to closer scrutiny than this during the 2001 Feast, when the State Judicial Police's special public security team patrolled in Ticuani, contributing to a more peaceful Feast.

The misdeeds of the *cholos*, proven or alleged, were openly discussed much more than the misbehavior of others. Many people stated with certainty that the *cholos* had killed the man who died before the start of the Feast in 2000, using this open secret to warn me away from them. This suspected killing was seen as absolutely aberrant and linked to the corrupting influence of New York. Yet during the same year, there were at least three other killings, all by a young man from a family associated with political assassination in Ticuani. These killings, which were not discussed openly, were seen as the unfortunate outcome of hot Ticuani blood and excessive alcohol.

The *cholos* feel both pride and pain in their social distance from returning regulars and economically comfortable Ticuani locals. They feel at once strongly attached to and alienated from Ticuani. In an interview with Griscelda Perez and me, Griscelda asked them, "Do you feel alienated when you come here?"

> DIONISIO: Yeah. We feel here the same way as when we arrive there. The people do not want us. And they don't accept us . . . they think we are bad, or they fear us for the fact that we have tattoos, we dress *cholo*. They think that we come to kill someone. . . . Here the people who have money . . . they don't dress *cholo*. They have a way of dressing with their little suits, like preppy . . . making their hair all nice, and kind of sissylike, you know, right? *(Laughter)* . . .
>
> RS: How does it feel to be alienated in both places? . . .
>
> D: It is that, like this, when we pass by, the people will not walk by you. . . .
>
> HORACIO: They see you as nothing more than something weird, as if you were some kind of freak. . . . They do not understand this. It is another mentality, totally different. . . .
>
> HOMERO: There are times when dead bodies arrive, and they have been killed there in *pandillas,* you know, they think that we are criminals. But no, right?
>
> D: We are peaceful gangs *[bandas palomitas]. (Laughter)* . . .
>
> HOMERO: They are afraid of us that they will die. But one knows what one does: You only mess with a man who is not in—
>
> HORACIO: You know, we are the best people, if nobody looks for problems. The sweetest guys. . . . But if you start to look for problems, then, yeah. . . .
>
> D: It's like with the women, I am a lover. But when they make me mad . . . —pssss. I am the worst man that you have known in your life. (Spanish, translated by the author)

The contradictory messages in this passage mirror the place of the *cholos* in the Ticuani transnational world. They painfully experience as class exclusion the superior attitude of those they call preppies and the social distance of people who do not even want to walk by them. Yet appended to their expressions of pain are expressions of anger and justifications for retributive violence against those who "look for problems" or "make me mad." Hence the *cholos'* exclusion is partly the result of the fear and dread they generate in others, of the ways in which they demand respect and threaten violence.

The *cholos'* alienation is not, however, based solely on others' fear of them. It also results from their limited success in embracing essential parts of the immigrant narrative of return, their rejection by other migrants and natives in Mexico and the United States, and what Paul Willis has called a "partial penetration" of structure: their understanding of how the immigrant condition is one of long odds and great vulnerabilities.[13] Thus *cholos* experience themselves, physically and emotionally, as misunderstood freaks isolated from the rest of Ticuani society. They experience this exclusion intensely as a group. Indeed, they experience most of their lives as part of a group: their emotional and physical proprioception is to an extreme degree social. They rarely walk alone either in Ticuani or in New York, because in their world to walk alone is to be vulnerable and to be nobody. Their experience is simultaneously that of aggrieved, alienated outsiders who see migrant life as dangerous and stacked against them and of dangerous, powerful men who gain pleasure from being feared. Even as they speak plaintively about no one "wanting" them, they project their aggressive presence through their posture, prolonged eye contact, and other means. They look sad when recounting their victimization but laugh after Dionisio says that they are "peaceful gangs."

The *cholos'* sense of belonging in Ticuani, and their claim of ownership, is interesting given that they are not natives of the town. Homero was the only member of this group born in Ticuani; he was raised elsewhere in Puebla. Horacio was born and raised elsewhere in Mexico but spent a lot of time in Ticuani as a youth and has many relatives from Ticuani who maintain links there. Dionisio was actually born in the United States but was raised with "all Mexicans" in the United States and strongly identifies as Mexican, not Mexican American or Chicano: "I was born there [the United States], but I was raised with all Mexicans, and I have never run around with a bunch of Americans or a bunch of Blacks . . . never. And for this, my Spanish is good. If not, now I would speak it all broken up." These backgrounds exemplify the negative experiences of teen migrants. Arriving in the United States as teenagers, Homero and Horacio experienced discrimination and dropped out of high school, instead joining and starting Mexican gangs. Although Dionisio was born in the United States, his closest friends were always Mexican teen migrants. Their experience of adolescence was his, too.

These Mixtecos Locos all say they feel deeply Ticuanense, and they return to Ticuani for the same reasons as the regulars: for vacation, to get away from the pressures of life in New York, and to enjoy the Antorcha and a closer link with Padre Jesús. All have run the Antorcha and participated in the dances, the *gallos,* and the *torros* (rodeos). Horacio told me: "I like it . . . I was not born here. But I consider myself a Ticuanense. . . . I like to come and see . . . the mountains. When I was little in the *cerros* [hills] there, I talked with myself . . . it's a long way from where I was before, and where I am now. Now, all that I have achieved and gained, I am a little bit proud of being a Ticuanense" (Spanish, translated by the author). Homero told me that Padre Jesús helps keep him safe during the Antorcha and in his daily life as a *pandillero.* He talks to Padre Jesús, especially in Ticuani: "The first thing that I do when I get to the Church is that . . . I cross myself and say, 'Padre Jesús, watch over me.'" Many regulars say similar prayers under different circumstances, such as preparing for a test in school. The *cholos* and the regulars give similar reasons for running the Antorcha, including fulfilling *promesas.*

Yet the narratives and histories of the *cholos* differ from those of most returning youths in two important ways. First, *cholos* do *promesas* for both conventional reasons and reasons associated with their gang membership. When asked what doing the Antorcha meant to him, one of the *cholos* said: "For me, it is a way of shaking off the sins I carry. . . . There are people who . . . hurt another person in a way that, well, your family can end up involved. . . . This is a form of getting rid of . . . the sins you carry. . . . It is not a thing of getting close to or paying God, but rather to carry a cross." For him the Antorcha serves as a penance for his *cholo* activities. Yet he quickly moves to normalize his return by invoking "normal" causes: "Sometimes it is not like this, sometimes it is no more than a simple thanks to God that one has had . . . a triumph. Many people go on the Antorcha for this. Sometimes someone's mother was sick, your grandmother is dying. . . . It is a belief we have." Religious ritual makes even *cholo* returnees feel integrated into Ticuani society, providing a language and practice of belonging. No matter what one's sins elsewhere, one can run the Antorcha.

The narrative, image, and actions of the *cholos* are nevertheless often at odds with those of the dominant culture of migration, even if they are also definitely its result. The *cholo* narrative contradicts the migrant culture of *superando,* or getting ahead. Migrants are supposed to leave and return victorious, with nicer clothes, better jobs, and more money and education. By doing so, they vindicate the risks they have run. Their U.S.-born children, likewise, are supposed to return better educated and better paid than their parents, living in nicer apartments and working at higher-status jobs. In short, they are supposed to return as what the *cholos* would call preppies.

The *cholo* narrative is different and embodies the journey teen migrants made in the 1990s.[14] It highlights different aspects of the problems of migrants and proposes radically different solutions. First, it perceives real danger, including that of deadly violence, in migrating to and settling in New York. Second, it responds differently, with violence. Third, most *cholos* are not drawn from the ranks of the earlier cohorts of adult migrants or from the 1.5 generation; growing numbers are teen migrants. This group simultaneously experiences the pressures on first-generation immigrants to earn money and on second-generation children of immigrants to do well in school and pursue a career. If they enroll in school, they feel severe pressure to leave and earn money. Moreover, teen migrants seem to be most likely to experience discrimination and mistreatment, especially, they report, by Puerto Rican and Black youths. These dueling images of first- and second-generation success push some teen migrants toward the *cholo* narrative.

Such dynamics are evident in Horacio's comments below, which link the *cholos'* negative reception in Ticuani to the dangers they have faced, and faced down, in New York. In talking about why people in Ticuani fear the *cholos,* Horacio explained that they do not understand life in New York: "You know, that this is . . . a way of life. . . . But they [in the pueblo] don't understand this. One has to unite to protect oneself from others. If you are not with nobody—everybody picks on you. So then, you have to join up with others to protect yourself from others." This response differentiates their experience as teen immigrants from that of first-generation immigrants, who perceive or wish to perceive their struggles as successful. In the migrant narrative, they have triumphed over obstacles such as language difficulties and overt discrimination. For teen migrants such as these *cholos,* however, the can-do immigrant mentality and the conflicting expectations for earning money and academic success make life keenly difficult, especially when they feel set upon by other groups because they are Mexican. While most teen migrants are able to negotiate these conditions successfully, increasing numbers are responding by turning to *pandillerismo,* creating a whole new set of problems for them and their families.[15]

Horacio observed that the need to protect oneself now extended into the Mixteca and commented that now "we have people there and here we also have people." This transnationalization of gangs means that the context of threat is reproduced in the Mixteca, thus recharging the possibilities for the performance of *cholo* masculinity, the emotional and physical experience of social exclusion, and the angry, righteous assertions of belonging.

The *cholos'* different self-understanding and sense of exclusion is reflected in their use of different names to describe themselves and the U.S.-

born children of immigrants. These differences resonate clearly with the cleavages in the Latino gang world in California as represented in films, especially *Blood In, Blood Out* and *American Me*. The following quotes are from a discussion of *American Me*. Although the main lesson of the film for most *pandilleros*, including these, is that Santana forms a gang to demand respect from Black and white gangs inside and outside prison, these Mixtecos Locos use the film to make a point about the difference between "Chicanos" and "Mexicans":

DIONISIO: Santana, truth be told, does not represent Mexico very much. Santana . . . was a Chicano mentality. The Chicano mentality and the Mexican mentality are very different. Because many Chicanos talk of what the *raza* is, but they do not know what it is. They don't even know where the Mexican language comes from.

RS: So how is the Mexican mentality different from the Chicano mentality? . . .

D: The Chicanos in Los Angeles—we have a nickname. . . . Blacks and . . . whites call us—"wetbacks." . . . So the Chicanos, because they are born in the United States, they do not have the same beliefs as the Mexicans. . . . They have American . . . citizenship. . . . They think they are Mexicans, but better. They never offer . . . a helping hand. They think they are powerful and do not want to give a chance to a Mexican. . . . [But] a Mexican who sees another Mexican will lend him a hand. . . .

HOMERO: In Los Angeles . . . Sur 13, the majority of them are Mexicans . . . and La Familia are Chicanos. . . . And to Sur 13 they call them "garbage" *[escrapa]*. (Spanish, translated by the author)

Here Homero invokes the split between large California gangs, composed mostly of immigrants—such as Sur 13—and of Chicanos—such as La Familia—to describe his own sense of being Mexican. The Mixtecos Locos refer to New York–born Mexican Americans as Chicanos, a label that almost none of our other informants used. A very few college students or graduates called themselves Chicanos or Xicanos (often pronounced with an indigenous-sounding *sch* for the *x*), but most called themselves Mexicans first, and then Hispanic or Latino. Most disavowed the label *Chicano* as a more politicized identity from California that did not describe their lives in New York. The Mixtecos Locos here try to reserve the term Mexican for themselves, thereby disputing the authenticity of the second generation's Mexican identity. Indeed, Dionisio argues that others "don't even know where the Mexican language comes from."

The Mixtecos Locos went on to apply a version of the immigrant analogy to their categories of Mexicans and Chicanos. They asserted that Puerto Ricans born in New York are racist for discriminating against Mexicans, though those born in Puerto Rico are not. I followed up by asking if there is a difference between the two kinds of Mexicans they discussed. Dionisio answered: "Yes, it's the same with the Mexicans born there [in New York], and the Mexicans born here. . . . Those born in New York are racists, the same as the children of those born there that are racists." In this formulation, even the U.S.-born grandchildren of Mexican immigrants are racist toward Mexican immigrants. Invoking the rivalry between Chicanos and recent immigrants in California provides an instant moral and ethical framework for their conflicts with U.S.-born Mexican Americans. It disputes the latter's authenticity as Mexicans and frames them as aggressors against struggling immigrants. It also paints them as people who think they are "Mexicans, but better," who refuse to help their brothers, instead disparaging them as "garbage." Such quasiracial tension informs interactions between recent immigrants and U.S.-born Mexicans in situations where it need not make any appearance. At the very least, it requires emotional labor to acknowledge and then fight the idea that one is garbage.[16]

CONFRONTATION AND RACIALIZATION: *PUERTORRIQUEÑOS* IN TICUANI

The racialization of opponents is a fascinating dimension of *cholo* self-understanding, manifested most clearly in the "puertoricanization" of their enemies during the conflicts between the *cholos,* the Buendias, and the Zavalas. Young men the *cholos* had stepped up to told me they had been addressed as "puertorriqueño." One *cholo* told Magda that he did not like "those puertorriqueños" coming into "his" Ticuani. The conflict on the night of the big dance was particularly interesting in its use of this appellation. During the large fistfight between the *cholos* and the Zavalas at the dance, the Zavalas told me that one of their number, Gabriel, was talking tough to a friend of the *cholos* who had talked tough to him. Hard looks had been exchanged, and, as the friend of the *cholos* taunted another Zavala, Nazario attacked. The fight quickly escalated but was broken up by older men, who pulled the two sides apart.

The Zavalas tell the story as a confrontation with *cholo* interlopers claiming the town as their own, while the *cholos* tell it as "puertorriqueños" attempting to victimize them. The Zavalas told me that Gabriel talked big but was unable to defend himself in a fight, so Nazario jumped to his defense. After the fight, Nazario told me, mixing bewilderment, consternation, and indignation, that the *cholos* had called him "puertorriqueño." They said he looked Puerto Rican, that they did not like Puerto Ricans, and that he should be careful in Ticuani. Nazario asked me: "Can you believe those guys?" He acknowledged that he was not born in Ticuani but in Brooklyn; but, he said, his parents are from here, and he had always come back here. "Who do those guys think they are? I am from here, and those guys are not even from here, and they are calling me a Puerto Rican?" (Neither of the people involved in this initial phase of the conflict was Puerto Rican; both had parents from Ticuani and El Ganado.)[17] In the Zavala version of events, there is no mention of a gold chain, a robbery, or any other disputed object, as in the *cholo* version, which follows.

The *cholo* version of the story starts with an attempt by the "Puerto Ricans" to steal their friend's gold chain and quickly escalates to the threat of a "world war." Dionisio begins by asking me if I heard about "the problem we had in the dance. . . . Some Puerto Ricans came along . . . [and] beat up a friend [and] took his chain. . . . See how many were there, ten of them." He continues to define the people on the other side as Puerto Ricans:

DIONISIO: . . . This Puerto Rican, he isn't even Mexican, right? . . . I think he was drinking, . . . and maybe he thought that he was in Brooklyn. . . . He wanted to rob him. He wanted to feel this way. . . .

HORACIO: *(With great energy, in English)* Like old times! . . .

RS: And the *bronca*, how was it resolved? . . .

D: I said to one of the Puerto Ricans that I know . . . "You know what? . . . You are in Mexico. And here in Mexico, we are not going to let you do this. If you don't calm down your friends, we are going to be ready, because you are going to see a world war." . . . They left because we were about forty of us waiting outside for them. But it was already too late because they had taken them away, their relatives. . . . He ran like a hen to Puebla, no? A little girl. Did you get that, Roberto? . . . He ran like a little girl to Puebla, the Puerto Rican. . . .

RS: Well, I guess to avoid what could happen. . . .

HOMERO: Right.

RS: So then, last night, the talk of the "squash"—did you re-
solve the *bronca?* . . .

HOMERO: Yes. For the time being. (Spanish, translated by the
author)

The phrase "Like old times" invokes the narrative of Mexican self-defense
against Puerto Rican aggression in New York to frame the current situation. By invoking this narrative, Horacio legitimizes any violence that is
used and sets up a structural antagonism between the Mixtecos Locos and
the Zavalas. Defining them as Puerto Ricans makes it seem natural that
there should be conflict with them. Moreover, this labeling racializes both
the Zavalas and the *cholos*, placing the *cholos* in the morally superior position, occupying the ethnic Mexican social location in contradistinction to
the racial, Puerto Rican location. They also assert that the "Puerto Ricans"
are stealing their friend's chain, a frequent complaint in the accounts of
why Mexican gangs emerged in New York: Puerto Ricans would steal Mexicans' chains and call them names. That gold chains are staples in the style
of returning Mexicans and Mexican Americans—*cholos* and regulars
alike—lends weight to this version of the story. Possessing an expensive
gold chain suggests that the immigrant or the child of immigrants has been
successful. A chain has similar connotations among U.S.-born Mexicans in
New York. Hence, to steal someone's gold chain is to try to steal from them
the symbol of their success, the justification of all the sacrifice and suffering, and warrants a very strong response—a "war," if need be.

Dionisio reinforces the *cholos'* Mexican authenticity not only by racializing his rivals as Puerto Ricans but also by saying they were drinking and
must have thought they were "in Brooklyn," enabling him to say that in
Mexico, his group makes the rules, and those Puerto Ricans will no longer
get away with stealing their gold chains. Being Puerto Rican is feminized,
portrayed as being "like a hen . . . like a little girl," a point Dionisio under-
scores for me. Finally, Homero says the conflict has been squashed "for
the time being," leaving open the possibility that it will be reopened, cast
again as Mexican strength and virtue withstanding Puerto Rican vice and
aggression.

This racial strategy of the *cholos* is an interesting intersection of social
proprioception, racialization, and male friendship. These encounters provide a conflict where the *cholos* can vanquish a racially constructed enemy
who was once more powerful than they in New York, to do so by asserting
ownership over a place that the regulars think they "own," and to do so in

a large group of other young men who feel similarly alienated by returning regulars. That they had "forty of us" waiting for the small number of "Puerto Ricans" must have provided a sense of physical and emotional power, but here that power is understood as defending themselves against racialized violence by an alien group.

CONCLUSION

The emergence of *cholos* as a recognized social group in Ticuani has profoundly altered Ticuani youth culture and the experience of return. The returning second generation experiences such changes as compromised freedom and the emotional labor of projecting a New York image to avoid appearing vulnerable. In this new context, they even walk differently, experiencing their emotions and bodies in a different way. Transnationalization of youth culture and then gangs occurs in three steps: the development of adolescent rituals for New Yorkers in Ticuani, followed by the emergence of gangs in New York resulting from the dual processes of migration and assimilation, and then their exportation back to Ticuani. Ticuani gives returning second-generation regulars a set of rituals and ownership of place that authenticate their Mexicanness. The *cholos* challenge this ownership of Ticuani public space and the second generation's sense of belonging and ownership.

The *cholos* also challenge the dominant narrative of migrant struggle and triumph. While this immigrant narrative includes a critique of assimilation, exclusion, and discrimination in New York, it does not reject the whole system, because it banks on the ultimate success of migrants and their children. (Social commentator David Brooks explains "Reagan Democrats" the same way: working-class white voters whose interests would seem to be better served by Democrats may vote Republican because they have not given up on the American dream of becoming rich.)[18] The *cholo* narrative is fundamentally different. It sees life in New York as inherently dangerous, with other ethnic groups—Puerto Ricans, and even U.S.-born "Chicanos"—constantly ready to victimize Mexicans, especially teen migrants, who also face other intense assimilative pressures. The "natural" response is to fight back. Hence *cholos*, especially, have embraced the image of strong gang members who force respect from Blacks, whites, and Chicanos. These have become models for how to be Mexican in New York and elsewhere on the East Coast because they resonate with youths' experience there. Such is also the case in cities throughout New Jersey, and even in remote places like Kennett Square, Pennsylvania, the site of my first field-work as an undergraduate nearly twenty years ago.

The emergence of *cholos* as a recognized category on the East Coast of the United States is a new development in Mexican social life and youth culture. Although James Diego Vigil cites the *cholo* identity as an importation of the marginalized status of premigration Indians in Mexico, especially Mexico City, to California, these East Coast teen migrants and second-generationers have formed their *cholo* identity by watching movies about California gangs and adopting the names of characters and gangs in them. In this view *cholos* in California represent the gold standard of Mexicanness. This *cholo* narrative, which poses a stark alternative to the lives of what *cholos* call *gente trabajador*, working people living out the immigrant narrative, has emerged from the fundamentally different experience of migrating to and being ethnically targeted in New York during the 1990s.

The transnationalization of gangs and the changes in Ticuani are logical outcomes of the processes of migration and assimilation. Research on migration tends to celebrate transnational life as a creative local response to oppressive globalization, politics, or racism. While this is so, transnational life has a darker side that has received less attention.[19] But while migration is facilitated through an impressive migrant culture of reciprocity, emerging over decades and rightly highlighted in the work of Douglas Massey and his colleagues, it has also contributed, in combination with harsh assimilation, to a great deal of suffering, confusion, and hardship. Transnational gangs are both symptom and cause of such outcomes, and I predict they will grow in other migrant regions in Mexico and Latin America.

That harsh assimilation pressures and the disorganizing effects of migration contribute to the formation of youth gangs is not a new story. Indeed, it is the same story that Frederick Thrasher told about the Italian, Polish, Irish, and other gangs he studied in Chicago in the 1920s, and it is consistent with other classic work on immigration from that age, which saw the related developments of a great migration and the birth and growth of sociology as a discipline in the United States.[20] This story reappears today in James Diego Vigil's research on Mexican, Central American, Asian, and Black gangs.[21] Here, however, I situate gangs in a transnational context, tracing their emergence in New York and exportation back to Mexico. It is unclear whether a similar transnationalization of youth gangs happened during the last great wave of migration from the 1880s to the 1920s. Clearly, organized crime gangs such as the Mafia operated transnationally during that period. Indeed, the United States even dispatched an agent to Italy to investigate transnational links between criminals in both countries.[22] But the historical studies I know of have not documented extensive second-generation transnational activity, gang-related or otherwise, even those studies focused closely on the second generation or return migration.[23] Because second-generation transnationalization seems to have been less extensive in the past than it is today, I suspect that the transnationalization of youth gangs was also less common. Ongoing work in historical retrieval may clarify the issue.

A final comment concerns writing social dislocation and hardship back into our collective understandings of migration, which have leaned toward emphasizing migration's functional aspects. By considering the different outcomes of migration, I reintroduce agency, contingency, and the possibility of change into the narrative of migrant lives. I emphasize this agency not to argue that teen migrants are making bad choices but rather to underline that human institutions, like gangs, are formed by people, whose actions and interpretations must be studied for the reality to be fully understood. Moreover, if these institutions influence people's futures, it should be possible to imagine different futures and create institutions that can help shape them in more positive ways.

Conclusions and Recommendations

I have studied transnational life by "going where the ducks are"—by intensively studying one transnational community for a decade and a half. In more academic language, I have "sampled on the dependent variable" by focusing on a community that exhibits a great deal of transnational life. I have also attempted to do what Howard Becker says good qualitative research should: to closely follow the action for a long time, tell stories accurately, and examine more and not less of the thing under study.[1] By analyzing three substantive themes—politics, gender, and the second generation—I trace the process of migration as it leads to and then coexists with settlement and assimilation.

This book offers a close look at people attempting to live meaningful, dignified lives under difficult circumstances, and largely succeeding. First-generation Ticuanense men and women are justifiably proud of all they have been able to accomplish for *el pueblo*. And both the first and second generations have negotiated hard and often conflicting choices regarding gender, race, and ethnicity in the United States and Mexico. Teen migrants and *cholos*, who have faced the most difficult circumstances considered here, have also created meaningful lives in a particular niche in American and Mexican society, though with sometimes negative results for themselves and others—an outcome I consider unnecessary and changeable.

The search for recognition and respect is an impetus common to all three spheres of transnational life analyzed in this book. The Committee seeks recognition for its efforts on behalf of Ticuani. Under the old ways of the religious cargo system, their sacrifices would have given them both recognition and power. But even this system was always refracted through local power politics, especially the cacique system. Had the Committee members stayed in Ticuani and worked as hard for the community as they have done in New York, they might in fact have earned less power and recognition, because they would not have had the same capacity to extract Ticuanense dollars in New York. Making their claim to recognition under the old rules, but in a transnationalized system, has helped redraw Ticuani's political system. As similar efforts are undertaken in hundreds of other *municipios*, the participation of migrants is profoundly changing Mexico's political system.

Men and women migrants seek the recognition and admiration of their peers of both sexes in a context where the rules are also changing. The first-generation men face challenges to their traditional male privilege, or, alternatively, to their management of their preserved and extended privileges in the United States (created through institutions such as the Committee). They must negotiate their status in new and unaccustomed ways with their wives and families. Women, too, demand respect but seek to do so without throwing out all that they value in the old ways. In the second generation, transnational space makes this quest for respect easier in some ways for the men, as it places them in a context where their imagined male privilege is more likely to be supported. But women confront a pair of incompatible images: the completely autonomous New York woman and the Ticuani ranchera who depends utterly on men. Finding a balance between these two positions is hard for second-generation women.

Finally, the gang members too seek recognition of their suffering, power, and manhood. They seek acknowledgment of the fact that they did not get the deal they were promised. Migration is not, for them, a dream of *superando* (overcoming odds by hard work) but an experience of hostility and humiliation to which they respond with social and physical violence. They feel that the rules they were supposed to play under were changed, and they are taking back what is theirs. For both the Committee and the *cholos*, the contest is between rival groups of men demanding a recognition of their sacrifice and the recognition they feel they are entitled to.

In academic terms, this book seeks to critique and improve on earlier thinking about transnational life, to which I have contributed. At its most strident, this early theory saw transnational life as a result of the globalization of the economy, posited it as a "third way" of being for immigrants that was fundamentally different from the lives of past migrants, and saw it as an alternative to assimilation. In contrast, I argue here that transnational life is the product of the processes of migration from the home country and assimilation in the United States and that we can understand it better by examining other factors that profoundly affect it, such as the life course, adolescence, gender, political change, and changes in patterns of migration and assimilation. Similarly, transnational life is not an alternative to assimilation but is rather both a result of it and a context in which negative or positive assimilation can take place: second-generation college students and gang members both go back to Ticuani. This means that although not every immigrant will live a transnational life, those who do may have their experience of assimilation profoundly affected; and there is reason to believe that increasing numbers will do so. Finally, transnational life has concrete consequences in all of the arenas of life studied: it has helped change electoral politics in the Mixteca (and elsewhere in Mexico),[2] it has facilitated renegotiation of the traditional gender bargain, and it has changed both adolescence and youth culture for those in Ticuani and for Ticuanenses in the United States. These effects reach well beyond the focus on identity lamented by my friend, the wise but sometimes cranky Roger Waldinger, in 1997.

Research on transnational life has had a curiously mixed career in the social sciences. While on the one hand it has grown to become a mainstay of migration research in several disciplines, on the other it has only recently worked its way into the mainstream of sociology, with the publication of an article by Alejandro Portes and his colleagues in 2003 in the *American Sociological Review* and a harsh critique of "transnationalism" by Roger Waldinger and David Fitzgerald in a 2004 article in the *American Journal of Sociology*. One reason for this cold reception is that use of the term has outpaced the theorizing about it, leading to what I call the "stapling problem"—some simply "staple" the adjective *transnational* in front of whatever they are studying, as if the analytical work were already done. Second, even thoughtful elaborations of transnational theory have sometimes failed to fully engage existing theories of migration and coined new terms such as *transmigrant* without demonstrating clear, enduring differences from migrants (though Portes and his colleagues have begun to do so). Third, as discussed briefly in the introduction, this research has faced Merton's "fallacy of adumbration," wherein a theoretical innovation is judged not to be true if it is new, and not new if it is true. This curious reasoning denies the possibility that a new theoretical lens will enable one to see "new" instances of a given phenomenon in history. A spate of historical work over the last decade has fleshed out historical instances of transnational life, and transnational theory has gained purchase on a variety of issues that the adumbrators cannot explain, though some continue to attack the straw man of the early, overreaching version of transnationalism. Fourth, theory about transnational life has faced important questions regarding its originality, durability, and significance.

Acceptance of transnational research has also been slowed because much work on it has been developed through case studies, using what Michael Burawoy calls "reflexive science," while most other influential, earlier theories of migration use what he calls "positive science." Positive science emphasizes objectively gathered data, reliability, replicability, and representativeness and views the ability to predict as essential to evaluating a theory, while reflexive science uses the engagement with informants as a key to insight, cannot easily be reproduced, cannot usually be shown to be representative of a population, cannot usually predict, and gains insight through the investigation of "anomalies"—phenomena that do not quite fit with preexisting theories or even one's own preconceived understandings of the thing under study.[3] Another way to approach this issue is by comparison with different models in the hard sciences.[4] Much talk about social science as a discipline uses the language of physics, implying that if we just do our work well enough, we should be able to uncover laws that, like physical laws, apply in almost any social situation. But the social world rarely offers the chance to do controlled experiments or provides complete sets of information to theorize, and its subject matter—human beings and their social world—does not behave the same way all the time. As a result, evolutionary biology seems a more apt model for social-science theorizing. The point here is not to endorse any form of social Darwinism, but rather to argue that evolutionary biologists theorize under constraints and in ways that are more similar to those of social scientists than physicists do. Most social-science theories, as well as the data on which they are based, are incomplete, but this does not mean they are wrong. Similarly, social-science research that cannot predict future outcomes is not bad social science. If it does a good job of explaining how a state of affairs came to be—retrodiction, rather than prediction[5]—it still contributes to our understanding of our world.

While this book uses both reflexive and positive science, it falls more into the reflexive category, whereas the work of Douglas Massey and his colleagues is largely positive science. Their theory of "cumulative causation" of migration details why migration happens, how and why it evolves, and how migration becomes one of its own strongest causes, through processes such as family reunification.[6] They rightly emphasize their ability to demonstrate their theory with empirical, quantitative data. Yet such theories and methods have yielded blind spots: there are some questions about transnational life that they cannot ask, much less answer.

The key method in the theory of cumulative causation has been the ethnosurvey, a technique of interviewing migrants conversationally that nevertheless yields data suitable for statistical analysis. (Massey generously shared his ethnosurvey interview schedule with me, and I used a modified version of it to gather much of the data for chapter 2 of this book.) This analysis is contextualized by ethnography and by conditions such as globalization, but the center of it is the database yielded by the ethnosurvey. Yet the kinds of questions asked and data yielded by the ethnosurvey limit its ability to identify and explain the aspects of transnational life analyzed in this book. It comprehensively documents patterns of migration and return among migrants, and, with a random sample, can establish the frequency of transnational practices within a population, as Alejandro Portes and his colleagues did recently.[7] But the ethnosurvey does not take account of the researcher's strong, evolving relationships with key informants over time or how post hoc interpretations of and gossip about events can bring about change in the future. In short, it cannot analyze the social glue holding transnational life together.

Rather than seek patterns in large data sets yielding law-like theories, as positive science would require, and as cumulative causation theory does in exemplary fashion, reflexive case studies can trace how transnational practices become structural. Hence, I analyze how adolescence is transnationalized and how it subsequently structures the lives of the second generation in Brooklyn as a coercive, Durkheimian social fact. For example, the anomalous splits in the Ticuani community in New York and Puebla during the 1998 elections were catalyzed by changes in Mexican national politics, especially the PRI's change in candidate selection practices. From this observation, I theorize that the sending nation plays a key role in creating transnational space and is not simply superseded by transnational actions, as others have proposed.

Case studies are often criticized as being unrepresentative and unable to generate larger insights. While on one level this is true—there can be no random sample—on another level this criticism displays a powerful lack of imagination, a lack of knowledge of how cases do their analytical work, and the preoccupation of positive science with representativeness to the exclusion of other dimensions of analysis.[8] Even otherwise acute observers sometimes take this position. Douglas Massey, then president of the American Sociological Association, raised this point in a conference on transnationalism in 2001 when he repeated a joke circulated among Mexican anthropologists: an anthropologist gives a long lecture on the intimacies of the village he has studied for many years. The anthropologists in the audience all respond, "It's not like that in my village." Massey's implication was that work on transnational life has not moved past the "not in my village" stage. However, that case studies, positively or reflexively studied, cannot generalize to an entire population as a random sample can is beside the point here. The extreme particularism of the "not in my village" stance is bad social science. In a reflexive-science model, cases acquire theoretical importance through three dialogues: between the researchers and informants; between the local dynamics of the subject under study and the larger structures within which it is embedded; and between analysis of the case and theory. In this book, I further refine and develop theory on transnational life by analyzing other processes affecting it, including adolescence, changes in the Mexican political system, gender, and generation.[9] A purely positive-science approach or methods would not be in the "ethnographic neighborhood" to ask the kinds of questions and obtain the kinds of data analyzed in this book. My point here is not that reflexive science is the right and positive science the wrong approach for analyzing transnational life. Both models offer potentially useful insights, and both should be used.

My extended case study of the transnational life of Ticuanense migrants and their children does several kinds of analytical work. First, it strengthens theorizing about transnational life by engaging with related theories of migration, politics, adolescence, gender, and generation. Hence I use theories of adolescence and the life course to show that second-generation transnational practices are not simple continuations of the first generation's attachment to Ticuani, but part of adolescence in New York. In contrast to a classic "immigrant adolescence"—caught statically between "Americanization" and preservation of Mexican customs—a set of more complex and interesting transnational adolescent practices, both positive and negative, has emerged. Mexican gangs have flourished in New York not simply because of "normal" assimilation pressures but also because of conditions created by changes in United States immigration law and resulting family reunification, by the hostile reception to Mexicans in New York, and by the especially difficult experience of teen migrants. In contrast, association with Ticuani helps others redefine their Mexicanness and do better in New York. Such an embedded analysis both takes account of larger structures and recognizes the roles of migrants and their children in creating transnational practices and life.

Transnational life is changing the assimilation experience for many, and this change requires a theoretical retooling. The invigorated version of assimilation offered by Richard Alba and Victor Nee captures some of the experience of second-generation Ticuanenses, and the notion of segmented assimilation as developed by Portes and his colleagues captures more of it by focusing on how ethnicity's meaning changes with social mobility. But for many second-generation Ticuanenses, Mexicanness is forged both in New York and in Mexico. While some returnees follow the same upward or downward assimilative paths in Ticuani as in New York, for others, return to Ticuani is transformative. In either case, their experience of adolescence cannot be understood properly without considering how it is transnationalized and how it in turn affects assimilation.

This transnationalization of second-generation adolescence seems to be historically new. Working in the 1920s and 1930s among Italian immigrants and their children, neither Caroline Ware nor Irvin Child noted a tendency for the children of immigrants to return to Italy, one clear sign of transnational life. This was so even among the more consciously Italian American set of second-generation youths noted by Child. Even though Child did his research during the Great Depression, when return would have been harder, one would at least expect discussion of the interruption of the pattern of return if it had existed before. Similarly, Ostergren's extremely thorough analysis of Swedish migration observes no second-generation pattern of return, despite its meticulous documentation of many kinds of first-generation return and reciprocity.[10] Yet some examples exist, such as the second- and third- or later-generation Polish Americans who volunteered to fight and die for Poland's nationalist cause during World War I as part of that country's diasporic Kosciusko Army.[11] In contrast, contemporary observers note that many children of immigrants return to their parents' home countries regularly during adolescence.[12] *Mexican New York* develops new theoretical tools to make sense of this new dimension of the immigrant experience.

DURABILITY, LIMITS, AND PROSPECTS FOR TRANSNATIONAL LIFE

This book also contributes to the understanding of durability and change in transnational life. I have documented strong transnational participation through the second generation, and some in the 2.5 or third generation, through the cases of pioneer migrant grandmothers caring for their U.S.-born grandchildren. Such intergenerational durability speaks to the vitality of transnational life, which here serves as a strategy facilitating upwardly mobile assimilation. As mentioned in the introduction, the scope of participation in Ticuani transnational life is surprising. I estimate that some 30 to 40 percent of all Ticuanenses return to Ticuani over the course of three years. Given that many who never return still participate in some aspects of transnational life in New York, I would say that a majority participate periodically in some form of transnational life. The percentage of people who do not participate in any way in transnational life—have never given money to a committee, for example—is small.

Yet there are limits to local-level transnational life. Ticuani has been transnationalizing for more than thirty years, with the New York Committee as a key institution. The kind of associational life that has emerged is somewhere between the concept of the seamless "natural community" posited in sociology in the 1920s or by anthropologist Robert Redfield in the 1920s through the 1950s, and the more voluntary type of association of a United States political club. In another twenty years, the first-generation men most involved in Ticuani politics will have retired from public life. Democratization in Mexican politics may prolong local-level transnational life by mobilizing younger first- and 1.5-generation migrants to participate in Ticuani politics, but I suspect that Ticuani transnational politics and Committee involvement will become less intense. Yet this still makes the case *for* rather than against the importance of a transnational lens: Many in the second and some in the third generation will have experienced United States assimilation differently as a result of several decades of transnational life, and Ticuani and the Mixteca are permanently changed. Just as early transnationalists erred in positing a "third way," so too do critics err in posing proof of a third way as the only evidence to show the importance of a transnational lens. Documenting thirty years of local level effects on important processes like assimilation, politics, adolescence, and gender should be enough to merit scholarly attention. My work comparing Mexican with Swedish, Italian, and Polish migration takes up these issues of durability.[13] The likely outcome is a less intense, but still enduring, Ticuanense transnational life that, like the Jewish religious camps and summer camps in the Catskills, may have a strong influence on individuals. Moreover, this is a spreading process. As new migrant towns are transnationalized throughout Mexico, they will experience many of the changes described here, transforming new Mexican sending areas and supporting their own forms of transnational life.

Macro-Level Factors Affecting Transnational Life

While this book purposely emphasizes *local*-level transnational life, macro-level institutions and forces will help to make transnational life a durable, probably permanent phenomenon. During the 1990s the Mexican state developed an impressive capacity for deepening relations with Mexicans and Mexican Americans in the United States. The main vehicle for this effort was the Program for Mexican Communities Abroad, formed in 1990 by President Salinas through the Ministry of Foreign Affairs. This program was extremely active during the 1990s and organized most of the existing hometown associations. The program was also used for political ends by the PRI, and migrants have also attempted to use it as a political space. Perhaps the biggest change in the macropolitical context is how Mexican migrants in the United States have become part of Mexico's imagined political community. Consistent with this reality, Mexico has cultivated relations with Mexican American and Mexican immigrant leaders, betting on their future prominence in U.S. politics. By bringing such leaders to visit Mexico, and keeping them informed about Mexican issues, the state of Mexico is laying the groundwork for a small but politically informed Mexican diaspora.

Mexico's strategy was well received by the United States before September 11, 2001. With Mexican Americans accounting for about two-thirds of the Latino population, the Bush administration was pushing for legalization for many undocumented Mexicans in the United States, with a vision of strengthening the relationship between the two countries. President Bush hoped to court Latino and Catholic votes in key electoral states like California, Texas, New York, and Florida. Thus the conditions for the emergence of an effective diasporic lobby were met: the United States target group had electoral power, and Mexico is significant in U.S. foreign policy.[14]

Although the subsequent focus on terrorism has eclipsed relations with Mexico in U.S. politics, long-term trends will support transnational and diasporic life. A cadre of Mexican immigrant leaders in the United States are either permanent U.S. residents or U.S. citizens and also hold elected office in Mexico. Andrés Bermudez, a U.S. citizen known as the "Tomato King," was elected mayor of the large city of Jerez, Zacatecas, in 2001. Although he was stripped of his post by the Mexican electoral authorities, this action was taken because he had failed to fulfill the requisite period of residence in Zacatecas; his U.S. citizenship was not the issue.[15] During summer 2003, several migrants in the United States ran for the Mexican Congress; significantly, they presented themselves as representatives of Mexican migrants in the United States. One, Manuel de la Cruz, earned enough votes to be selected by his party but was passed over as a deputy for the left-leaning Party of the Democratic Revolution (PRD).

These migrant candidates in July 2003 were different from Eddie Baron, a Mexican national and U.S. permanent resident, who was elected by the PRI in 2000 and moved back to Mexico to take up his post. De la Cruz, like the other half-dozen or so migrant candidates, had grown tired of waiting for President Vicente Fox to enact his promised promigrant agenda and had lobbied political parties directly to be put up for election to the *plurinominal* or regional district congressional seats. They vowed to run and govern as migrants, pushing to implement their constitutional right to vote for president from abroad and to gain political recognition for their contributions to Mexico. While none were actually elected, their candidacies helped foster a reimagination of Mexico's political community, and more such candidates will follow in the next congressional elections.

This transnationalization of Mexican political life can be usefully viewed through a globalist lens, but not the one that would read these developments simply as a manifestation of global trends toward democracy. Rather, I would adapt Saskia Sassen's analysis.[16] She sees economic globalization as requiring the commitment and legislative backing of nation-states; she also sees the nature of state sovereignty as having changed. Similarly, I see the sovereignty of the Mexican political system—understood as having its politics conducted in Mexico by Mexican actors—as changing. The Mexican political system now has Mexican national actors acting extraterritorially, but still within the Mexican political system. This is different from the older notion of outside actors, such as the United States, influencing Mexican politics. Mexico has given its emigrant citizens a constitutional right to political representation, in part because of the demands these citizens made and continue to make on Mexico and in part because of its commitment to becoming "modern." In this view, the Mexican state's actions helped to create and strengthen the transnational public sphere within which demands on the state are made.

Such transnational mobilization will likely also increase immigrants' participation in American politics and spur the adoption of American citizenship (or dual citizenship), as happened among Dominicans in New York.[17] All of the migrants who ran for the Mexican Congress in 2003 have been financially successful in the United States, deeply involved in community service, or both. De la Cruz, a driving force behind the Zacatecas Federation for many years, also quietly worked with other leaders to organize baseball and other sports leagues for Mexican immigrants and second-generation youths, in part because he saw them as an important counterweight to gangs in Los Angeles. Similarly, immigrant entrepreneurs who conduct their business transnationally are more likely to be U.S. citizens and to be more successful educationally and occupationally than are those whose business is all done in the United States.[18]

Deepening integration between Mexico and the United States is also likely to support transnational life. New populations will migrate in response to industrialization, and NAFTA may evolve into a closer form of integration with freer movement of people across borders, along the lines of the European Union. Moreover, the continuing departure of working-age migrants from large regions of rural Mexico in states like Zacatecas, Jalisco, Guanajato, and Michoacán has created what Mexican officials privately call ghost towns, in which the elderly people and children living there need services that must be supported by migrants.[19] I suspect that Mexican leaders will increasingly emphasize to Mexicans in the United States the ways links with Mexico can help them retain their authentic Mexicanness, and also how improvements in Mexico increase the pleasure of returning to the hometown in Mexico.

Mexico's falling population growth could undermine one basis for transnational life. Although for at least the next twenty years the number of workers entering the Mexican economy will exceed the number of jobs, after that Mexico should be able to significantly increase its investment in human capital and could, in thirty years, become a first-world economy. Migration tends to slow when there is about a five-to-one wage differential between countries; the differential between the United States and Mexico is now about ten to one.[20] Extensive development and slower population growth would decrease the migration pressure that supports transnational life, though existing transnational life could persist. The Italian case is instructive here. To alleviate the fear of massive Italian migration anticipated when Italy joined the European Community (now the European Union) in the 1960s, the EC invested heavily in development in Italy. Italy is today a country of immigration. While Italy stood closer, in economic terms, to the EC in the 1960s than Mexico does to the United States today, such a vision for Mexican–United States integration would help guide a process that is taking place anyway. However, the United States would have to give Mexico grants of about US$25 billion per year to support an analogous economic integration, a move that seems highly unlikely. Regardless of what happens, emigration from the Mixteca and similar regions seems likely to continue until the supply of new migrants is exhausted, a prospect that could become reality within thirty years.[21]

Another, somewhat ironic, form of transnational life could develop if large numbers of retired American citizens move to Mexico. As regions within Mexico increasingly offer first-class health care along with inexpensive housing, domestic help, golf, and other pleasures of retirement, increasing numbers of retired Americans—both Mexican Americans and Anglos—are likely to relocate there. The political effects in both countries could be fascinating. One can imagine the politically powerful AARP opening chapters in Mexico.

POLICY IMPLICATIONS

Below, I discuss the policy implications of two themes discussed extensively in the book: civic and political associational life between the United States and Mexico, and the transnational and local dimensions of youth and family issues. I take the view of a well-intentioned bureaucrat seeking feasible interventions. Some issues could be addressed with a minimum of additional institutional or financial involvement, simply by employing strategic thinking. Other interventions would require both thinking differently and creating new institutions or programs, some of which are transnational in scope and more expensive.

Civic and Political Associational Life between the United States and Mexico

Mexican political parties and social movements span both countries, addressing issues ranging from indigenous rights, neoliberalism, and NAFTA to customs officials' abuse of returning migrants. Mexico's Program for Mexican Communities Abroad has registered more than six hundred community-of-origin committees, and hundreds more exist. One challenge is to channel the energies of these myriad organizations into making positive contributions to the American and Mexican political systems.

First, we should rationalize and harness some of the economic power of remittances to Mexico for more positive ends in both countries. Some US$15 billion was transferred to Mexico in 2004, much sent via unsafe or usurious methods. Following the recommendations of Rudy del la Garza,[22] the two countries should establish facilities that would remit funds free or for a nominal fee but hold the money for two days in order to collect interest. The income from this float could be used for educational and development projects in Mexico and in Mexican American communities in the United States, and parties in both countries would benefit from cheaper, safer transfer of remittances.

Second, further institutionalizing the relations between Mexicans or Mexican Americans in Mexico and the United States would help sustain diasporic ties, which could aid assimilation in the United States. For example, a program putting Mexican American youths to work in public education or social programs of their relatives' hometowns, or in internships with the Mexican government or businesses, could promote a positive definition of Mexicanness. Rather than thwart assimilation in the United States, as many fear could happen, transnational life, including spending time in the home country, has the potential to help mitigate negative assimilation pressures and promote positive assimilation for these youths. Mexico should also greatly expand its educational exchanges with U.S.-born Mexican Americans. The United States could help by being more cooperative in granting nonprofit status to Mexican civic organizations. This would make it easier to contribute to projects in Mexico, obtain the cooperation of American institutions, and direct energy toward issues in communities in the United States as well. A new policy in Mexico allows wealthy Mexican or Mexican American entrepreneurs in the United States to "adopt a microregion," investing in actual or potential sending areas. While limited in its potential for large-scale change, this program may bring about positive changes. The United States could also facilitate such investments under the rationale of promoting development in Mexico.

The policies regarding Mexicans' voting from abroad should be rationalized. This is a major issue, and a tricky one. Migrants press their demand to vote in Mexican municipal or state elections on the basis that their ongoing contributions to projects and families in Mexico entitle them to a voice in politics. Critics object that migrants no longer understand local problems and, as absentee voters, would not have to live with the consequences of their vote. Voting from abroad presents logistical challenges but could be managed by establishing voter registries in the consulates or perhaps using the Internet. The PRI has thus far prevented enactment of the constitutional right to vote for president from abroad because it fears migrants will vote against the PRI. Other issues include the potentially negative reaction in the United States to the exercise of the Mexican vote in the United States— though technically on Mexican soil, if it is done in the consulates[23]—by very large numbers of Mexicans, which some will no doubt paint as an infringement of United States sovereignty. One solution suggested has been the establishment of some kind of extraterritorial republican or electoral college system, by which migrants in the United States would elect representatives to vote for them in Mexico. This is less likely to inspire negative reactions in the United States. However, as discussed above, migrants are not waiting for Mexico to decide what to do. As migrants have sought and gained spots as *plurinominal* or regional congressional representatives, mainly through the PRD, they are entering directly into Mexican politics and will no doubt press their demands for inclusion from inside the *periférico*, Mexico City's equivalent of the Washington Beltway. Hence, even if Mexico does not implement the right to vote from abroad, which seems quite possible, returning migrants or migrant *diputados* (congressional representatives) living in the United States will exert increasing political pressure in Mexico, amplified by migrant dollars and prestige.

Finally, American political parties should read up on American immigration history and begin to cultivate relationships with Mexican migrant organizations. It was much easier for immigrants to vote during the last great wave of immigration, between the 1860s and the 1920s. These electoral mechanisms, while often used by political machines to subvert democratic ends, ultimately speeded the successful integration of these new immigrant groups. Given this history, it is amazing to me that the immense network of immigrant organizations that now exists should have so few links with the American political system. While such relationships have begun to develop, a more systematic effort is required. We should remember that assimilation is a two-way process: newcomers must be given the chance to become full members of society.

Youth and Family Issues and Policies

Teen migrants and children of migrants need to feel they belong and have good prospects in the United States. Gangs are the most serious risk they face, though the interventions I recommend go beyond discouraging gang activity. Stronger law enforcement itself is not an adequate solution. In the Mixteca, local authorities have built larger jails and selectively deployed the state police to deal with gangs. While these steps did decrease violence in Ticuani, they also gave gang members tangible targets for their resentment of the state, their absent parents, and adult authority, and jailing them briefly made it "cooler" to be a gang member. The walls of Ticuani's new jail are covered with gang graffiti.[24] Mexico's attempts to coordinate its policing of gangs with the efforts of the New York City Police Department have so far been unreciprocated.

A broader approach would consider the needs of returning teen migrants and children of migrants. While the relationship of Israel with American Jews is often invoked by Mexican officials, its example is not much followed. Mexico and the United States should dedicate resources toward programs for returning regulars and *pandilleros,* especially during school vacations. Local towns could adapt or develop customs to include these youths as authentic members of the towns, and not as tourists. Holiday camps, sporting activities, and volunteer programs could be established in migrant-sending regions for the returning second generation. Such camps could establish close links with Mexico to the second generation and beyond. Such steps would strengthen diasporic Mexican identity and could aid positive assimilation in the United States while also helping local communities.

Mexico should also reinvigorate and expand the student exchanges coordinated during the mid-1990s through the Program for Mexican Communities Abroad, and the United States should support this effort. The two countries, with the aid of private groups, could also expand opportunities for Mexican Americans to attend university in Mexico, enabling them to understand not only their own Mexicanness but also Mexico–United States relations while getting a first-class international education at an affordable price. A large number of scholarships could be established with some small percentage of the float from US$15 billion of remittances each year, and that investment would be returned many times over when these young Mexican Americans returned to the United States to work in their communities. (Such is one of the goals of the nonprofit organization I cofounded, the Mexican Educational Foundation of New York.)

To aid assimilation, Mexican government agencies, including local sections of the Integrated Family Development Department (DIF), should promote closer relationships with local authorities and institutions in United States migrant destinations. A judicious expansion of the sister cities program might prove useful.

The stated policy of the United States is to facilitate the acquisition of full, active U.S. citizenship for immigrants and their children. Obstacles to citizenship hurt American social and civic life by creating a large, disenfranchised population of undocumented people.[25] In my view, encouraging citizenship acquisition among immigrants and their families is not inconsistent with their maintaining a relationship with their homeland and will have many positive long-term impacts in the United States. Moreover, assimilation problems in the United States reflect larger difficulties in how it meets the needs of its youths, especially lower-income urban youths. Instead of just an immigration policy—which determines only who gets in— the United States needs an *immigrant* policy that helps newcomers to become citizens, learn English, participate fully in American institutions, and help their children to do the same. Such a policy would help those coming into difficult environments to rise above them and to change those environments themselves. Finally, the United States should simplify its procedures for becoming a legal immigrant and a U.S. citizen, while taking all necessary steps to ensure national security: this step would benefit the United States as well as the individuals affected.

A final issue, mentioned incidentally in the book, merits inclusion here because it illustrates how small-scale, local interventions could greatly improve people's lives: migrant men abandoning their wives and children in Mexico. Abandonment can be either total—as when the man leaves and neither sends money nor visits, and may form another family with a new partner in the United States—or emotional—as when the man sends money but never returns. These are sometimes selfish exercises of power but may also result from the man's own desperate situation. Many migrant men feel depressed, have alcohol problems, and see no way to bring their families to the United States. They have gone to the United States to prosper, feel ashamed that they are still struggling, and cannot bear their families to witness this perceived failure, even if it means not seeing them for years and years.

Regarding men who have completely abandoned their families, U.S. laws empower women to garnish errant fathers' wages.[26] There is no legal obstacle to Mexican women's doing this. However, most women in Mexico do not know they have this right and are unable to act on it. During the late 1990s, the DIF in Tamaulipas created a pilot program with Texas to enforce child-support obligations. To implement a similar program on a larger scale, Mexican institutions must inform women in sending regions of their rights and then create a mechanism by which errant fathers could be compelled to fulfill their obligations. Such a mechanism could operate through social networks, a Web-based registry of "deadbeat migrant dads," or legal measures. Large-scale arrangements could even be negotiated as side agreements to NAFTA, utilizing an existing binational institution.

These are just three issues for which combined local, national, and transnational interventions are possible. Other problems, including public health issues such as tuberculosis, AIDS, and drug abuse, could also be addressed through such an approach. Too often, well-intentioned scholars seduced by transnational or global analyses declare that only transnational or global solutions can address problems, while well-intentioned policymakers think only within their immediate jurisdiction. I advocate the combination of any and all methods that enable well-designed interventions at strategic sites.

Coda

The Mexican Educational Foundation of New York

At the urging of my editor at the University of California Press, the energetic, insightful, and funny Naomi Schneider, here I describe briefly the Mexican Educational Foundation of New York (MexEd), a 501(c)(3) nonprofit organization. MexEd's goals are to foster Mexican and Mexican American leadership and progress in New York by promoting educational achievement, mentorship, and positive definitions of Mexicanness. I cofounded it with Sandra Lara, a Ph.D. student at Teachers College at Columbia University (now Dr. Lara-Cinisomo and an analyst at the RAND Corporation in California). For the past several years, we have served on the organization's board with two dedicated friends, Jorge Suárez and Sven Kaludzinksi-Trevino, a Mexican and Mexican American, respectively, who both work in finance. Part of the impetus for starting this organization was my own frustration at watching so much potential in this community thwarted by obstacles large and small. This frustration deepened the further I got into the study of second-generation Mexican Americans at work and at school in New York. I had previously worked as a volunteer English teacher, amnesty counselor, and expert witness with the Mexican community and had taken time off during graduate school to work as a community organizer. Yet these efforts did not have much cumulative effect.

The story of forming MexEd in New York actually starts with Sandra's own story of coming to the United States as a young child, growing up in difficult circumstances in Los Angeles, getting into and through college by dint of character and intelligence, and then charging through a master's degree at Harvard in the same way. Sandra then returned to Los Angeles to start LEGAL (Latinos Encouraging Graduation among Latinos), which had goals similar to MexEd's. She then came to New York to attend Teachers College and worked on my project on second-generation work and school-

293

ing. Her experience and work on LEGAL, and my wish to find an appropriate outlet to help the community, led to the founding of MexEd. We met Jorge and Sven, who were also searching for a way to help the community, and the rest, as they say, is history.

MexEd is a young organization with big plans based on experience and extensive research. We have begun by running a mentorship program to help Mexican and Mexican American youth learn about college and about internship opportunities in professional, community, and business settings. The strategy is to have all MexEd students work with Mexicans or Mexican American mentors in New York or in Mexico to increase the social capital in the community. We focus first on the rapid advancement of a few selected MexEd scholars, while working to increase college attendance by Mexicans and Mexican Americans. We also raise funds for college scholarships.

In addition to promoting these concrete goals, we work to challenge limiting images and beliefs. For example, we aim to reverse the pernicious perception encountered over and over again in the second-generation study that college is good but "Mexicans don't go to college." We want Mexicans and Mexican Americans in New York to take it for granted that Mexicans go to college. In addition to our mentoring and internship programs, we would like to help send some students to Mexico for college, for public service and internships, and for paid work. Such experiences could redefine Mexicanness in a very positive way, even for those for whom it already has positive meanings, as we have seen documented in this book, and expand these youths' social capital—contacts and networking—in ways that are not possible in the United States. A program like this would also stretch scholarship dollars, promote United States–Mexico understanding, and strengthen links between Mexico and its diaspora in the United States. It could become instrumental in fighting negative assimilation and promoting positive assimilation. It is negative assimilation pressures that pose the greatest danger to the individual futures of these youths and to their collective future in American society. MexEd could foster the formation of a cadre of Mexican and Mexican American leaders in New York who both understand the problems of the community and issues in Mexico–United States relations and have the skills to address these issues. Programs such as MexEd wishes to develop could make an important difference in these young people's lives, too, by helping them to both identify and act on a compelling project outside themselves.

Anyone wishing to learn more about MexEd or to contribute to its programs can contact me at robert_smith@baruch.cuny.edu or at the Mexican

Educational Foundation of New York, c/o Professor Robert Smith, School of Public Affairs, Baruch College, D-0901, 135 East 22nd Street, New York, NY 10010. One hundred percent of contributions will go to MexEd programs. Half of my royalties from this book will be donated to MexEd and other Mexican organizations, especially in New York.

Notes

CHAPTER 1. TRANSNATIONAL LIFE IN
ETHNOGRAPHIC PERSPECTIVE

1. Lamont (2000) offers a different but fascinating analysis of moral maps.

2. To emphasize the importance of Ticuani in anchoring transnational life, and also the insistence of those in Ticuani that they have the right to define who is and is not authentically Ticuanense, I use the term *local* mainly to refer to people now living in Ticuani. For Ticuanenses living in New York who visit, I use *returnees* or a similar term. For interactions in New York, especially with those with other ethnic groups that have been in a neighborhood longer than Mexicans, I usually use racial and ethnic terms, which are more salient in such encounters. See Jess and Massey 1995 on how power determines the definition of *local*.

3. See R. Smith 2003a,b, 1998a,b, 1993, 2001b; Goldring 2001; Guarnizo 1998; Portes 1999; Espinosa 1998; Moctezuma Longoria 2003a,b; Delgado Wise 2003.

4. Harvey (1989) argues that new technology and ways of organizing economic life "compress" time and space so that distances no longer have the same meaning. International economic transactions that previously took weeks now take seconds. Sassen (1999), Pessar and Mahler (2003), Massey, Goldring, and Durand (1994), and Doreen Massey and Jess (1995) note that time-space compression is not simply a matter of technology but also of having access to such technology. Ticuanenses are a relatively powerless group in the sense that their actions do not significantly affect global capitalism. But because of their location in the United States and in migrant-sending regions of Mexico where such technologies now coexist with older forms of economic and political organization, they have become powerful in their own community.

5. On earlier diasporas, see Cohen 1995; Gabaccia 2000; Glick-Schiller 1999; Foner 1997, 1999; R. Smith 2000, 2003b.

6. This mutual constitution of structure and agency implies a flexibly structured evolution wherein particular contexts present opportunities that speed up changes in structure. This dialectic approach accommodates change over time better than one focusing on structure itself. Ewa Morawska's work (2001, 1989) on structuration in migration theory has been especially useful. In taking up structuration, I also carry on in the tradition of Sahlins's work on generative historical structures (1981), Braudel's multistoried historical structures (1981), Durkheim's work on social facts (1984), and Giddens's work on structuration (1976, 1984), and I draw on Emirbayer and Goodwin 1994, Emirbayer and Mische 1998, Swidler 1986, Tilly 1997, Venkatesh 2000a, Sewell 1992, and Doreen Massey 1995a,b.

The analysis in this book can be read as symbolic interactionist in that it is consistent with Blumer's "three premises of symbolic interaction: that we know things by their meanings, that meanings are created through social interaction, and that meanings change through interaction" (Fine 1993: 64). I analyze how belonging, masculinity, and Mexicanness are negotiated collectively and evolve over time, though I see meaning-making processes as much affected by external context (see Weigert 1991; Fine 1993: 70). I draw on Denzin's (1985) argument that emotions are lived through physical bodies in my analysis of *promesas,* and on Flaherty's (1999) work on the experience of time in my analysis of "accelerated social time" in Ticuani. I use Goffman's (1963) concept of stigma management and Hochschild's (1983) concept of emotion work in analyzing the evolving presentation and experience of self for *cholos* and regulars.

7. "Making the facts understandable" and prediction are sometimes referred to, respectively, as the Aristotelian or finalistic tradition and the causal-mechanistic or Galilean tradition in science. See Ragin 2000; von Wright 1971; and workshop notes, National Science Foundation meeting, "The Scientific Bases of Qualitative Research," July 11–12, 2003.

8. The ethnographic work of Sara Guerrero-Rippberger, Sandra Lara, Agustín Vecino, Griscelda Perez, Carolina Perez, and Lisa Peterson was invaluable for many reasons, not least that it facilitated my work with teenage informants.

9. Although this book was fully drafted long before Burawoy published his article on revisiting field sites (2003), my return visits have been both realist—I was able to see how the object of knowledge had changed—and constructivist—my knowledge of the object and my theorizing about it have changed.

10. Similarly, Thomas and Znaniecki's *The Polish Peasant in Europe and America* (1927) emphasizes the disruption of familial and communal social structures resulting from migration. It does, however, discuss the concept of Polonia and links between Poland and Poles abroad. I thank David Fitzgerald for raising this point.

11. Portes et al. 2003; Guarnizo et al. 2003.

12. See especially Basch, Glick-Schiller, and Blanc-Szanton 1994; Glick-Schiller, Basch, and Blanc-Szanton 1992; Glick-Schiller and Fouron 2001a. In

this last book, the authors argue that even those who never leave their homes in the United States or Haiti are also transmigrants because they imagine themselves to be so, even two or three generations removed from the initial migration.

13. See, for example, Kearney 1991; Glick-Schiller et al. 1992; Rodriguez 1996; and especially David Gutiérrez 1994 on the concept of a "Third Space" in "Greater Mexico."

14. See Ortner 1995; Mitchell 1997.

15. This differentiation is for my own purposes and does not reflect the quite varied usage of the term. I distinguish between *transnational* and *global* to make my analysis more precise.

16. Portes, Guarnizo, and Landholt 1999.

17. As used here, *home* means one's birthplace and *host* means the country to which one migrates.

18. On "transnational," see Guarnizo 1998; Portes, Guarnizo, and Landholt 1999; Glick-Schiller 1999; Levitt 2001a,b; Goldring 1997; R. Smith 2000, 2003a,b. Suttles (1968) argues that the research on "natural community" by Park, Burgess, and McKenzie (1925) and Park (1952) has been misunderstood by others who construe it as too literal and geographical a notion of community.

19. Rumbaut 1999.

20. I refer to the concept of segmented assimilation as formulated by Alejandro Portes, Min Zhou, Ruben Rumbaut, and their colleagues. They posit three routes to assimilation, each giving race and ethnicity a different meaning: loss of ethnicity and upward assimilation into the white middle class; downward mobility into the Black "underclass" or "rainbow underclass"; and upward mobility through the retention of ethnicity as a resource creating human capital. Assimilation is thus segmented into upward and downward paths. I both use and critique this theory in later chapters. See Portes and Zhou 1993; Portes and Rumbaut 2001; Zhou 1999.

21. The random-sample study by Portes and his colleagues (2002) found transnational entrepreneurs in the United States to earn more money and have larger businesses and more education than their counterparts whose businesses were conducted strictly in the United States. Levitt (2001a,b), Graham (2001), and Rivera Salgado (2001) had similar findings.

22. See Ostergren's description of the Swedish temperance movement and the movement to extend the franchise, whose spread he traces in part to the efforts of the reformist editor Isidor Kjellberg, who had earlier spent time in the American Midwest. Ostergren 1988, especially 302–3 and 362n.18.

23. See Suttles 1968, 1972.

24. See Foner 2001a,b, 1999, 1997; Glick-Schiller 1999; R. Smith 2000, 2003a,b.

25. Zolberg 1999. Cecilia Menjivar (2002b) points to the state's power to limit movement as a significant factor in her pessimistic assessment of the prospects for transnational life among second-generation Guatemalans in the United States.

26. This paragraph draws on Massey and Durand et al. 1998, 2001, 2002; and Sassen 1998, 1988.

27. Douglas Massey and Espinosa 1997.

28. See, for example, Douglas Massey et al. 2002.

29. Escobar Latapi 1998.

30. Levitt (2001a,b) is a notable exception.

31. See Merton 1968: 16, cited in Portes 2001: 184.

32. Doreen Massey and Jess (1995) use this phrase in their introduction.

33. My conceptualization of social space as simultaneously geographical location, enduring social relations between people, and particular, episodic convergences of people engages various theories about place and space. Gieryn's work (2000, 2002) analyzes place in contradistinction to space, which he says is a unique geographical locale that has been given meaning by people. My discussion of Ticuani and the importance of the zocalo for those in New York, while it frames these locations as geographical space, resonates strongly with Gieryn's notion of place. This notion is also illustrated by the lengths to which my informants go to create Mexican social space in New York, where there is nothing like the zocalo, a place that they feel they can possess. My analysis also takes seriously Herb Gans's (2002) charge that sociologists should go beyond simply asserting that space is socially constructed to specifying how, including the ways particular kinds of space encourage particular social interactions. Here I discuss, for example, the importance of the zocalo in facilitating or staging particular kinds of social interaction in Ticuani. In positing that social space can simultaneously exist in geographical form and in enduring as well as ephemeral social form, and how it can be used to express dominance and hierarchy, I also tread the same path as those who theorize "spatiality," emphasizing how spaces are created with particular goals by particular interests. See Zukin 2002: 345, 1991; Sassen 2002; Bourdieu 1989; LeFebvre 1991; Pries 1999; Gottdiener 1985; Harvey 1985, 2001; Foucault 1977; Flores and Benmayor 1997.

34. See Flores and Benmayor 1997. The quote is from Gottdiener 1985: 123. On belonging, see also Espinosa 1998.

35. See B. Anderson 1991. On Fox and Mexico's imagined community, see R. Smith 2003a,b; Moctezuma Longoria 2003a,b; Delgado Wise 2003.

36. Appadurai 1996. While I disagree with Appadurai's stance on the state, his scholarship has opened up scholarly thinking about forms of transnational realities and processes in fascinating ways that often go unappreciated by his critics, including his insights on how transnational space is imagined and experienced by migrants.

37. Hirschman (1970) focuses on how members of states, firms, and organizations sometimes exercise exit (leaving), voice (protest with the threat of leaving), or loyalty (loyal opposition). My point here is that migrants have been able to exit Mexico physically and thus voice their concerns from the United States, whether as dissenters, loyal opposition, or part of or in association with the power structure.

38. My argument resonates with Sassen's (1998) point that although economic globalization transcends the state, it must be legislated, managed, and "instantiated" by the state in global cities. The state is thus not obsolete but rather is necessary to globalization.

39. Gerald Suttles's (1968) insight that community sentiment forms when a group is perceived by other groups—through its "foreign relations"—was derived by observing local group interactions in the Addams neighborhood of Chicago. Although Suttles used the word metaphorically, it is ironic that the current application of this local process of community sentiment literally does involve a foreign government. See also Gans 2002.

40. See Portes and his colleagues' special issue of *Ethnic and Racial Studies,* especially the introduction. Douglas Massey et al. (1987, 2002) also have an epistemological inclination toward taking the individual as their unit of analysis because of their emphasis on individual data drawn from their ethnosurvey. Community, as such, figures in their analysis as a factor affecting the migration process and its development as measured by individual data. The focus is not on the interaction between members of various parts of a community or group.

41. Most work on transnational life has focused on the public sphere and politics, emphasizing analysis of the activities of men, while most work on gender in migration has focused on women, as if only women were gendered. (Goldring 2001 and Levitt 2001a,b are important exceptions.) This book focuses more on men than on women, treating men as gendered, and on male-male friendship and male-female romantic relationships.

42. I thank Greta Gilbertson for suggesting this phrase to me.

43. See Hondagneu-Sotelo 1994; Hagan 1994; Doreen Massey 1995; Espinosa 1998; and especially Pessar and Mahler 2003. Menjivar 2002a also analyzes how men and women use different kinds of power within migrant networks. See also Mahler 1995.

44. Sara Guerrero-Rippberger's 1999 Barnard College senior thesis in sociology offers an insightful analysis of these processes, and her work on this project helped in the development of these ideas.

45. Menjivar (2002a: 230) cites Hondagneu-Sotelo and Avila (1997) in making the point that intergenerational tensions are often overlooked in more functionalist analyses of migration and discusses the "triple burden of simultaneously entering adolescence, a new society, and reconstituted families with little resemblance to those they knew before." See Mahler 1995.

46. I acknowledge the work and intellectual generosity of Marcelo and Carola Suarez-Orozco (1995, 2001) and Ricardo Ainslie (2002).

47. My book's tracing of the development and contestation over different meanings of place resonates strongly with the work of Doreen Massey and Jess (1995).

48. Fascinating work on the ways Mexicans as a group are negotiating Mexican public and religious life and undocumented status can be seen in Galvez (2004) and Rivera Sanchez (2003) on Asociación Tepeyac. See also R.

Smith 2001a,b, 2002. Cortina and Gendreau (2003) draws mainly on census data.

49. See Burawoy 1991, 1998.

50. See the work of Gaspar Rivera Salgado (2001), Luin Goldring (2001), Luis Guarnizo (1994), David Kyle (2001), Alejandro Portes (2001), Nina Glick-Schiller (1999), and Pamela Graham (2001).

51. These estimates come from Cortes Sanchez (2002, 2003) and from my work (2001a, 2002, 2003a,b,c).

CHAPTER 2. DUAL CONTEXTS FOR TRANSNATIONAL LIFE

1. This section draws on a previous brief history in R. Smith 1996b and 2001a and a longer history in R. Smith 1995.

2. Estimates of the ages of the population come from Valdes de Montano and Smith (1994) and R. Smith (1995). I derive the figure of 100,000 from the census's undercount estimate and an estimate by the New York City Planning Department in the early 1990s. Later estimates draw on the 1998 and 1999 Current Population Surveys. The census official Jorge del Piñal predicts Mexicans will become the largest minority on the East Coast (Alonso-Zaldivar 1999). I thank John Mollenkopf and Joseph Salvo for furnishing both data and expert advice.

3. I thank Francisco Rivera-Batiz and Hector Cordero-Guzman for sharing Emergency Immigrant Census data.

4. Alonso-Zaldivar 1999.

5. Rivera-Batiz 2003.

6. Massey, Durand, and Malone 2002; Cornelius 1994.

7. Valdes de Montano and Smith 1994; R. Smith 1995; McNees, Siulc, Smith, and Flores 2003.

8. Pare 1975, 1972.

9. Cornelius 1986.

10. Presidencia de la República 1982.

11. R. Smith 1994, 1995; Kim 1999.

12. Douglas Massey and Espinosa 1997.

13. Kraly and Miyares 2001.

14. Cortés Sánchez 2002, 2003.

15. See Douglas Massey, Goldring, and Durand 1994; Douglas Massey and Espinosa 1997.

16. Douglas Massey, Durand, and Malone 2002.

17. See Binford 1998, 2004; Cornelius 1994.

18. Valdes de Montano and Smith 1994.

19. This observation comes from fieldwork done for my second-generation project by Agustín Vecino (1999).

20. See R. Smith 2001a, 2005b; Roediger 1991; Ignatiev 1995; Jacobson 1996.

21. See M. Waters 1999.

22. See Portes and Rumbaut 2001; Portes and Zhou 1993; Zhou 1999.

23. Willis 1977; Gans 1992.

24. See Neckerman, Lee, and Carter 1999.

25. The only other Latino group to experience a nominal drop was Colombians, whose per capita incomes dropped 3.4 percent; incomes among Dominicans increased 11.7 percent, among Puerto Ricans 6.4 percent, and among Ecuadorans 14.5 percent.

26. Cohort analysis considers the same category of people in two different census data sets, here 1980 and 1990, enabling one to disaggregate Mexican and Mexican American populations. The method is subject to the risk that excessive mobility or morbidity will affect the assumption that one obtains data on the same people. But I agree with Myers (Myers and Cranford 1998; Myers 1998) that it is preferable to the static methods normally used.

27. My thanks to Joe Salvo and Peter Lobo of the New York City Planning Department for sharing these data.

28. Rivera-Batiz 2003.

29. Myers and Cranford 1998; Myers 1998; Moss and Tilly 1996.

30. See especially Waldinger 1996; also Portes and Bach 1985; Portes and Zhou 1993; Alba and Nee 2003.

31. Waldinger and Bozorgehr 1996.

32. Rivera-Batiz 2003: 42.

33. See Waldinger 1996; Portes and Rumbaut 2001.

34. See Waldinger 1996.

35. See Blalock 1956, 1958.

36. See T. Waters 1999 on the structural roots of immigrant gangs.

37. On the production or constitution of space, see Lefebvre 1991; Massey, Goldring, and Durand 1994; Doreen Massey and Jess 1995; Pessar and Mahler 2003.

38. This quote is from memory.

39. See Pinderhughes 1993.

40. See Portes and Rumbaut 2001.

41. "Doubly bounded solidarity" is my adaptation, developed in my unpublished 1994 paper, of the concept of bounded solidarity. See Portes 1995a,b; Zhou 1999.

42. R. Smith 1996b.

43. Myers and Cranford 1998.

44. See Moss and Tilly 1996.

45. On Korean-Mexican relations, see Smith 1995; Kim 1999. For a different but interesting approach to the issue of how context affects racialization and ethnic identity, see Rodriguez and Cordero-Guzmán 1992 and Rodriguez 2000. They asked informants how they would describe themselves racially and ethnically and then asked how they thought Americans would label them. The results were quite different. See also Oboler 1995.

46. This quote is from memory.

47. See Ostergren 1988; Wyman 1993.

48. See R. Smith 2000, 2001b.

49. Ostergren 1988; Massey et al. 1987; Massey, Goldring, and Durand 1994; Massey et al. 2002.

50. Kearney 1991, 2000; Mora 1982; Cederstrom 1993.

51. Carrasco 1969; Pare 1972, 1975; Bartra and Calvo 1975; Huerta Jaramillo 1985; Joachim 1979.

52. I chose the fictional name *Ticuani* for the village I studied because it celebrated the Dance of the Tecuanis, but I adapted the spelling to differentiate it from that other meaning. An exhibit on the Dance of the Tecuanis can be seen at the Puebla installations of the Instituto Nacional de Antropológia y Historia.

53. See Sahlins 1981 on generative historical structures.

54. I estimate population loss in two ways. First, if there were 3,975 people in 1958 and 218 births in 1959, then the population in 1970, when there were 251 births, would be about 4,578. But according to the INEGI (the Mexican census), the population fell to 3,857 in 1980 and 2,483 in 1990. A house-by-house count in 2000 by my researchers yielded a soft estimate of about 1,800 people. Even if not completely accurate, these figures show a marked population decrease. The 1,800 people in Ticuani in 2000 represent only 39 percent of the 4,578 who were there in 1970, before migration began in earnest, for a net population loss of 61 percent from the peak in 1970. Second, INEGI figures show a net loss of population of 1,354 between 1980 and 1990, or 35 percent of the population. This figure underestimates the total loss because many had left before 1980.

55. The *municipio* is the basic unit of government in Mexico, corresponding to the county in the United States. It usually has a *cabecera*, or county seat, hosting the government and police, and one or more agricultural hamlets known as *ranchos*. The survey reported here gathered information on 100 dwellings, 79 households, and 290 Ticuanenses, yielding information such as current domicile, migration and work history, and legal status of household members, including those residing in New York. These 290 people represent some 10 percent of the population of the *cabecera*. Local Ticuanenses estimated in 1993 that 1,500 of the *municipio's* 2,483 people live in the *cabecera*. If 1,500 people equals the 48 percent in Ticuani, then 1,272 equals the 41 percent in New York, yielding a total of 2,772 Ticuanenses from the *cabecera* in both New York and Ticuani. The 290 on whom we have information represent 10.4 percent of 2,772. This rough method falls short as demography but, given the large percentage of the population surveyed, suffices for our purposes.

56. One qualified for amnesty either by being able to document having worked ninety days in agriculture in the United States between May 1985 and May 1986 or by having lived in the United States continuously since 1981. Mexicans reportedly applied at higher rates than other nationalities.

57. My survey shows a steady outflow of migration punctuated by three large jumps: between 1969 and 1972, when the first wave of younger migrants left, partly in response to political repression in Mexico; following the first

large peso devaluation in 1976; and, by far the largest, during the years of the amnesty from 1986 to 1988.

58. These statistics were generously computed for me by Joe Salvo and Peter Lobo. Some of them appear in Peter Arun Lobo and Joseph J. Salvo, *The Newest New Yorkers, 2000* (New York: New York City Department of City Planning, 2004).

59. The number of births in Ticuani has also fallen, to just 107 in 1997, compared with 131 in 1900, 199 in 1919, 157 in 1954, and 251 in 1973. This decrease is due both to a falling birthrate and a shrinking population.

60. Foweraker 1993; Pare 1975.

61. See R. Smith 1995.

62. See Durand and Parrado 1996. They give the 10 percent estimate for 1992.

63. Mines 1981; Douglas Massey et al. 1987; Castaneda 1996.

64. See Castaneda 1996.

65. Douglas Massey et al. 1987, 2001, 2002.

CHAPTER 3. "LOS AUSENTES SIEMPRE PRESENTES"

1. Glick-Schiller and her colleagues (Basch, Glick-Schiller, and Blanc-Szanton 1994) dismissed the concept of community when first theorizing about transnational life, and many have shied away from it since. Others use *community* to cover many different kinds of association.

2. See R. Smith 1995, 1998c.

3. Vanderbush 1998: 4; Cornelius 1996: 500.

4. Neiburg 1988; Pare 1975; Bartra and Calva 1975.

5. Carrasco 1969. See Kearney 1995; Rivera Salgado 1998; Smith 1995, 1998a,b,c.

6. Huerta Jaramillo 1985; Joachim 1979.

7. See Bartra and Calva 1975; Neiburg 1988; Pare 1972, 1975.

8. See also Silva 1993.

9. Don Trinidad's disagreements with the Committee led to a cold initial reception for me because he associated me with them. When we met, I came bearing a letter of introduction from the Committee. But as he saw me participate in the life of the town over time, he became increasingly friendly.

10. Breton 1964; Levitt 2001a,b.

11. The Committee had a list of donors that numbered more than two hundred households in the mid-1990s,and even included those few Ticuanenses living outside New York. I have listened to Committee conference calls to Ticuanenses in Las Vegas or California, seeking contributions.

12. Flores, Benmayor, and Renaldo (1997) discuss the creation of such sacred, secular spaces.

13. See Jones-Correa 1993.

14. Rodriguez, Rosenbaum, and Gilbertson 1993; R. Smith 2001a,b.

15. See R. Smith 2003a,b.

16. See especially the work of Carlos Gonzalez Gutiérrez, a high-ranking Mexican bureaucrat in the Secretariat of Foreign Relations.

17. This speech was given in Spanish. In my translation, I have edited and abridged the remarks slightly for ease of reading. In particular, I have moved this remark from higher up in the speech to improve its flow in the text.

18. See this insight as applied to the rise of national states in displacing local identities as developed in Tilly, Tilly, and Tilly 1975.

19. My other work examines other routes of involvement of Mexicans in New York politics; see Smith 2001a,b.

CHAPTER 4. THE DEFEAT OF DON VICTORIO

1. Years of terms have been changed for confidentiality.

2. See R. Smith 2003a,b.

3. Formally, there are now four mechanisms to pick party candidates for municipal president: (1) "usual means and customs" *(usos y costumbres)*, whereby locally chosen committees pick presidents, especially in indigenous communities; (2) a "consultation of the base," a large assembly of all the voters who pick by show of hands; (3) a political council, wherein the people chose a council to pick a president; and (4) direct vote via a secret primary election.

4. I draw on Pansters 1990.

5. See R. Smith (2003a,b) on global and transnational approaches. See also the well-done ethnography by Rhacel Salazar Parreñas (2001) of Filipina domestic workers, which uses a globalization lens.

6. See Meyer et al. 1997; Soysal 1994.

7. See especially Sassen 1998, as well as 1988, 1991, 1996; and Thrift 1996, chapter 6.

8. The idea of a "moral economy" originated with Adam Smith and David Hume in the eighteenth century. They hoped that emerging capitalist markets would promote individual freedom, reward judicious investment, and punish greed, thus promoting self-regulation. Contemporary usages include those of Scott (1976, 1985) and E. P. Thompson (1963).

9. To preserve confidentiality, I report only percentages, not actual numbers of votes.

10. These figures come from a variety of conversations with state officials, including Mario Riestra, who served as Governor Morales Flores's adviser on migration and who headed CONOFAM.

11. See G. Thompson 2001.

CHAPTER 5. GENDER STRATEGIES, SETTLEMENT, AND
TRANSNATIONAL LIFE IN THE FIRST GENERATION

1. See Artico's insightful analysis (2003) of the constructed meaning of parental absence, as abandonment or sacrifice, for stay-behind youth.

2. I benefit here from Hochschild 1989, Hondagneu-Sotelo 1994, and especially Connell 1995, as well as from Beth Bernstein's intellect and generosity.

3. Hondagneu-Sotelo 1994; Hagan 1994; Mummert 1994, 1999; Salazar Parreñas 2001; Espinosa 1998; Binford and d'Abeterre 2000.

4. The meaning of *mandilón* lies somewhere between the polite *henpecked* and the vulgar *pussy-whipped*. See Matt Gutmann's insightful 1996 book.

5. See Mummert 1993, 1994, 1999; Hirsch 2003.

6. Although in Spanish one would refer to *la masculinidad ranchera* because *masculinidad* is a feminine noun and the adjective must take a feminine ending (though the noun *ranchero* is masculine), in English I adopt the terms *ranchero masculinity* and *ranchera femininity* to simplify the issue of gender.

7. In defining hegemonic masculinity, I paraphrase closely from Connell 1995: 77.

8. Gutmann's useful critique of an early version of this chapter argued that the division of space between men and women is less rigid in Mexico than is reported in much of the research literature. He is right, but I still think that these *images* of what male and female space and conduct should be strongly influence how people act.

9. See Hondagneu-Sotelo 1994; Hagan 1994; Rouse 1995.

10. See Besserer 2000, 2004.

11. A companionate marriage emphasizes a psychologically close friendship cemented by sexual intimacy. In respect marriages, sexuality is seen as a woman's duty and is not discussed. See Mummert 1993, 1994; Hirsh 2003. Ranchera femininity resonates with the notion of *marianismo*, sometimes understood as being like the Virgin Mary—without sexual desire, deferential to one's husband and other male relatives, constant in virtue, and pure. The Mariana is often contrasted with La Malinche, the indigenous woman who became Hernán Cortés's lover—sexually voracious, disloyal, and unpredictable. See Stevens 1994; Gutierrez 1991; Leal 1993; Bocchi 2000.

12. Katz 1999: 144.

13. "Crisis of masculinity" is Greta Gilbertson's phrase.

14. Hondagneu-Sotelo 1994; Hagan 1994; Espinosa 1998; Binford and d'Abeterre 2000.

15. Zhou and Bankston 1998; Kibria 1993; Portes and Rumbaut 2001.

16. On homosexuality, see Prieur 1998; Kulik 1997; Lancaster 1992; Cantu 2000; Almaguer 1991.

17. I have known Don Gerardo since the late 1980s and have spoken with him many times, but he always evaded my requests for a formal interview. Hence he is not quoted at length in this chapter.

18. Being *novios* literally translates into being boyfriend and girlfriend but implies a more serious commitment, assuming eventual marriage.

19. See Brandes 2002.

20. See Hays 1996.

21. On other kinds of prayer groups in New York, see Galvez 2004 and Rivera Sanchez 2003.

22. Material from this section comes from the field notes of Sandra Lara, Sara Guerrero-Rippberger, Agustín Vecino, and myself in Ticuani in 1999.

23. See Flaherty 1999.

24. See Goldring 2001.

25. Gutmann 1996; Mummert 1994, 1999; Hirsch 2003; Binford and d'Abeterre 2000.

26. See Hondagneu-Sotelo 1994.

CHAPTER 6. "IN TICUANI, HE GOES CRAZY"

1. This chapter draws on my own research over many years, work by Sara Guerrero-Rippberger over more than two years, and work by other team members, including Griscelda Perez and Sandra Lara. Unless otherwise noted, fieldwork observations come from my own notes.

I first came to know Toño as the son of a Committee member, and I interviewed him and his sister and their father and mother in 1997 when I began in earnest my research on the second generation. He was then reinterviewed for the NSF-funded part of the project by Sara, who also came to know his girlfriend Julia and her sisters well. Sara and I also did ethnography with them in New York and Ticuani. Sara interviewed Julia and her sisters for her 1999 Barnard College senior thesis (Guerrero-Rippberger 1999). Over several years of fieldwork, we observed the evolution of Toño and Julia's relationship, especially during return trips to Ticuani by Toño in 1999 and 2001 and Julia in 1999 and 2000.

2. See Zhou and Bankston's (1998) and Kibria's (1993) work on Vietnamese youths in the United States.

3. See Gilligan 2002. Connell 1995, Messerschmidt 1993, Messner 1997, Kimmel 1996, and Leadbeater and Way 1996 also discuss these incompatible demands.

4. Guerrero-Rippberger (1999: 24) makes this point nicely. Her thesis directed me to Phipher's work.

5. Suarez-Orozco and Suarez-Orozco 1995, C. Suarez-Orozco 1999, M. Suarez-Orozco and Paez 2002, and Ainslie 2002 write persuasively on these points. Guerrero-Rippberger also writes about the immigrant bargain.

6. See M. Suarez-Orozco and Paez 2002.

7. Zhou and Bankston 1998; Kibria 1993.

8. In retrospect, it would have been interesting to compare, for example, Toño's gender bargains with his girlfriend and sisters to those of others. While other gender strategies were observed—Leo's refusal to chastise his sister is one example—no similarly rich case presented itself. Leo, who was younger, more restricted in his movements, and without a girlfriend, did not offer a valid comparison to Toño. Toño's relations with Julia and his family fascinated me, and I was in a position to study them because of my long-standing relation-

ships with those involved. Moreover, their theoretical importance emerged only as the action unfolded. My work here thus reflects an ethnographic reality whereby selecting cases is not always possible: instead one follows the stories as they unfold and then attempts to make theoretical sense of them.

9. Guerrero-Rippberger 1998–2000.

10. According to Zhou and Bankston (1998) and Kibria (1993), Vietnamese parents similarly accommodate their second-generation children. For example, Zhou and Bankston explain that fathers view their daughters' educational and occupational mobility as an indirect sign of obedience. Their mothers see it as a way to make them better able to fight the hard gender-role strictures they face in the Vietnamese community.

11. Guerrero-Rippberger 1998–2000.

12. Guerrero-Rippberger 1998–2000.

13. Guerrero-Rippberger 1998–2000: 7.

14. Guerrero-Rippberger 1998–2000.

15. Quote taken from an interview done by Sara Guerrero-Rippberger for her 1999 thesis.

16. Guerrero-Rippberger 1998–2000: 9.

17. Guerrero-Rippberger 1998–2000.

18. Ticuani field notes from 2000 by Guerrero-Rippberger, G. Perez, and R. Smith.

19. Men also noticed these dynamics. One young man who now lives in New York told me that if he had a girlfriend like Julia, he would not spend so much time away from her.

20. Katz 1988.

21. Flores and Resaldo (1997) cite Gottdiener (1985) in discussing a different but similar notion of places that come to have sacred, nonreligious meanings.

22. See Zhou and Bankston 1998; Kibria 1993.

CHAPTER 7. "PADRE JESÚS, PROTECT ME"

1. For embodied experience, I draw on Klawiter 1999; Katz 1999.

2. See Comer 1993: 205.

3. I draw on Taylor, Jacobs, and Roberts 2000; Furstenberg 1993; Furstenberg et al. 1999; Dornbusch, Ritter, and Steinberg 1991; Dornbusch et al. 1987; Baldwin, Baldwin, and Cole 1990; Lamborn, Dornbusch, and Steinberg 1996; Lamborn et al. 1991; and Anderson 1991.

4. This emerging consensus on adolescence as a hard transition requiring guidance contradicts the popular notion of it as a time of necessary and inherent conflict with parents and authority, derived from the work of Anna Freud and G. G. Hall. The view emphasizing transition draws on Erikson's stage theory (1963), Marcia's (1980) identity-status model, and Phinney's (1989, 1998) three-stage ethnic-identity model. In my discussion of how adolescence becomes transnationalized, I have benefited from Suarez-Orozco and Suarez-

Orozco 1995; Ainslie 2002; Furstenberg et al. 1999; Eccles and Harold 1993; Eccles et al. 1997; Furstenberg 2000; Montemayor, Adams, and Gullotta 1990, 2000. Furstenberg (2001) and Kmec and Furstenberg (2002) show that effects of neighborhood become more important in later adolescence.

5. Comer 1993; Montemayor, Adams, and Gullotta 2000; Ainslie 2002.

6. Furstenberg and his colleagues (1999) accept that parents have less control over their children's environment in adolescence but argue that parents still make consequential choices about schools, neighborhoods, and after-school programs. By Furstenberg's criteria, sending one's children to Ticuani is a feasible intervention.

7. This observation comes from Sara Guerrero-Rippberger.

8. Pilgrimages such as the Antorcha are common throughout central Mexico, functioning as religious acts of devotion, reaffirmations of community membership, and protests against subordination in the United States. See Lopez and Cederstrom 1991: 16; Mora 1982; Shadow and Rodriguez 1990.

9. See Massey and Jess (1995) on the power to leave a place.

10. Omi and Winant (1986), drawing on Blauner (1972), write that the immigrant analogy is the "assumption, critical in contemporary thought, that there are no essential long-term differences—in relation to the larger society— between the third world or racial minorities and the European ethnic groups" (10). See also Roediger 1991; Feagin and Sikes 1994.

11. Massey and Denton 1993.

12. See R. Smith 1995, 1996b, 2005a, 2005b.

13. See Lamont 2000.

14. See Comer 1993.

15. C. Suarez-Orozco 1999.

16. Such thinking is not exclusively "Mexican"; it is common in white American households too. But all groups understand such rules as ethnically and culturally distinctive: this is how "we" do it.

17. See Katz 1999: 104. Katz's notion that our experience of our bodies and emotions is mediated by our perceptions of others seeing us, and is thus profoundly social, completed the theoretical pattern I had started to discern by analyzing my informants' data, using Klawiter's concept of embodied emotion and refitting Sacks's concept of proprioception to social life. I also thank the Merleau-Ponty scholar Taylor Carmen for his intellectual agility and generosity.

18. See also Denzin 1985; Fine 1992.

19. Klawiter 1999: 122; Katz 1999.

20. This project developed into a long-term relationship with Ceydi. Sara Guerrero-Rippberger did one-on-one interviews with Ceydi and her brother and followed her in school. Separately and together, Sara and I hung out with Ceydi and her friends at parties, at home, and at school, and we accompanied them to Ticuani. We did the same with Jericho and Napoleon, except in school, and conducted a separate interview with Napoleon and Jericho. Over more than two years we came to know them and their families and friends well.

21. See Hondagneu-Sotelo and Messner 1996.
22. See Goodwin, Jasper, and Polletta 2001.

CHAPTER 8. "I'LL GO BACK NEXT YEAR"

1. Ethnography and life-course analysis are rarely combined because of the burdens of first-person observation over the long term. I have been able to combine them because I have lived in New York and hung out with Ticuanenses since I began graduate school in my early twenties.

2. See Erikson 1968, 1963; Elder 1985, 1999; Giele and Elder 1998.

3. Few studies analyze how life course affects transnational life. I first used the concept in a paper presented at a conference organized by Mary Waters and Peggy Levitt at Harvard in 1997. Levitt (2001a,b) uses the concept in a somewhat different way.

4. Recent work on early adulthood in sociology (Furstenberg et al. 2002; Cook and Furstenberg 2002) and "emerging adulthood" in psychology (Arnett 2004) argues that it is a new phase in the life course, distinct from adolescence and full adulthood. These researchers focus on the fact that early adults have gone through some but not all of the transitions to full adulthood, usually finishing their education, getting full-time jobs, and establishing independent households, but not necessarily marrying and having children as their counterparts in the 1950s and 1960s would already have done.

5. See also chapter 7 and the work of Erikson, M. Suarez-Orozco, C. Suarez-Orozco, Ainslie, Montemayor, and Phinney cited there.

6. This upward mobility also brought accusations of elitism. One critic called the group a "bunch of fucking snobs" *(pinches presumidos)*; others have stressed to me in interviews that they are not in the crowd of snobs.

7. See Friedman and Davis 1998; Richman 1998; P. Brown 1998; Stamm 2001.

8. Studies show that reliance on family day care is more common among Latinos than Blacks and more common among Blacks than whites in the United States.

9. This quote is from memory and may not be verbatim.

10. These new housing-construction styles may reflect changing preferences resulting from migration; construction in parts of Sweden and Italy revealed extensive changes in materials and styles as a result of returning migrants' preferences. See Ostergren 1988; Wyman 1993.

11. Hondagneu-Sotelo and Avila 1997.

12. See www.brown.edu/Research/Catskills_Institute (accessed October 2002).

13. For example, only 38 percent of respondents in the 1990 National Jewish Population Study said they attended synagogue, whereas 92 percent of NCSYers did. Friedman and Davis report that "33% of married former NCSYers married other former NCSYers, and 17% actually met each other via NCSY." And while 52 percent of Jews in the United States marry non-

Jewish partners, 98 percent of NCSYers married other Jews. Friedman argues that meeting a future spouse is a "latent function" of NCSY. See www.ou.org/publications/ja/5759winter/ncsy.htm.

14. The *shabbaton* is an intense set of religious observations, common meals, and Torah study in which young Jews gather from a variety of places. Outside their normal environments, participants are focused on the religious rituals and on doing them together.

15. Stamm 2001.

16. Menjivar 2002b.

17. R. Smith 2000.

18. See Child 1943.

19. Zake 1981; Pienkos 1991.

20. Unless otherwise cited, the material in this paragraph comes from Pienkos 1991.

21. See Taagepera 1993.

CHAPTER 9. DEFENDING YOUR NAME

1. Agustín Vecino first made this distinction in our ethnographic discussions. See Vecino 1999.

2. The crews I know of resemble adolescent youth friendship groups, with some "deviant" behavior, more than gangs. Unlike the groups documented in Hagedorn (1988), Vigil (1988), and Moore et al. (1978), they do not have recognized steps by which their members advance to full gang membership.

3. See Lopez Castro 1985; Hernandez Leon 1999.

4. Escobar Latapi 1999.

5. On West Indians, see Mattei and Smith 1998. See also the ongoing work of Nina Siulc and Dave Brotherton.

6. See Cruz and Portillo Pena 1998; Santacruz Giralt 2001.

7. See Elder 1980 and the overview in Furstenberg et al. 1999.

8. Hernandez Leon 1999; Quinones 2001.

9. Hondagneu-Sotelo and Avila (1997) and Menjivar (2002a) both discuss the difficulties facing such young migrants and their parents in the context of family reunification.

10. Thrasher (1927) saw gangs resulting from social disorganization caused by migration and from the "interstitial" social and physical locales in which the second generation was raised. When immigrant families moved out of "gangland" into nicer neighborhoods, gang formation ceased by the third generation. Hence, 70 percent of the gangs Thrasher studied were composed of newer immigrants, mainly Italian, Polish, and Irish, while only 4 percent and 2 percent were German and Swedish, respectively. Fully 87 percent of gangs were composed of "foreign stock"—immigrants or their first-generation children. Vigil (1988, 2002) and Joan Moore (2001) extend Thrasher's argument by showing how "multiple marginalities" prevent later generations from moving out of "gangland."

11. See Venkatesh 1997, 2000; Jankowski 1991.

12. See Vigil 2002, 1988; Moore et al. 1978; Moore 1991.

13. See Levitt 2001a,b.

14. This discussion engages cultural citizenship theory, which often presumes that Latinos claim space in relation to dominant white society. They also claim space in relation to Blacks and other Mexicans and Latinos, with whom they are more likely to share schools and public spaces. See Flores and Resaldo 1997; Flores and Benmayor 1997. The assimilative pressure I identify, in the form of the Hollywood movies portraying gangs as the way to be authentically Mexican, could be seen as a pressure working against Latinos' claiming existential belonging.

15. See Vigil (1988) and Moore et al. (1978) on gangs as institutions of reception.

16. See Merton 1938, 1968.

17. See Katz 1988; E. Anderson 1999, 1990, 1978; Jankowski 1991; Horowitz 1983; Gilligan 1991; Connell 1995.

18. Bourgois 1995: 79.

19. See Mutter 1999.

20. Katz 1988.

21. See MacLeod 1995.

22. Latino cultural citizenship theory analyzes ethnically understood space; see Flores and Benmayor 1997, especially pp. 15–23. For theorizing on space, see Pries 1999; Gans 2002; Gieryn 2000; Bourdieu 1989; Gottdiener 1985; Zukin 1991; Sassen 2002; and Foucault 1977.

23. Hence their constitution and control over space invokes both Flores and Benmayor's (1997) discussion of symbolically important space and also the emphasis on hierarchy and dominance being expressed in spatial relations, as in Zukin 1991, 2002; Foucault 1977; and others.

24. See Vigil 1988, 2002; E. Anderson 1999; Katz 1988; Horowitz 1983.

25. The introduction in Pries (1999) offers an overview of this literature.

26. A zoned school is a public school that must accept all students in a specific geographic zone. The zones for high schools are larger than those for the earlier grades, so, on entering high school, students from smaller ethnic groups, as Mexicans were in the early 1990s, may find themselves in school with a good number of coethnics for the first time. Second, in many New York City neighborhoods, the zoned high school is not very good, and stronger students transfer to better schools in other parts of New York, or to "magnet" schools that do not draw on a specific geographical area. See R. Smith 2002a,b,c.

27. Ragin 2000.

28. See Geertz 1973. For broader structural analyses of how images of Latinos are produced in the United States, see C. Rodriguez 1997; Davila 2001; Oboler 1995. My argument here focuses on what happens to these images once they are produced: why and how Mexican youths use images of Mexican gangs in making their own lives.

29. ¡Simón! or ¡Simón Bolívar! is a slang exclamation of agreement, referring to the historical liberator of the Americas.

30. We have interviewed more informants for the project on second-generation work and school mobility, but for this chapter I used the first sixteen interviews that reported gang or crew involvement.

31. Paz 1961.

CHAPTER 10. RETURNING TO A CHANGED TICUANI

1. E. Anderson 1998. *Preppy* and *cholo* are terms that Ticuanenses and *cholos* both use. *Regular* is not strictly a folk category, because the regulars do not use it in everyday talk. But many did use it in describing their identity to me, either with respect to *cholos* or with respect to ethnic groups in New York, and immediately understood my usage.

2. Hochschild 1983.

3. For example, the *pandilleros* from the marginalized rancho discussed in chapter 4 were involved in the murder of a taxi driver in 1996. But these generalizations are not universally valid. Not all members of the regular group we followed most closely were wildly successful, and at least one of the *cholos* was economically very successful. However, the images of the *cholos* as less successful and the regulars as more successful influence social life because people accept them as true.

4. See Massey and Jess (1995) on the power to leave.

5. Of course, the kinds of emotional work required of Napoleon and of me, as an adult, white American academic, are significantly different.

6. I draw loosely on Csikszentmihalyi 1990, 2000.

7. G. Perez 2000: 5.

8. This analysis of how the zocalo fosters social interaction fits with Gans's (2002) call to learn about how physical spaces affect social life.

9. The situation was described to me shortly afterward by Jericho and Napoleon, and then again in a later interview with them both, as well as by other members of the research team who attended the wedding (Sara Guerrero-Rippberger 1998–2000; C. Perez 2000; G. Perez 2000).

10. Jack Katz 1988; E. Anderson 1998.

11. My reading of this behavior draws on Katz 1999.

12. Horowitz 1983.

13. See Willis 1977.

14. Menjivar 2002a, chapter 7, insightfully discusses how some children of immigrants adopt incorporational and some oppositional identities, leading to different intergenerational relations with their immigrant parents. See also Hondagneu-Sotelo and Avila 1997; Esteva 1999.

15. See Valenzuela (1999) on tension between recent immigrant and Mexican American students.

16. The *cholos* draw their moral map by closely guarding the distinction between being Mexican, and thus virtuous, and being Chicano, and thus corrupted by America, in ways that resonate with Michelle Lamont's analysis of

the drawing of racial boundaries by white and Black Americans and white and Muslim immigrant French men. See Lamont 2000.

17. One of the Zavala group was half Puerto Rican, half Ticuanense, but he was not involved in this conflict.

18. Brooks 2003.

19. Hondagneu-Sotelo 1994, Hagan 1994, and Levitt 2001a,b are exceptions.

20. Work on social disorganization by Robert Parks, W. I. Thomas, Florian Znaniecki, and others influenced Thrasher's work.

21. Vigil 2002.

22. See Petacco 1972. I thank Donna Gabaccia for this citation.

23. See Child 1943. On return migration, see Wyman 1993 and Cinel 1991.

CONCLUSIONS AND RECOMMENDATIONS

1. Becker 2003.

2. See R. Smith 2003a,b.

3. See Lichterman 1998; Burawoy 1998; Burawoy et al. 1991.

4. Here I apply some insights from Lieberson and Lynn 2002.

5. See Katz 1999.

6. See Douglas Massey et al. 1987; Massey and Espinosa 1997; Douglas Massey et al. 1998.

7. Portes et al. 2003 have documented transnational practices of immigrant entrepreneurs, and Guarnizo et al. 2003 have analyzed transnational political practices using a large sample, quantitative techniques, and a positive-science approach.

8. See Ragin 2000.

9. See, of course, Giddens 1984, 1976; Burawoy 1998; Morawska 2001.

10. Ostergren 1988.

11. See R. Smith 2003b, which draws heavily on Pienkos 1991 and the sources he cites.

12. See Portes and Rumbaut 2001; Fitzgerald 2000; R. Smith 2000, 2001a,b.

13. See Smith 2000, 2001a,b, 1998, 1997.

14. On the importance of such factors in producing meaningful diasporic lobbying, compare the fates of the largely successful lobbying efforts of the Jewish diaspora and the largely unsuccessful ones of the Armenian diaspora in the United States. See Kokot, Tololyan, and Alfonso 2004; de la Garza 1997, 1983; Sheffer 1986.

15. See R. Smith 2003a,b.

16. See Sassen 1998.

17. Graham 2001; Guarnizo 1998.

18. See Portes, Guarnizo, and Landholt 1999; Graham 2001; Pessar 1999.

19. G. Thompson 2001; Douglas Massey, Durand, and Malone 2002.

20. See Cornelius, Martin, and Hollifield 1995.

21. This paragraph draws on Zolberg and Smith 1996; R. Smith 2001c.

22. See de la Garza et al. 1997; de la Garza and DeSipio 1998.

23. See Ruggie 1993.
24. See Venkatesh 2000.
25. See Jones-Correa 1997a,b.
26. On migrant-child separation, see the work of Carola and Marcelo Suarez-Orozco; Gail Mummert 1999, 1996; Zendejas Romero 2004; Artico 2003; Faulstich Orellana et al. 2001; Salazar Parreñas 2001.

Bibliography

Acquarone, Alberto. 1990. The Impact of Emigration on Italian Public Opinion and Politics. In *The Italian Emigration to the United States, 1880–1930*, ed. F. Cordasco and M. V. Cordasco. Fairview, NJ, and London: Junius-Vaughn Press.

Acuña, Rodolfo. 1996. *Anything but Mexican: Chicanos in Contemporary Los Angeles*. New York: Verso.

Ainslie, Ricardo. 2002. The Plasticity of Culture and Psychodynamic and Psychosocial Processes in Latino Immigrant Families. In *Latinos: Remaking America*, ed. Marcelo Suarez-Orozco and Mariela Paez. Berkeley: University of California Press.

Alarcón, Rafael. 2000. Remesas de migrantes zacatecanos. In *Migración internacional y desarollo regional*, ed. Hector Rodriguez and Miguel Moctezuma Longoria. Mexico City and Zacatecas: Senate of Mexico and Universidad Autónoma de Zacatecas.

Alba, Richard. 1996. Italian Americans: A Century of Ethnic Change. In *Origins and Destinies*, ed. Silvia Pedraza and Ruben Rumbaut. New York: Wadsworth.

Alba, Richard, and Victor Nee. 1999. Rethinking Assimilation Theory for a New Era of Immigration. In *The Handbook of International Migration: The American Experience*, ed. Charles Hirschman, Philip Kasinitz, and Josh DeWind. New York: Russell Sage Foundation.

———. 2003. *Remaking the American Mainstream: Assimilation and Contemporary Immigration*. Cambridge, MA: Harvard University Press.

Almaguer, Tomás. 1991. Chicano Men: A Cartography of Homosexual Identity and Behavior. *Differences: A Journal of Feminist and Cultural Studies* 3 (2): 75–100.

Alonso-Zaldivar, Ricardo. 1999. Big Apple Takes on a Flavor of Mexico. *Los Angeles Times*. February 19.

Amparo Casar, María, and Ricardo Raphael de la Madrid. 1998. Las elecciones y el reparto del poder. *Nexos* 247 (July).

Anderson, Benedict. 1991 [1983]. *Imagined Communities: Reflections on the Growth and Spread of Nationalism.* New York and London: Verso.

Anderson, Elijah. 1978. *A Place on the Corner.* Chicago: University of Chicago Press.

————. 1990. *Streetwise: Race, Class, and Change in an Urban Community.* Chicago: University of Chicago Press.

————. 1991. Neighborhood Effects on Teenage Pregnancy. In *The Urban Underclass,* ed. C. Jencks and P. E. Peterson. Washington, DC: Brookings Institution.

————. 1999. *Code of the Street: Decency, Violence, and the Moral Life of the Inner City.* New York: Norton.

Appadurai, Arjun. 1996. *Modernity at Large: Cultural Dimensions of Globalization.* University of Minnesota Press.

Arnett, Jeffrey Jensen. 2004. *Emerging Adulthood: The Winding Road from the Late Teens through the Twenties.* New York: Oxford University Press.

Arteaga Dominguez, Efrain, and Manuel Garcia Hernandez. Zacatecas. In *1994: Las elecciones en los Estados,* ed. Silvia Gomez Tagle, 325–49. México, DF: Centro de Investigaciones Interdisciplinarias en Ciencias y Humanidades, Universidad Autónoma Nacional de México.

Artico, Ceres. 2003. *Latino Families Broken by Immigration.* New York: LFB Scholarly Publishing.

Baca Zinn, Maxine. 1998. "Chicano Men and Masculinity." In *Men's Lives,* ed. Michael Kimmell and Michael Messner, 25–34. Boston: Allyn and Bacon.

Baldwin, A. L., C. Baldwin, and R. E. Cole. 1990. Stress-Resistant Children. In *Risk and Protective Factors in the Development of Psychopathology,* ed. J. Rolf, A. S. Masten, D. Cicchetti, K. Neuchterlein, and S. Weintraub. Cambridge: Cambridge University Press.

Barbalet, J. M. 1988. *Citizenship: Rights, Struggle, and Class Inequality.* Milton Keynes: Open University Press.

Bartra, Roger. 1975. Campesinado y poder politico en México. In *Caciquismo y poder politico en el Mexico rural,* ed. Roger Bartra. México, DF: Instituto de Investigaciones Sociales, Universidad Nacional Autónoma de México.

Bartra, Roger, and Pilar Calvo. 1975. Estructura de poder, clases dominantes y lucha ideológica en el Mexico rural. In *Caciquismo y poder politico en el Mexico rural,* ed. Roger Bartra. México, DF: Instituto de Investigaciones Sociales, Universidad Nacional Autónoma de México.

Basch, L., N. Glick-Schiller, and C. Blanc-Szanton. 1994. *Nations Unbound: Transnational Projects, Postcolonial Predicaments, and Deterritorialized Nation States.* Sydney: Gordon & Breach.

Baubock, Rainer. 1994. *Transnational Citizenship: Membership and Rights in International Migration.* Aldershot: Edward Elgar.

Baumrind, D. 1971. Current Patterns of Parental Authority. *Developmental Psychology Monograph,* part 2, 4 (7): 1–103.

Becker, Howard. 1998. *Tricks of the Trade: How to Think about Your Research While You're Doing It.* Chicago: University of Chicago Press.

————. 2003. The Problems of Analysis. Paper presented at National Science Foundation workshop "Scientific Bases of Qualitative Analysis," Arlington, VA.

Bermudez Viramonte, Andrés. 2001. *Open Letter to President Vicente Fox.* September 15. Zacatecas: Universidad Autónoma de Universidad Autónoma de Zacatecas.

Bernstein, Elizabeth. 2001. The Meaning of the Purchase: Desire, Demand, and the Commerce of Sex. *Ethnography* 2 (3): 391–420.

Besserer, Federico. 1997. La transnacionalización de los oaxacalifornianos: La comunidad transnacional y multicentrica de San Juan Mixtepec, Oaxaca. Paper presented at Michoacán XIX Coloquio de Antropología e Historia Regionales, El Colegio Michoacán, Zamora, Michoacán.

————. 1998. Notes on the case of Felipe Sanchez. Personal communication.

————. 2000. Sentimientos (in) apropiados de la mujeres migrantes: Hacia una nueva ciudadania. In *Migración y relaciones de genero en México,* ed. Dalia Barrera Bassols and Cristina Cehmichen Bazan, 371–89. México, DF: Universidad Nacional Autónoma de México.

————. 2004. *Topografías transnacionales: Una geografía para el estudio de la vida transnacional.* Universita Autónoma Metropolitana Unidad Iztapalapa/Plaza y Valdés.

Binford, Leigh. 1998. Accelerated Migration from Puebla. Paper presented at conference "Mexicans in New York and Mexico: New Analytical Perspectives on Migration, Transnationalization, and Immigrant Incorporation," Barnard College and the New School for Social Research, New York.

————. 2004. *La económia politica de migración aceleradad: Siete estudios de caso.* Puebla and Mexico City: Universidad Autónoma de Puebla and Consejo Nacional de la Ciencia y Tecnología.

Binford, Leigh, and Maria Eugenia D'Abeterre, eds. 2000. *Conflictos migratorios transnacionales y respuestas comunitarias.* Puebla, Mexico: Gobierno del Estado de Puebla/Consejo Estatal de Población/Instituto de Ciencias y Humanidades—Benemerita Universidad Autónoma de Puebla.

Blalock, Hubert M. 1956. Economic Discrimination and Negro Increase. *American Sociological Review* 21: 581–88.

————. 1958. Percent Nonwhite and Discrimination in the South. *American Sociological Review* 22 (6): 677–82.

Blanc-Szanton, Cristina. 1998. The Philippine State and Its Diaspora. Paper presented at conference on States and Diasporas, Columbia University.

Blauner, Bob. 1972. *Racial Oppression in America.* New York: Harper and Row.

Bocchi, Steven. 2000. The Meanings of Marianismo in Mexico. www.lclark.edu/~woodrich/Bocchi_marianismo.html. Accessed January 2005.

Bourdieu, Pierre. 1977. *Outline of a Theory of Practice.* Trans. Richard Nice. Cambridge: Cambridge University Press.

————. 1989. Social Space and Symbolic Power. *Sociological Theory* 7 (1): 14–25.

Bourgois, Philippe. 1995. *In Search of Respect.* New York: Cambridge University Press.

Brandes, Stanley. 2002. *Staying Sober in Mexico City.* Austin: University of Texas Press.

Braudel, Fernand. 1981. *Structures of Everyday Life: The Limits of the Possible.* New York: Harper and Row.

Breton, Raymond. 1964. Institutional Completeness of Ethnic Communities and the Personal Relations of Immigrants. *American Journal of Sociology.* 70 (2): 193–205.

Brimelow, Peter. 1995. *Alien Nation.* New York: HarperPerennial.

Brooks, David. 2003. The Triumph of Hope over Self-Interest. *New York Times,* January 12.

Brotherton, David. 1998. The Evolution of New York City Street Gangs. In *Crime and Justice in New York City,* ed. A. Karmen, 40–55. New York: Mc-Graw-Hill.

Brown, Mary. 1996. *The Scalabrinians in North America (1887–1934).* New York: Center for Migration Studies.

Brown, Phil. 1998. *Catskill Culture: A Mountain Rat's Memories of the Great Jewish Resort Area.* Philadelphia: Temple University Press.

Brubaker, Rogers. 1989. *Immigration and Politics of Citizenship in Europe and North America.* Lanham, MD: University Press of America.

———. 1993. Political Dimensions of Migration from and among Soviet Successor States. In *Eastern European Migrations,* ed. Myron Weiner, 39–64. Boulder, CO: Westview.

Brysk, Allison. 1996. Turning Weakness into Strength. *Latin American Perspectives* 23 (2): 38–57.

Burawoy, Michael. 1976. The Functions and Reproduction of Migrant Labor: Comparative Material from Southern Africa and the United States. *American Journal of Sociology* 81: 1050–87.

———. 1998. The Extended Case Method. *Sociological Theory* 16 (1): 4–33.

———. 2003. Revisits: Toward a Theory of Reflexive Ethnography. *American Sociological Review* 68 (5): 645–79.

Burawoy, Michael, et al. 1991. *Ethnography Unbound: Power and Resistance in the Modern Metropolis.* Berkeley: University of California Press.

Butler, Judith. 1997. *Excitable Speech: A Politics of the Performative.* New York: Routledge.

———. 1999 [1990]. *Gender Trouble: Feminism and the Subversion of Identity.* New York: Routledge.

Calhoun, Craig. 1994. *Social Theory and the Politics of Identity.* Oxford and Cambridge, MA: Blackwell.

Cannistraro, Philip. 1975. Fascism and Italian Americans in Detroit. *International Migration Review* 9 (1): 29–41.

Cannistraro, Philip, and Gianfausto Rosoli. 1979. Fascist Emigration Policy in the 1920s. *International Migration Review* 13 (4): 673–93.

Cano Lopez, Gustavo. 2000. Personal communication.

Cantu, Lionel. 2000. Entre Hombres/Between Men: Latino Masculinities and Homosexualities. In *Gay Masculinities,* ed. Peter Nardi, 224–46. Thousand Oaks, CA: Sage.

———. 2001. A Place Called Home: A Queer Political Economy of Mexican Immigrant Men's Family Experiences. In *Queer Families and the Politics of Visibility,* ed. Mary Bernstein and Renate Reimann. New York: Columbia University Press.

Carpizo, Jorge. 1998. El peligro del voto de los mexicanos en el extranjero. *Nexos* 247 (July): 11–12.

Carpizo, Jorge, and Diego Valades. 1998. *El voto de los mexicanos en el extranjero.* México, DF: Universidad Nacional Autónoma de México, Instituto de Investigaciones Juridicoas.

Carrasco, Pedro. 1961. The Civil-Religious Hierarchy in Meso-American Communities: Pre-Spanish Background and Colonial Development. *American Anthropology* 63: 483–97.

———. 1969. Central Mexican Highlands: Introduction. In *Handbook of Middle American Indians,* special issue of *Ethnology* 8, part 2 (31): 579–602.

Castaneda, Jorge. 1996. Mexico's Circle of Misery: How U.S. Bailouts Postpone Reform. *Foreign Affairs* (July–August): 92–105, www.foreignaffairs.org.

Cederstrom, Thoric Nils. 1993. The Potential Impacts of Migrant Remittances on Agricultural and Community Development in the Mixteca Baja Region of Mexico. Ph.D. diss., University of Arizona.

Child, Irving. 1943. *Italian or American? The Second Generation in Conflict.* New Haven, CT: Yale University Press.

Chin, Margaret May. 2001. When Coethnic Assets Become Liabilities: Mexican, Ecuadoran, and Chinese Garment Workers in New York City. In *Migration, Transnationalization, and Race in a Changing New York,* ed. Héctor Cordero-Guzmán, Robert C. Smith, and Ramón Grosfoguel. Philadelphia: Temple University Press.

Cinel, Dino. 1991. *The National Integration of Italian Return Migration, 1870–1929.* New York: Cambridge University Press.

Cohen, Robin. 1995. *Global Diasporas.* Seattle: University of Washington Press.

Coleman, James. 1988. Social Capital in the Creation of Human Capital. *American Journal of Sociology, Supplement* 94: S95–S120.

Coles, Robert. 1967. *Children of Crisis.* Boston: Little, Brown.

Coltrane, Scott. 1998. Stability and Change in Chicano Men's Family Lives. In *Men's Lives,* ed. Michael Kimmel and Michael Messner, 520–36. Boston: Allyn and Bacon.

Comer, James P. 1993. The Potential Effects of Community Organization on the Future of Our Youth. In *Adolescence in the 1990s: Risk and Opportunity,* ed. Ruby Takanashi. New York: Teachers College Press.

Connell, Robert W. 1995. *Masculinities.* Berkeley: University of California Press.

Conner, Walker. 1986. The Impacts of Homelands upon Diasporas. In *Diasporas in Modern International Politics,* ed. Gabriel Sheffer. London: Croom Helm.

Cook, Thomas, and Frank Furstenberg. 2002. Explaining Aspects of the Transition to Adulthood in Italy, Sweden, Germany, and the United States: A

Cross-Disciplinary, Case Synthesis Approach. In *Early Adulthood in Cross-National Perspective. Annals of the American Academy of Political and Social Science,* ed. Frank Furstenberg, 257–87. Thousand Oaks, CA: Sage Publications.

Cornelius, Wayne. 1994. Los Migrantes de la Crisis: The Changing Profile of Mexican Migration to the United States. In *Social Responses to Mexico's Economic Crisis of the 1980s,* ed. M. Gonzalez de la Rocha and A. Escobar Latapi. San Diego, CA: Center for U.S.-Mexican Studies.

————. 1996. Mexican Politics in Transition: The Breakdown of a One-Party Dominant Regime. San Diego, CA: Center for U.S.-Mexican Studies.

Cornelius, W. A., Anne Craig, and Jonathan Fox, eds. 1994. *Transforming State-Society Relations: The National Solidarity Strategy.* San Diego, CA: Center for U.S.-Mexican Studies.

Cornelius, Wayne, J. Gentleman, and P. Smith. 1989. *Mexico's Alternative Political Futures.* San Diego, CA: Center for U.S.-Mexican Studies.

Cornelius, Wayne, P. Martin, and J. Hollifield, eds. 1995. *Controlling Immigration: A Global Perspective.* Stanford, CA: Stanford University Press.

Cortés Sánchez, Sergio. 2002. Migration by Residents of the State of Puebla in the Decade of the 1990s. Paper presented at conference "Haciendo Historia," City University of New York.

————. 2003. Migrants from Puebla in the 1990s. In *Immigrants and Schooling: Mexicans in New York,* ed. Regina Cortina and Monica Gendreau, 183–202. New York: Center for Migration Studies.

Cortina, Regina, and Monica Gendreau, eds. 2003. *Immigrants and Schooling: Mexicans in New York.* New York: Center for Migration Studies.

Cruz, José Miguel, and Nelson Portillo Pena. 1998. *Solidaridad y violencia e la pandillas del gran San Salvador: Mas alla de la vida loca.* San Salvador: Universidad Centroamerica.

Csikszentmihalyi, Mihaly. 1990. *Flow: The Psychology of Optimal Experience.* New York: HarperPerennial.

Csikszentmihalyi, Mihaly, and Barbara Schneider. 2000. *Becoming Adult: How Teenagers Prepare for the World of Work.* New York: Basic Books.

D'Agostino, Peter. 1994. Italian Ethnicity and Religious Priests in the American Church: The Servites, 1870–1940. *Catholic Historical Review* 80 (4): 714.

————. 1997a. The Scalabrini Fathers, the Italian Emigrant Church, and Ethnic Nationalism in America. *Religion and American Culture: A Journal of Interpretation* 7 (1): 121–59.

————. 1997b. "Fascist Transmission Belts" or Episcopal Advisors? Italian Consuls and American Catholicism in the 1930s. Cushwa Center for the Study of American Catholicism: Working Paper Series. Spring.

————. 1998a. The Triad of Roman Authority: Fascism, the Vatican, and Italian Religious Clergy in the Italian Emigrant Church. *Journal of American Ethnic History* 17 (3): 3–38.

————. 1998b. The Crisis of Authority in American Catholicism: Urban Schools and Cultural Conflict. *Records of the American Catholic Historical Association of Philadelphia.* Fall–Winter.

Davila, Arlene. 2001. *Latinos, Inc.* Berkeley: University of California Press.

de la Garza, Rodolfo O. 1982. Chicano-Mexican Relations: A Framework for Research. *Social Science Quarterly* 63 (1): 115–30.

———. 1997. Foreign Policy Comes Home: The Domestic Consequences of the Program for Mexican Communities Abroad. In *Beyond the Border: Mexico's New Foreign Policy*, Rodolfo de la Garza and Jesús Velasco. Lanham, MD: Rowman and Littlefield.

de la Garza, Rodolfo O., and Louis DeSipio. 1998. Interests Not Passions: Mexican American Attitudes toward Mexico and Issues Shaping U.S.-Mexico Relations. *International Migration Review* 32 (Summer).

de la Garza, Rodolfo, and C. Vargas. 1992. The Mexican Origin Population of the United States as a Political Force in the Borderlands. In *Changing Boundaries in the Americas*, ed. Lawrence A. Herzog. San Diego, CA: Center for U.S-Mexican Studies.

Delgado Wise, Raul, ed. 2003. *Migración y Desarrollo*. No. 1. Zacatecas, Zacatecas: Universidad Autónoma de Zacatecas.

Delgado Wise, Raul, Miguel Moctezuma Longoria, and Hector Rodriguez Ramirez. 2000. Informe final de investigación: Evaluación de programas y proyectos comunitarios y productivos con participación de los migrantes: El caso de Zacatecas. Zacatecas: Universidad Autónoma de Zacatecas.

Denzin, Norman K. 1985. Emotion as Lived Experience. *Symbolic Interaction* 8: 223–40.

DeSipio, Louis. 1998. *Making Americans/Remaking America: Immigrants and Immigration in the Contemporary United States*. Boulder, CO: Westview.

Dominguez, Jorge. 1982. *Mexico's Political Economy: Challenges at Home and Abroad*. Beverly Hills, CA: Sage Publications.

Dominguez, Rufino. 1995 and other years. Autobiographical notes and materials from the Organización del Pueblo Explotado y Oprimido.

Dornbusch, S. M., P. L. Ritter, P. H. Leiderman, D. F. Roberts, and M. J. Fraleigh. 1987. The Relation of Parenting Style to Adolescent School Performance. *Child Development* 58: 1244–57.

Dornbusch, S. M., P. L. Ritter, and L. Steinberg. 1991. Community Influences on the Relations of Family Status to Adolescent School Performance among African Americans and Non-Hispanic Whites. *American Journal of Education* 99: 543–67.

Dresser, Denise. 1991. *Neopopulist Solutions to Neoliberal Problems: Mexico's National Solidarity Program*. San Diego, CA: Center for U.S.-Mexican Studies.

———. 1996. Treading Lightly and without a Stick: International Actors and the Promotion of Democracy in Mexico. In *Beyond Sovereignty: Defending Democracy in the Americas*, ed. Tom Farer, 317–41. Baltimore: Johns Hopkins University Press.

DuBois, W. E. B. 1992 [1935]. *Black Reconstruction in America: 1860–1880*. New York: Atheneum.

Durand, Jorge, and Douglas Massey. 1992. Mexican Migration to the United States: A Critical Review. *Latin American Research Review* 27 (2): 3–43.

————. 1996. Migradollars and Development: A Reconsideration of the Mexican Case. *International Migration Review* 30 (114).

Durand, Jorge, and Emilio Parrado. 1999. The New Era of Mexican Migration to the United States. *Journal of American History* 86: 518–36.

Durkheim, Émile. 1984 [1897]. *The Division of Labor in Society.* New York: Free Press.

Eccles, Jacquelynne, and R. D. Harold. 1993. Parent-School Involvement during the Early Adolescent Years. *Teachers College Record* 94: 568–87.

Eccles, J. S., E. Lord, R. W. Roeser, B. L. Barber, and D. M. H. Josefowicz. 1997. The Association of School Transitions in Early Adolescence with Developmental Trajectories through High School. In *Health Risks and Developmental Transitions during Adolescence,* ed. J. Schulenberg, J. Maggs, and K. Hurrelman, 283–320. New York: Cambridge University Press.

Elder, Glen H. Jr. 1980. Adolescence in Historical Perspective. In *Handbook of Adolescent Psychology,* ed. J. Adelson. New York: Wiley.

————, ed. 1985. *Life Course Dynamics: Trajectories and Transitions, 1968–1980.* Ithaca, NY: Cornell University Press.

————. 1999. *Children of the Great Depression: Social Change and Life Experience.* Boulder, CO: Westview.

Emirbayer, Mustafa, and Jeff Goodwin. 1994. Network Analysis, Culture, and the Problem of Agency. *American Journal of Sociology* 99 (6): 1411–54.

Emirbayer, Mustafa, and Ann Mische. 1998. What Is Agency? *American Sociological Review* 103: 962–1023.

Erikson, Eric. 1963. *Childhood and Society.* New York: Norton.

————. 1968. *Identity and the Life Cycle.* New York: Norton.

————. 1975. *Life History and Historical Moment.* New York: Norton.

Escobar Latapí, Agustín. 1999. Comments at conference on Transnational Family, El Colegio de la Frontera Norte, Tijuana.

Espinoza, Victor. 1998. *El dilema del retorno: Migración, genero y pertenencia en un contexto transnacional.* Zamora, Michoacán, Mexico: El Colegio de Jalisco and El Colegio de Michoacán.

————. 1999. La Federación de Clubes Michoacanos en Illinois: Historia y perspectivas a futuro de una organización civil mexicana en Estados Unidos. Report of the Chicago-Michoacán Project, Heartland Alliance for Human Needs and Human Rights, Chicago.

Esteva, Juan. 2003. Urban Street Activists: Gang and Community Efforts to Bring Peace and Justice to LA's Neighborhoods. In *Gangs and Society: Alternative Perspectives,* ed. Louis Kontos, David Brotherton, and Luis Barrios. New York: Columbia University Press.

Faulstich Orellana, Marjorie, et al. 2001. Transnational Childhoods: The Participation of Children in Processes of Family Migration. *Social Problems* 48 (4): 573–92.

Feagin, Joe R., and Melvin P. Sikes. 1994. *Living with Racism: The Black Middle-Class Experience.* Boston: Beacon.

Feldman-Bianco, Bela. 1992. Multiple Layers of Time and Space: The Construction of Class, Race, Ethnicity, and Nationalism among Portuguese Immigrants. In *Towards a Transnational Perspective on Migration*, ed. Nina Glick-Schiller, Linda Basch, and Cristina Blanc-Szanton. New York: Annals of the New York Academy of Sciences, vol. 645.

Fine, Gary Alan. 1992. Wild Life: Authenticity and the Human Experience of "Natural" Places. In *Investigating Subjectivity: Research on Lived Experience*, edited by C. Ellis and M. G. Flaherty, 156–75. Newbury Park, CA: Sage.

———. 1993. The Sad Demise, Mysterious Disappearance, and Glorious Triumph of Symbolic Interactionism. *Annual Review of Sociology* 19: 61–87.

Fitzgerald, David. 2000. *Negotiating Extra-Territorial Citizenship: Mexican Migration and the Transnational Politics of Community*. CCIC Monograph No 2. San Diego, CA: Center for U.S.-Mexican Studies. University of California, San Diego.

Flaherty, Michael G. 1999. *A Watched Pot: How We Experience Time*. New York: New York University Press.

Flores, William, and Rena Benmayor. 1997. *Latino Cultural Citizenship*. Boston: Beacon.

Flores, William, and Renato Resaldo. 1997. Identity, Conflict, and Evolving Latino Communities: Cultural Citizenship in San Jose, California. In *Latino Cultural Citizenship*, ed. William Flores and Rena Benmayor. Boston: Beacon.

Foerster, Robert. 1919. *The Italian Emigration of Our Times*. Cambridge, MA: Harvard University Press.

Foner, Nancy. 1997. What's So New about Transnationalism? New York Immigrants Today and at the End of the Century. *Diaspora* 6 (3): 354–75.

———. 1999. The Immigrant Family: Cultural Legacies and Cultural Changes. In *The Handbook of International Migration: The American Experience*, ed. Charles Hirschman, Philip Kasinitz, and Josh DeWind. New York: Russell Sage Foundation.

———. 2001a. *From Ellis Island to JFK*. New Haven: Yale University Press.

———. 2001b. Transnationalism Then and Now: New York Immigrants Today and at the Turn of the Twentieth Century. In *Migration, Transnationalization, and Race in a Changing New York*, ed. Héctor Cordero-Guzmán, Robert C. Smith, and Ramón Grosfoguel. Philadelphia: Temple University Press.

Fonte, John. 2002. Men with Two Countries: Points That American Negotiators Should Keep in Mind while They Consider How Best to Help Mexico. *National Review Online*. www.nationalreview.com. March 21.

Foweraker, Joe. 1993. *Popular Mobilization in Mexico: The Teachers' Movement, 1977–87*. New York: Cambridge University Press.

Fox, Jonathan. 1994a. The Difficult Transition from Clientelism to Citizenship. *World Politics* 46 (2): 151–84.

———. 1994b. Targeting the Poorest: The Role of the National Indigenous Institute in Mexico's Solidarity Program. In *Transforming State-Society Relations in Mexico*, ed. W. Cornelius, A. Craig, and J. Fox. San Diego, CA: Center for U.S.-Mexican Studies.

——. 1996. How Does Civil Society Thicken? *World Development* 24 (6): 1089–1103.

Freud, Anna. 1965. *Normality and Pathology in Childhood.* New York: International Universities Press.

Friedman, Nathalie, and Perry Davis. 1998. *Faithful Youth: A Study of the National Conference of Synagogue Youth.* New York: National Conference of Synagogue Youth.

Furstenberg, Frank. 1993. How Families Manage Risk and Opportunity in Dangerous Neighborhoods. In *Sociology and the Public Agenda,* ed. William Julius Wilson. Newbury Park, CA: Sage.

——. 2000. The Sociology of Adolescence and Youth in the 1990s: A Critical Commentary. *Journal of Marriage and the Family* 62: 896–910.

——. 2001. Managing to Make It: Afterthoughts. *Journal of Family Issues* 22 (2): 160–62.

——, ed. 2002. *Early Adulthood in Cross-National Perspective. Annals of the American Academy of Political and Social Science.* Thousand Oaks, CA: Sage Publications.

Furstenberg, Frank, Thomas D. Cook, Jacquelynne Eccles, Glen Elder Jr., and Arnold Sameroff. 1999. *Managing to Make It: Urban Families and Adolescent Success.* Chicago: University of Chicago Press.

Gabaccia, Donna. 2000. *Italy's Many Diasporas.* Seattle: University of Washington Press.

Galvez, Alyshia. 2001. The Right to Have Rights: How Undocumented Mexican Participants in Guadalupan Devotional Organizations Redefine the Terms of Citizenship. Paper presented at conference "Haciendo Historia," City University of New York.

——. 2004. In the Name of Guadalupe: Religion, Politics, and Citizenship among Mexicans in New York. Ph.D. diss., New York University.

Gandreau, Monica. 1998. *Media and Imagination of Transnational Space.* Paper presented at conference on Mexican Migration to New York, Barnard College.

Gans, Herbert. 1979. Symbolic Ethnicity: The Future of Ethnic Groups and Cultures in America. *Ethnic and Racial Studies* 2 (1): 1–20.

——. 1992. Second-Generation Decline: Scenarios for the Ethnic and Economic Futures of Post-1965 American Immigrants. *Ethnic and Racial Studies* 15 (2): 173–92.

——. 1999. Toward a Reconciliation of "Assimilation" and "Pluralism": The Interplay of Acculturation and Ethnic Retention. In *The Handbook of International Migration: The American Experience,* ed. Charles Hirschman, Philip Kasinitz, and Josh DeWind. New York: Russell Sage Foundation.

——. 2002. The Sociology of Space: A Use-Centered View. *City and Community* 1 (4): 329–39.

Garcia Acevedo, Rosa María. 1996. Aztlán and Mexico. In *Chicanas/Chicanos at the Crossroads: Social, Economic, and Political Change,* ed. David Maciel and Isidro Ortiz. Tucson: University of Arizona Press.

Garcia Sanchez, Celerino. 1992. Oaxaca-Sinaloa-Estados Unidos: En transito a San Quintin. *Ojarasca.* (October.)

Geertz, Clifford. 1973. *The Interpretation of Cultures.* New York: Basic Books.

Gibson, Margaret. 1988. *Accommodation without Assimilation.* Ithaca, NY: Cornell University Press.

Giddens, Anthony. 1976. *New Rules of Sociological Method.* New York: Basic Books.

———. 1984. *The Constitution of Society.* Berkeley: University of California Press.

Giele, Janet Z., and Glen H. Elder, Jr., eds. 1998. *Methods of Life Course Research: Qualitative and Quantitative Approaches.* Thousand Oaks, CA: Sage Publications.

Gieryn, Thomas F. 2002. Give Place a Chance. *City and Community* 1 (4): 341–45.

Gilligan, Carol. 1991. *In a Different Voice: Psychological Theory and Women's Development.* Cambridge: Harvard University Press.

———. 2002. *The Birth of Pleasure.* New York: Alfred A. Knopf.

Gilligan, James. 1996. *Violence: Our Deadly Epidemic and Its Causes.* New York: G. P. Putman's Sons.

Gledhill, John. 1994. *Neoliberalism, Transnationalization, and Rural Poverty: A Case Study of Michoacán, Mexico.* Boulder, CO: Westview.

Glick-Schiller, Nina. 1999. Transmigrants and Nation-States: Something Old and Something New in the Immigrant Experience. In *The Handbook of International Migration: The American Experience,* ed. Charles Hirschman, Philip Kasinitz, and Josh DeWind, 94–120. New York: Russell Sage Foundation.

Glick-Schiller, N., L. Basch, and C. Blanc-Szanton. 1992. *Towards a Transnational Perspective on Migration.* Annals of New York Academy of Science, vol. 645.

Glick-Schiller, Nina, and Georges Fouron. 2001a. *Georges Woke Up Laughing: Long-Distance Nationalism and the Search for Home.* Durham, NC: Duke University Press.

———. 2001b. The Generation of Identity: Redefining the Second Generation within a Transnational Social Field. In *Migration, Transnationalization, and Race in a Changing New York,* ed. Héctor Cordero-Guzmán, Robert C. Smith, and Ramón Grosfoguel. Philadelphia: Temple University Press.

Gobierno de Mexico. Plan de desarollo, 1995–2000. Secretária de Relaciones Exteriors. México, DF.

Goffman, Erving. 1961. *Asylums: Essays on the Social Situation of Mental Patients and Other Inmates.* New York: Anchor Books.

———. 1963. *Stigma: Notes on the Management of Spoiled Identity.* New York: J. Aronson.

Goldring, Luin. 1992. Diversity and Community in Transnational Migration: A Comparative Study of Two Mexico-U.S. Migrant Circuits. Ph.D. diss., Cornell University.

———. 1996. Blurring Borders: Reflections on Transnational Community. *Research in Community Sociology* 6: 69–104.

———. 1998a. The Power of Status in Transnational Social Fields. In *Transnationalism from Below*, 165–95. New Brunswick, NJ: Transaction.

———. 1998b. From Market Membership to Transnational Citizenship? *L'ordinaire latino-americano* 173–74 (July–December): 167–72.

———. 1999. El estado mexicano y las organizaciones transmigrantes: Reconfigurando a nación, ciudadania, y relaciones entre estado y sociedad civil? In *Fronteras fragmentadas*, ed. Gail Mummert, 297–316. Zamora, Michoacán: El Colegio de Michoacán.

———. 2001. From Market Membership to Transnational Citizenship: The Changing Politicization of Transnational Social Spaces. In *Transnational Social Spaces*, ed. Ludger Pries, 162–86. New York: Routledge.

Gonzalez de la Rocha, Mercedes. 1994. *The Resources of Poverty*. London and Oxford: Blackwell.

Gonzalez Gutierrez, Carlos. 1993. The Mexican Diaspora in California: The Limits and Possibilities of the Mexican Government. In *The California-Mexico Connection*, ed. K. Burgess and A. Lowenthal, 221–33. Berkeley: University of California Press.

———. 1997. Decentralized Diplomacy: The Role of Consular Offices in Mexico's Relations with Its Diaspora. In *Bridging the Border: Transforming Mexico-U.S. Relations*, ed. Rodolfo de la Garza and Jesus Velazquez, 49–67. Lanham, MD: Rowman and Littlefield.

———. 1998. The Mexican Diaspora: Current Challenges for the Mexican State. Paper presented at conference on States and Diasporas, Columbia University.

Goodwin, Jeff, James Jasper, and Francesca Polletta, eds. 2001. *Passionate Politics: Emotions and Social Movements*. Chicago: University of Chicago Press.

Gordon, Milton. 1964. *Assimilation in American Life*. New Haven, CT: Yale University Press.

Gottdiener, Mark. 1985. *The Social Production of Urban Space*. Austin: University of Texas Press.

Graham, Pamela. 1997. Nationality and Political Participation within the Context of Dominican Transnational Migration. In *Caribbean Circuits*, ed. Patricia Pessar, 91–127. Staten Island, NY: Center for Migration Studies.

———. 2001. Political Incorporation and Re-Incorporation: Simultaneity in the Dominican Migrant Experience. In *Migration, Transnationalization, and Race in a Changing New York*, ed. Héctor Cordero-Guzmán, Robert C. Smith, and Ramón Grosfoguel. Philadelphia: Temple University Press.

Granovetter, Mark. 1973. The Strength of Weak Ties. *American Journal of Sociology* 78: 1360–80.

Grindle, Merilee. 1988. *In Search of Rural Development in Mexico*. Cambridge, MA: Harvard University Press.

Grosfoguel, Ramón, and Chloé Georas. 1996. The Racialization of Latino Caribbean Migrants in the New York Metropolitan Area. *CENTRO: Journal of the Center for Puerto Rican Studies* 8: 192–201.

Guarnizo, Luis. 1994. Los Dominicanyorks: The Making of a Binational Society. In *Annals of the Academy of Political and Social Science* 533: 70–86.

———. 1998. The Rise of Transnational Social Formations: Mexican and Dominican State Responses to Transnational Migration. *Political Power and Social Theory* 12: 45–94.

Guarnizo, Luis, A. Portes, and W. Haller. 2003. "Assimilation and Transnationalism." *American Journal of Sociology* 108 (6): 1211–48.

Guarnizo, Luis, Arturo Roach, and Elizabeth Roach. 1999. Mistrust, Fragmented Solidarity, and Transnational Migration: Colombians in New York City and Los Angeles. In *Ethnic and Racial Studies* 22 (2): 367–97.

Guarnizo, Luis, and Michael Peter Smith. 1998. The Locations of Transnationalism. In *Transnationalism from Below*, ed. Michael Peter Smith and Luis Eduardo Guarnizo, 3–34. New Brunswick, NJ: Transaction.

Guerrero-Rippberger, Sara. 1999. But for the Day of Tomorrow: Negotiating Femininity in a New York Mexican Identity. Senior thesis, Barnard College.

———. 1998–2000. Notes for Rob Smith's Second-Generation Project.

Gutiérrez, David. 1999. Migration, Emergent Ethnicity, and the So-Called Third Space: The Shifting Politics of Nationalism in Greater Mexico. *American Journal of History* 86 (2): 481–517.

Gutiérrez, José Angel. 1986. The Chicano in Mexicano–North American Foreign Relations. In *Chicano-Mexican Relations*, ed. Tatcho Mindiola Jr. and Max Martinez. Houston, TX: Mexican American Studies Program, University of Houston.

Gutierrez, Ramon A. 1991. *When Jesus Came, the Corn Mothers Went Away: Marriage, Sexuality, and Power in New Mexico, 1500–1846*. Stanford, CA: Stanford University Press.

Gutmann, Matthew. 1996. *The Meanings of Macho: Being a Man in Mexico City*. Berkeley: University of California Press.

Hagan, Jacqueline. 1994. *Deciding to Be Legal*. Philadelphia: Temple University Press.

———. 1998. Social Networks, Gender, and Immigrant Settlement: Resource and Constraint. *American Sociological Review* 63 (1): 55–67.

Hagedorn, John M. 1988. *People and Folks: Gangs, Crime, and the Underclass in a Rustbelt City*. Chicago: Lake View.

———. 2001. Globalization, Gangs, and Collaborative Research. In *The Eurogang Paradox: Street Gangs in the U.S. and Europe*, ed. Malcolm Klein, Hans-Jürgen Kerner, Cheryl L. Maxson, and Elmar G. M. Weitkamp. Boston: Kluwer.

Hall, G. Stanley. 1904. *Adolescence: Its Psychology and Its Relations to Physiology, Anthropology, Sociology, Sex, Crime, Religion, and Education*. New York: D. Appleton.

Hanagan, Michael. 1997. Recasting Citizenship. *Theory and Society*, special issue, ed. Charles Tilly and Michael Hanagan, 26 (4): 397–402.

———. 1998. Irish Transnational Social Movements, Deterritorialized Migrants, and the State System: The Last One Hundred and Forty Years. *Mobilization: An International Journal* 3 (1): 107–26.

———. 1999. Introduction. In Charles Tilly and Michael Hanagan, *Expanding Citizenship, Reconfiguring States*. Lanham, MD: Rowman and Littlefield.

Handlin, Oscar. 1951. *The Uprooted: The Epic Story of the Great Migrations That Made the American People*. Boston: Little, Brown.

———. 1959. *Immigration as a Factor in American History*. Englewood Cliffs, NJ: Prentice-Hall.

Hapak, J. 1981. The Polish Military Commission. *Polish American Studies* 38 (2): 26–38.

Harvey, David. 1989. *The Condition of Postmodernity: An Enquiry into the Origins of Cultural Change*. Cambridge, MA: Blackwell.

Hays, Sharon. 1996. *The Cultural Contradictions of Motherhood*. New Haven, CT: Yale University Press.

Heisler, Barbara Schmitter. 1984a. Immigrant Settlement and the Structure of Emergent Immigrant Communities in Western Europe. *Annals of the American Academy of Political and Social Science* 48: 76–86.

———. 1984b. Sending States and Immigrant Minorities: The Case of Italy. *Comparative Studies of Society and History* 26 (2): 325–34.

Hernández, Ernesto. 2002. Masculinidades y transnacionalidad en una comunidad transnacional mixteca. Paper given at conference "Transnationalism: An Ethnographic and Interdisciplinary Look," Universidad Autónoma Metropolitana, Mexico City.

Hernández-Leon, Ruben. 1999. ¡A la aventura! Jovenes, pandillas y migración de la conexión Monterrey-Houston. In *Fronteras fragmentadas*, ed. Gail Mummert. Zamora, Michoacán, Mexico: El Colegio de Michoacán.

Hirsch, Jennifer. 2003. *A Courtship after Marriage: Sexuality and Love in Mexican Transnational Families*. Berkeley: University of California Press.

Hirschman, Albert O. 1970. *Exit, Voice, and Loyalty*. Cambridge, MA: Harvard University Press.

Hochschild, Arlie. 1983. *The Managed Heart*. Berkeley: University of California Press.

———. 1989. *The Second Shift*. New York: Avon.

Hondagneu-Sotelo, Pierrette. 1994. *Gendered Transitions: Mexican Experiences of Migration*. Berkeley: University of California Press.

———. 2001. *Doméstica: Immigrant Workers Cleaning and Caring in the Shadows of Affluence*. Berkeley: University of California Press.

Hondagneu-Sotelo, Pierrette, and Cristina Avila. 1997. "I'm Here but I'm There": The Meanings of Transnational Motherhood. *Gender and Society* 11 (5): 548–71.

Hondagneu-Sotelo, Pierrette, and Michael Messner. 1996. Gender Displays and Men's Power: The "New Man" and the Mexican Immigrant Man. In *Theorizing Masculinities*, ed. Harry Brod and Michael Kaufman, 200–218. Thousand Oaks, CA: Sage.

Horowitz, Ruth. 1983. *Honor and the American Dream: Culture and Identity in a Chicano Community*. New Brunswick, NJ: Rutgers University Press.

———. 1990. Sociological Perspectives on Gangs. In *Gangs in America,* ed. C. Ronald Huff, 37–54. Newbury Park, CA: Sage.

Huerta Jaramillo, Ana María de. 1985. *Insurreciones rurales en el estado de Puebla, 1868–1870.* Puebla, Mexico: Universidad Autónoma de Puebla, Centro de Estudios Historicos y Sociales.

Ignatiev, Joel. 1995. *How the Irish Became White.* New York: Routledge.

Instituto Electoral Federal. 1998. *Informe final que presenta la comisión de especialistas que estudia las modalidades del voto de los mexicanos residentes en el extranjero.* México, DF.

Jacobson, David. 1996. *Rights across Borders: Immigration and the Decline of Citizenship.* Baltimore, MD: Johns Hopkins University Press.

Jankowski, Martín Sánchez. 1991. *Islands in the Street.* Berkeley: University of California Press.

———. 1995. The Significance of Status in Race Relations. In *The Bubbling Cauldron: Race, Ethnicity, and the Urban Crisis,* ed. Michael Peter Smith and Joe R. Feagin, 77–89. Minneapolis: University of Minnesota Press.

Jess, Pat, and Doreen Massey. 1995. The Contestation of Place. In Doreen Massey and Pat Jess, *A Place in the World: Places, Cultures, and Globalization.* New York: Oxford University Press.

Joachim, Benoit. 1979. *Perspectivas hacia la historia social latinoamericana.* Puebla, Mexico: Universidad Autónoma de Puebla, Centro de Estudios Historicos y Sociales.

Jones-Correa, Michael. 1997a. *Between Two Islands?* Ithaca, NY: Cornell University Press.

———. 1997b. Comments at conference on Second-Generation Transnationalism, Harvard University.

Kao, Grace, and Marta Tienda. 1995. Optimism and Achievement: Educational Performance of Immigrant Youth. *Social Science Quarterly* 76 (1): 1–19.

Kasinitz, Philip. 1992. *Caribbean New York.* Ithaca, NY: Cornell University Press.

Kasinitz, Philip, and Milton Vickerman. 2001. Ethnic Niches and Racial Traps: Jamaicans in the New York Regional Economy. In *Migration, Transnationalization, and Race in a Changing New York,* ed. Héctor Cordero-Guzmán, Robert C. Smith, and Ramón Grosfoguel. Philadelphia: Temple University Press.

Katz, Jack. 1988. *Seductions of Crime.* New York: Basic Books.

———. 1999. *How Emotions Work.* Chicago: University of Chicago Press.

Kearney, Michael. 1991. Borders and Boundaries of State and Self at the End of Empire. *Journal of Historical Sociology* 4: 52–74.

———. 1995. The Local and the Global: The Anthropology of Globalization and Transnationalism. *Annual Review of Anthropology* 24: 547–66.

———. 1996. *Reconceptualizing the Peasantry: Anthropology in Global Perspective.* Boulder, CO: Westview.

———. 2000. Transnational Oaxacan Indigenous Identity: The Case of Mixtecs and Zapotecs. *Identities* 7 (2): 173–95.

Kibria, Nazli. 1993. *Family Tightrope: The Changing Lives of Vietnamese Families.* Princeton, NJ: Princeton University Press.

Kim, Dae Young. 1999. Beyond Co-Ethnic Solidarity: Mexican and Ecuadorean Employment in Korean-Owned Businesses in New York City. *Ethnic and Racial Studies* 22 (3): 581–605.

Kimmel, Michael. 1996. *Manhood in America: A Cultural History.* New York: Free Press.

Kindlon, Daniel J., and Michael Thompson, with Teresa Barker. 1999. *Raising Cain: Protecting the Emotional Life of Boys.* New York: Ballantine.

Klawiter, Maren. 1999. Racing for the Cure, Walking Women, and Toxic Touring: Mapping Cultures of Action within the Bay Area Terrain of Breast Cancer. *Social Problems* 46 (1): 104–26.

Klein, Malcolm. 1995. *The American Street Gang: Its Nature, Prevalence, and Control.* New York: Oxford University Press.

———. 2001. Resolving the Eurogang Paradox. In *The Eurogang Paradox: Street Gangs in the U.S. and Europe,* ed. Malcolm Klein, Hans-Jürgen Kerner, Cheryl L. Maxson, and Elmar G. M. Weitkamp. Boston: Kluwer.

Kmec, J. A., and F. F. Furstenberg. 2002. Racial and Gender Difference in the Transition to Adulthood: A Follow Up Study of the Philadelphia Youth. In *New Perspectives on the Life Course,* vol. 7: *New Frontiers in Socialization,* ed. R. Settersten and T. J. Owen. London: JAI.

Kokot, Waltraud, Khachig Tololyan, and Carolin Alfonso. 2004. *Diaspora, Identity, and Religion: New Directions in Theory and Research.* New York: Routledge.

Kraly, Ellen Percy, and Inés Miyares. 2001. Immigration to New York: Policy, Population, and Patterns. In *New Immigrants in New York,* ed. Nancy Foner, 33–80. New York: Columbia University Press.

Kulik, Don. 1997. The Gender of Brazilian Transgendered Prostitutes. *American Anthropologist* 99 (3): 574–84.

Kwong, Peter. 1987. *The New Chinatown.* New York: Hill and Wang.

———. 1997. *Forbidden Workers: Illegal Chinese Immigrants and American Labor.* New York: New Press.

Kyle, David. 1999. The Otavalan Trade Diaspora: Social Capital and Transnational Entrepreneurship. *Ethnic and Racial Studies* 22 (2): 422–47.

———. 2001. *The Transnational Peasant: The Social Construction of International Economic Migration and Transcommunities from the Ecuadoran Andes.* Baltimore: Johns Hopkins University Press.

Lamborn, S. D., S. M. Dornbusch, and L. Steinberg. 1996. Ethnicity and Community Context as Moderators of the Relations between Family Decision Making and Adolescent Adjustment. *Child Development* 67: 283–301.

Lamborn, S. D., N. Mounts, L. Steinberg, and S. Dornbusch. 1991. Patterns of Competence and Adjustment among Adolescents from Authoritative, Authoritarian, Indulgent, and Neglectful Families. *Child Development* 62: 1049–65.

Lamont, Michelle. 2000. *The Dignity of Working Men.* New York: Russell Sage Foundation, and Cambridge, MA: Harvard University Press.

Lancaster, Roger N. 1992. *Life Is Hard: Machismo, Danger, and the Intimacy of Power in Nicaragua.* Berkeley: University of California Press.

Lara, Sandra. 2000–2001. Notes from Rob Smith's Second-Generation Project.

Leadbeater, Bonnie J. Ross, and Niobe Way. 1996. *Urban Girls: Resisting Stereotypes, Creating Identities.* New York: New York University Press.

Leal, Luis. 1983. Female Archetypes in Mexican Literature. In *Women in Hispanic Literature: Icons and Fallen Idols,* ed. Beth Miller, 227–42. Berkeley: University of California Press.

Lee, Jennifer. 2001. Entrepreneurship and Business Development among African Americans, Koreans, and Jews: Exploring Some Structural Differences. In *Migration, Transnationalization, and Race in a Changing New York,* ed. Héctor Cordero-Guzmán, Robert C. Smith, and Ramón Grosfoguel. Philadelphia: Temple University Press.

Lefebvre, Henri. 1991. *The Production of Space.* Trans. Donald Nicholson-Smith. Oxford: Blackwell.

Lessinger, Johanna. 2001. Class, Race, and Success: Two Generations of Indian Americans Confront the American Dream. In *Migration, Transnationalization, and Race in a Changing New York,* ed. Héctor Cordero-Guzmán, Robert C. Smith, and Ramón Grosfoguel. Philadelphia: Temple University Press.

Levitt, Peggy. 1997. Transnational Community Development: The Case of Boston and the Dominican Republic. *Nonprofit and Voluntary Sector Quarterly* 26: 509–26.

———. 2001a. *The Transnational Villagers.* Berkeley: University of California Press.

———. 2001b. Transnational Migration: Taking Stock and Future Directions. *Global Networks: A Journal of Transnational Affairs* 1 (3): 195–216.

Levitt, Peggy, and Mary Waters. 2002. Introduction. In *The Changing Face of Home,* ed. Peggy Levitt and Mary Waters, 1–32. New York: Russell Sage Foundation.

Lieberson, Stanley, and Freda Lynn. 2002. Barking Up the Wrong Branch: Scientific Alternatives to the Current Model of Sociological Science. *Annual Review of Sociology* 29: 1–19.

Lichterman, Paul. 1996. *The Search for Political Communities: American Activists Reinventing Commitment.* Princeton, NJ: Princeton University Press.

———. 1998. What Do Movements Mean? The Value of Participant Observation. *Qualitative Sociology* 21 (4): 401–18.

Lopez, Gustavo Angel, and Thoric Cederstrom. 1991. Moradores en el purgatorio: El regreso periódico de los migrantes como una forma de peregrinación. *Memoria del Simposio Internacional de Investigaciones Regionales.* Centro Regional de Puebla, Puebla: Instituto Nacional de Antropología e Historia.

Lopez Castro, Gustavo. 1985. *La casa dividida.* Zamora, Michoacán: El Colegio de México.

MacLeod, Jay. 1995 [1987]. *Ain't No Makin' It.* Boulder, CO: Westview.

Mahler, Sarah. 1995. *American Dreaming.* Princeton, NJ: Princeton University Press.

———. 1998. Theoretical and Empirical Contributions toward a Research Agenda for Transnationalism. In *Transnationalism from Below,* ed. M. P. Smith and L. Guarnizo, 64–102. New Brunswick, NJ: Transaction.

———. 2001. Suburban Transnational Migrants: Long Island's Salvadorans. In *Migration, Transnationalization, and Race in a Changing New York,* ed. Héctor Cordero-Guzmán, Robert C. Smith, and Ramón Grosfoguel. Philadelphia: Temple University Press.

Mangione, Silvia. 1998. The Need for the Vote from Abroad for Italians. Paper presented at conference on States and Diasporas, Columbia University.

Marcia, J. E. 1980. Identity in Adolescence. In *Handbook of Adolescent Psychology,* ed. J. Adelson, 159–87. New York: John Wiley.

Marshall, T. H. 1950. *Citizenship and Social Class.* Cambridge: Cambridge University Press.

Martínez, Jesús. 1998. In Search of Our Lost Citizenship: Mexican Immigrants, the Right to Vote, and the Transition to Democracy in Mexico. Paper presented at conference on States and Diasporas, Columbia University.

———. 1999. El voto "extraterritorial": Respuesta a carpizo. *Nexos* (October): 13–14.

Massey, Doreen. 1995. *Space, Place, and Gender.* Minneapolis: University of Minnesota Press.

Massey, Doreen, and Pat Jess, eds. 1995. *A Place in the World: Places, Cultures, and Globalization.* New York: Oxford University Press.

Massey, Douglas. 1999. Comments at conference on New Developments in Transnational Scholarship on Transnational Migration, Princeton University.

Massey, Douglas, Rafael Alarcón, Jorge Durand, and Humberto Gonzalez. 1987. *Return to Aztlán: The Social Process of Transnational Migration from Western Mexico.* Berkeley: University of California Press.

Massey, Douglas, and Nancy Denton. 1993. American Apartheid: Segregation and the Making of the Underclass. Cambridge, MA: Harvard University Press.

Massey, Douglas, Jorge Durand, and Nolan Malone. 2002. *Beyond Smoke and Mirrors: Mexican Immigration in an Era of Economic Integration.* New York: Russell Sage Foundation.

Massey, Douglas, and Kristin Espinosa. 1997. What's Driving Mexico-US Migration? A Theoretical, Empirical, and Policy Analysis. *American Journal of Sociology* 102 (4): 939–99.

Massey, Douglas, Luin Goldring, and Jorge Durand. 1994. Continuities in Transnational Migration: An Analysis of Nineteen Mexican Communities. *American Sociological Review* 99: 1492–1533.

Massey, Douglas, et al. 1998. *Worlds in Motion: Understanding International Migration at the End of the Millennium.* New York: Oxford University Press.

Mattei, Linda Miller, and David Smith. 1998. Belizean Boys 'n the Hood: Garifuna Labor Migration and Transnational Identity. In *Transnationalism from Below,* ed. Michael Peter Smith and Luis Eduardo Guarnizo, 270–90. New Brunswick, NJ: Transaction.

McAdam, Doug. 1998. On International Origins of Domestic Political Opportunities. In *Social Movements in American Political Institutions*, ed. A. Constain and A. McFarland. New York: Rowman and Littlefield.

McNees, Molly, Nina Siulc, Robert Smith, and T. Flores. 2003. Mexicans and Health in New York. Final Report to the United Hospital Fund. New York: Lutheran Medical Center.

Menjivar, Cecilia. 2002a. *Fragmented Ties: Salvadoran Immigrant Networks in America*. Berkeley: University of California Press.

———. 2002b. Living in Two Worlds? Guatemalan-Origin Children in the United States and Emerging Transnationalism. *Journal of Ethnic and Migration Studies* 28 (3): 531–552.

Merton, Robert. 1938. Social Structure and Anomie. *American Sociological Review* 3: 672–82.

———. 1968 [1957]. *Social Theory and Social Structure*. New York: Free Press.

Messner, Michael A. 1997. *Politics of Masculinities: Men in Movements*. Thousand Oaks, CA: Sage.

Messerschmidt, James. 1993. *Masculinities and Crime*. Lanham, MD: Rowman and Littlefield.

Meyer, J., J. Boli, G. Thomas, and F. Ramirez. 1997. World Society and the Nation State. *American Journal of Sociology* 103 (1): 144–81.

Miller, Mark J. 1981. *Immigrants in Europe: An Emerging Political Force*. New York: Praeger.

Mines, Richard. 1981. Developing a Community Tradition of Migration: A Field Study of Rural Zacatecas, Mexico, and California Settlement Areas. Monograph No. 3. San Diego, CA: Center for U.S.-Mexican Studies.

Mitchell, Katharyne. 1997. Transnational Discourse: Bringing Geography Back In. *Antipode* 29 (2): 101–14.

Moctezuma Longoria, Miguel. 1998. La producción de fuera de trabajo-migrante y la organización de los clubes de zacatecanos en los EU. Ph.D. diss., Colegio de la Frontera Norte.

———. 2001a. *Claves para la ley Bermudez*. Zacatecas, Mexico: Universidad Autónoma de Zacatecas.

———. 2001b. *Andrés Bermudez: Un símbolo zacatecano binacional*. Zacatecas, Mexico: Universidad Autónoma de Zacatecas.

———. 2002. *Iniciativa de reforma a la constitución politica del estado libre y soberano de Zacatecas sobre el ejercito pleno de los derechos politicos de los migrantes*. Zacatecas, Mexico: Universidad Autónoma de Zacatecas.

———. 2003a. La voz de los actores: Sobre la ley migrante de Zacatecas. *Migración y Desarrollo* 1: 100–103.

———. 2003b. Territorialidad de los clubes de Zacatecas en Estados Unidos. *Migración y Desarrollo* 1: 49–73. Zacatecas: Universidad Autónoma de Zacatecas.

Moctezuma Longoria, Miguel, and Hector Rodriguez, eds. 1999. *Migración internacional y desarollo regional*. Zacatecas and Mexico City: Senate of Mexico and the Universidad Autónoma de Zacatecas.

Mollenkopf, John H. 1999. Urban Political Conflicts and Alliances: New York and Los Angeles Compared. In *The Handbook of International Migration: The American Experience*, ed. Charles Hirschman, Philip Kasinitz, and Josh DeWind. New York: Russell Sage Foundation.

Montemayor, Raymond, Gerald Adams, and Thomas Gullotta. 2000. *Adolescent Diversity in Ethnic, Economic, and Cultural Contexts*. Thousand Oaks, CA: Sage.

————, eds. 1990. *From Childhood to Adolescence: A Transitional Period?* Newbury Park, CA: Sage.

————, eds. 1992. *Adolescent Identity Formation*. Newbury Park, CA: Sage.

————, eds. 1998. *Delinquent, Violent Youth: Theory and Interventions*. Thousand Oaks, CA: Sage.

Monti, Daniel J. 1991a. Gangs in More- and Less-Settled Communities. In *Gangs*, ed. Scott Cummings and Daniel J. Monti. Albany: State University of New York Press.

————. 1991b. Origins and Problems of Gang Research. In *Gangs*, ed. Scott Cummings and Daniel J. Monti. Albany: State University of New York Press.

————. 1994. *Wannabe: Gangs in Suburbs and Schools*. Cambridge, MA, and Oxford: Blackwell.

Moore, Joan. 1991. *Going Down the Barrio: Homeboys and Homegirls in Change*. Philadelphia: Temple University Press.

Moore, J., R. Garcia, C. Garcia, L. Cerda, and F. Valencia. 1978. *Homeboys: Gangs, Drugs, and Prison in the Barrios of Los Angeles*. Philadelphia: Temple University Press.

Mora, Teresa V. 1982. *La Mixteca Baja, su migración: Nieves Ixpantepec y San Nicolas Hidalgo, Oaxaca*. Cuadernos No. 30. México, DF: Departamento de Etnología y Antropología Social, Instituto Nacional de Antropología y Historia.

Morawska, Ewa. 1989. Labor Migrations of Poles in the Atlantic World Economy, 1880–1914. *Comparative Studies in Society and History* 31 (2): 237–70.

————. 1994. In Defense of the Ethnic Assimilation Model. *Journal of American Ethnic History* 13 (2): 76–87.

————. 2001. Structuring Migration: The Case of Polish Income-Seeking Travelers to the West. *Theory and Society* 30: 47–80.

Moss, P., and C. Tilly. 1996. "Soft" Skills and Race: An Investigation of Black Men's Employment Problems. *Work and Occupations* 23 (3): 252–76.

Mummert, Gail. 1993. Changes in the Formation of Western Rural Families: Profound Modifications. *DemoS* 6: 23–24.

————. 1994. From *Metate* to *Despate*: Rural Women's Salaried Labor and the Redefinition of Gendered Spaces and Roles. In *Women of the Mexican Countryside, 1850–1990*, ed. H. Fowler-Salamini and M. K. Vaughn, 192–209. Tucson: University of Arizona Press.

————. 1996. Cambios en la estructura y organización familiares en un contexto de emigración masculina y trabajo asalariado femenino: Estudio de caso en un valle agricola de Michoacán. In *Hogares, families: Desigualdad, conflicto, redes solidarias y parentales,* 39–46. México, DF: SOMEDE.

———. 1999. Juntos o despartados: Migración transnacional y la fundación del hogar. In *Fronteras fragmentadas,* ed. Gail Mummert, 451–74. Zamora, Michoacán: El Colegio de Michoacán.

Mutter, Nicole. 1998. The Symbolic Violence of Violence-Prevention Programs. Senior thesis, Barnard College.

Myers, D. 1998. Dimensions of Economic Adaptation by Mexican-Origin Men. In *Crossings,* ed. Marcelo Suarez-Orozco. Cambridge, MA: Harvard University Press.

Myers, D., and C. Cranford. 1998. Temporal Differentiation in the Occupational Mobility of Immigrant and Native-Born Latina Workers. *American Sociological Review* 63 (1): 68–93.

Nagengast, Carol, and Michael Kearney. 1990. Mixtec Ethnicity: Social Identity, Political Consciousness, and Political Activism. *Latin American Research Review* 25 (2): 61–91.

Nagler, Stuart. 1958. Notes from Quaker Work Camp in Ticuani. Quaker Archives, Philadelphia.

Nash, June. 1970. In the Eyes of the Ancestors: Belief and Behavior in a Maya Community. New Haven, CT: Yale University Press.

Neckerman, Kathryn, Sara Lee, and Prudence Carter. 1999. Minority Cultures of Mobility. *Ethnic and Racial Studies* 22 (6): 945–65.

Neiburg, Federico G. 1988. *Identidad y conflicto en la sierra mazateca: el caso del Consejo de Ancianos de San Jose Tenango.* México, DF: Instituto Nacional de Antropología e Historia, Escuela Nacional de Antropología e Historia.

Newburn, Tim, and Elizabeth Stanko. 1994. *Just Boys Doing Business? Men, Masculinities, and Crime.* London: Routledge.

Oboler, Suzanne. 1995. *Ethnic Labels, Latino Lives: Identity and the Politics of (Re)presentation in the United States.* Minneapolis: University of Minnesota Press.

O'Brien, Denise. 1958. Report on Puebla Trip. Unpublished paper.

Omi, M., and M. Winant. 1986. *Racial Formation in the United States: From the 1960s to the 1980s.* New York: Routledge & Kegan Paul.

Ortner, Sherry B. 1995. Resistance and the Problem of Ethnographic Refusal. *Comparative Studies in Society and History* 37 (1): 172–93.

Ostergren, Robert. 1988. *A Community Transplanted: The Trans-Atlantic Experience of a Swedish Immigrant Settlement in the Upper Midwest, 1835–1915.* Madison: University of Wisconsin Press.

Pansters, Wil. 1990. *Politics and Power in Puebla: The Political History of a Mexican State, 1937–1987.* Amsterdam: Center for Latin American Studies.

———. 2001. Institutional Politics and Reform in Mexican Higher Education: The Example of the Universidad Autónoma de Puebla. Paper presented at annual meeting of the Latin American Studies Association, Washington, DC.

Pare, Luisa. 1972. Diseno teoretico para el estudio del caciquismo en México. *Revista mexicana de sociologia* 34, no. 2 (April–June).

———. 1975. Caciquismo y estructura de poder en la Sierra Norte de Puebla. In *Caciquismo y poder political en el Mexico rural,* ed. Roger Barta. México, DF: Instituto de Investigaciones Sociales, Universidad Autónoma de México.

Park, Robert. 1952. *Human Communities: The City and Human Ecology.* Glencoe, IL: Free Press.

Park, Robert, Ernest W. Burgess, and Roderick D. McKenzie. 1925. *The City.* Chicago: University of Chicago Press.

Paz, Octavio. 1961. *Labyrinth of Solitude: Life and Thought in Mexico.* Translated by Lysander Kemp. New York: Grove.

Perez, Carolina. 2000. Notes on Rob Smith's Second-Generation Project.

Perez, Griscelda. 2000. Notes on Rob Smith's Second-Generation Project.

———. 2001. Notes on Rob Smith's Second-Generation Project.

Perez Godoy, Mara. 1997. Transnational Migration and the Institutionalization of Mobilization: The Role of a Political Party in a Social Movement. *Revista iberoamericana* 27 (1–4): 715–31.

———. 1998. Social Movements and International Migration: The Mexican Diaspora Seeks Inclusion in Mexico's Political Affairs, 1968–1998. Ph.D. diss., University of Chicago.

Perlman, Joel, and R. Waldinger. 1997. Second Generation Decline? Children of Immigrants, Past and Present: A Reconsideration. *International Migration Review* 31 (Winter): 893–922.

Perlmutter, Ted. 1998. Contemporary and Historical Politics of Italians' Abroad Right to Vote. Paper presented at conference on States and Diasporas, Columbia University.

Pessar, Patricia. 1999. The Role of Gender, Households, and Social Networks in the Migration Process: A Review and Appraisal. In *The Handbook of International Migration: The American Experience,* ed. Charles Hirschman, Philip Kasinitz, and Josh DeWind. New York: Russell Sage Foundation.

Pessar, Patricia, and Sherri Grasmuck. 1991. *Between Two Islands.* Berkeley: University of California Press.

Pessar, Patricia, and Sarah Mahler. 2003. Transnational Migration: Bringing Gender Back In. *International Migration Review* 37 (3): 812–46.

Petacco, Arrigo. 1972. *Joe Petrosino, 1860–1909.* Milan: A. Mondori.

Philips, Bruce. n.d. *Re-Examining Intermarriage: Trends, Textures, and Strategies.* New York: Susan and David Wilstein Institute of Jewish Policy Studies and the American Jewish Committee.

Phinney, Jean. 1985. A Three Stage Model of Ethnic Identity Development in Adolescence. In *Ethnic Identity: Formation and Transmission among Hispanics and Other Minorities,* ed. Martha Bernal and George P. Knight. Albany: State University of New York Press.

———. 1989. Stages of Ethnic Identity in Minority-Group Adolescents. *Journal of Early Adolescence* 9: 34–49.

————. 1998. Ethnic Identity in Adolescents and Adults: Review of Research. In *Readings in Ethnic Psychology*, ed. Pamela Balls Organista, Kevin Chun, and Gerardo Marin, 73–99. New York: Routledge.

Pienkos, Donald E. 1991. *For Your Freedom through Ours: Polish American Efforts on Poland's Behalf, 1863–1991*. Boulder, CO: East European Monographs. Distributed through Columbia University Press.

Pinderhughes, Howard. 1993. Down with the Program: Racial Attitudes and Group Violence among Youth in Bensonhurst and Gravesend. In *Gangs: The Origins and Impact of Contemporary Youth Gangs in the United States*, ed. Scott Cummings and Daniel J. Monti. Albany: State University of New York Press.

Polanyi, Karl. 1957. The Economy as an Instituted Process. In *Trade and Market in the Early Empires*, ed. K. Polanyi, C. Arensberg, and H. Pearson. Chicago: Henry Regnery.

Polk, Kenneth. 1994. Masculinity, Honour, and Confrontational Homicide. In *Just Boys Doing Business?*, ed. Tim Newburn and Elizabeth Stanko. London: Routledge.

Portes, Alejandro. 1995a. *The Economic Sociology of Immigration: Essays on Networks, Ethnicity, and Entrepreneurship*. New York: Russell Sage Foundation.

————. 1995b. Economic Sociology and the Sociology of Immigration: An Overview. In *The Economic Sociology of Immigration*, ed. A. Portes. New York: Russell Sage Foundation.

————. 1996. Transnational Communities: Their Emergence and Significance in the Contemporary World System. In *Latin America in the World Economy*, ed. R. P. Korzeniewicz and W. C. Smith, 151–68. Westport, CT: Greenwood.

————. 1998. Social Capital: Its Origins and Applications in Modern Sociology. *Annual Review of Sociology* 24: 1–24.

————. 1999. Conclusion: Towards a New World—The Origins and Effects of Transnational Activities. *Ethnic and Racial Studies*, special issue, 22 (2): 463–77.

————. 2001. The Debates and Significance of Immigrant Transnationalism. *Global Networks: A Journal of Transnational Affairs* 1 (3): 181–94.

Portes, Alejandro, and Robert Bach. 1985. *Latin Journey*. Berkeley: University of California Press.

Portes, A., L. Guarnizo, and P. Landholt. 1997. Summary of Results and Conclusion from Informant Interviews for Research Project, Transnational Communities: Their Origins and Effects among Latin American Immigrants in the US. Unpublished manuscript.

————. 1999. Introduction: Pitfalls and Promise of an Emergent Research Field. *Ethnic and Racial Studies* 22 (2): 217–38.

Portes, Alejandro, William J. Haller, and Luis Eduardo Guarnizo. 2003. Transnational Entrepreneurs: An Alternative Form of Immigrant Economic Adaptation. *American Sociological Review* 67 (2): 278–98.

Portes, Alejandro, and Dag MacLeod. 1996. Educational Progress of Children of Immigrants: The Roles of Class, Ethnicity, and School Context. *Sociology of Education* 69 (4): 255–75.

Portes, Alejandro, and Ruben Rumbaut. 1994. *Immigrant America*. Berkeley: University of California Press.

———. 2001. *Legacies*. Berkeley: University of California Press.

Portes, Alejandro, and Min Zhou. 1993. The New Second Generation: Segmented Assimilation and Its Variants. *Annals of the American Academy of Political and Social Science* 22 (2): 217–38.

Presidencia de la República. 1982. *Geografía de la marginalización en Mexico*. Coordinación General del Plan Nacional de Zonas Deprimidas y Grupos Marginados. México, DF.

Pries, Ludger. 1999. *Migration and Transnational Social Spaces*. Aldershot: Ashgate.

Prieur, Annick. 1998. *Mema's House, Mexico City: On Transvestites, Queers, and Machos*. Chicago: University of Chicago Press.

Quinones, Sam. 2001. *True Tales from Another Mexico*. Albuquerque: University of New Mexico Press.

Ragin, Charles. 2000. *Fuzzy Set Social Science*. Chicago: University of Chicago Press.

Redfield, Robert. 1930. *Tepoztlán, a Mexican Village: A Study of Folk Life*. Chicago: University of Chicago Press.

———. 1955. *The Little Community: Viewpoints for a Study of the Human Whole*. Chicago: University of Chicago Press.

Resaldo, Renato. 1997. Cultural Citizenship, Inequality, and Multiculturalism. In *Latino Cultural Citizenship*, ed. William Flores and Rena Benmayor, 27–38. Boston: Beacon.

———. 2003. Introduction: The Borders of Belonging. In *Cultural Citizenship in Island Southeast Asia*, ed. Renato Resaldo, 1–15. Berkeley: University of California Press.

Richman, Irwin. 1998. Online article at www.brown.edu/Research/Catskills _Institute. Accessed October 2002.

Rivera-Batiz, Francisco. 1996. *The Education of Immigrant Children: The Case of New York City*. New York: Immigrant New York Series, International Center for the Study of Migration, Ethnicity and Citizenship, New School for Social Research.

———. 2003. Manhatítlan. Unpublished paper.

Rivera Salgado, Gaspar. 1998. Political Activism among Mexican Transnational Indigenous Communities and the Mexican State. Paper given at conference on States and Diasporas, Columbia University.

———. 1999. Migration and Political Activism: Mexican Transnational Indigenous Communities in a Comparative Perspective. Ph.D. diss., University of California, Santa Cruz.

———. 2001. Transnational Political Strategies: The Case of Mexican Indigenous Migrants. In *Immigration Research for a New Century: Multidiscipli-

nary Perspectives, ed. Nancy Foner, Ruben Rumbaut, and Steven Gold. New York: Russell Sage Foundation.

Rivera Sanchez, Lillian. 2003. Asociación Tepeyac. Paper presented at conference "Haciendo Historia," City University of New York.

Roberts, Bryan, Reanne Frank, and Fernando Lozano-Ascencio. 1999. Transnational Migrant Communities and Mexican Migration to the US. In *Ethnic and Racial Studies*, special issue, 22 (2): 238–66.

Rodriguez, Clara. 1997. *Latin Looks: Latina and Latino Images in the U.S. Media*. Boulder, CO: Westview.

———. 2000. *Changing Race: Latinos, the Census, and the History of Ethnicity in the United States*. New York: New York University Press.

Rodriguez, Clara, and Héctor Cordero-Guzmán. 1992. Placing Race in Context. *Ethnic and Racial Studies* 15 (4): 523–42.

Rodriguez, Nestor. 1996. Autonomous Migration, Transnational Communities, and the State. *Social Justice* 23 (3): 21–37.

Rodriguez, Orlando, Emily Rosenbaum, and Greta Gilbertson. 1993. *Nuestra Nueva York: Latino Immigrants' Perspectives on Politics*. New York: Hispanic Research Center, Fordham University.

Roediger, David. 1991. *The Wages of Whiteness*. New York: Routledge.

Rouse, Roger. 1989. Mexican Migration to the US: Family Relations in a Transnational Migrant Circuit. Ph.D. diss., Stanford University.

———. 1991. Mexican Migration and the Social Space of Postmodernism. *Diaspora* 1 (1): 8–24.

———. 1992. Making Sense of Settlement: Class, Transformation, Cultural Struggle, and Transnationalism among Mexican Migrants in the US. In *Towards a Transnational Perspective on Migration: Race, Class, Ethnicity, and Nationalism Reconsidered*, ed. Nina Glick-Schiller, Linda Basch, and Cristina Blanc-Szanton. New York: Annals of the New York Academy of Sciences, vol. 645.

———. 1995. Thinking Through Transnationalism: Notes on the Cultural Politics of Class Relations in the Contemporary United States. *Public Culture* 7: 2.

Ruggie, John G. 1993. Territoriality and Beyond: Problematizing Modernity in International Relations. *International Organizations* 47 (1): 139–74.

Ruiz Hernandez, Margarito Xib. 1993. Todo indigenismo es lo mismo. *Ojarasca*, July.

Rumbaut, Rubén. 1994. The Crucible Within: Ethnic Identity, Self-Esteem, and Segmented Assimilation among Children of Immigrants. *International Migration Review* 28 (4): 748–94.

———. 1997. Assimilation and Its Discontents: Between Rhetoric and Reality. *International Migration Review* 31 (4).

———. 1998. Second Generation Assimilation and Language Retention and the Limits of a Transnational Perspective. Paper presented at conference on Second-Generation Transnationalism, Harvard University.

Sahlins, Marshall. 1981. *Historical Metaphors and Mythical Realities: Struc-*

ture in the Early History of the Sandwich Islands Kingdom. Ann Arbor: University of Michigan Press.

Salazar Parreñas, Rhacel. 2001. Servants of Globalization: Women, Migration, and Domestic Work. Stanford, CA: Stanford University Press.

Salvo, J., and A. P. Lobo. 1996. The Newest New Yorkers, 1990–94. New York: New York City Planning Dept.

———. 1998. The Newest New Yorkers, 1995–96. New York: New York City Planning Dept.

Sanchez, Arturo Ignacio. 1997. Transnational Political Agency and Identity Formation among Colombian Immigrants. Paper presented at conference "Transnational Communities and the Political Economy of New York City in the 1990s," New School for Social Research, New York.

Santacruz Giralt, María. 2001. Barrio adentro: La solidaridad violento de las pandillas. San Salvador: Universidad Centroamericana.

Sassen, Saskia. 1988. The Mobility of Capital and Labor. New York and London: Oxford University Press.

———. 1991. The Global City: New York, London, Tokyo. Princeton, NJ: Princeton University Press.

———. 1995. Immigration and Local Labor Markets. In The Economic Sociology of Immigration, ed. A. Portes. New York: Russell Sage Foundation.

———. 1996. Losing Control? Sovereignty in an Age of Globalization. The 1995 Columbia University Leonard Hastings Schoff Memorial Lectures. New York: Columbia University Press.

———. 1998. Globalization and Its Discontents. New York: New Press.

———. 1999. Guests and Aliens. New York: New Press.

———. 2002a. Scales and Spaces. City and Community 1 (1): 48–50.

———. 2002b. Global Changes and Their Implications for Social Organization. Paper presented at conference on Gangs and the Global City, Chicago.

Schneider, Eric C. 1999. Vampires, Dragons, and Egyptian Kings: Youth Gangs in Postwar New York. Princeton, NJ: Princeton University Press.

Scott, James. 1976. The Moral Economy of the Peasant: Rebellion and Subsistence in Southeast Asia. New Haven, CT: Yale University Press.

———. 1985. Weapons of the Weak: Everyday Forms of Peasant Resistance. New Haven, CT: Yale University Press.

Sewell, William. 1992. A Theory of Structure: Duality, Agency, and Transformations. American Journal of Sociology 98: 1–29.

Shadow, Robert. 1994. La peregrinación religiosa en América Latina: Enfoques y perspectivas. In Procesiones y peregrinaciones: Una aproximación, ed. Carlos Garma and Robert D. Shadow. México, DF: Universidad Autónoma Metropolitana-Iztapalapa.

Shadow, Robert, and María J. Rodríguez V. Rodriguez. 1990. Símbolos que amarran, símbolos que dividen: Hegemonía e impugnación en una peregrinación, en campesina a Chalma. Mesoamerica 19: 33–72.

Sheffer, Gabriel. 1986. Modern Diasporas in International Politics. London: Croon Helm.

Sherman, Rachel. 1999. From State Introversion to State Extension: Modes of Emigrant Incorporation in Mexico, 1900–1996. *Theory and Society* 28 (6): 835–78.

Smith, Michael Peter, and Luis Eduardo Guarnizo. 1998. Introduction. In *Transnationalism from Below*, ed. Michael Peter Smith and Luis Eduardo Guarnizo. New Brunswick, NJ: Transaction Publishers.

Smith, Robert C. 1993. De-Territorialized Nation Building: Transnational Migrants and the Re-Imagination of Political Community by Sending States. Seminar on Migration, the State and International Migration. Occasional Papers Series, New York University, Center for Latin American and Caribbean Studies. Spring.

———. 1994. Bounded Solidarity. Draft manuscript.

———. 1995. "Los Ausentes Siempre Presentes": The Imagining, Making, and Politics of a Transnational Community. Ph.D. diss., Columbia University.

———. 1996a. Domestic Politics Abroad, Diasporic Politics at Home: The Mexican Global Nation, Neoliberalism, and the Program for Mexican Communities Abroad. Paper presented at the meeting of the American Sociological Association.

———. 1996b. Mexicans in New York City: Membership and Incorporation of New Immigrant Group. In *Latinos in New York*, ed. S. Baver and G. Haslip Viera. Notre Dame, IN: University of Notre Dame Press.

———. 1997. Transnational Migration, Assimilation, and Political Community. In *The City and the World*, ed. Margaret Crahan and Alberto Vourvoulias-Bush, 110–32. New York: Council on Foreign Relations Press.

———. 1998a. The Changing Nature of Citizenship, Membership, and Nation: Comparative Insights from Mexico and Italy. Paper given at Transnational Communities Programme, Manchester, England.

———. 1998b. Reflections on the State, Migration, and the Durability and Newness of Transnational Life: Comparative Insights from the Mexican and Italian Cases. *Soziale Welt* 12: 197–220.

———. 1998c. Transnational Localities: Technology, Community, and the Politics of Membership within the Context of Mexico-US Migration. In *Transnationalism From Below*, ed. Michael Peter Smith and Luis Guarnizo, 196–240. New Brunswick, NJ: Transaction Publishers.

———. 2000. How Durable and New Is Transnational Life? Historical Retrieval through Local Comparison. *Diaspora* 9 (2): 203–34.

———. 2001a. Mexicans: Economic, Political, and Educational Problems and Prospects. In *New Immigrants in New York*, ed. Nancy Foner. New York: Columbia University Press.

———. 2001b. Local Level Transnational Life in Rattvik, Sweden, and Ticuani, Mexico: An Essay in Historical Retrieval. In *Transnational Social Spaces*, ed. Ludger Pries, 187–219. London: Routledge.

———. 2001c. Current Dilemmas and Future Prospects of the Inter-American Migration System. In *Global Migrants, Global Refugees: Problems and Solutions*, ed. Aristide Zolberg and Peter Benda, 121–71. New York: Berghahn Books.

———. 2002a. Gender, Ethnicity, and Race in School and Work Outcomes of Second Generation Mexican Americans. In *Latinos Remaking America,* ed. Marcelo Suarez-Orozco and Mariela Paez. Berkeley: University of California Press.

———. 2002b. Globalization, Adolescence, and the Transnationalization of Mexican Gangs between New York and Mexico. Paper presented at the meeting of the American Sociological Association. Chicago.

———. 2002c. Black Mexicans, Nerds, and Cosmopolitans: Successfully Negotiating Badly Segmented Assimilation within New York City's School and Racial Hierarchies. Unpublished paper.

———. 2002d. Social Location, Generation, and Life Course as Social Processes Shaping Second Generation Transnational Life. In *The Changing Face of Home,* ed. Peggy Levitt and Mary Waters, 145–68. New York: Russell Sage Foundation.

———. 2003a. Migrant Membership as an Instituted Process: Migration, the State, and the Extra-Territorial Conduct of Mexican Politics. *International Migration Review* 37 (2): 297–343.

———. 2003b. Diasporic Memberships in Historical Perspective: Comparative Insights from the Mexican and Italian Cases. In Josh DeWind, Steven Vertovec and Peggy Levitt, eds. *International Migration Review,* special issue, 37 (3): 724–59.

———. 2003c. Imagining Alternative Educational Futures for Mexicans in New York City. In *The Schooling of Mexican Children in New York State,* ed. Regina Cortina, 93–124. New York: Center for Migration Studies.

———. 2005a. Racialization and Mexicans in New York City. In *New Destinations for Mexican Migration,* ed. Ruben Hernandez Leon and Victor Zuñiga. New York: Russell Sage Foundation.

———. 2005b. Actual and Possible Uses of Cyberspace by and among States, Diasporas, and Migrants. In *Virtual Diasporas and Global Problem Solving,* ed. Jason Hunter and Peter Hayes. Berkeley, CA: Nautilus Institute.

Smith, Robert C., Héctor Cordero-Guzmán, and Ramón Grosfoguel. 2001. Introduction: Migration, Transnationalization and Racial Dynamics in a Changing New York. In *Migration, Transnationalization, and Race in a Changing New York,* ed. Héctor Cordero-Guzmán, Robert C. Smith, and Ramón Grosfoguel. Philadelphia: Temple University Press.

Somers, Margaret. 1993. Citizenship and the Place of the Public Sphere: Law, Community, and Political Culture in the Transition to Democracy. *American Sociological Review* 58 (5): 587–620.

Soysal, Yasemin N. 1994. *Limits to Citizenship: Migrants and Postnational Membership in Europe.* Chicago: University of Chicago Press.

———. 1997. Changing Parameters of Citizenship and Claims-Making: Organized Islam in European Public Spheres. *Theory and Society* 26: 511–28.

Spener, David. 1996. Small Firms, Small Capital, and the Global Commodity Chain: Some Lessons from the Tex-Mex Border in the Era of Free Trade. In

Latin America in the World Economy, ed. R. P. Korzeniewicz and W. C. Smith, 77–100. Westport, CT: Greenwood.

Spergel, Irving. 1995. *The Youth Gang Problem.* New York: Oxford University Press.

Stahler-Sholk, Richard. 1998. The Lessons of Acteal. *NACLA Report on the Americas* 31 (5): 11–15.

Stamm, Alan. 2001. Camp Life. www.brown.edu/Research/Catskills_Institute. Accessed October 2002.

Stevens, Evelyn P. 1994. Marianismo: The Other Face of Machismo in Latin America. In *Confronting Change, Challenging Tradition: Women in Latin American History,* ed. Gertrude Yeager, 3–17. Wilmington, DE: Jaguar Books on Latin America.

Suarez-Orozco, Carola. 1999. Adolescence and Gender in the Second Generation. Address to the annual meeting of the American Psychological Association.

———. 2001. Psychocultural Factors in the Adaptation of Immigrant Youth: Gendered Responses. In *Women, Gender, and Human Rights: A Global Perspective,* ed. Marjorie Agosín, 170–88. Piscataway, NJ: Rutgers University Press.

Suarez-Orozco, Carola, and Marcelo Suarez-Orozco. 1995. *Transformations: Immigration, Family Life, and Achievement Motivation among Latino Adolescents.* Stanford, CA: Stanford University Press.

Suarez-Orozco, Marcelo. 1989. *Central American Refugees in US High Schools: A Psychosocial Study of Motivation and Achievement.* Stanford: Stanford University Press.

Suarez-Orozco, Marcelo, and Mariela Paez. 2002. *Latinos: Remaking America.* Berkeley: University of California Press.

Suarez-Orozco, Marcelo, and Carola Suarez-Orozco. 2001. *Children of Immigration.* Cambridge, MA: Harvard University Press.

Suttles, Gerald. 1968. *The Social Order of the Slum.* Chicago: University of Chicago Press.

———. 1972. *The Social Construction of Communities.* Chicago: University of Chicago Press.

Swidler, Ann. 1986. Culture in Action: Symbols and Strategies. *American Sociological Review* 51 (2): 273–86.

Taagepera, Rein. 1993. Running for President of Estonia: A Political Scientist in Politics. *PS: Political Science and Politics* 26: 302–4.

Takanashi, Ruby, ed. 1993. *Adolescence in the 1990s: Risk and Opportunity.* New York: Teachers College Press.

Tarrow, Sidney. 1998. *Power in Movement: Social Movements and Contentious Politics.* New York: Cambridge University Press.

Taylor, Ronald, Leanne Jacobs, and Debra Roberts. 2000. Ecological Correlates of the Social and Emotional Adjustment of African American Adolescents. In *Adolescent Diversity in Ethnic, Economic, and Cultural Contexts,* ed. R. Montemayor, G. Adams, and T. Gullotta. Thousand Oaks, CA: Sage.

Thomas, William Isaac, and Florian Znaniecki. 1927. *The Polish Peasant in Europe and America.* New York: Alfred A. Knopf.

Thompson, E. P. 1963. *The Making of the English Working Class.* London: Victor Gollancz.

Thompson, Ginger. 2001. An Exodus of Migrant Families Is Bleeding Mexico's Heartland. *New York Times.* June 17, 1.

Thrasher, Frederick. 1927. *The Gang: A Study of 1,313 Gangs in Chicago.* Chicago: University of Chicago Press.

Thrift, Nigel. 1996. *Spatial Formations.* London: Sage.

Thurstone, L. L. 1927. The Method of Paired Comparison for Social Value. *Journal of Abnormal and Social Psychology* 21: 384–400.

Tilly, Charles. 1978. *From Mobilization to Revolution.* Reading, MA: Addison-Wesley.

———, ed. 1996. *Citizenship, Identity, and Social History.* Cambridge: Cambridge University Press.

———. 1997. *Roads from Past to Future.* Boulder, CO: Rowman and Littlefield.

———, ed. 1999. Why Worry about Citizenship? In *Expanding Citizenship, Reconfiguring States,* ed. C. Tilly and M. Hanagan. Boulder, CO: Rowman and Littlefield.

Tilly, Charles, Louise Tilly, and Richard H. Tilly. 1975. *The Rebellious Century, 1830–1930.* Cambridge, MA: Harvard University Press.

Tololyan, K. 1996. Rethinking Diaspora(s): Stateless Power in the Transnational Moment. *Diaspora* 5 (1): 3–36.

———. 1999. Diaspora as a Concept and a Metaphor. Paper presented at Barnard Forum on Migration, Barnard College.

U.S. Department of Labor. Bureau of Labor Statistics. *Current Population Survey,* various years.

Valdes de Montano, Luz María, and Robert Smith. 1994. Mexicans in New York. Final Report to the Tinker Foundation.

Valenzuela, Angela. 1999. *Subtractive Schooling: U.S.-Mexican Youth and the Politics of Caring.* Albany: State University of New York Press.

Vanderbush, Walt. 1999. Assessing Democracy in Puebla: The Opposition Takes Charge of Municipal Government. *Journal of Latin American and World Affairs* 41 (2): 1–27.

Vecino, Agustín. 1999. Gangs and Crews. Notes for Rob Smith's Second-Generation Project.

Velasco Ortiz, Laura. 1999. Comunidades transnacionales y conciencia etnica: Indigenas migrantes en la frontera Mexico–Estados Unidos. Ph.D. diss., El Colegio de Mexico.

———. 2002. *El regreso de la comunidad: Migración indigena y agentes etnicos.* Tijuana, Mexico: El Colegio de la Frontera Norte.

Venkatesh, Sudhir Alladi.1997. The Social Organization of Street Gang Activity in an Urban Ghetto. *American Journal of Sociology* 103 (1): 82–111.

———. 2000a. *American Project: The Rise and Fall of a Modern Ghetto.* Cambridge, MA: Harvard University Press.

———. 2000b. Are We a Family or a Business? History and Disjuncture in Chicago's Street Gangs. *Theory and Society* 29: 427–62.

———. 2002. Neo-Liberalism and the American Street Gang. Paper presented at conference on Gangs and the Global City, Chicago.

Vertovec, Steven. 1999a. Conceiving and Researching Transnationalism. *Ethnic and Racial Studies* 22 (2): 446–62.

———. 1999b. Three Meanings of Diaspora, Exemplified among South Asian Religions. *Diaspora* 6 (3): 277–99.

Vigil, James Diego. 1988. *Barrio Gangs: Street Life and Identity in Southern California*. Austin, TX: University of Texas Press.

———. 1990. Cholos and Gangs: Culture Change and Street Youth in California. In *Gangs in America*, ed. C. Ronald Huff, 116–28. Newbury Park, CA: Sage.

———. 1991. The Established Gang. In *Gangs*, ed. Scott Cummings and Daniel J. Monti. Albany: State University of New York Press.

———. 2002. *A Rainbow of Gangs*. Austin: University of Texas Press.

von Wright, Georg Henrick. 1971. *Explanation and Understanding*. Ithaca, NY: Cornell University Press.

Wacquant, Loïc. 2002. The Punishing City Revisited: On the Metropolis as Incubator of Neo-Liberal Penalty. Paper presented at conference on Gangs and the Global City, Chicago.

Waldinger, Roger. 1996. *Still the Promised City? African-Americans and New Immigrants in Postindustrial New York*. Cambridge, MA: Harvard University Press.

———. 1997. Comments at conference on Transnationalization, Race, and Migration, New School for Social Research, New York.

Waldinger, Roger, and M. Bozorghehr, eds. 1996. *Ethnic Los Angeles*. New York: Russell Sage Foundation.

Waldinger, Roger, and David Fitzgerald. 2004. Transnationalism in Question. *American Journal of Sociology* 109 (5): 1177–95.

Waldinger, Roger, and Michael Lichter. 2003. *How the Other Half Works: Immigration and the Social Organization of Labor*. Berkeley: University of California Press.

Ware, Carolyn. 1935. *Greenwich Village, 1920–1930: A Comment on American Civilization in the Post-War Years*. Boston: Houghton Mifflin.

Warner, W. Lloyd, and Leo Srole. 1945. *The Social Systems of American Ethnic Groups*. New Haven, CT: Yale University Press.

Waters, Mary. 1994. Ethnic and Racial Identities of Second Generation Black Immigrants in New York City. *International Migration Review* 28 (4): 795–820.

———. 1996. The Intersection of Gender, Race, and Ethnicity in Identity Development of Caribbean American Teens. In *Urban Girls*, ed. B. Leadbeater and N. Way. New York: New York University Press.

———. 1999. *Black Identities: West Indian Immigrant Dreams and American Realities*. New York: Russell Sage Foundation.

Waters, Tony. 1999. *Crime and Immigrant Youth*. Thousand Oaks, CA: Sage Publications.

Weber, Max. 1964. Politics as a Vocation. In *From Max Weber,* ed. H. H. Gerth and C. Wright Mills. New York: Oxford.

Weigert, A. J. 1991. Transverse Interaction: A Pragmatic Perspective on Environment as Other. *Symbolic Interaction* 11: 353–63.

Weiner, Antje. 1997. Making Sense of the New Geography of Citizenship: Fragmented Citizenship in the European Union. *Theory and Society* 26: 531–59.

Willis, Paul. 1977. *Learning to Labor: How Working Class Kids Get Working Class Jobs.* New York: Columbia University Press.

Wilson, William Julius. 1987. *The Truly Disadvantaged.* Chicago: University of Chicago Press.

———. 1996. *When Work Disappears: The World of the New Urban Poor.* New York: Alfred A. Knopf.

Wolf, Eric. 1957. Closed Corporate Peasant Communities in Mesoamerica and Central Java. *Southwestern Journal of Anthropology* 13 (1).

———. 1959. *Sons of the Shaking Earth.* Chicago: University of Chicago Press.

Wyman, Mark. 1993. *Round-Trip to America: The Immigrants Return to Europe, 1880–1930.* Ithaca, NY: Cornell University Press.

Zabin, Carol, and Allie Hughes. 1995. Economic Integration and Labor Flows: Stage Migration in Farm Labor Markets in Mexico and the United States. *International Migration Review* 29 (2): 395–422.

Zake, L. 1981. The National Department and the Polish American Community, 1916–1923. *Polish American Studies* 38 (2): 16–25.

Zendejas Romero, Sergio. 2004. Política local y formación del estado: Procesos políticos y de identidad social en torno a zonas rurales mexicanas, 1890–1998. Unpublished manuscript.

Zhou, Min. 1999. Segmented Assimilation: Issues, Controversies, and Recent Research on the New Second Generation. In *The Handbook of International Migration: The American Experience,* ed. Charles Hirschman, Philip Kasinitz, and Josh DeWind. New York: Russell Sage Foundation.

Zhou, Min, and Carl Bankston III. 1998. *Growing Up American.* New York: Russell Sage Foundation.

Zolberg, Aristide. 1999. Matters of State: Theorizing Immigration Policy. In *The Handbook of International Migration: The American Experience,* ed. Charles Hirschman, Philip Kasinitz, and Josh DeWind, 94–120. New York: Russell Sage Foundation.

Zolberg, Aristide, and Robert Smith. 1996. Migration Systems in Comparative Perspective: An Analysis of the Inter-American Migration System with Comparative Reference to the Mediterranean-European System. Report to U.S. Department of State, Bureau of Population, Refugees, and Migration.

Zolberg, Aristide, Astri Suhrke, and Sergio Aguayo. 1989. *Escape from Violence: Conflict and the Refugee Crisis in the Developing World.* New York: Oxford University Press.

Zukin, Sharon. 2002. What's Space Got to Do with It? *City and Community* 1 (4): 345–48.

Zuñiga, Victor, and Rubén Hernández-León, eds. *New Destinations for Mexican Migration*. New York: Russell Sage Foundation.

Methodological Appendix

Mexican New York has used a variety of methods over its long gestation. In this appendix, I describe both my relationships with Ticuanenses in New York and Ticuani and the methods I used, both alone and with research assistants, with special focus on ethnography and interviews. Ethnography, more than any other social science method, is subjective, and this subjectivity is one of its strengths. By this, I mean that the quality of the data and analysis depend extensively on the relationships that the ethnographer develops with his informants (since I am a man, I will use the pronoun *he* in this appendix). Moreover, the interactions in which the ethnographer becomes involved are ways he can come to see social processes that might otherwise remain hidden. The ethnographer, to some extent, is his own research tool. This point can be illustrated by discussing my initial entry into Ticuani society in New York and Ticuani.

My first encounter with Ticuani came through the neighboring town of El Ganado, to which I had gone on the invitation of Fernando Sanchez, "El Gordo," a *tortillero* (owner of a tortilla factory) in Brooklyn, where I had met him. He invited me to El Ganado to see the Feast during August 1988, and so I spent most of July and August in El Ganado, returning to New York in early September. I spent a good deal of time with Ticuanenses, whom I added to my study, which was still in its initial stages. Returning to New York, where I was immersed in coursework and some service work to the Mexican community, I continued my relationships with Ticuanenses. I first met the Committee in late 1990 at one of their meetings. Through my research, I had come to know a Ticuanense married to a Ganadero, and the Ticuanense had invited me to the Committee's meeting to discuss my research. I summarized my research and asked for their approval. The discussion was vigorous, with Committee members wanting to

351

know how it would benefit the community, what I would use it for, and other questions. Younger Ticuanenses in the Youth Group gave me their blessing and urged the Committee to do the same, which in the end they did, even giving me a letter of introduction to the Ticuani president.

When I got to Ticuani and delivered this letter to the president, I expected him to ask how he could help. Instead, he looked at the letter, placed it in a drawer without commenting on it, and sat stiffly. Sensing that doors were closing, I told him that I had met only once with the Committee and that they had okayed my project, and then I excitedly told him that I was going to run in the Antorcha. I inquired if perhaps we could speak in two days, when I got back. He smiled, remarking that it was good that I was doing the Antorcha. He warmed up considerably after this, telling me in future conversations that the Committee had no right to demand things of him, and had forgotten its place in doing so.

This was my first introduction to the power-laden relations between the Committee and the *municipio*, which turned out be a major theme in this book, but my response was one I would use repeatedly. People liked the fact that I really wanted to learn about Ticuani life and to actively participate in its rituals and collective life in New York and Ticuani. And my participation put me at the site of social action that I would not have been able to learn about as well by, for example, interviews. And almost all Ticuanenses aided my work in ways large and small. This initially reticent municipal president helped me a great deal in the end, introducing me to people and including me in what he could have kept as private conversations. He even wrote a letter asking that Ticuanenses participate in a house-to-house survey we were conducting. I think part of the reason all sides talked to me is because they wanted to be heard in whatever my telling of their story would be.

I cultivated my relationship with the Committee and with other people involved in politics in New York and Ticuani. During my first years of fieldwork, in the early 1990s, I attended at least one of the all-day Sunday meetings per month, and during times of high or particularly interesting activity, I attended them every week. I also helped the Committee by, for example, locating a lawyer and serving as their guide as they secured nonprofit status in New York State. This experience, too, was revealing. Despite the fact that I had worked with the Committee for several years, Don Manuel warned me directly that if I tried to trick them, that would end our relationship. Other Committee members told me not to worry about his comments; it was simply Don Manuel's *desconfianza* (mistrust), the view that animated many of his interactions with the world. Still, Don Manuel understood and supported my project in his own way. He would never do an individual interview with me because the Committee was a collective enterprise. All the quotes from him in this book come from my recordings of collective meetings or from fieldnotes. Yet he was generous in interpreting events for me, and even had me tend bar and handle money for the Committee. I remained engaged with the Committee to one degree or another during the entire time I worked on this study, from the late 1980s through 2003. While I did not attend all their meetings during my second intensive stint of fieldwork, from 1997 to 2002, I did attend public events and town meetings; I went to Ticuani with them, too, and did many interviews.

Within the Committee, I developed some particularly close friendships, which grew to include my friends' entire families. These friendships inadvertently prompted questions for me and gave me access to the data to answer them. Don Emiliano and Tomás Maestro and their families took special care to make sure I knew what was going on and to include me. Insights from Doña Selena, Eliana, Victoria, and Mia and their own families were key in developing my ideas on life course, transnational life, and intrafamily dynamics. Their patient explanations of and expansive comments on events in Ticuani were instructive. My relationships with Doña Xochitl, Magda, Marisol, and Toño similarly led me to form ideas about the immigrant bargain, gender, and transnational life. The longevity of my relationship with the family came out in humorous form during a 2001 interview with Magda, Marisol, and Xochitl. In reviewing our common history, we realized that when we first met, thirteen years earlier, I had been the same age as her brother Toño was at the time of the interview—twenty-four. "Wow! So basically you watched us grow up!" Magda exclaimed. I had watched them move from adolescence to young adulthood as I had moved from young adulthood to full adulthood. We also laughed at how the interview had been arranged. During an earlier visit to their house, I had spoken to Xochitl about interviewing her and her daughters about gender issues in the family. As she and I talked, I said that I wanted to interview her when Tomás was not home, and then began to explain my reasoning—that he always answered for her and she did not really get a chance to talk. But before I could say this, she and I both laughed. My request, by its words alone, sounded like I should not have asked this and she should have refused, but she understood exactly what I meant. She responded: "Yes, I know, he will not let me talk"—thus letting me off the hook and acknowledging our common understanding and friendship. It is this kind of deep ethnographic relationship that has made possible the insights in this book, such as they are.

These long-term relationships meant that even when I spoke to people I did not know at a party, there was likely to be someone they knew who knew me, often for years. This was very important with the children of immigrants in Ticuani and New York. I could not have done the work on adolescence, gangs, life course, and return in the same way without these preexisting relationships.

During this long involvement with Ticuanenses in New York and Ticuani, I was also active in the larger Mexican community in New York, with selected groups in California, and with various levels of government and community in other migrant-sending Mexican states, especially Zacatecas. Hence, my discussions of the Mexican state's motives in pursuing policies are not mere speculation but are based on observations of the creation and implementation of programs. I even advised then president-elect Vicente Fox's transition team on how it might develop relations between Mexico and its diaspora in the United States. I have also worked with several New York–based Mexican civic groups in New York: Casa México, Casa Puebla, the Mexican American Students Alliance, the Mixteca Organization, and Asociación Tepeyac. I taught English in basements and took time off from graduate school to work as a community organizer. I also filed an affidavit in a lawsuit seeking greater educational access for undocumented immigrant students at the City University of New York, and supported the New York State law that ultimately carried out this project to some degree. I have also served as an expert witness in deportation cases and advised the Catholic Church and various public schools and departments of education on how to address the Mexican population. I reached this widely in my research in part to achieve what Mitchell Duneier might call a "transnational extended place" approach: by knowing how the federal government in Mexico was thinking and acting about migrants, I could better understand the larger context of Ticuani transnational life. But I also did these things because my life is quite bound up with the Mexican community in New York, and I feel it is my honor and duty to try to help, thus reciprocating in small measure the *confianza* migrants and their children have offered by telling me their stories.

During most of this long research project, I worked alone. But I have benefited from research assistance from Mexican, American, and Mexican American friends and students. In my early research, Mexican anthropologist Arturo Mota, from the National Institute of Anthropology and History in Mexico City, helped me do interviews for two weeks, and two undocumented (in the United States) Mexican immigrant friends from New York helped me do a large survey in Ticuani during one week in 1993.

Starting in 1998, work on the second generation was facilitated greatly, and to some extent done, by excellent undergraduate researchers and one graduate student, whom I hired with funding from the National Science Foundation Sociology Program and the Social Science Research Council's Program on International Migration.

I used two techniques for collective ethnography—"piggybacking" and a "Rashomonic team approach"—both of which underline the central assertion that quality of ethnographic analysis depends largely on the relationships ethnographers develop with their informants. Piggybacking worked in two ways. Every researcher whose work appears in this book was personally introduced by me to the research community and their work facilitated by drawing—piggybacking—on my longstanding relationships. Usually, I introduced them to families where I had a close relationship with more than one member of the family, such as in the case of Tomás and Xochitl Maestro. We then did fieldwork together and separately, discussing both findings and emerging areas to investigate. Sara Guerrero-Rippberger's work was especially helpful in developing the gender analysis in this book. When starting in the field, Sara read materials for the project, including my doctoral dissertation and other papers and proposals. She also brought great ethnographic instincts honed in childhood at her dissertation-writing mother's knee. I introduced her to Madga, Toño, and Marisol; she became deeply engaged with them and with Julia, Tomás's girlfriend, and she opened space for me to do further work with them. Moreover, the approach of our team—including, in various years, Sara, Sandra Lara, Griscelda Perez, Carolina Perez, and myself—enabled us to get different, Rashomonic perspectives on Toño and Julia's relationship and others' perceptions of them. While Sara had become close to Julia, whom I also came to know, I drew on my long-term relationships with Toño, Tomás Maestro, and Magda, who turned out to be an especially insightful social observer and friend. Similarly, parents of teens called me to ask whether a particular researcher was working with me, and gave their okay to the interviews once they knew this was so. Moreover, the social meaning of me as a man in his midthirties hanging out with girls or boys in their late teens or early twenties changed because the parents knew me as a friend and researcher and because my students were also involved in these relationships. Sara also opened up relationships with second- and 1.5-generation and teen migrants whom I did not know, making it possible for me to develop relationships with them.

Similarly, I introduced Griscelda Perez into the community, but she developed relationships beyond these initial ones. She was especially skillful in doing the gang interviews and research in Ticuani, drawing on life experience with such young men in California. She danced with them at parties and joked with them in the zocalo. They knew me from various years hanging around in New York and Ticuani, playing pool and going to parties. These informal interactions led to the interviews Griscelda and I did and to later ethnographic work I did with them. Here, piggybacking on Griscelda's ethnographic relationships enabled me to develop new or deepen existing research relationships, and thus to do further research. Hence, I kept in touch with the Mixtecos Locos and went to Homero's 2001 wedding in Ticuani, even marching with him to deliver a goat to his fiancée's house the night before the wedding, when the civil ceremony took place. In the same vein, long after Sara had left New York to work with Teach for America, I pursued themes in the dynamics of the Maestro family through interviews and fieldwork. I drew similarly on Sandra Lara's extension of preexisting relationships and creation of new ones with some of the "pioneer" women migrants. Because the second-generation project unfolded over the course of more than five years of fieldwork, these researchers did their work at different times, following and joining different friendship groups among the Ticuani second-, 1.5-, and teen generations. I was the constant on the research team.

This project drew on various kinds of data. First, fieldnotes and ongoing relationships were used to develop cases and trace out processes. I followed particular cases over time and used what I knew from the past to guide future research. I also used what I call "grounded ethnographic interviews." These involve asking informants about particular events or themes that have emerged in past research with these and other informants. They usually involve informants with whom the researcher has solid preexisting relationships, and usually informants have been interviewed before, at least for long life-history interviews. I found such interviews to be especially useful after I had gained some sense of what was going on in the larger community, after many interviews and much ethnography had been done and my considered ideas were forming. A main advantage of this kind of interview is that you get informants' versions of events rather than simply relying on your own interpretations. With apologies to Geertz, one might say that one gets to ask the native if he blinked, winked, or had something in his eye.

I also did "grounded group interviews" that enabled me to gain access to social dynamics among informants. For example, I knew from talking to and watching Napoleon and Jericho that they had different understandings of masculinity. They responded very differently to perceived aggression by *cholos:* the former was ready to fight, and the latter ignored it and did not let it register on his social radar. Hence, I asked them to do a group interview to discuss this issue, including specific examples of their differing reactions. While we were waiting to start the interview, two passing Mexicans "stepped up" to Napoleon and Jericho. I was standing abut ten to fifteen feet away during the encounter, and hence the other youths did not see me with Napoleon and Jericho. Their reactions were predictable: Jericho shrugged the encounter off as misguided macho, while Napoleon was outraged. Hence, I started the group interview by asking them to explain to me what had just happened. We then moved into retrospectively discussing various interactions in Ticuani and New York, some of which are reported in this book. This kind of grounded interview presupposes ethnographic immersion but goes beyond that to ask informants to interpret and reflect on events that the ethnographer observed. In group interviews, you can get informants with different perspectives to challenge each other, frame their understandings differently, or otherwise capture some of the dynamic quality of the social life observed.

It would be hard to quantify the hours of observation this project draws on. My own work involved long interviews, usually more than one, with at least sixty adult or young adult Ticuanenses and twenty-five to thirty of their U.S.-raised children, as well as extensive longitudinal work with a smaller group who are most actively involved in its transnational life. It also draws on more than one hundred life-history interviews for the second-generation project; seven long group interviews; and ethnographic fieldwork in schools, public places, and homes, as well as countless hours of supervision of more than a dozen students during three years of fieldwork in New York and Mexico. Similarly, it would be hard to count the times I have been welcomed in the Maestro household in New York and Don Emiliano's and Doña Selena's in Ticuani, as well as many other homes. The main payoff of this work, I think, comes from close observation of a relatively small number of people over a long period of time, first by me and later by two or three especially good research assistants, and I was also able to cast a larger data net through other research assistants.

My writing of the text developed alternately in ways that can be roughly described as "sailing with instruments" versus "dead reckoning." (I prefer these metaphors to the naturalistic metaphors, which invoke Darwin's exhaustive exercise in *The Origin of Species*, used by Jack Katz, Eli Anderson, and Stanley Lieberson and Freda Lynn, though those metaphors work well, too.) The former refers to navigation using instruments, while the latter describes simply sailing by one's own knowledge of the stars and sea. Per this analogy, my analysis of gender and of coconstitution of masculinity and Mexicanness in emergent space drew first on a dead reckoning with the data and then on an explicit engagement with the instruments, the theories. While this overstates the case—one always works with theories and ideas in mind when gathering and engaging data—my experience in, for example, comparing the meaning of Don Gerardo's and Don Emiliano's absences was really one of discovery. I had no explicit intention to write such a comparison when I was hanging out with or interviewing them. It was only later that the comparative insights emerged as I reread the notes and interviews with members of the two families. Having these insights into these two cases enabled me to go back and wrestle again with theories on gender and migration, to gain some purchase on them, and to guide further research. Similarly, my analysis of the coconstitution of space emerged without conscious consideration of theories of space. In the end, my analysis emerged from my repeated readings of the fieldnotes and interviews and my own personal, but visceral and almost preconceptual, sense of what was going on at those various sites. Theories of space came in only after the manuscript had been written and revised. But I realized that the literature was describing processes very similar to those I had described through ethnographic dead reckoning, such as my analysis of the ways that gangs were coconstituting masculinity, Mexicanness in *sonidos* and Mexican parties. In my work on transnational politics and the Mexican state, I had a more ready framework formed from my earlier work. The exciting part here was rethinking these issues in light of new developments—for example, seeing how changes in Mexican national politics in 1998 affected local Ticuani politics in Brooklyn in the summer of the same year. While my analysis evolved as I wrote and rewrote the manuscript, my insights here felt more like getting the complete story than like clearly seeing something for the first time, as with the gender and space analysis.

A final note here involves combining life-course analysis and ethnography. These two methods are rarely used together because the former requires tracking movement from one phase of life to another, and the latter requires that one be present to observe and discuss changes with informants. Because this study began early in my graduate career and lasted another decade and a half, I have been able to follow my informants for a very long time. I joke with my friends that without the virtue of being any smarter, I have been able to gain greater insight by seeing how things turned out in the end. My own life course has moved ahead steadily during this time. It has been a great pleasure to share this journey with my Ticuanense friends, both grownups and children, in the United States and Mexico. To them, I offer a large thank-you and an *abrazote*.

Index

Italicized page numbers indicate figures, tables, and maps.

voice, concept of, 55, 67, 114, 300n37
voting, 65–66, 77, 82–84, 89–90, 193, 286, 289–90. *See also* electoral politics, Mexican

wages, 26–28. *See also* per capita incomes; salaries
Waldinger, Roger, 16, 28, 279
"wannabes," 243, 247–48, 259
Ware, Caroline, 283
water project. *See* potable water project
Waters, Mary, 24, 311n3
weddings, 227, 244, 249–50, 254–55, 314n9
welfare, 166, 168
wigs for Padre Jesús, 149, *150*, 310n7
Willie, 147, 157
Willis, Paul, 25, 266
wolf (in Dance of the Tecuanis), 43, *156*
Wolf, Eric, 41
women, 21, 26; and job opportunities, 26, 28, 36; settlement practices of, 115–22. *See also* working women
work ethic, 23, 29, 36–37, 124–25, 164, 166–67, 220
working women: first-generation migrants as, 97, 99, 103, 107, 111,

115–16, 179; second-generation migrants as, 125, 128–29, 131, 194, 196

Xavier, 195, 200–1
Xochitl, 128–30, 134, 141, 353, 355

Yonny, 100
youth immigration. *See* teen migrants

Zacatecas Federation, 286
Zavala, Erving, 260
Zavalas, 143–44, 260, 262, 270–72, 315n17
Zhou, Min, 25, 99, 299n20, 309n10
Znaniecki, Florian, 298n10
zocalo (Ticuani), 10, 12, 300n33; and gender strategies of second generation, 2, 127, 135, 140–42; and New York Committee, 54–56, 87; and "regulars" (nongang youth), 253–54, *254*, 314n8; and returned *cholos*, 213, 235, 244–45, 253, 260, 263; and returned migrant population, 65, 159, 171, 199
Zolberg, Aristide, 9
zoned schools, 225, 313n26
Zoriano, Don, 60

Text:	10/13 Aldus
Display:	Aldus
Cartographer:	Bill Nelson
Compositor:	Sheridan Books, Inc.
Printer and Binder:	Sheridan Books, Inc.